The Faber Pocket Guide to Haydn

Richard Wigmore is a distinguished musicologist, specialising in the Viennese Classical period and Lieder. He has written many CD notes, concert programme notes, newspaper and magazine articles on Haydn.

He writes for *Gramophone*, *BBC Music Magazine* and the *Daily Telegraph*, lectures frequently and broadcasts regularly on BBC Radio 3. His previous publications include *Schubert: The Complete Song Texts* and many articles for reference books, including *The New Grove Dictionary of Music and Musicians*.

D0488885

THE FABER POCKET GUIDE TO
Haydn

Richard Wigmore

faber and faber

First published in 2009
by Faber and Faber Limited
3 Queen Square, London WC1N 3AU

Typeset by RefineCatch Limited, Bungay, Suffolk
Printed in England by CPI Bookmarque, Croydon CRO 4TD

A CIP record for this book
is available from the British Library

ISBN 978-0-571-23412-7

10 9 8 7 6 5 4 3 2 1

To Ali

Contents

Foreword

All great composers are fascinating; it goes with the job description. Some of them have been great men, rising heroically to all the challenges that life has thrown at them; some have been enigmas; some have been pains. And then there's Franz Joseph Haydn, surely one of the most lovable personalities of all time. Papa Haydn, beloved of almost all men and women (the exceptions being, perhaps, the unfortunate Mrs Haydn and a few publishers); Haydn the wit; Haydn the devoted protector of all his musicians; Haydn the musical inventor; Haydn, the kindest of men.

But, as Richard Wigmore points out, Haydn's adorable character has at times almost undermined his reputation. True, he is the funniest of the great composers; true that he was criticised for the cheerfulness of his religious music (properly devout people evidently considering their faith a matter for gloom); and true that he expressed no pretentious aims for his art. But Haydn has *everything*: his moments of pain are as tragic as any in music; his joy can be overwhelmingly powerful; and his capacity for musical experiment is infinite – no composer has been more original.

There are any number of sides to Haydn, in fact; but the effect of his art, no matter how dark or strange it may become, is always positive. His music is life-enhancing. In this book, containing answers to many of the questions that one might have wanted to ask about the man and his work had one thought of them, one can delve deeper into the extraordinary creative life of a phenomenon: the so-called father of the symphony and the string quartet, whose music became more profound, but also – paradoxically – ever more youthful, as he reached an age twice that at which most of his contemporaries had taken up the permanent occupation of pushing up daisies. There is an endless amount to learn about Haydn. This book should prove to be an excellent starting point, an enthusiastically springy diving board from which the reader can plunge into the music.

STEVEN ISSERLIS

A Haydn 'Top 20'

Absurd as it is to cull a mere twenty works from his vast, protean output, here are the Haydn pieces I could least live without:

The Creation
The Seasons
The Seven Last Words (original orchestral version)
Mass in D minor, 'Nelson'
Mass in B flat, 'Harmoniemesse'
Piano Sonata No. 20 in C minor
Piano Sonata No. 52 in E flat
Variations in F minor, 'Un piccolo Divertimento'
Piano Trio No. 28 in E major
Piano Trio No. 30 in E flat
String Quartet in D, Op. 20 No. 4
String Quartet in G, Op. 76 No. 1
String Quartet in E flat, Op. 76 No. 6
String Quartet in F, Op. 77 No. 2
Symphony No. 44 in E minor, 'Mourning'
Symphony No. 88 in G
Symphony No. 92 in G, 'Oxford'
Symphony No. 93 in D
Symphony No. 99 in E flat
Symphony No. 104 in D, 'London'

Things people said about Haydn

JOHN GREGORY (*The State and Faculties of Man*) 1766
The style of Haydn sometimes pleases by its spirit and a wild luxuriancy . . . but possesses too little of the elegance and pathetic expression of music to remain long in the public taste.

EMPRESS MARIA THERESA 1772
There is a certain Haydn, who has unusual ideas, but he is just a beginner.

MOZART (ATTRIBUTED)
There is no one who can do it all – to joke, to terrify, to evoke laughter and profound sentiment – and all equally well: except Joseph Haydn.

ERNST LUDWIG GERBER 1790
Every harmonic artifice is at [Haydn's] command, even those from the Gothic age of the grey contrapuntists. But instead of their former stiffness, they assume a pleasing manner as soon as he prepares them for our ears. He has a great gift for making a piece sound familiar. In this way, despite all the contrapuntal artifices therein, he achieves a popular style and is agreeable to every music lover.

CHARLES BURNEY
It is well known how much [Haydn] contributed to our delight, to the advancement of his art, and to his own fame, by his numerous productions in this country, and how much his natural, unassuming and pleasing character, exclusive of his productions, endeared him to his acquaintances and to the nation at large.

ALBERT CHRISTOPH DIES (1810)
Haydn had a moderately strong bone structure; the muscles were slight. His hawk nose (he suffered much from a nasal polyp which had doubtless enlarged this part) and other

features, too, were heavily pock-marked, his nose even seamed so that the nostrils each had a different shape. Haydn considered himself ugly.

E. T. A. HOFFMANN (1810)

[Haydn's] symphonies lead us through infinite green forest groves, through a jolly, bustling crowd of happy people. A rapid succession of young men and girls dance past; laughing children lie in wait behind tress and rosebushes, teasingly throwing flowers at each other. A life of eternal youth, full of love and bliss, as if before the Fall.

THOMAS BUSBY (1819)

If in any one of the melodies of *The Creation* I could discover the celestial grace of Sacchini, in the recitatives the profound science of Sebastian Bach, or in the choruses, a single example of that transcendent force of imagination, profound adjustment of parts, or sublimity of aggregate effect, so uniformly conspicuous in Handel, I would allow Haydn to be an oratorio composer.

JOHN KEATS (1820)

Haydn is like a child, for there is no knowing what he will do next.

JEAN INGRES

Whoever studies music, let his daily bread be Haydn . . . Haydn the great musician, the first, who created everything, discovered everything, taught everything to the rest.

MILY BALAKIREV (1860)

Haydn, that genius of vulgar music who induces an inordinate thirst for beer.

HUGO WOLF (1885)

What a spirit of childlike faith speaks from the heavenly pure tones of Haydn's music.

JOHANNES BRAHMS (1896)

What a man; beside him we are just wretches.

J. CUTHBERT HADDEN (1902)

Haydn lacked the true dramatic instinct. His placid, easy-going, contented nature could never have allowed him to rise to great heights of dramatic force. He was not built on a heroic mould; the meaning of tragedy was unknown to him.

DONALD FRANCIS TOVEY

[Of Symphony No. 99] This adagio is typical of that greatness in Haydn which moved Cherubini to tears, and of that freedom which taught Beethoven's inmost soul more than he, the uncouth pupil, could learn from Haydn the tired teacher.

ALDOUS HUXLEY

Haydn lived to a ripe old age and his right hand never forgot its cunning; but it also failed to learn a new cunning. Peter-Pan-like, he continued, as an old man, to write the sort of thing he had written 20, 30 and 40 years before.

WILFRID MELLERS

In a work such as the *Harmoniemesse* he rebuilds the Church in a spirit of the Enlightenment which he celebrates in his greatest instrumental works.

HANS KELLER

Alone among geniuses, the old Haydn was in clear possession of the advantages of all his biographical stages – that, perhaps just because he matured so incomprehensibly late, he was the only composing genius who reached a prolonged, consistent, late climax during which he was, simultaneously, young, middle-aged, and old.

ALFRED BRENDEL

We easily forget that the solemn Adagio [of Schubert] – also that of early Beethoven – originated in Haydn, and that the first of all great C minor piano sonatas was Haydn's.

ROBIN HOLLOWAY

He is music's supreme intellectual.

DANIEL CHUA

If you hear only happiness in Haydn, then the joke is on you.

Haydn in 2009

> The whole performance went off wonderfully well.
> Between the various sections, tumultuous applause . . .
> When it was over, people cried out, 'Papa Haydn to the
> front!' Finally the old man came forward and was greeted
> with tumultuous Applaudissement and cries of 'Long live
> Papa Haydn, long live music!' Their imperial majesties
> were all present, and joined in the calls of 'bravo'.

The writer of these lines was Johan Fredrik Berwald, a cousin
of the Swedish composer Franz, the work in question *The
Creation*, whose public premiere in Vienna's Burgtheater on
19 March 1799 was the most spectacular triumph of Haydn's
career. For nigh on two decades he had been an international
superstar, fêted from Edinburgh to Naples, from Lisbon to
St Petersburg. No composer, not even Handel, certainly not
Mozart, had ever been as widely celebrated in his own lifetime.
Now *The Creation*, Haydn's joyous celebration of the universe,
an idyllic vision that contrasted poignantly with the turbulence
of the Napoleonic Wars, set the final seal on his fame.

Yet even before Haydn's death just ten years later, while
French troops were bombarding Vienna, reaction had begun
to set in. By then Beethoven and Mozart, in that order, had
usurped Haydn's pre-eminence. This hierarchy, and with it a
progressive notion of musical history, was famously enshrined
by that weaver of fantastic tales, E. T. A. Hoffmann, in an 1810
essay on Beethoven's Fifth Symphony: 'Haydn's compositions
are dominated by a feeling of childlike optimism . . . a world of
love, of bliss, of eternal youth . . . no suffering, no pain; only
sweet, melancholy longing for the beloved vision.' (Had he
never heard the 'Trauer' or 'La Passione' symphonies, *The
Seven Last Words*, or the F minor keyboard variations?) Mozart,
moving beyond Haydn, led 'deep into the spirit realm' and, in
Don Giovanni, afforded a glimpse of the demonic in music. At

the end of the evolutionary chain, Beethoven evoked awe, fear and terror, awakening 'the infinite yearning which is the essence of Romanticism'.

Haydn's later music was never in serious eclipse. Most of the 'London' symphonies, plus a handful of those composed for Paris, remained repertoire staples throughout the nineteenth century – though until the 1840s they were more popular in France, Germany and Britain than in Austria. In the German-speaking lands, *The Creation* and *The Seasons* fulfilled the same role as *Messiah*, *Israel in Egypt* and *Samson* in Britain and North America. *The Seasons*, especially, reinforced the notion of Haydn as the composer *par excellence* of rural culture, with mud on his boots and roots in Croatian and Austro-Hungarian folk song. Riding official critical disapproval and the 'back-to-Palestrina' Cecilian movement which sought to 'purify' church music, Haydn's masses, like Mozart's, never went out of favour in Austria and Catholic Germany (though as late as the Haydn centenary of 1909 Bavarian and Austrian delegates were squabbling over whether the masses were liturgically acceptable). His keyboard sonatas were indispensable teaching fare; and his string quartets, available (unlike the symphonies) in a complete edition, formed the bedrock of the repertoire, both for amateur players and that new breed, the professional string quartet. The Op. 20 quartets of 1772 were virtually Haydn's only pre-1780 works known outside church and schoolroom.

Yet while Haydn, or at least post-1780 Haydn, was still heard with pleasure, by the 1820s the image was fixed of the composer as a blithe precursor, who created the symphony and string quartet for others to build on: a figure of 'childlike optimism' and prelapsarian innocence in a century that revered heroes, rebels and tragic victims, preferably all rolled into one. Coexisting with Haydn the childlike was the perception of Haydn the avuncular funster. The once-affectionate nickname 'Papa' (which apparently even Haydn's parrot caught on to) was now used condescendingly of a composer who – in contrast to the mercurial, ultimately 'tragic' Mozart and the fist-shaking, destiny-defying Beethoven – had spent his career as a liveried servant of the discredited aristocracy. Even when he had tasted 'freedom' in London, he still returned, dutifully, to his post as Esterházy Kapellmeister. Writing in 1895, that arch-Wagnerian Ernest Newman castigated Haydn as 'pacific and timorous', someone whose spirit was 'almost emasculated by undue seclusion from the active life of men'. (Ironically, and inconveniently for the Romantics, Beethoven intermittently longed for a Kapellmeister's position in the service of a supportive prince.)

Among musicians of the nineteenth and early twentieth centuries Haydn always had his admirers, notably the tradition-revering Brahms, who near the end of his life lamented that 'people understand almost nothing about Haydn any more'. On playing the soaring melody of the Largo of Symphony No. 88 he allegedly exclaimed: 'I want my Ninth Symphony to sound like this!' Another, more surprising, Haydn enthusiast was Richard Wagner, as revealed in Cosima's Diaries, though he still defined Haydn's music in terms of its relationship to Mozart and Beethoven. Cosima's entry for 19 October 1873 (quoted in the final volume of Robbins Landon's *Haydn: Chronicle and Works*), apropos the Andante of Symphony No. 104, gives E. T. A. Hoffmann's evolutionary trope a new twist: 'Haydn, inspired after the death of Mozart by the latter's genius, becomes the real predecessor of Beethoven; rich and yet so finely worked orchestration, everything "speaks", everything is inspiration . . .'

Many nineteenth-century musicians, though, especially those who counted themselves 'progressives', were ambivalent, indifferent or even hostile towards Haydn. After a Leipzig performance of one of his symphonies in 1836, Schumann praised the music's 'sunny clarity' and 'childlike joy'. (Beginning with E. T. A. Hoffmann, the epithets 'kindlich' – childlike – and 'heiter' – serene, or cheerful – would run like a mantra through German Haydn criticism.) Five years later he was more barbed: 'One can learn nothing more from [Haydn]; he is like a regular house friend, always gladly and respectfully received; but he no longer has any deeper interest for our age.' Berlioz, predictably, had even less time for Haydn. *The Creation* came under repeated attack in France (and for that matter in Britain, where it was measured against the all-conquering Handel and found wanting). But in a private letter of 1859 Berlioz, true to form, outdid all the competition in vitriol: 'I have always felt a profound antipathy for this work . . . its lowing oxen, its buzzing insects, its light in C which dazzles like a Carcel lamp; and then its Adam, Uriel, Gabriel, and the flute solos and all the amiabilities really shrivel me up – they make me want to murder someone.' In 1852 the German music historian Franz Brendel even went so far as to attribute the supposed narrow range of Haydn's music to a stunted psychological development, arguing that, in contrast to Mozart, his unhappy marriage rendered him incapable of expressing human love!

Blurring his perception of the composer's allegedly 'spotless' morality with musical aesthetics, Nietzsche, in *Menschliches, Allzumenschliches*, summed up the century's patronising attitude to Haydn: 'So far as genius can exist in a thoroughly virtuous man, Haydn had it. He goes to the edge of the line that morality prescribes for the intellect; he just makes music that has "no past".' Haydn, then, was the esteemed inventor, the developer of the sonata style, without whom Mozart and Beethoven would have been impossible. But in failing to transcend conventional morality, he – unlike Beethoven – could never create music of spiritual and emotional depth. Carl Ferdinand Pohl, in his multi-volume biography (the third volume, dealing with the London and post-London years, was unfinished on his death in 1887) and his influential 1879 *Grove* article, took the same stance, praising Haydn the innovator while repeatedly emphasising, *à la* E. T. A. Hoffmann, his 'childlike cheerfulness'.

What Robbins Landon has called 'the nadir of Haydn's biographical existence', certainly in the English-speaking world, came with the publication of J. Cuthbert Hadden's influential *Master Musicians* volume in 1899, revised in 1934 and still to be found in second-hand bookshops. He blithely dismissed the ninety-odd pre-'London' symphonies as 'of practically no account', and wrote of the quartets: 'It would be too much to say that even Haydn fully realised the capacities of each of his four instruments. Indeed, his quartet writing is often bald and uninteresting.' In a final *coup de grâce* he added: 'But at least he did write in four-part harmony.' Phew!

Although the 1909 centenary celebrations prompted no significant revaluation of Haydn, between the wars public perception of the composer began to shift, in part because of a wider reaction against the febrile, neurasthenic atmosphere of late Romanticism (this was the era of Les Six and the neoclassical Stravinsky). Most crucial in the English-speaking world, though, was the passionate championship of Sir Donald Francis Tovey. For Cobbett's *Cyclopaedia of Chamber Music* (1929), Tovey wrote a brilliant extended article on Haydn's string quartets that, unprecedentedly, identified and celebrated the unique mastery of each work. For the concerts of the Reid Orchestra he founded in Edinburgh he penned his still widely read series of analytical essays on eleven late symphonies (Nos. 88 and 92 plus nine of the London twelve). Here was Haydn as consummate master rather than warm-up act to Mozart and Beethoven: Haydn the supreme original, Haydn the intrepid adventurer, heedless of 'rules'; a Haydn of kittenish playfulness and tigerish power (two of his favourite tropes) who traded in the inspired-unexpected and raised wit to the level of the sublime. Most significantly, and most controversially for the nay-sayers, Tovey's Haydn was also a composer of emotional profundity who (in the slow introduction of No. 104) could 'strike one of those tragic notes of which [he] knows the depth as well as or better than the gloomiest artists'. In sum, here was a Haydn who would not be cowed by Mozart, Beethoven or anyone else.

Tovey's understanding of Haydn, as revolutionary in its way as Hermann Abert's debunking in the German-speaking world of the sentimentalised rococo image of Mozart, has crucially coloured the attitudes of later generations of scholars and music-lovers. But it was with good reason that Tovey dubbed Haydn 'the Inaccessible'. With whole swathes of his music, especially works from his early and middle years, not even in print, scholarship on Haydn lagged far behind that on any other eighteenth- and nineteenth-century composer of comparable stature. Only after the Second World War, thanks to the efforts of Jens Peter Larsen (who had earlier weeded out numerous spurious symphonies marketed under Haydn's name) and, above all, that prodigious and indefatigable scholar-populariser H. C. Robbins Landon, has most of Haydn's vast output become available in a reliable critical edition – though at the time of writing (2008), the collected edition prepared by the Joseph Haydn-Institut in Cologne and published by Henle Verlag is still several years from completion. Beginning with the records he produced for the Haydn Society he founded in 1949, Robbins Landon also initiated many Haydn recordings and broadcast performances. Today we can hear on CD over ninety per cent of Haydn's music, more than anyone bar the composer himself could have heard during his own lifetime.

Two centuries after his death, the composer's stock has never been higher among scholars – for whom Haydn the subversive, Haydn the paradoxical, Haydn the peerless master of complex and subtle cerebral games holds a unique fascination – professional musicians (including many composers) and a growing band of aficionados. Like Mozart, he has benefited immeasurably from historically aware performances, often on 'period' instruments, that aim to recreate the colours, balances and articulations of the late eighteenth century. The results have been to make Haydn's works sound even more fiercely original, certainly less comfortable, with the un-Mozartian rough edges in his music relished rather than planed. No one can hear, say, Trevor Pinnock's recordings of the so-called *Sturm und Drang* symphonies, or Nikolaus Harnoncourt's 'Paris' set, and still talk patronisingly of dear old 'Papa Haydn'.

And yet . . . Not even the most fanatical Haydn-lover could claim him as a truly popular composer, with the iconic status of Bach, Mozart, Beethoven, Schubert or Wagner. Tovey notwithstanding, comparisons with Mozart – usually adverse –

even now colour many people's perception of Haydn, as irrel-
evant comparisons with Brahms long dogged Bruckner. Ask
any concert promoter or recording executive and you will still
hear the old cliché that Haydn – apart from *The Creation* and,
in German-speaking lands, *The Seasons* – spells death at the box
office/CD store. Three period-instrument symphony cycles
(from Roy Goodman, Christopher Hogwood and Bruno Weil)
were bravely begun and then abandoned as commercial fail-
ures. Alan George, viola player in the Fitzwilliam String
Quartet, has written, from experience, that replacing a Haydn
quartet with one by Mozart is almost certain to boost ticket
sales. No one in their right mind would fancy living on the
profits of a Peter Shaffer/Milos Forman *Joseph*.

One problem, of course, is the undeniable lack of romantic
appeal in Haydn's long life. Although far from the naive,
unreflective countryman of popular imagination, he is still the
victim of the amiable persona he presented to the world, and
of a working life spent largely in seclusion as Esterházy
Kapellmeister: no scurrilous letters, no rebellion against the
status quo, no scandal or intrigue (the odd mistress was de
rigueur in eighteenth-century court circles), no 'stranger in
black' or deathbed Requiem, no tragically premature end.
Haydn's life, unlike Mozart's, has defied mythification.

Haydn ended his brief Autobiographical Sketch of 1776
with the words: 'My sole wish is to offend neither my neighbour, nor my gracious prince, nor above all our merciful
God.' Modesty – twisted by the Romantics into a cringing
meekness – love of order, a strong sense of duty and a devout,
yet never dogmatic, Catholic faith were instilled from early
childhood. His neatly written autograph scores are typically
headed 'In nomine Domini' and signed off with 'Laus Deo'.
As to the deep-seated sense of duty that so riled the nineteenth century, at least until the late 1780s Haydn easily reconciled service to Prince Nicolaus with an acute sense of his
own creative worth. He famously told Griesinger, 'My prince
was happy with all my works . . . I could, as head of an orchestra, experiment, see what enhanced and what weakened an

effect . . . I was set apart from the world, there was nobody nearby to confuse or annoy me in my course, so I couldn't help becoming original.'

In childhood Haydn acquired a reputation as something of a prankster. On a (usually) more sophisticated plane, this love of practical jokes is evident in so much of his music (as I write these words I chuckle inwardly at the 'clap if you dare' false ending of Symphony No. 90). Griesinger wrote that 'a guileless roguery, what the English call *humour*, was among Haydn's out-standing characteristics'. Dies observed in his character 'a genial, witty, teasing strain, but with it always the innocence of a child'. Yet as in his music, his humour can have a wry, acerbic edge, as manifested, inter alia, in his letters to Maria Anna von Genzinger and his London Notebooks.

While it would be absurd to 'deconstruct' Haydn and pres-ent him as a tragic or misunderstood figure, his personality, like his music, was less bucolically uncomplicated than the nineteenth century, and much of the twentieth, liked to imag-ine. That he was affable, considerate to his fellow musicians (among whom he was always popular) and a kindly father fig-ure to his pupils, is irrefutable. Beyond this he never seems to have lacked self-belief, became a shrewd diplomat as Esterházy Kapellmeister and, in later years, mixed easily with people of all classes – though as he told a visitor late in life, he preferred to associate with people of his own status rather than aristo-crats or royalty. Witnesses testify to his predominant cheerful-ness. Yet as his letters to Frau von Genzinger, especially, reveal, he could be prey to loneliness and depression, both in the wilds of Eszterháza (which by 1790 he had come to loathe) and in London. With or without the consolation of Luigia Polzelli, he must often have felt isolated and embittered in his marriage to an ill-educated woman who was utterly indifferent to his music. The much-maligned Constanze Mozart was a model of enlightened understanding by comparison. Haydn's modesty, remarked on by many contemporaries, coexisted with a justified pride in his achievements. But until late in life he remained surprisingly touchy about attacks, usually emanating from Berlin or Hamburg, on the 'comic fooling' of his symphonies, quartets and sonatas. It also rankled that his music never found favour with Joseph II and his entourage. Haydn's hostility to Leopold Hofmann (whom he accused of slandering him) was surely fuelled by the fact that Hofmann, a third-rate talent, was a Habsburg court 'insider'.

From his impecunious freelance years in Vienna around 1750, Haydn was always acutely aware of the value of money, as countless letters to publishers reveal. No one, not even Beethoven, was more adept at driving a favourable bargain, or at selling 'exclusive' rights to two or more publishers or patrons. The absence of copyright protection can be offered in partial mitigation here, though not when Haydn shamelessly passed off two keyboard trios by his pupil Pleyel as his own. From several contemporary comments, we can infer that Haydn would not, perhaps, have been the first to buy his round in the pub. That said, he was generous to those closest to him (some have cited a 'peasant's instinct' here), supporting his youngest brother Johann Evangelist for many years, and providing for his relatives and servants, and even his ex-mistress Luigia Polzelli, in his will.

The writer Caroline Pichler, who met both Haydn and Mozart at the Viennese salons of her father, Franz Sales von Greiner (and in 1795 penned a terrible poem in praise of Haydn), recorded that they were men of absolutely no intellectual distinction outside music. Others, including Griesinger, have stressed Haydn's lack of literary culture. Yet Haydn was au fait with contemporary trends in Enlightenment literature, aesthetics and philosophy, stimulated by his contact with writers and intellectuals in Vienna and, later, London. His avowed favourite among poets (also much admired by C. P. E. Bach and Beethoven) was Christian Fürchtegott Gellert (1715–69), whose deftly crafted verses treat moral questions and religious truths with a light, popular, sometimes witty touch. Besides musical treatises, encyclopaedias and books on astronomy (in England he was fascinated by Herschel's telescope) and agriculture, Haydn's library contained, inter alia, a German translation of Pope's *Essay on Man*, volumes of German poetry, and a number of works he had acquired, probably as gifts, in England. These include Burney's *General History*, Sterne's *A Sentimental Journey through France and Italy* (Haydn was more than once compared to the Irish master of the comic, the antic and the paradoxical), Edmund Burke's *A Philosophical Inquiry into the Origin of Our Ideas of the Sublime and Beautiful*, Adam Smith's *The Theory of Moral Sentiments* and an annotated edition of Shakespeare's plays.

In line with the aesthetic thought of Burke and Smith, Haydn was intent that music should be a medium not just of entertainment but of moral and philosophical contemplation. He told Griesinger that he portrayed 'moral characters' in his music. And as the American musicologist David Schroeder and others have convincingly demonstrated, in his later music, especially, he sought not merely to entertain and move, but to take the listener on a journey of intellectual and ethical enlightenment, thus encouraging reflective, 'philosophical' listening. That habit was lost in the nineteenth century, which placed a premium on the confessional, the erotic and the apocalyptic.

Haydn's questing, rigorously argumentative, ultimately optimistic art rarely admits of the operatically inspired lyrical sweetness and pathos with which Mozart captivates the most casual listener, though we might be thankful that this has at least saved Haydn from mobile ringtones and shopping malls. So much of Mozart's music is opera by other means. Beethoven, with his ethically charged idealism, characteristically evokes a sense of forces confronted and heroically overcome. While moral enlightenment may have been Haydn's goal in his later symphonies, his instrumental works, except for obvious pictorialisms and the unique case of *The Seven Last Words*, are quintessentially music about music. He is arguably the most sophisticated manipulator and subverter of musical forms in history – one aspect of his appeal to modern composers. His greatest symphonies, quartets, sonatas and piano trios are among the marvels of civilised art, endlessly unpredictable in their strategies and structure, dazzling in their sheer speed of thought, breathtaking in their expressive range. Their themes may be innocent, their treatment never. And *The Seven Last Words* and the fathomless, harmonically visionary slow movements of the late quartets and masses, where Haydn's religious impulse is coloured by a Romantic sense of the sublime and the ineffable, should scotch once and for all the notion that he was incapable of evoking the most exalted spiritual states.

Perhaps this supremely companionable yet at times (especially in some of the string quartets, of all periods) curiously ascetic composer, rarely as straightforward as he seems, sometimes eccentric to the point of perversity and only 'naive' when it suits him, will never quite match the popular appeal of Mozart and Beethoven. Yet in our fractured and neurotic age, his humane, life-affirming vision, expressed with consummate mastery of the sonata style he did more than anyone to perfect, has a unique power to refresh and uplift the spirit. It is tempting to suggest, with composer Robin Holloway, that the full extent of his greatness is a ticking time bomb that has yet to go off. 'When its hour comes the explosion, rather than a Big Bang, will be a still small voice that tells of the vast within the modest, the dark within the bright, and vice versa: the essence of human experience in essentially musical terms.'

HAYDN: THE LIFE

A biographical sketch

What sparse information we have on Haydn's youth and early manhood derives largely from four sources: his own Autobiographical Sketch of 1776, carefully fashioned for *Das gelehrte Österreich*, a kind of Austrian 'Who's Who'; and the three relatively brief biographies of Georg August Griesinger, Albert Christoph Dies and Giuseppe Carpani, all based on conversations with Haydn during the last decade of his life. The most dependable account is by the diplomat (he became Royal Councillor to the Saxon Legation in Vienna) and journalist Griesinger, whose avowed aim was 'to sketch Haydn as faithfully as possible as he lived and as he was'. Dies, professor of landscape painting at the Imperial Academy in Vienna, writes more vividly on Haydn's life (especially in old age) and character, though he only knew the composer from 1805 onwards, when his memory was often shaky. Least reliable of all is the epistolary biography *Le Haydine* by the Italian *littérateur* Carpani, always more interested in a piquant anecdote than in getting his facts right. To these early sources we can add the music historian Carl Ferdinand Pohl (1819–87), author of a monumental, multi-volume Haydn biography (the third and final volume was completed by Hugo Botsiber in 1927), who drew on many documents that are now lost.

Boyhood and youth, 1732–c.1749

'I was born on the last day of March 1733 in the market village of Rohrau, Lower Austria, near Prugg an der Leytha' [nowadays spelt Bruck an der Leitha], wrote Haydn in his Autobiographical Sketch. Dates are never the strongest point in these early sources. Dies gets the year, 1732, right but has Haydn born prematurely on 30 March. As usual Griesinger is the most reliable, giving the date as 31 March 1732 – though many contemporary sources state 1 April, the day Haydn was baptised. Situated some forty kilometres east of Vienna on the western bank of the River Leitha that then divided Austria from Hungary, Rohrau was, and in essence remains, a tranquil one-street village set amid low-lying countryside of marshes (the Leitha would often overflow its banks), woods and vine-yards. When the dying Beethoven was given a lithograph of the single-storey thatched farmhouse where Haydn was born, he allegedly exclaimed: 'Strange, that such a great man should have come from such a poor cottage.' The birthplace, rebuilt after being gutted by fire in 1899, survives in a rather pretti-fied, sanitised form as a small Haydn museum.

Haydn, who with mingled touchiness and pride liked to emphasise his humble origins, would doubtless have appreci-ated Beethoven's encomium. But while his family was several notches lower down the social scale than Mozart's, the Haydns were not quite the impoverished 'peasants' of popular mythol-ogy. Although there were partisan attempts in the nineteenth century to claim the composer as Croatian, Hungarian or Slovakian (this corner of the sprawling Habsburg Empire had long been an ethnic melting pot), his ancestors on both sides were of South German stock. (The etymological origin of 'Haydn' is *Heide*, meaning either 'heath' or 'heathen'. In his lifetime his name was variously spelt 'Heiden', 'Haiden', 'Heydn', 'Hayden' or 'Haidn'.) Haydn's father's family had lived for two generations in the nearby town of Hainburg. His father Matthias (1699–1763) was a respected master wheel-wright, following in the footsteps of his own father Thomas, who had narrowly escaped the marauding Turks in July 1683. Matthias's standing in Rohrau was acknowledged in 1741 when he became the village's elected magistrate, or *Marktrichter*, responsible for supervising the market, arranging the rota for fire-guard duty, ensuring that the roads and fences were in good repair, and seeing that people paid their dues promptly to the local lord of the manor.

The lord in question was Count Karl Anton von Harrach (1692–1758), who provided Matthias with plenty of work repairing and repainting coaches, and had employed Joseph's mother, née Anna Maria Koller (1707–54), as a cook at Schloss Harrach before her marriage in 1728. Dies wrote of her concern for 'neatness, diligence and order, qualities she sternly required of her children at a tender age'. There were twelve children in all, born between 1730 and 1745, six of whom (three sons and three daughters) survived to adulthood: an unusually high proportion in those days, and a tribute to Anna Maria's standards of hygiene. Joseph – usually known by the Austrian diminutive 'Sepperl' – was the second child and the eldest son. His two younger brothers, Johann Michael (1737–1806) and Johann Evangelist (1743–1805), would likewise become professional musicians.

Haydn wrote that his father was 'a great lover of music by nature'. Although Matthias had no formal training, he had taught himself to play the harp as a journeyman wheelwright in Frankfurt-am-Main. He also had a pleasant tenor voice, and in the evenings often accompanied himself and Anna Maria in folk songs. In Dies's words, 'All the children had to join in his concerts, to learn the songs and to develop their singing voices. When the father sang, the five-year-old Joseph used to accompany him, as children will, by playing with a stick on a piece of wood; his childish imagination turned this into a violin.'

Though he was hardly a Wunderkind à la Mozart, Joseph's musical gifts manifested themselves early. In his Autobiographical Sketch he wrote that 'as a boy of 5 I correctly sang all [my father's] simple little pieces'. In late 1737 or early 1738 his singing talent, and his ability to keep time accurately, were spotted by Matthias's friend and cousin-by-marriage Johann Matthias Franck, a schoolteacher and choir director in Hainburg. Franck proposed that Joseph should go and live with him and his wife, 'in order that I might learn the rudiments of music and other juvenile necessities'. After long deliberations his parents agreed, though at that stage Anna Maria was set on her clever eldest son becoming a priest. Around his sixth birthday the boy moved into Franck's cramped, shabby home-cum-schoolhouse in the walled fortress town on the Danube.

If various anecdotes are to be believed (in presenting a rags-to-riches life story, the aged Haydn always enjoyed dwelling on his early hardships), Franck ran his school with an iron hand, like a cross between Dickens's Gradgrind and Mr Squeers. Nor does personal hygiene seem to have been a priority in the Franck household, as Haydn told Dies:

> I could not help noticing, to my distress, that I was gradually getting very dirty, and although I took great pride in my small person [even in childhood he habitually wore a wig for cleanliness], I could still not prevent stains on my clothes, which made me very ashamed . . .

Yet the composer would look back on his time in Hainburg with gratitude, if not affection. In Griesinger's words:

> He received instruction in reading and writing, in the catechism, in singing, and on almost all the string and wind instruments, even the timpani: 'I shall be indebted to this man even in the grave', Haydn often said, 'that he taught me so much, even though in the process I received more thrashings than food.'

'When I was 7 the late Capellmeister von Reutter passed through Haimburg [sic] and quite by chance heard my weak but pleasant voice,' recalled Haydn in his Autobiographical Sketch. 'He immediately took me to the choir school where, apart from my studies, I learnt the art of singing, the harpsichord and the violin from very good masters.' As Griesinger has it, Joseph was eight when Georg Reutter the younger, Kapellmeister of St Stephen's Cathedral in Vienna, 'auditioned' him during a talent-scouting mission, tipped off by the local parish priest. What seems to have clinched the appointment was the boy's rapid mastery of the trill, lured by handfuls of cherries from the priest.

Dies agrees with Haydn's own dating of the audition, but adds that Reutter insisted he wait until his eighth birthday and in the meantime diligently practise his scales. So it was probably in the late spring or summer of 1740 that Haydn, like

Schubert after him, became one of six trebles in Vienna's élite choir school, singing, in his own words, 'both at St Stephen's and at court to great applause'. Life in the choir house, adjacent to the mighty cathedral (described by Charles Burney in 1772 as 'a dark, dirty, and dismal old Gothic building, though richly ornamented'), was apparently even more spartan than at Franck's, making the frequent concerts at homes of the nobility, where food was provided, all the more welcome. Crucially, though, the boy imbibed a vast amount of music both ancient and modern at St Stephen's. In his daily routine he sang masses and motets by composers ranging from Palestrina and Allegri (whose celebrated *Miserere* was a staple), through Alessandro Scarlatti, Johann Joseph Fux and the Italian-born honorary Viennese Antonio Caldara, to living figures such as the imperial court composer Georg Christoph Wagenseil, Johann Adolf Hasse, and Kapellmeister Reutter himself. Regular services were augmented by lavish Habsburg ceremonies, such as the requiem mass for Emperor Charles VI in October 1740.

Griesinger writes that 'apart from scanty instruction customary at that time in Latin, religion, arithmetic and writing, Haydn had in the choir school very capable instructors on several instruments, and particularly in the art of singing'. All the sources state that the boy received scant training in music theory. (Haydn always stressed that he learned primarily from listening to the works of others rather than formal study.) According to Griesinger, Reutter gave him just two lessons, though in partial mitigation he did 'encourage him to make whatever variations he liked on the motets and *Salves* that he had to sing in church, and this practice soon led him to ideas of his own which Reutter corrected'. What scant spare time Joseph had seems to have been devoted to composition, though unlike the meticulously trained and supervised Mozart, his reach in those early years exceeded his grasp. Griesinger and Dies each tell a similar story (with minor variants) of the ambitious fledgling composer. As Dies has it:

Reutern [*sic*] surprised him once just as he had spread out a *Salve regina* in twelve parts on a sheet of paper more than one ell long. 'Hey boy, what are you doing?' Reutern looked over the long sheet, laughed heartily at the numerous repetitions of the word 'Salve' and still more at the ridiculous idea that he could compose in twelve parts [Griesinger has sixteen]. He added, 'You silly lad, aren't two parts enough for you?'

Several anecdotes testify to the boy's sense of fun and adventure. At Whitsun 1745 the six choirboys augmented the court choir at the Habsburg summer palace of Schönbrunn, then in the final stages of reconstruction. Dies relates how

Except for the church services, he used to play with the other boys, climbing the scaffolding and making a terrible din on the staging. What happened? The boys suddenly beheld a lady. It was the Empress Maria Theresa herself, who ordered someone to get the noisy boys off the scaffolding and to threaten them with a thrashing if they were caught there again. The next day, driven by curiosity, Haydn climbed the scaffolding alone, was caught, and duly collected the promised thrashing.

Haydn would remind the amused empress of the incident when she visited Eszterháza in 1773.

By 1745 Joseph was the choir's star treble, soon to be joined by his talented eight-year-old brother Michael. A year or two later Reutter proposed to 'make the young Haydn's fortune' by turning him into a 'permanent soprano'. The plan was foiled when Matthias Haydn swiftly appeared and, relieved to find his son still intact, forbade the operation. A much-quoted story tells how, before a ceremony at the Augustinian monastery of Klosterneuburg in November 1748, the Empress had rejected the sixteen-year-old Joseph as treble soloist, announcing to Reutter that he 'doesn't sing any more; he crows'. The solos went instead to brother Michael. Croaky, adolescent Joseph was now of little use to Reutter, though his inevitable dismissal from St Stephen's seems to have been hastened when he cut off the pigtail of another choirboy. (The future author of the 'Joke' Quartet and the bassoon raspberry in Symphony No. 93 was already renowned for his prankish humour.) So some time between the end of 1748 and November 1749 (the precise date given by Pohl) Haydn left the choir school for the last time.

Freelance in Vienna, c. 1749–1761

Pohl recounts, doubtless with more than a touch of romantic exaggeration, how the penniless seventeen-year-old Haydn spent that first damp November night on a bench in the open. Yet while his life as a freelance musician in Vienna was initially hard (he would write of these galley years that he was 'forced to eke out a wretched existence by teaching young people'), Haydn never seems to have contemplated returning to the parental home in Rohrau. His first lodgings were in the garret of an acquaintance, Johann Michael Spangler, a tenor at the Michaelerkirche opposite the entrance to the Hofburg. Spangler's wife's pregnancy put an end to this arrangement after a few months, though Haydn would repay the debt many years later by engaging the daughter they were expecting, Maria Magdalena, as a soprano in the Esterházy opera troupe.

Griesinger and Dies both tell of Haydn's pilgrimage, possibly in the spring of 1750, to the Benedictine church of Mariazell in the Styrian Alps, whose statue of the Black Virgin drew vast numbers of pilgrims. Already confident of his prowess as a composer, he took with him some 'motets' (perhaps including his earliest surviving composition, the *Missa brevis* in F) and asked the choirmaster if his choir might sing them. The request was refused, though at a service the next day Haydn made his mark by devious means, snatching a copy from one of the soloists and singing with such panache that he was rewarded with sixteen gulden. Two of Haydn's later masses were to have associations with Mariazell.

Swapping one garret for another, Haydn moved from the Spanglers to a squalid, leaky attic room in the so-called Michaelerhaus on the Kohlmarkt, next to the Michaelerkirche. (The building still stands today.) In Dies's account, 'the utter loneliness of the place, the complete lack of anything to encourage a spirit unemployed, and his altogether desperate situation led him to such gloomy speculation that he was obliged to take refuge in his worm-eaten clavichord or his violin to play away his cares.' He would compose zealously well into the night; and drawing on friends and contacts made at St Stephen's, he initially scraped a living by giving lessons and playing the violin in orchestras and in street serenade parties, a favourite activity in Maria Theresa's hedonistic Vienna.

In those days the higher up the social scale you were the lower down you lived. And as luck had it, the elegant ground-floor apartment of the Michaelerhaus was occupied by Pietro Metastasio, court poet and the century's most celebrated librettist. Metastasio was tutor to the eight-year-old Marianne von Martínez, the future singer and composer who would play duets with Mozart at her salons in the 1780s. In return for free meals, Haydn was engaged by the poet to teach Marianne keyboard and singing.

About the same time his alfresco music-making led to a chance encounter with the popular Viennese comedian and impresario Joseph Felix von Kurz, known by his stage persona 'Bernardon'. One evening, after Haydn and his accomplices had serenaded Kurz's wife, the actor asked for the composer of the piece just performed. Haydn came forward, and was immediately commissioned, for the handsome sum of twenty-five ducats, to write numbers for Kurz's new play with music, *Der krumme Teufel* (The crooked devil). The show – probably the first public performance of any of Haydn's works – was successfully staged at the Kärntnerthor Theatre in May 1753 before being banned, allegedly because of its satirical references to an Italian theatre director, Giuseppe Afflisio. Neither libretto nor score survives, though we can glean a flavour of the story – a typical *Hanswurst* farce replete with topical gags – from its follow-up, *Der neue krumme Teufel*, set by Haydn for a Kärntnerthor production in November 1759. Again the music is lost.

During the winter of 1752–3, Metastasio introduced Haydn to the crusty old opera composer Nicola Porpora, recently arrived in Vienna from Dresden. As Griesinger put it, 'Porpora was giving voice lessons to the mistress of the Venetian ambassador, Correr; however, because he was too grand and too fond of his ease to accompany her on the harpsichord himself, he entrusted this business to our Giuseppe.' (In later life Haydn would routinely use the Italian form of his name.) The composer recalled 'many taunts of *Ass, Idiot, Rascal*, and pokes in the ribs. But I put up with them because I profited greatly from Porpora in singing, composition and Italian.'

In his Autobiographical Sketch we read that through Porpora Haydn 'learnt the true fundamentals of composition'. Perhaps at Porpora's behest he honed his mastery of traditional contrapuntal techniques by working his way through the standard textbooks: *Gradus ad Parnassum* (1725) by the Viennese Baroque composer and theoretician J. J. Fux, and Johann Mattheson's *Der vollkommene Kapellmeister* (1739). Haydn would later use *Gradus ad Parnassum* as the basis of his own teaching. Both Griesinger and Dies date Haydn's excited discovery of the sonatas and theoretical writings of Carl Philipp Emanuel Bach to this period, though research by the American musicologist A. Peter Brown has revealed that little, if any, of Bach's music was available in Vienna until the following decade. Through Porpora Haydn made contact with other eminent figures in the Viennese musical scene, including Gluck and Wagenseil, the latter an important influence on Haydn's early style.

By about 1755, with growing access to patronage – crucial to any aspiring young musician in the imperial capital – the twenty-three-year-old Haydn's fortunes were definitely on the up. He was now earning a tolerable living, primarily through teaching, leading the orchestra in the Leopoldstadt church of the Barmherzige Brüder (for which he earned sixty gulden a year) and playing the organ in the chapel of Count Haugwitz in the Bohemian Chancellery. He also sang tenor in the Hofkapelle in Lent, played the violin at court balls during the carnival season and began to sell manuscript copies of his keyboard divertimenti. With a growing tally of female pupils, Haydn gradually increased his monthly fee from two to five ducats. He repaid a loan of 150 gulden, and was able to leave the Michaelerhaus for more salubrious lodgings in the Seilerstätte. Shortly after the move all his clothes were stolen. From his father (Matthias remarried in 1755 after Anna Maria's death the previous year) he received only a seventeen-kreutzer coin and pious advice to 'fear God and love thy neighbour'. But, in Griesinger's words, 'Haydn soon saw his loss restored by the generosity of good friends; one had a dark suit made for him, another gave him shirts and underclothes, and Haydn recovered through a stay of two months with Baron Fürnberg that cost him nothing.'

Haydn probably came to know the music-loving government official Carl Joseph von Fürnberg when he was engaged to give music lessons to his children. The Baron owned an estate at Weinzierl, near the picturesque wine village of Weissenkirchen in der Wachau, about fifty kilometres west of Vienna. Here he often hosted summer music parties with a more or less regular group of players, including Haydn; and it was for these occasions, probably some time between 1754 and 1757, that the young composer produced his first divertimenti for string quartet, alighting 'by accident' (Haydn's words) on the genre which he would raise to supreme heights. It is likely, too, that many of the early string trios were also composed for Weinzierl. According to Dies, 'the quartets and other pieces won him the increasing favour of amateur musicians, so that he became recognised everywhere as a genius'.

In the tight-knit world of Viennese musical patronage one contact led to another; and it was on Fürnberg's recommendation, probably (that word again) in 1757 or 1758, that Haydn landed his first full-time appointment: as Kapellmeister to a Count Morzin – either Franz Ferdinand Maximilian or his son Carl Joseph Franz – at a salary of two hundred gulden, plus free lodging and board at the officer's table. Griesinger wrote that the composer 'was at last able to enjoy the happiness of a care-free existence; he was quite contented. Winters were spent in Vienna, summers in Bohemia [at the count's palace at Lukavec, near Pilsen].' For Morzin's small band of a dozen or so players Haydn composed his earliest symphonies, and assorted divertimenti for wind ensemble.

During the summers at Lukavec Haydn acquired a passion for hunting and fishing, though, as Griesinger reports, 'in riding he developed no skill, because after he had fallen from a horse on the Morzin estate, he never trusted himself again to mount'. Otherwise little is known of these years except that at a service in St Stephen's Cathedral on 26 November 1760 Haydn married Maria Anna Aloysia Apollonia Keller (1729–1800), elder daughter of the wigmaker Johann Peter Keller. On the recommendation of his brother Georg Ignaz, a violinist in the St Stephen's *Kapelle*, Keller had for a time employed Haydn as music teacher. It was testimony to the composer's thrift and growing financial security that he was able to deposit a thousand gulden as a so-called 'matching-sum' for his wife's dowry.

Several years earlier Haydn had fallen in love with Maria Anna's sister, Therese. But as often happened with the younger daughters of devout Catholic families, she was encouraged, perhaps even compelled, by her parents to enter a nunnery. So, like Mozart and Dvořák after him, Haydn married the sister of his first love. Unlike theirs, though, his marriage was a story of growing indifference, petty quarrels and infidelities on both sides.

By Haydn's own account, his wife was ill-educated, unmusical (he told Griesinger that 'it's all the same to her whether her husband is a cobbler or an artist'), shrewish, irresponsible with money and religious to the point of bigotry. While her unsympathetic image has doubtless been exaggerated in the Haydn literature, other witnesses confirm her lack of culture. In his memoirs, the Swedish violinist and composer Johan Fredrik Berwald recalled visiting the Haydns as a boy in 1799:

> When the conversation fell on that excellent work, *The Creation*, which we had heard yesterday, she said, 'People say it's supposed to be good, I wouldn't know.' We gathered from the old lady's words that she was neither educated nor musical. They say in Vienna that Haydn's rather unhappy and childless marriage is the reason why he composed so much.

In the early 1770s Maria Anna had an affair with the Esterházy court painter Ludwig Guttenbrunn. A few years later Haydn began a lengthy liaison with the singer Luigia Polzelli. In a defence that would hardly have stood up in court, Haydn told Griesinger: 'My wife was unable to bear children, and I was therefore less indifferent to the charms of other women.' Ironically, Therese would choose a secular life after her Viennese convent was dissolved in the 1780s.

Dies relates how Haydn had to conceal his marriage from Count Morzin, who expressly forbade members of his musical establishment to wed. By then, though, the spendthrift count found himself virtually bankrupt, and was soon forced to dismiss his musicians. His Kapellmeister had already come to the attention of Prince Paul Anton Esterházy, head of the dynasty whose unswerving loyalty to the Habsburg crown had helped make it second only to the royal family in wealth and influence. Griesinger tells how the prince (whom he confuses with his younger brother Nicolaus), in the process of enlarging his musical entourage and needing an assistant to his aged Kapellmeister Gregor Joseph Werner, was so delighted by a performance of Haydn's Symphony No. 1 that he offered the composer a job on the spot. Whatever the exact truth, in March 1761 Haydn took up the post of vice-Kapellmeister at the Esterházys' Viennese palace in the Wallnerstrasse, a stone's throw from the Michaelerkirche. On 1 May he signed a three-year formal contract, renewable at the prince's pleasure. His official annual salary was four hundred gulden, double what he had earned as Kapellmeister to Count Morzin, though a recently discovered document in the Esterházy archives reveals that he received an extra two hundred gulden, initially paid 'under the counter' so as not to offend Werner. Haydn would remain in the service of the Esterházys, either actively or nominally, until his death nearly half a century later.

Esterházy vice-Kapellmeister, 1761–1766

The Romantics would pointedly contrast Haydn's long years of willing 'servitude' at the Esterházy court with the 'emancipated' Mozart and, especially, Beethoven. Yet for the twenty-nine-year-old Haydn in 1761, the Esterházy appointment, with its promise of imminent promotion (Werner was sixty-eight, and in weakening health), represented the triumphant fulfilment of his youthful ambition.

Members of the Austro-Hungarian nobility were forever vying with each other in status-enhancing ostentation. Prince Paul Anton's desire to expand his musical establishment, though, was not merely cultural one-upmanship but impelled by a passionate and informed love of music. As 'Ober-Kapellmeister', Werner remained in charge of music for the church. Haydn's contract – deemed debasing by later generations, but typical of the century (compare J. S. Bach's duties in Leipzig) – stipulated that 'in all other circumstances, where any sort of music is to be made, everything relating to the music, in general and in particular, is the responsibility of the said vice-Kapellmeister'. As a 'house officer' (rather than a servant) Haydn had to ensure the good behaviour of his musicians, and to 'avoid undue familiarity in eating and drinking or otherwise in his relations with them, lest he should lose the respect due to him'. He was obliged to 'compose such pieces of music as his Serene Highness may command', and forbidden from writing for anyone else. Twice a day he was required to appear before Prince Paul Anton to learn what music was wanted for his Highness and his guests. He was also responsible for engaging new instrumentalists (some of whom he may have recruited from Morzin's disbanded orchestra), supervising the music library, purchasing musical instruments, and coaching the female singers at the court.

Haydn's first works for the expert Esterházy orchestra of around fifteen musicians were the 'times of day' symphonies, Nos. 6–8. A sure-fire success with the prince (who had apparently suggested to Haydn a follow-up to Vivaldi's *Four Seasons*), these were also guaranteed to endear Haydn to his players. By now, though, Paul Anton was a sick man. He died, childless, on 18 March 1762, and was succeeded by his younger brother Nicolaus, destined to be Haydn's employer for twenty-eight years. Like Paul Anton, Nicolaus had distinguished himself as a soldier in the Habsburg army, showing outstanding bravery at the head of a cavalry regiment at the Battle of Kolin (1757) during the Seven Years War. Like his older brother, too, he tended to run his court like a more or less benign military establishment, with his estates manager Peter Ludwig von Rahier as his first lieutenant. But in his fanatical passion for music (he was a fine violinist) and theatre, and his love of display, Nicolaus left Paul Anton standing. His taste for sumptuous ceremony led Goethe to coin the phrase 'das Esterházysche Feenreich' (the Esterházy Fairy Kingdom) and quickly earned him the nickname 'Nicolaus the Lover of Magnificence'.

Unlike his brother, Prince Nicolaus preferred rural to urban living. Although he initially spent a few months each winter in Vienna, he transferred the court's base to the Esterházys' summer castle in provincial Eisenstadt, a predominantly German-speaking town in what was then Hungary, some forty-five kilometres south-east of Vienna. A vast, ungainly slab of a building, Schloss Esterházy originated as a medieval fortress and was rebuilt between 1663 and 1672 as a Baroque palace, complete with four bulky corner towers topped by onion domes, and a frescoed hall (now known as the Haydnsaal) where Haydn would premiere many of his symphonies and chamber works. Nicolaus also liked to spend as much time as possible at Süttor, his roomy hunting lodge in reclaimed malarial swampland south-east of Lake Neusiedl, where he could indulge his passion for duck-shooting. Many an eighteenth-century prince dreamt of creating his own Versailles. Nicolaus Esterházy was one of the few with the means to turn fantasy into reality. And with the Viennese architect Melchior Hefele, he was soon hatching plans to transform the unhealthily sited hunting lodge into a rococo Italianate showpiece that would rival the Habsburg palace of Schönbrunn.

For all his hauteur and pomposity, Nicolaus was to prove a generous and appreciative patron to Haydn, who until he bought his own house in 1766 lived with his wife in an apartment in the 'Old Apothecary', just up the hill from the Esterházys' Eisenstadt castle. His works during these early years were mainly instrumental: symphonies, concertos for members of the orchestra, divertimenti and dances. There were also congratulatory cantatas for His Highness, the *festa teatrale*, *Acide e Galatea*, and four short comic operas, of which only a fragment of *La Marchesa Nespola* survives.

As a buffer between the princely administration and the musicians, the modest yet quietly self-confident composer quickly became an accomplished diplomat. In September 1765 a fraught situation developed when some impromptu bird-shooting from flautist Franz Sigl set fire to one of the prince's houses, with near-disastrous consequences for the whole town. The irascible estates manager Rahier – never Haydn's favourite member of the Esterházy establishment – summarily arrested and imprisoned Sigl. When the composer protested, Rahier reported him to Prince Nicolaus, who delivered a severe reprimand. Haydn's reply to the prince, in which he also defends the disgraced tenor Carl Friberth (accused by Rahier of failing to doff his hat!), is a carefully judged balance of tact and firmness, and one of many testimonies to his concern for his musicians' welfare. The prince and his estates manager calmed down; and though Sigl was dismissed, he was later reinstated.

Another crisis at court rapidly followed. In October 1765 Werner, by now bed-ridden and, we can infer, jealous of his young vice-Kapellmeister's success, wrote a notorious let-ter to the prince accusing Haydn of lax administration. Inter alia, he complained that the instruments and music archives were not properly maintained, the orchestra was idle and the chorus a bunch of libertines (*plus ça change*, some will say). Haydn, naturally easy-going in his relations with the musi-cians, probably was too slack over discipline, though given his phenomenal workload as composer, vocal coach and per-former, it is a wonder that he found any time for what must have seemed tedious administrative tasks.

Werner's letter duly prompted a seven-point admonishment from Prince Nicolaus dealing with each complaint in turn. Then, in what seems to us an outrageous postscript, the prince enjoined Haydn to 'apply himself to composition more diligently than hitherto, and especially to write such pieces as

can be played on the gamba, of which we have seen very few up
to now'. By 'gamba' Nicolaus meant that strange new preoccupation of his, the baryton. Duly chastened by this slight,
Haydn knuckled down. (Unlike Mozart in Salzburg, he kept
any smouldering resentment under wraps.) Partly, perhaps, to
remind the prince of his industry as a composer, he initiated a
thematic catalogue of his works, the so-called *Entwurf-Katalog*;
and he responded dutifully to Nicolaus's demand for baryton
music by presenting him with a set of three trios on 4 January
1766 and keeping up a more or less regular production of trios
over the next decade.

Kapellmeister, 1766–1775

With Werner's long-anticipated death on 3 March 1766, Haydn
was automatically promoted to the top job. Although his salary
remained unchanged (it was already higher than Werner's had
been), he now added church music to his responsibilities. His
most monumental work to date, the so-called *Missa Cellensis*,
begun in 1766, was probably the result of an outside commission, like the *Applausus* cantata he had composed in 1768 for the
monastery of Zwettl. But his next two completed masses, the
'Grosse Orgelsolomesse' (1768–9) and the *Missa Sancti Nicolai*
(1772), were both composed for the Esterházy court, as were the
G minor *Salve regina* (1771) and, possibly, the imposing *Stabat
mater* of 1767, destined to become one of his greatest international successes. During the year of his promotion Haydn
moved out of the apartment in the 'Old Apothecary' into a
charming two-storey house of his own in Klostergasse (now
Josef-Haydngasse), down the hill from Schloss Esterházy. It was
twice destroyed by fire, in 1768 and 1776, and each time rebuilt
at Prince Nicolaus's expense. Like the Rohrau birthplace, the
house is now a Haydn museum.

By 1766 the prince's spectacular conjuring act in the
Hungarian swamps was well advanced. From now on Nicolaus
would spend most of the year at Eszterháza, as he decreed the
new summer palace would be called. Then, in the autumn of

1768, he celebrated the completion of his four-hundred-seat opera house with Haydn's new comic opera *Lo speziale*. He had already assembled a small, permanent opera troupe; from 1769, he engaged a theatrical company each summer to perform repertoire ranging from Shakespeare to contemporary farces. A new marionette theatre, intricately fashioned as a jewel-encrusted grotto, was inaugurated in 1773 with *Philemon und Baucis*, during festivities in honour of the visiting Empress Maria Theresa that also saw the premiere of Haydn's *burletta per musica*, *L'infedeltà delusa*. As Prince Nicolaus surely knew, his fairy-tale extravaganza was the only European palace with *two* purpose-built opera houses: a flamboyant statement of cultural power and prestige, guaranteed to make aristocratic visitors go goggle-eyed with mingled admiration and envy.

After visiting Eszterháza in 1784, the Swiss Baron Johann Kaspar Riesbeck marvelled in his *Briefe eines reisenden Franzosen über Deutschland*:

> The castle is enormous, and filled to bursting with luxurious objects. The garden contains everything that human fantasy can conceive to enhance or, if you will, undo the work of nature. Pavilions of all kinds stand like the dwellings of voluptuous fairies, and everything is so far removed from normal human activity that one looks upon it as if in the middle of a wonderful dream.

He also observed that the palace gardens were surrounded by a wilderness 'where the people live like animals in underground caves or like Mongols in tents ... The clearest proof that a country is unhappy is the confrontation between the greatest magnificence and the most wretched poverty, and the greater the confrontation, the unhappier the country.' Prince Nicolaus enjoyed the exotic local colour provided by his singing, dancing serfs at Eszterháza entertainments. But reports confirm that he was one of the harshest of landlords, impervious to the reforms introduced by Maria Theresa to alleviate the lot of the peasantry.

Meanwhile his Kapellmeister continued his prolific production of instrumental music with symphonies, sonatas and string quartets (the three sets Opp. 9, 17 and 20) of increasing ambition and expressive reach. For all the zest and colour of his early symphonies, if Haydn had died in 1767 at thirty-five – the same age as Mozart – we should rate him no higher than several other Austrian symphonists, notably his gifted but unambitious younger brother Michael, contentedly ensconced at Salzburg, and Johann Baptist Vanhal. But over the next four or five years, beginning with works such as the 'Maria Theresa' and 'La Passione' symphonies (Nos. 48 and 49), he emerged as incontestably the greatest instrumental composer of his generation.

The proliferation of minor-key works, by Haydn and other composers, around 1770 has spawned the label *Sturm und Drang* (storm and stress), though the German literary movement of that name, kick-started by Goethe's rampaging 1773 drama *Götz von Berlichingen* and his sensational epistolary novel *Die Leiden des jungen Werther*, lay in the future. Few of the major-key quartets and symphonies of these years could be described as stormy or stressful. Yet virtually every work, major or minor, testifies to the increased expressive and intellectual power of Haydn's sonata thinking. He now begins to exploit the dramatic energy latent within his often laconic musical material, with a mingled freedom and logic that no other composer around 1770 could match. Haydn the master of the eccentric and surprising has also become the supreme master of long-range strategy.

According to Griesinger, Haydn suffered from a 'raging fever' in 1770 or early 1771, doubtless as a result of his unhealthy surroundings and/or sheer overwork. As a token of thanksgiving to the Virgin Mary, he composed the G minor *Salve regina*, not the *Stabat mater*, as the composer claimed in old age. By then the prince's 'summer' season at Eszterháza would often stretch well into the autumn, to the increasing frustration of the instrumentalists and singers, who until the completion of a new music building were required to leave their wives behind in Eisenstadt. The only personnel exempt from this rule were Haydn himself (ironically, given the state of his marriage), the orchestra leader Tomasini, and the tenors Leopold Dichtler and Carl Friberth, who were married to the company's two sopranos.

Things came to a head in the autumn of 1772, when the Eszterháza season dragged on even longer than usual, and the musicians' distress at their separation from their families was aggravated by the prince's threats of a pay cut or dismissal. In Griesinger's account:

> [T]he loving husbands . . . went to Haydn and asked for his advice. Haydn had the inspiration of writing a symphony . . . in which one instrument after the other is silent. This symphony was performed as soon as possible in front of the Prince, and each of the musicians was instructed, as soon as his part was finished, to blow out his candle and leave with his instrument under his arm. The Prince and his entourage instantly understood the meaning of this pantomime, and the next day came the order to leave Esterhaz [*sic*].

Nicolaus also abandoned his plans for reductions in expenditure. Haydn the diplomat-cum-shop steward had prevailed again, and charmingly – though the symphony as a whole is anything but charming.

During the late 1760s and 1770s Haydn's reputation steadily advanced both within and beyond the Habsburg lands. In 1768, the year he wrote the *Applausus* cantata for Zwettl Abbey, he obtained special permission from the prince to direct a performance of his *Stabat mater* in Vienna, accompanied by his close friend, the court cellist Joseph Weigl, and the tenor Carl Friberth. Although the terms of his 1761 contract with Prince Paul Anton forbade him from composing 'for any other person without prior knowledge and gracious consent', Prince Nicolaus began to grant him much more leeway, fully aware that his Kapellmeister's fame could only enhance his own *éclat*. In February 1774 Haydn first benefited financially from publication of his works when the Viennese firm of Kurzböck issued a set of keyboard sonatas (Nos. 21 to 26 in Hoboken's catalogue). Later the same year, he received his most prestigious commission to date: an Italian oratorio for the biannual Lenten concerts of the Viennese Tonkünstler-Societät in aid of the widows and orphans of musicians. Premiered with huge forces on 2 April 1775, *Il ritorno di Tobia* was an artistic triumph and raised the handsome sum of 1,712 gulden.

Opera director: 1776–1784

As Prince Nicolaus's obsession with the baryton waned, doubtless to Haydn's relief (arthritic fingers may have played their part here), so his passion for all things theatrical, especially Italian *opera buffa*, reached insatiable levels. In 1776, the year seven new Italian singers were engaged, the prince inaugurated a regular Eszterháza theatre and opera season that could stretch to ten months or more. The singers, players and their families were by now decently accommodated in the 250-room Musicians' Building. Haydn, too, lived here for most of the year after selling his Eisenstadt house in 1778 and using part of the proceeds to buy an annuity. Five operas were staged in 1776, all comedies except for Gluck's by now famous *Orfeo ed Euridice*. In 1778, the first year for which full records have survived, there were 184 evenings devoted to plays and fifty-two to operas and marionette operas. The ratio then gradually shifted in favour of staged opera (marionette operas were rarely given after 1778), culminating in 1786 in a staggering 125 performances of seventeen different works. All the most celebrated Italian composers of the day, plus a few Austrians such as Dittersdorf, were represented, with Cimarosa, Anfossi and Paisiello heading the list.

Prince and Kapellmeister would choose much of the repertoire between them during their brief winter sojourns in Vienna, where a lucrative trade in Italian operas had developed. Haydn would then get to work organising the copying of parts, cutting, altering or recomposing arias to suit the available personnel, coaching the singers, and rehearsing and directing performances from the keyboard. Between 1776 and 1790 he supervised eighty-eight different opera productions, including six works of his own: *Il mondo della luna* (premiered in 1777), *La vera costanza* (1779), *L'isola disabitata* (1779), *La fedeltà premiata* (1781),

Orlando paladino (1782) and *Armida* (1784). Not surprisingly, Haydn's prodigious operatic activities left little time for composition in other genres. Between 1772 and 1785 he composed a single set of string quartets, Op. 33 of 1781, and just two liturgical works, the 'Little Organ Mass' of *c.*1777–8, and the 'Mariazellermesse' of 1782. Sets of keyboard sonatas appeared in 1776, 1780 and 1784, while symphonic production was spasmodic until 1782, when Haydn's creative focus began to shift towards instrumental music for international publication.

On New Year's Day 1779 Haydn signed a new contract allowing him to accept outside commissions and to enter into negotiations with publishers, thus formally enshrining a situation that had more or less existed for several years. Other restrictive clauses from the 1761 contract were removed, including 'he shall take good care to conduct himself in an exemplary fashion, refraining from undue familiarity and from vulgarity in eating, drinking and conversations'; and his annual salary was raised from 600 to 782 gulden and thirty kreutzer, augmented by substantial supplies of grain, meat, wine and fuel. (A comfortable middle-class salary at this time was reckoned to be 500–550 gulden.)

Later that year, on the morning of 18 November, a devastating fire gutted the opera house after a stove exploded in the Chinese ballroom. Haydn's autograph of *La vera costanza* was destroyed, along with the scores and parts of several marionette operas and the orchestral parts of many symphonies. Unfazed, the opera-mad prince immediately decreed that the season would continue in the marionette theatre, and gave orders for the reconstruction of the opera house. The new building was ready early in 1781, several months behind schedule, and inaugurated on 25 February with Haydn's *La fedeltà premiata*.

The year 1779 was significant in other ways, too. In March an Italian couple, the twenty-nine-year-old singer Luigia Polzelli and her much older, consumptive violinist husband, Antonio, joined the musical establishment. Neither was overly talented. When Nicolaus dismissed both Polzellis at the end of

1780, Haydn intervened and had them reinstated. His motives, though, were not strictly professional. He and Luigia had by then become lovers, and would remain so, albeit with diminishing ardour on both sides, for the next decade.

The unhappily married composer, attractive to women despite his self-professed ugliness (attributed by Dies to 'deeply pockmarked skin and a brownish complexion'), had doubtless had the odd more or less discreet affair before 1779. Dies reported that 'in his younger years he is said to have been very receptive to love'. Fragmentary evidence suggests that around 1767–70 he had a liaison with a 'Mademoiselle Catherine Csech', a lady-in-waiting to Princess Grassalkovics in Pressburg (present-day Bratislava), to whom he left a thousand gulden in his will. But his affair with Luigia, of the dark, vivacious eyes and shapely figure (all that we know of her appearance comes from her passport description), quickly became common knowledge. Luigia apparently believed that her younger son, Antonio, born in 1783, was Haydn's. While he never commented on the matter, the otherwise childless composer seems to have harboured a paternal affection for Antonio and his elder brother Pietro, who would die of consumption, aged just nineteen, in 1796. He taught both boys music and in 1803 engaged Antonio as a violinist in the Esterházy orchestra. Luigia's modest vocal credentials can be gauged from the music she sang. Haydn created only one role for her, the ingénue Silvia in *L'isola disabitata* (December 1779). She was then confined to minor soubrette parts in revivals of other composers' operas, for which Haydn composed several sprightly, technically undemanding 'insertion arias'.

By the early 1780s publishers were falling over each other to acquire rights in Haydn's latest symphonies and quartets. Illegal copying was rife, and dozens of symphonies by composers including Vanhal and Haydn's brother Michael were issued under Haydn's name by firms quick to exploit his commercial cachet. From now on all his instrumental music was conceived primarily for circulation beyond the Esterházy court. In 1780 he sold six keyboard sonatas (No. 20 and

Nos. 35–9) to the Viennese firm of Artaria, initiating a long and mutually profitable relationship. The following year, using the British ambassador in Vienna as go-between, he sold symphonies for the first time to William Forster in London, destined to become his most faithful British publisher. Negotiations with publishers in Paris, Leipzig and other cities quickly followed. In an age before strict copyright laws, Haydn, like Beethoven after him, was not above selling 'exclusive' rights to two or more publishers simultaneously. There were occasional protests, but the usual reaction was to turn a blind eye.

Relieved of his obligation to offer everything he wrote to the prince, Haydn would also sell multiple subscription copies of works to patrons, as exemplified by the Op. 33 quartets of 1781. With his by now shrewdly developed commercial sense (and some musical justification), he famously announced that the quartets were composed 'in a completely new and special way'. He would use similarly persuasive sales talk when offering his three 'beautiful, elegant and by no means over-long symphonies' of 1782, Nos. 76–8, to the Parisian publisher Boyer. Haydn had composed these for a projected visit to England, where his popularity had been further boosted by the sensational success in 1781 of Symphony No. 53, the enigmatically titled 'L'Impériale'. The *Morning Herald* even reported that 'the Shakespeare of musical composition is hourly expected'. But Prince Nicolaus evidently withheld his permission, if indeed Haydn ever asked it. According to Dies, the composer was so touched by Nicolaus's generosity after he had twice paid for the rebuilding of his Eisenstadt house that 'he swore to the prince to serve him till death should end the life of one or the other, and never leave him even if he were offered millions'.

International fame: 1784–1790

Haydn composed his last stage work for Eszterháza, the *opera seria*, *Armida*, in the winter of 1783–4. For the next seven years he led something of a double life as provincial Kapellmeister and European celebrity. At court he continued to adapt, rehearse and direct a vast tally of (mainly comic) operas. For the international market he composed a steady stream of keyboard trios (a newly popular domestic genre, especially in England) and symphonies (Nos. 79–92), while the sets published as Op. 50 (1787), Opp. 54/55 (1788) and Op. 64 (1790) both satisfied and further stimulated the demand among players and publishers for string quartets. In 1784 or early 1785 Haydn received a particularly lucrative commission to compose symphonies for the Parisian Concert de la Loge Olympique. The upshot was the 'Paris' set, Nos. 82–7, symphonies both worldly and profound, with catchy, popular-style melodies and a new grandeur of effect calculated to please a broad public.

More unlikely commissions arrived from further afield. Just when Haydn must have thought he had finished for good with oddball instruments, along came a request from King Ferdinand IV of Naples for concertos and *notturni* for the *lira organizzata*, a sort of hurdy-gurdy with attitude. Around the same time, either in 1785 or 1786, he received an equally eccentric commission from a canon of Cádiz: for a series of orchestral reflections on The Seven Last Words of Christ to be performed in a black-draped church during Holy Week. Haydn later stressed the enormous challenge of writing seven Adagios (eight, including the *Introduzione*) 'without tiring the listeners'. He succeeded, triumphantly.

After the flute-playing Earl of Abingdon had failed to net Haydn for the 1782–3 London season, *The Gazetteer & New Daily Advertiser* of 17 January 1785 proposed a more radical strategy:

> *Haydn*, the simplest as well as the greatest of men, is resigned to his condition, and in devoting his life to the rites and ceremonies of the Roman Catholic Church . . . is content to live immured in a place little better than a dungeon, subject to the domineering spirit of a petty Lord, and the clamorous temper of a scolding wife. Would it not be an achievement equal to a pilgrimage, for some aspiring youths to rescue

him from his fortune and transplant him to Great Britain, the country for whom his music seems to be made?

A few months later the *Morning Herald* (16 September 1785) gloomily predicted that Haydn would 'never honor the land of *heresy* with his presence. This great genius is so great a bigot to the ceremonies of religion, that all his leisure moments are continuously engaged in the celebration of masses and the contemplation of purgatory.' News of Haydn's affair with La Polzelli had evidently not filtered through to London.

'The universality of Haydn's genius cannot be more strongly proved than by the vast demand for his works all over Europe,' proclaimed the *European Magazine and London Review* of October 1784. Yet amid the general adulation there were dissenting voices. In his Autobiographical Sketch Haydn had defended himself at length against certain anonymous 'Berliners', who accused him of bizarre effects and 'comic fooling' (though he had plenty of admirers in North Germany). Complaints of 'caprice' and 'triviality' crop up elsewhere, too. Nor was Haydn ever truly in favour at the Habsburg court. Maria Theresa had been virtually unaware of his music until she heard *L'infedeltà delusa* at Eszterháza in 1773, while the reforming zeal of her son Joseph II coexisted with decidedly conservative musical tastes. He was ambivalent towards Mozart's music, which he seems to have found dense and 'difficult' (in this he was not alone); and his opinion of Haydn tended to echo that of the more hostile Berliners. In a conversation reported by Carl Ditters von Dittersdorf, Haydn's old friend from Viennese street-serenading days, the Emperor asked 'Don't you think he sometimes trifles [*tändelt*] far too much?', to which Dittersdorf deftly countered, 'He has the gift of trifling, without, however, debasing the art.' Joseph remained unimpressed.

It was either in 1783 or 1784 that Haydn first met Mozart, perhaps at one of Mozart's subscription concerts, or at a musical-literary salon in the home of the former Court War Secretary Franz Sales von Greiner, where both composers were frequent guests, or at one of two performances of *Il ritorno di Tobia* during Lent 1784, where all five soloists had sung or would sing in Mozart opera premieres. Although Haydn's duties at Eszterháza limited their encounters to a few weeks each winter or early spring, they formed one of the most celebrated of all musical friendships.

Like Mozart and many other Viennese artists and intellectuals in sympathy with Enlightenment ideals, Haydn became a Freemason, though after his initiation in the lodge 'Zur wahren Eintracht' (True Harmony) on 11 February 1785 (Mozart had joined its sister lodge, 'Zur Wohltätigkeit', the previous December) he attended no further meetings; and except, obliquely, in *The Creation* and the final trio and chorus of *The Seasons*, Freemasonry barely impinged on his music. Information about meetings between the two composers is sketchy. If the Irish tenor Michael Kelly, the first Basilio and Curzio in *Figaro*, is to be believed, in 1784 they played quartets together at the Viennese home of the composer Stephen Storace, brother of Nancy, Mozart's first Susanna. 'The players were tolerable,' remarked Kelly coyly in his unreliable ghosted *Reminiscences* of 1826. 'Not one of them excelled on the instrument he played, but there was a little science among them, which I dare say will be acknowledged when I name them: The First Violin . . . Haydn; Second Violin . . . Baron Dittersdorf; Violoncello . . . Vanhall [*sic*]; Tenor . . . Mozart.'

More securely documented are the occasions when Mozart unfurled the string quartets he would dedicate to 'my dear friend Haydn'. All six quartets were played on 15 January 1785. After the last three (K458, K464 and K465) were repeated on 12 February, Leopold Mozart famously reported to his daughter Nannerl: 'Herr Haydn said to me: "I tell you before God and as an honest man, that your son is the greatest composer known to me either in person or by name. He has taste and, what is more, the most profound knowledge of composition." '

We know, too, that Haydn attended rehearsals of *Così fan tutte* and at least one performance of *Le nozze di Figaro* in the winter of 1789–90. Their meetings seem to have been at their most frequent towards the end of 1790, when Haydn decamped to Vienna after Prince Nicolaus's death. Many years later the composer and musical chronicler Abbé Maximilian Stadler recalled playing Mozart's string quintets with Mozart and Haydn. When Johann Peter Salomon engaged Haydn for London, it was apparently agreed that Mozart would join him for the 1792 season. Both Griesinger and Dies report on the meal between the three men just before Haydn's departure for London. According to Dies, when Mozart expressed his concern that his friend knew little of the world and spoke too few languages, Haydn replied with ingenuous confidence – and some truth – that 'my language is understood throughout the whole world'. In a passage that gave the green light to future romantically inclined biographers, Dies continued:

> [A]t the moment of parting [Mozart] said, 'We are probably saying our last adieu in this life.' Tears welled in both men's eyes. Haydn was deeply moved, for he applied Mozart's words to himself. It never occurred to him that the threads of Mozart's life would be cut by the inexorable Parcae the very next year.

Never one to go overboard about fellow musicians, Mozart admired Haydn above all other living composers. There are various stories of him praising his friend's music and defending it in the face of hostile criticism. Haydn's influence, exhaustively debated in the literature, is patent in Mozart's string quartets (including the teenaged works of 1772–3) and in pieces like the 'little' G minor Symphony, K183 (modelled on Haydn's No. 39 in the same key), and the two late string quintets, K593 and K614. The latter, popular in tone yet faintly ascetic, is arguably the most Haydnesque of all Mozart's mature works. Haydn's spirit is also manifest in finales like those of the E flat Symphony, No. 39, and the piano concertos K451 and K459.

Pace biographers such as Karl Geiringer and Rosemary Hughes, both drawing on Pohl, it is much harder to detect any reciprocal influences. (Hughes goes so far as to suggest that recognition of Mozart's superiority initially disturbed Haydn's 'artistic balance'.) Even Haydn's increasing use of chromaticism from the early 1780s onwards, often attributed to Mozart's example, has parallels in the music of other Austrian composers. There are half-echoes of the 'Jupiter' Symphony in the Adagio cantabile of Haydn's Symphony No. 98, perhaps written in tribute to his deceased friend, and overt reminiscences of Symphony No. 40, the Requiem and *Die Zauberflöte* in *The Seasons*. One or two numbers in *The Creation* also evoke *Die Zauberflöte*. The famous 'dissonant' slow introduction to Mozart's String Quartet K465 is distantly felt in the Allegretto of Haydn's G major Quartet Op. 54 No. 1, and seems to have been the starting point for 'Chaos' in *The Creation*. But neither of these movements sounds remotely Mozartian.

Haydn did, though, return his friend's compliment and revere Mozart as the greatest living composer, himself included. He, more than anyone else, was in a position to penetrate the full extent of the younger man's genius. He may even have been a little overawed by Mozart, especially as an opera composer. In an unauthenticated letter of 1787 replying to a request for a new comic opera, he wrote: 'I should be risking a good deal, for scarcely any man can brook comparison with the great Mozart.' He went on: 'If only I could impress on the soul of every music lover . . . how inimitable are Mozart's works, how musically intelligent, how extraordinarily sensitive . . . why, then nations would vie with each other to possess such a jewel within their borders.' In London, in the presence of Charles Burney, Haydn remarked: 'I have often been flattered by my friends that I have some genius; but he was much my superior.' When he learnt of Mozart's death, he wrote to their mutual friend Michael Puchberg, 'For some time I was quite beside myself at [Mozart's] death and could not believe that Providence would transport so irreplaceable a man to the other world.'

In sharp contrast to Mozart's effusive, touching, sometimes bawdy letters, Haydn's correspondence makes pretty sober reading on the whole. Most surviving letters from the 1780s are to publishers and patrons, though we might smile at his occasional attempts to wriggle out of awkward situations and put a favourable gloss on his double-dealing. His most self-revealing letters by far are those he wrote to Maria Anna von Genzinger. Haydn seems to have first visited the Viennese home of the society doctor (and Prince Nicolaus's physician) Peter Leopold von Genzinger and his wife during the spring of 1789. In June Frau von Genzinger – cultured, warm-hearted and a talented pianist to whom Haydn gave occasional lessons – sent the composer her own keyboard arrangement of a 'beautiful Andante' from one of his symphonies or quartets (we do not know which); and over the following months their friendship burgeoned into something deeper, at least on Haydn's part. Although the relationship almost certainly remained platonic, Maria Anna became Haydn's confidante, as Luigia Polzelli could never be, and the recipient of his most intimate, spontaneous and, on occasion, poignant letters.

Haydn wrote for her his E flat Sonata, Hoboken No. 49, with its tender and impassioned Adagio; and he took an affectionate interest in the musical education of her children, especially the eldest, sixteen-year-old Josepha ('Pepperl', or 'Pepi'), to whom (in a letter of 14 March 1790) he offered tips on the interpretation of his new cantata *Arianna a Naxos*. In that same letter, Haydn told Maria Anna of Prince Nicolaus's 'melancholy state' after the death of his wife on 23 February, further heightened 'when he heard my favourite Adagio in D' – probably the slow movement of either Symphony No. 88 or No. 92.

By now Haydn was feeling ever more acutely the contrast between his sojourns in the capital and his isolated existence in the Hungarian *puszta*. As a guest in the homes of the enlightened Viennese aristocracy and haute bourgeoisie he had tasted a society where differences of rank counted for little. Fourteen years earlier, in his Autobiographical Sketch, he had pledged his loyalty to the Esterházy family 'in whose service I wish to live and die'. Now, in his late fifties, he had simply outgrown the life of a Kapellmeister in a hierarchical princely establishment. He poured out his disillusionment, not without a certain wry humour, in a much-quoted letter to Frau von Genzinger of 9 February 1790:

> Well, here I sit in my wilderness – forsaken like a poor waif – almost without human company – sad – full of memories of past glorious days . . . and who knows when these days will return again. Those wonderful parties? – where the whole circle is one heart, one soul – all the beautiful musical evenings . . . for three days I did not know if I was Kapellmeister or Kapell-servant. Nothing could console me, my whole house was in disorder, my fortepiano, which I usually love, was perverse and disobedient . . . and then, just when I was happily dreaming that I was listening to *Le nozze di Figaro*, the ghastly north wind woke me up and almost blew my nightcap off my head.

He goes on to compare the fine food on offer *chez* Genzinger with the character-forming diet at Eszterháza: 'Instead of that delicious slice of beef, a slab of 50-year-old cow; instead of ragout with little dumplings, an old sheep with carrots; instead of a Bohemian pheasant, a leathery joint.'

Haydn's frustration in his 'wilderness' is evident in other letters from the spring and summer of 1790. 'If only I could be with Your Grace for a quarter of an hour,' he wrote on 30 May, 'to pour out all my troubles to you, and hear your comforting words. I have to endure many irritations from the court here, yet must accept them in silence.' A month later he lamented to Frau von Genzinger that 'it is sad always to be a slave, but Providence wills it so'.

Providence willed it otherwise sooner than Haydn could have hoped. The disconsolate Prince Nicolaus died in Vienna, after a short illness, on 28 September 1790. His son Prince Anton immediately dismissed the musical and theatrical personnel except for the wind-band (*Harmonie*), required for hunts and other ceremonies. Kapellmeister and orchestral leader Tomasini remained on the payroll, albeit on reduced salaries (Haydn also had his pension of a thousand gulden a year), and were free to seek work elsewhere. The composer hastily left for Vienna, where he lodged with an acquaintance, Johann Nepomuk Hamberger. Here he completed the set of six string quartets published as Op. 64. He was not short of invitations from, inter alia, King Ferdinand in Naples and Prince Grassalkovics, who tried to lure him with the post of Kapellmeister at his court in Pressburg.

Meanwhile the violinist-impresario Johann Peter Salomon was scouring the continent for singers for his forthcoming London season. Hearing of Prince Nicolaus's death, he travelled post-haste from Cologne to Vienna and announced himself to Haydn with the now-famous words, as reported by Dies, 'I am Salomon from London and have come to fetch you. Tomorrow we will conclude an *accord*.' The following day, 8 December, Haydn signed a contract on highly favourable terms. He would receive £300 for six symphonies (equal to approximately £25,000 in 2009), and the same sum for an opera for Sir John Gallini's newly rebuilt King's Theatre. In the event the opera, *L'anima del filosofo*, never saw the stage after Gallini failed to secure a theatre licence. He was also promised £200 for twenty smaller works, £200 for the rights to their publication, and £200 for a benefit concert. On 15 December, after the 'merry meal' (Griesinger) with Salomon and Mozart, the fifty-eight-year-old Haydn, who had never journeyed more than 120 kilometres from Vienna, embarked on the greatest adventure of his life.

London, 1791–1795

Haydn and Salomon travelled from Vienna via Munich and Salomon's home town of Bonn, where the composer met the promising young Ludwig van Beethoven, then a viola player and organist in the elector's service. They reached Calais on New Year's Eve, and the following day embarked for Dover. As Haydn wrote to Anna Maria von Genzinger:

> I stayed on deck during the whole crossing, so as to gaze

my fill of that mighty monster, the ocean. As long as it was
calm, I wasn't afraid at all, but towards the end, when the
wind grew stronger and I saw monstrous high waves
surging towards us, I became a little frightened, and slightly
ill, too.

On 2 January 1791 he arrived in London, by far the most
populous and cosmopolitan city in Europe: a clamorous, vora-
cious metropolis of around a million inhabitants (five times
the size of Vienna), seething with commerce, spectacle and
crime. Like all foreign visitors, Haydn was overwhelmed by
'this endlessly huge city . . . whose beauties and marvels have
quite astounded me'. In time he would also be repelled by the
squalor of the urban proletariat. After spending his first two
nights in London with the publisher John Bland and his wife,
he took rooms at 18 Great Pultney Street, the house where
Salomon lived. He was also given a studio in Broadwood's
piano shop, where he composed *L'anima del filosofo* and
Symphonies Nos. 95 and 96 – though he would later move to
the (then) sylvan tranquillity of Lisson Grove, on the city's
northern fringes.

From the outset Haydn was lionised by London's musical
and social elite. Prominent among the former was the music
historian Charles Burney (father of the novelist and diarist
Fanny), who had long been intent on luring Haydn to
England. Through Burney he came to know the amateur
composer and Moravian minister Christian Ignatius Latrobe,
who wrote that '[Haydn] appeared to me to be a religious
character, & not only attentive to the forms & usages of his
own Church, but under the influence of a devotional spirit'.
The *Daily Advertiser* reported that in the ballroom in
St James's Palace Haydn was publicly recognised by all the
royal family without being introduced – a far cry from the
rigid etiquette at the Esterházy court. 'The Prince of Wales
first observed him, and upon bowing to him, the Eyes of all
the Company were upon Mr Haydn, every one paying him
Respect.' As the composer told Frau von Genzinger in that

same letter of 8 January, 'Everyone wants to know me. I had to dine out six times up to now, and if I wanted I could have an invitation every day; but first I must consider my health, and second my work. Except for the nobility, I admit no callers till 2 in the afternoon.'

With his abiding sense of curiosity, Haydn was fascinated by English customs and mores. During his London visits he kept notebooks (four in all) in which he jotted down anything that intrigued him, from the inhabitants' reckless consumption of alcohol (an observation repeatedly echoed over the following century, not least by Dostoevsky, who in 1862 wrote of London that 'everyone is in a hurry to drink himself into insensibility') to the cost of living, the weather ('the fog was so thick that you could have spread it on bread', he noted in December 1791) and the oddities of the legal system: 'If anyone steals £2 he is hanged; but if I trust anyone with £2000 and he runs off with it, he is acquitted.' Perhaps repeating an after-dinner bon mot, he observed: 'In France the girls are virtuous and the wives are whores; in Holland the girls are whores and the wives virtuous; but in England they remain whores all their lives.' On occasion English history could leave him bemused: 'On 5th Nov the boys celebrate the days on which the Guys set the town on fire.'

London's concert life in the 1790s was far more extensive and democratic than Vienna's. Nobles and commoners alike could attend an opera or subscription concert virtually every evening, while societies of amateurs and professionals like the Nobleman's and Gentlemen's Catch Club and the Anacreontic Society would perform regularly in the city's taverns. Salomon's Friday concert series in the Hanover Square Rooms (seating around five hundred in comfort) opened on 11 March with the usual motley array of symphonies, concertos and vocal items. The main attraction for the audience ('numerous and very elegant') was a new symphony by Haydn, conducted by the composer. As Nos. 95 and 96 were not yet ready (they were first performed in April or May), the symphony played was almost certainly No. 92, new to London audiences, though not to

Parisians. 'A new grand overture by HAYDN was received with the highest applause, and universally deemed a composition as pleasing as scientific,' enthused the *Diary or Woodfall's Register* of 12 March. The symphony quickly became a favourite, and was chosen for the occasion of Haydn's receiving an honorary doctorate at Oxford in July. Of the degree ceremony he later told Dies, 'I felt very silly in my gown . . . But I have a lot – I might say everything – to thank this doctor's degree in England; because of it I became acquainted with the first men in the land and gained entrance to the greatest houses.'

Interspersed with Salomon's concerts were other musical activities, including private concerts at court, the promised benefit concert on 16 May and a concert on 30 May at which Haydn conducted his *Seven Last Words* and two symphonies. That same week he was profoundly stirred by monster performances of *Israel in Egypt*, *Messiah*, *Zadok the Priest* and excerpts from other choral works in Westminster Abbey. Carpani recounted that he 'confessed . . . that when he heard the music of Hendl [*sic*] in London he was struck as if he had been put back to the beginning of his studies . . . He pondered every note and drew from those most learned scores the essence of true musical grandeur.' The first seeds were sown for *The Creation*.

In the summer of 1791 Prince Anton Esterházy, in need of a new *opera seria* for an official ceremony, demanded to know when his nominal Kapellmeister intended to return to Vienna. Haydn feared the worst, writing to Frau von Genzinger, 'Now, unfortunately, I expect to be dismissed, and hope God will give me the strength to make up for this loss.' As it turned out, the rift was soon healed. The composer recuperated from the feverish pace of London life at the country estate, near Hertford, of the banker Nathaniel Brassey and his family. Living 'as if in a monastery', as he told Frau von Genzinger, he spent most of his time composing (probably Symphony No. 93 and parts of Nos. 94 and 98) and taking solitary walks in the woods with his English grammar.

On his return to London, he was invited by his principal royal patron, the Prince of Wales (the future George IV), to visit his newly married brother and sister-in-law, the Duke and Duchess of York, at their country estate Oatlands, near Weybridge in Surrey. Haydn observed in his London Notebook: 'The little castle, 18 miles from London, lies on a slope and commands the most glorious views. Among its many beauties is a most remarkable grotto which cost £25,000 sterling and which was 11 years in the building.' (Haydn was always fascinated by the precise cost of things.) In the same entry he noted: 'The Prince of Wales wants my portrait.' The upshot was the famous painting by John Hoppner – Haydn as urbane, dignified man of the world – housed today in the Royal Collection.

Defying competition from the Professional Concert directed by Haydn's former pupil Ignaz Pleyel – a friendly musical rivalry whipped up by the press into a gladiatorial contest – Salomon's 1792 concert series eclipsed even the previous year's triumphs. Four new symphonies, Nos. 93, 94, 97 and 98, were rapturously received, with No. 94 causing the greatest furore of the entire season. Yet his hectic existence threatened to take its toll on his health and spirits, as his letters to Luigia Polzelli and Maria Anna von Genzinger reveal. On 17 January he wrote to Frau von Genzinger:

[I]f only Your Grace could see how tormented I am here in London, having to attend all sorts of private concerts . . . and by the enormous amount of work heaped on my shoulders . . . I have never in my life written as much in one year as I have here during the past one, but now I am completely exhausted, and it will do me good to be able to rest a little when I return home.

What Haydn did not reveal was his relationship with one of his piano pupils, Rebecca Schroeter (née Scott), the forty-year-old widow of the composer Johann Schroeter. Haydn's letters to her have not survived. But we can guess the nature of their mutual feelings from her increasingly passionate letters to him, and from his explanation to Dies after the artist came upon copies of her letters in his London Notebook:

> Haydn smiled and said, 'Letters from an English widow in London, who loved me; but though she was already sixty [she was in fact only forty-four when Haydn left London for the last time!], she was still a beautiful and charming woman, and I would have very easily married her if I had been single then.'

Although there are no letters from his second London visit (probably, as Robbins Landon has suggested, because he installed himself near her house in James Street, Buckingham Gate), we can guess that they revived their affair. Haydn dedicated to Rebecca three of his finest piano trios, including the 'Gypsy Rondo', No. 25, and the F sharp minor, No. 26, the latter perhaps a melancholy farewell to his English lover. They would remain in touch after Haydn's return to Vienna.

In April 1792 he wrote to Prince Anton informing him that Salomon's concerts would finish at the end of June, after which he would return home immediately. He travelled to Vienna via Bad Godesberg, near Bonn, where he renewed his acquaintance with Beethoven. It was agreed that the twenty-one-year-old composer would come to Vienna later in the year to study harmony and counterpoint with Haydn.

The eighteen months (July 1792 to January 1794) Haydn spent in Vienna and Eisenstadt form a relatively tranquil interlude between the two high-pressure London sojourns. His duties for Prince Anton were minimal. He lodged again in Hamberger's house and caught up with old friends. Here he composed dance music for a charity ball in the Redoutensaal and began work on a set of string quartets (published in groups of three as Op. 71 and Op. 74) for the 1793 London season. He also introduced his newest symphonies to the Viennese, though unlike in England the concerts barely registered in the newspapers. In the event Haydn would delay his projected return to England by a year, citing as an excuse the painful removal of a polyp on his nose. The real reason was probably Prince Anton's reluctance to let his Kapellmeister disappear again so quickly (according to Dies, the prince deemed that 'Haydn had acquired enough fame for himself'). Perhaps, too, the composer was unwilling to make what he saw as a potentially hazardous continental journey after the execution of Louis XVI in January 1793.

By then Beethoven had arrived on schedule from Bonn to commence his course of study. The mythology suggests that the two men, nearly two generations apart, were a disastrous fit: Haydn a lax teacher, too busy with his own compositions to take trouble over the young man's exercises, the hot-headed Beethoven increasingly frustrated and truculent.

The master was certainly unsystematic in his written correction of Beethoven's counterpoint exercises, based, like Haydn's own studies with Porpora, on Fux's *Gradus ad Parnassum*. But there is no reason to suppose that he did not discuss salient technical points, together with wider compositional questions. As Maynard Solomon put it in his biography of Beethoven:

> [To] study with Haydn was to learn not merely textbook rules of counterpoint and part writing, but the principles of formal organization, the nature of sonata writing, the handling of tonal forces . . . thematic development, harmonic structure – in short, the whole range of high-Classic musical ideas and techniques.

According to his pupil Ferdinand Ries, Beethoven maintained that he never learnt anything from Haydn. Ries also reported that Haydn's music 'rarely got away without a few digs' from Beethoven – though it is worth remembering that he was writing in the 1830s, when Haydn's stock was on the wane. Yet even if we did not know that Beethoven copied out several Haydn works for close study, his incalculable debt to his erstwhile teacher is writ large in his music, especially the symphonies (No. 4 pays overt homage to Haydn) and chamber music.

Haydn, for his part, admired many of Beethoven's earlier works, though not surprisingly he seems to have found his music after 1800 increasingly baffling. Although, like everyone else, he could find the 'Grossmogul' (his half-affectionate, half-exasperated nickname for Beethoven) alarmingly head-strong, master and pupil were on friendly terms throughout 1793. Haydn even took Beethoven with him to Eisenstadt during that summer. In December 1795, after his return from London, he invited Beethoven to play a piano concerto (either No. 1 or No. 2) at a benefit concert in the Redoutensaal that included three of his 'London' symphonies – a sure mark of the esteem in which he held his former pupil. They also gave concerts together on other occasions. In 1796 Haydn was the dedicatee of Beethoven's Op. 2 piano sonatas. But although there was no overt antagonism, from about 1798 their relationship became more distant and uneasy as Beethoven consolidated his independence from his former teacher. One or two anecdotes even suggest that the ambitious and competitive younger composer may have been a little jealous of the success of *The Creation*.

We have no account of Haydn's reactions to the death of Maria Anna von Genzinger, aged only forty-two, on 20 January 1793, though his grief at the loss of his closest confidante may have found expression in the violent and tragic coda of the F minor keyboard variations. Meanwhile he continued to correspond with the manipulative Luigia Polzelli, occasionally acceding to her requests for money (though increasingly, and disingenuously, pleading shortage of funds), and telling her that his wife was 'ill most of the time, and always in the same foul temper, but I don't really care any more'. Luigia even got Haydn to promise to marry her if he were to become free, though it is doubtful whether he ever seriously entertained the idea. He would remember his ex-mistress in his will. But by the time his wife died in 1800, he had no intention of marrying Luigia or anyone else.

After entrusting Beethoven's tuition to the famous pedagogue Johann Georg Albrechtsberger, Haydn finally departed for London on 19 January 1794 in a carriage lent by Baron Gottfried van Swieten, director of the Imperial Library and the musical patron who would compile the librettos of *The Creation* and *The Seasons*. He took with him his assistant and copyist Johann Elssler; and in his trunk were trios, the Opp. 71 and 74 quartets, the F minor keyboard variations, the completed score of Symphony No. 99 and parts of two other symphonies, Nos. 100 and 101. Travelling via Passau (where he may have heard a choral arrangement of his *Seven Last Words*) and Wiesbaden, they arrived in London on 4 February.

Haydn settled into his lodgings in Bury Street, St James's, and immediately plunged into the round of weekly concerts in the Hanover Square Rooms, now held on Mondays rather than Fridays, with an orchestra that, unlike in 1791–2, included clarinets. As the *Oracle* reported, 'The Professional is dropt, – in consequence Salomon's will be entirely unopposed until after Easter.' After Haydn, Salomon's star attractions were the violinist-composer Giovanni Battista Viotti and the *basso profundo* Ludwig Fischer, who in 1782 had created the role of Osmin in Mozart's *Die Entführung aus dem Serail*. Haydn's new Symphony No. 99 was premiered at the opening concert on 10 February; and press reaction was, if anything, even more euphoric than in earlier seasons. 'The incomparable HAYDN produced an Overture of which it is impossible to speak in common terms,' wrote the *Morning Chronicle*. 'It is one of the grandest efforts of art that we ever witnessed. It abounds with ideas, as new in music as they are grand and impressive.' The 'Clock', No. 101 (premiered on 3 March), provoked a comparable orgy of superlatives, while the 'hellish roar of war' in the Allegretto of the 'Grand Military Overture', No. 100 (31 March) – a direct response to the spirit of the times – ensured that it was quite simply *the* sensation of the season, as the 'Surprise' had been in 1792.

After a benefit concert for Salomon on 28 May, Haydn spent the English summer recuperating, travelling and composing: a new symphony (No. 102) for the following season, keyboard trios – always eagerly sought by publishers – and sonatas for the professional pianist Therese Jansen. A year later Haydn would be a witness at her marriage to the picture-dealer

Gaetano Bartolozzi, son of the famous engraver Francesco. He also composed songs to poems by his friend Anne Hunter, recent widow of the famous Scottish surgeon Dr John Hunter, who in 1792 had offered to remove Haydn's nasal polyp. Dies tells of the doctor's brawny assistants vainly trying to force the composer into a chair for the operation.

Haydn's fascination with ships, prompted by his friendship with several English naval men, was further stirred by reports of Lord Howe's victory over the French on the 'Glorious First of June' (though he was alarmed at the violent celebrations that followed), and by his visit to Portsmouth in July. Here he went aboard a captured French vessel, 'terribly shot to pieces', observed a 'most magnificent ship-of-the-line with 110 cannons called *The Prince of Wales*', and – a wheelwright's son to the last – noted the precise specifications of various ships, even making a sketch of a fireship's grappling irons. In August he travelled to Bath and Bristol with Andrew Ashe, flautist in Salomon's orchestra. In Bath (then a twelve-hour journey from London by mail coach, as Haydn duly noted) he lodged with the retired castrato Rauzzini for whom Mozart had composed the motet *Exsultate, jubilate*, and admired the city's 'many beautiful squares, on which stand the most magnificent houses'. The following month he recorded in his notebook details of the plot to assassinate George III with a poisoned arrow.

With star continental singers reluctant to cross the Channel in wartime, Salomon merged for the 1795 season with Viotti's new Opera Concert, which performed in the Great Concert Room of the King's Theatre, Haymarket (Salomon would resume his own concerts in 1796). 'His genius . . . is inexhaustible. In harmony, modulation, melody, passion and effect, he is wholy unrivaled [*sic*],' enthused the *Morning Chronicle* of Symphony No. 102, premiered on 2 February. The previous evening Haydn had been invited by the Prince of Wales to Carlton House, one of many royal musical soirées he attended. 'Nothing except my own compositions was played,' he recorded. 'I sat at the fortepiano; finally I had to sing too. The King, who hitherto would hear only Handel's music, was attentive; he chatted with me and introduced me to the Queen, who paid me many compliments.' (In *Le Haydine* Carpani remarked that the King 'throughout his life loved only a single woman and a single music – the Queen and the works of Handel (an extremely rare instance of constancy in both genres)'.)

After the premiere of No. 103 on 2 March, the *Morning Chronicle*, by now running out of adulatory epithets, praised the symphony's 'continual strokes of genius, both in air and harmony'. The season's climax was the composer's benefit concert on 4 May, featuring, uniquely, two major Haydn premieres: the *Scena di Berenice*, composed for the celebrated prima donna Brigida Giorgi Banti; and Symphony No. 104, 'the twelfth and last of the English', as he wrote in his notebook with pride; perhaps, too, a touch of relief at the fulfilment of his contract. Haydn was less than enamoured of La Banti's performance of his *Scena di Berenice*, noting (in English) that 'she song very scanty'. But the concert was the greatest triumph of his career to date. 'The whole company was thoroughly pleased, and so was I,' he wrote in his London Notebook. 'I made four thousand gulden this evening. Such a thing is only possible in England.'

After the concert season ended in June Haydn remained in London for another two months, completing three keyboard trios for Rebecca Schroeter and a new batch of songs. According to Griesinger:

> Haydn often repeated that he first became famous in Germany because of his reputation in England . . . he regarded his time in England as the happiest of his life. He was everywhere appreciated there; it opened a new world to him, and he could, through his handsome earnings at last escape the restricted circumstances in which he had grown grey.

Although he only seems to have craved 'escape' during his final year or two as Kapellmeister to Prince Nicolaus, he had indeed made undreamed-of sums in London. His net earnings of fifteen thousand gulden amounted to nearly twenty times his not insubstantial Esterházy salary.

Haydn certainly had many incentives to settle there permanently: the adulation of press, public and fellow musicians, his liaison with Rebecca Schroeter, a wide circle of friends, including Burney, Anne Hunter and Therese Bartolozzi, and the support of the royal family. Griesinger relates that Queen Charlotte had even offered him rooms for the summer in Windsor Castle if he would agree to settle in England, 'adding slyly, "and then sometimes we'll make music tête-à-tête" '. But at sixty-three, Haydn plumped for a return to his homeland and a less frenetic life in the service of the latest Esterházy prince, Nicolaus II (his father Prince Anton had died in January 1794). To the King and Queen, he gave the excuses of attachment to his prince, his homeland, and, incredibly, his wife. When the King offered to have her sent over, Haydn scotched the idea in a flash: 'She won't even cross the Danube, let alone the ocean.'

1795–1809: *Celebrity in Vienna and old age*

Leaving London on 15 August, Haydn and Elssler avoided the war zones of the Austrian Netherlands and the Rhineland by sailing to Hamburg. From here they travelled to Vienna via Berlin and Dresden, arriving in early September. According to Haydn's pupil Sigismund Neukomm, in Passau they heard the local choirmaster's choral arrangement of *The Seven Last Words*, though the performance in question may have taken place on the outward journey in 1794. During the Viennese interlude of 1793 Haydn's wife had encouraged him to buy a single-storey house in the Kleine Steingasse (later renamed Haydngasse) in the then quiet, leafy suburb of Gumpendorf, some three kilometres south-west of the old city. Only in 1796, after the construction of an additional floor, did Haydn and his wife, together with Elssler and several servants, finally move into the property (it became the Vienna Haydn Museum in 1904). For the time being he took rooms on the Neuer Markt, close to the winter palace of Prince Schwarzenberg where his late oratorios would be premiered.

Two factors clinched Haydn's decision to return to the service of the Esterházys: the knowledge that the family would provide well for him in his old age, and the light nature of his duties to Prince Nicolaus II. For most of the year he was free to lead an independent existence in Vienna, composing, conducting his 'London' symphonies and, later, his oratorios, and capitalising on the enhanced celebrity that his English triumphs had brought him. Although it was hardly true that Haydn 'first became famous in Germany [by which he also meant Austria] because of his reputation in England' (we can glimpse here his pique at the relative indifference of the imperial family), he returned from London not as the Esterházys' esteemed Kapellmeister but as a national and international hero.

Much to everyone's relief, Nicolaus II had no desire to return to his grandfather's summer palace which, though occasionally used as a hunting lodge, took on an increasingly forlorn air. Commandeered as a Russian army hospital in 1945, Eszterháza has gradually been restored to much of its former glory. There are even plans to build a replica of the opera house, demolished in the nineteenth century.

Nicolaus and his wife, Princess Marie Hermenegild, spent most of the year in their Wallnerstrasse palace, decamping to Eisenstadt during the late summer and autumn. The prince was far more interested in the visual arts than in music, spending much of his diminishing fortune in amassing a vast collection of paintings. At Eisenstadt he employed a small body of strings, a wind octet (*Harmonie*) and eight singers, including Haydn's youngest brother Johann Evangelist, who had entered the Esterházys' service as a twenty-one-year-old in 1765. Although Haydn was responsible for the musical establishment, his duties were largely confined to the months of September and October, during the festivities surrounding the name-day of Princess Marie Hermenegild. His chief task was to produce a new mass for performance on the first Sunday after the name-day itself, 8 September. Except for the 'Paukenmesse' and the *Missa in angustiis* ('Nelson' Mass), the late masses received their first performances during the name-day service in Eisenstadt's chubby rococo Bergkirche.

In contrast to the sympathetic princess, Prince Nicolaus was austere, arrogant and hot-tempered. As a serial lecher he comfortably out-womanised even the Prince of Wales, reportedly leaving a trail of some two hundred mistresses and a hundred illegitimate children. The government official Carl von Zinzendorf, a sharp observer of the social scene, noted that he even kept his own personal brothel (*'un temple dédié à la débauche'*, as he elegantly put it) in the Landstrasse. Forced into a loveless dynastic marriage at fifteen, the princess consoled herself in friendships with the Empress Marie Therese and other aristocratic ladies, writing sentimental poetry in several languages and taking the occasional lover.

Prince Nicolaus's initial instinct was to treat Haydn as a superior lackey, addressing him *de haut en bas* in the third person ('Er') – something understandably resented by a Doctor of Music from Oxford who had been treated as an equal by the English aristocracy. Pohl tells a story of an orchestral rehearsal at which the prince brusquely criticised the composer. In front of the players Haydn countered, 'Your Highness, that is *my* business,' whereupon the prince stormed out of the room. With a little diplomatic help from the princess, relations between the two men gradually improved. Musically limited though he was, the prince could hardly fail to appreciate the lustre his Kapellmeister brought to the house of Esterházy.

Despite requests for symphonies, No. 104 was to remain Haydn's last. The principal compositions of 1796 were the first two of the late masses (the 'Paukenmesse' and 'Heiligmesse'), a piano trio (No. 30), some beautiful part-songs and the ebullient Trumpet Concerto. Early the following year Haydn scored a huge popular and political triumph with the patriotic hymn 'Gott erhalte Franz den Kaiser', distributed throughout the Austro-Hungarian monarchy and sung in cities from Kraków to Trieste on the Emperor's twenty-ninth birthday, 12 February 1797. The hymn enshrined Haydn as Austria's national composer and consolidated his prestige in imperial circles, some compensation after the relative indifference of Maria Theresa and Joseph II. A few months later he reused the 'Volkslied', as he called it, in the String Quartet Op. 76 No. 3. This was one of a set of six commissioned by his friend Count Joseph Erdödy, who enjoyed more or less exclusive use of the new works until their publication in 1799.

Prince Nicolaus was among the aristocratic backers of the Gesellschaft der Associierten, founded in the 1780s by the lordly Baron Gottfried van Swieten primarily to promote the music of Handel. At Swieten's behest Mozart had re-orchestrated *Messiah* and other works for the society. The baron had been trying to coax an oratorio from Haydn since the Gesellschaft's performance of his chorus *The Storm* in 1793. As something of a warm-up, he provided the text for the com-poser's choral arrangement of *The Seven Last Words*, much admired on its premiere on 26 March 1796.

By then plans were being hatched for the masterpiece Haydn intended would seal his lasting fame. In London he had acquired, via Salomon, an anonymous English libretto entitled *The Creation of the World*. On being shown the text, Swieten immediately saw the opportunity to anoint Haydn as Handel's successor. (He seemed to be grooming Mozart for the same role in the late 1780s.) The Gesellschaft der Associierten guaranteed the composer five hundred ducats; and the baron's German translation of the libretto was ready by autumn 1796. Haydn worked on the oratorio for much of 1797, completing it in Eisenstadt in the late autumn, and later telling Griesinger:

> It was not until I reached the halfway point in my work that I noticed that it had turned out well; I was never so devout as during the time when I was working on *The Creation*; every day I fell on my knees and asked God to give me strength to pursue the work to its successful conclusion.

The Gesellschaft sponsored the first, semi-private performance of *The Creation* in the Schwarzenberg palace on 30

April 1798, following an open rehearsal the previous day. Haydn himself conducted, and court Kapellmeister Salieri played the fortepiano continuo. The largely aristocratic audience was overwhelmed. The Swedish diplomat Fredrik Silverstolpe reported that 'in the moment when Light broke forth for the first time, one would have said that light-rays darted from the composer's blazing eyes. The enchantment of the electrified Viennese was so profound that the performers could not continue for several minutes.'

With anticipation at fever pitch, the *Creation*'s public premiere, at the Imperial Burgtheater, finally took place on 19 March 1799. The performance was on an opulent scale, though just how opulent is a moot point: the *Allgemeine musikalische Zeitung* stated that 'singers and orchestra consisted of more than 180 persons'; in his memoirs, the Swedish composer-violinist Johan Fredrik Berwald, then a child prodigy of eleven, gave the figure at four hundred. It caused a predictable sensation. Receipts broke all box-office records for Viennese theatres, and the oratorio quickly became a national cultural monument. Like *Messiah* in England, *The Creation* raised huge sums for charity, initially in the performances Haydn conducted for the widows' and orphans' fund of the Tonkünstler-Societät. Writing to the publishers Breitkopf und Härtel of a performance in aid of wounded soldiers, Griesinger observed that 'this music seems to have been made to help collect money for good works'.

According to Pohl, the sustained effort involved in composing the oratorio and the stress associated with its first performances left the hitherto robust Haydn feverish and debilitated. During his convalescence he composed the most famous of his masses, the so-called 'Nelson' Mass, conducting the first performance in Eisenstadt on 23 September. On his return to Vienna in late October he spent several days with his brother Michael, cathedral organist in Salzburg, whom he had probably not seen since the 1760s – though Michael had contemplated visiting Joseph in the winter of 1770–1 after learning of his brother's serious illness. Together they attended two concerts in the Theater auf der Wieden, the first of which featured Beethoven in one of his piano concertos (either No. 1 or No. 2) and a performance of Haydn's 'beliebte Sinphonie', probably the 'Surprise', No. 94.

From his mother Haydn had inherited an intense – psychiatrists might say obsessive – love of order, neatness and cleanliness, qualities he demanded from his entire household. In later years he adhered to an unchanging routine, as described by his live-in copyist and factotum Johann Elssler. Note that there is no mention of his wife, with whom he lived in a state of indifference until her death in 1800.

In the summer he rose at 6.30 a.m. The first thing he did was shave, which he did for himself up to his 73rd year. Then he finished dressing. If a pupil was present he had to play his lesson on the keyboard to Herr v Haydn while the master dressed. All mistakes were immediately corrected and a new task set . . . At eight o'clock sharp breakfast had to be on the table, and immediately afterwards Haydn sat down at the keyboard, improvising and working out sketches of his latest composition . . . At 11.30 visits were paid or received, or he went for a walk until 1.30. The hour from 2 till 3 was reserved for lunch, after which Haydn always occupied himself with some small domestic task or went into his little library and read a book. At 4 o'clock Haydn returned to his music scoring the sketches he had been working on that morning . . . At 8 in the evening Haydn usually went out, returning home at nine, when he sat down to write out a score or took a book and read until 10. At 10 he had supper, which consisted of bread and wine. Haydn made it a rule only to have bread and wine at night, and broke it only when he was invited out for dinner. He enjoyed light, entertaining conversation at table. At 11.30 Haydn went to bed, in his old age even later.

On 24 March 1799, five days after the *Creation*'s public premiere, the *Allgemeine musikalische Zeitung* announced that Haydn was 'working on a great new work, which the worthy

Herr Geheimrath Freyherr van Swieten has arranged metrically from Thomson's "Seasons", and of which he has already completed the first part, "Spring". The curiosity of all music lovers is already stretched to breaking point.' In his excitement, the newspaper correspondent had run ahead of himself. Although the baron had been quick to propose a follow-up to *The Creation*, Haydn began work on *The Seasons* only in the autumn of 1799, after composing the 'Theresienmesse' for the princess's name-day festivities and two string quartets dedicated to another quartet-loving aristocrat, Prince Lobkowitz, part of a projected set of six. In the event these two works, published in 1802 as Op. 77, would be his last completed quartets.

'Haydn is now writing with new zeal, since he has had the good luck to lose his nasty wife,' reported Silverstolpe to his family on 5 April 1800. Maria Anna Haydn's death 'from severe arthritis' in the spa of Baden on 20 March may have come as a welcome release to her husband of forty years. Yet while at work on *The Seasons* during 1800 Haydn frequently complained of 'nervous exhaustion'. Relations with Swieten, too, were sometimes strained, as when the baron tried to bully Haydn into dropping the quotation from the 'Surprise' Symphony in favour of a tune from a popular opera. After finally completing the oratorio around the end of the year he suffered an attack of fever; and the planned semi-private premiere, again in Prince Schwarzenberg's palace, had to be postponed until 24 April 1801. The performance was twice repeated, 'with unparalleled success', as Haydn informed his one-time pupil and London rival Ignaz Pleyel. Dies relates how audience opinion was evenly divided over the relative merits of *The Seasons* and *The Creation*. Although the hall was barely half full – a premonition, Robbins Landon suggests, of Haydn's gradually waning popular appeal in Vienna over the next decade – the public premiere in the Redoutensaal on 29 May was enthusiastically received.

Silverstolpe remarked of the oratorio that 'the subject is much more limited than that of *The Creation* but closer to Haydn's own taste'. Haydn's own words suggest the opposite. He wrote to the composer-publisher Muzio Clementi in

London that 'many prefer it to *The Creation* because of its greater variety'. Conversely, he derided the libretto's triviality, even more so after critics (North Germans, as usual, to the fore) had attacked the passages of onomatopoeic imitation. In the new Romantic aesthetic that abhorred naive 'tone-painting', the pictorialisms in *The Creation* were also coming under fire. According to Dies, when the Emperor asked the composer which of the two oratorios he preferred, he replied: '*The Creation.*' 'And why?' 'In *The Creation* angels speak and tell of God, but in *The Seasons* only Simon speaks.'

Haydn conducted regular charity performances of his late oratorios until his final public appearance with *The Seven Last Words* on 26 December 1803. As Esterházy Kapellmeister he continued to perform his light administrative duties. Documents reveal that he still had to mediate occasionally in disputes, usually over pay, between the prince and the musicians. In 1801 and 1802 he composed two final masses for Princess Marie Hermenegild, the 'Schöpfungsmesse' and the 'Harmoniemesse'. Far from betraying creative 'burn-out' after *The Seasons*, both are works of undimmed power and inventiveness that find new solutions to the setting of the mass text.

Apart from the brief, pungent National Hungarian March, the 'Harmoniemesse' was destined to be Haydn's last completed work. (We can discount the profitable Scottish folk-song arrangements, which by now he was farming out to pupils without coming clean to his publishers.) He still hoped to complete the set of quartets for Prince Lobkowitz, and in the summer of 1803 even managed to compose the two middle movements of a planned D minor quartet, eventually published as Op. 103. 'It is my last child,' he told Griesinger, 'but it still looks like me.' He toyed with the idea of another oratorio, on the subject of The Last Judgement – a tantalising prospect – and a Cecilian ode based on Dryden entitled *Polyhymnia, oder die Macht der Töne* (Polyhymnia, or the power of music). But at seventy-one he no longer had the stamina.

Haydn retired as Esterházy Kapellmeister around the end of

1803, shortly after his final appearance as conductor. After his brother Michael had refused the post of vice-Kapellmeister, Haydn's duties were divided between Tomasini, Johann Fuchs, a local musician in the service of the Esterházys, and the brilliant pianist-composer Johann Nepomuk Hummel. Haydn spent his remaining years quietly at his house in Gumpendorf. Heaped with honours, he was host to a stream of visiting musicians, including the young Carl Maria von Weber, who early in 1804 noted: 'Except for the weaknesses of old age he is still cheerful and light-hearted, is happy to talk about his affairs, and is especially pleased to talk to pleasant young artists.'

In August of the same year, however, Griesinger reported to the publishers Breitkopf und Härtel that 'Haydn has stopped all work because of his health, and a quartet of which he has completed two movements is all he cares for, and to which he sometimes devotes a quarter of an hour'. By now the composer was increasingly prone to melancholia and depression, and plagued by musical ideas which he was too weak to elaborate at the keyboard (his habitual method of working). Yet his famed sense of humour could still surface. Early in 1805 rumours circulated in France of his death, and Cherubini composed a funeral cantata for a planned commemorative event. Pohl recounts Haydn's reaction: 'I am much indebted to them for this unexpected honour. If I had known of the ceremony, I would have gone there to conduct the mass [i.e. the cantata] in person.'

Intent on gathering material for a biography, the landscape painter Dies first visited Haydn in April 1805, and left the following sketch of the old composer:

[A]lthough sick for a long time, and with both legs swollen, he gave me both his hands and received me with a cheerfulness that spread over his whole features and with such an intelligent look that I was surprised. This lively expression, the brownish (tinged with red) facial colouring, the exceptionally neat clothing . . . his powdered wig and, despite the swelling, the boots he was wearing and the gloves; all this made one forget any trace

of illness and gave the old man of seventy-three the look
of a fifty-year-old, which was enhanced by his medium
height and the fact that he was not at all heavy.

Dies goes on to relate how Haydn liked to watch his neighbour's children playing in his housekeeper's room, noting
'their jokes make him forget his sad condition . . . He admits
his spirit is weak. He cannot think, cannot feel, cannot write,
cannot hear music.'

Suffering from arteriosclerosis, Haydn rarely left his house
from 1806 onwards. In August that year he was profoundly
distressed by news of his brother Michael's death. He spent
much of his time praying, reminiscing about his years in
England, reading the newspapers and checking household
accounts. In the evenings he discussed the daily news with
his neighbours and occasionally played cards with them, forti-
fied by the Malaga wine which Prince Nicolaus regularly sent
as a gift. His last public appearance was on 27 March 1808, at
the famous performance of *The Creation* (in Carpani's Italian
translation) mounted in honour of his seventy-sixth birthday
in the Great Hall of Vienna University. Salieri conducted. It
was attended by the cream of Viennese society, intent on paying a final homage to the master. In a gesture of reconciliation,
Beethoven is said to have kissed Haydn's hand. The *Allgemeine
musikalische Zeitung* reported how 'thunderous applause' interrupted the performance at the words 'And there was light',
whereupon Haydn, 'tears streaming down his pallid cheeks . . .
raised his trembling arms to Heaven, as if in prayer to the
Father of Harmony'. After the first part the composer was so
overwhelmed that he asked to be taken home.

In November 1808 Haydn's favourite pupil Sigismund
Neukomm found the composer further weakened, and trying
to console himself by reharmonising his 'Emperor's Hymn' at
the piano. The following February he amended his will of 1801
(his estate, including the Gumpendorf house, totalled some
fifty-five thousand gulden). On 11 May Napoleon's troops
began to bombard Vienna, causing Beethoven – then grappling

with the 'Emperor' Concerto – to retreat to a cellar and muffle his ears to protect what remained of his hearing. Elssler tells how after a series of explosions had shaken the house, Haydn, though seized with trembling, comforted the terrified servants with the words: 'Children, don't be frightened, for where Haydn is no harm can come to you.' A few days later he was deeply moved when a French officer visited him and sang the aria 'In native worth' from *The Creation*. After playing through the 'Emperor's Hymn' three times on 26 May, Haydn took to his bed and never left it. He died peacefully in his sleep shortly after midnight on 31 May, and was buried in the nearby Gumpendorf cemetery the following day – the French invasion obviously precluded an elaborate funeral. On 2 June a mass by his brother Michael was performed – 'lamentably', according to one witness – in the local church. A more worthy memorial service was held in the Schottenkirche on 15 June, with a performance of Mozart's Requiem, attended by the Viennese élite and many French army officers.

A chronology

1732 Franz Joseph Haydn born in the village of Rohrau, Lower Austria, 31 March. Baptised 1 April.

1737 Brother Johann Michael born 13 or 14 September.

1738 Joseph (known as 'Sepperl') receives his first formal musical instruction from Johann Matthias Franck in Hainburg.

1740 Enters the choir school of St Stephen's Cathedral in Vienna under Johann Reutter.

***c.*1743** Earliest efforts at composition, intermittently supervised by Reutter.

1745 Brother Michael joins the choir school.

1748 or **1749** Dismissed from the choir school after his voice breaks.

1749 or **1750** Composes *Missa brevis* in F, his earliest surviving work.

1750 Ekes out a living in Vienna teaching and playing the organ and violin. Possible visit to the Benedictine church of Mariazell.

1753 Plays for Nicola Porpora's singing lessons and receives informal instruction from him in composition. First stage work, *Der krumme Teufel*, produced at the Kärntnerthor Theatre.

1754 Death of mother Anna Maria in Rohrau.

***c.*1754–6** Composes first string quartets for Baron Fürnberg.

1755 His father Matthias remarries.

1757 or **1758** First salaried post, as music director to Count Morzin. Composes first symphonies.

1760 Marries Maria Anna Aloysia Apollonia Keller, a wigmaker's daughter, 26 November.

1761 Appointed vice-Kapellmeister to the Prince Paul Anton Esterházy. Composes the 'times of day' symphonies, Nos. 6–8.

1762 Death of Prince Paul Anton Esterházy, who is succeeded by his younger brother Nicolaus.

1763 Haydn's *festa teatrale*, *Acide e Galatea*, produced in Eisenstadt. Symphonies Nos. 12, 13, 40 and 72. Death of father Matthias in Rohrau.

1764 Symphonies Nos. 21–4.

1765 Symphonies Nos. 28–31. Haydn reprimanded by Prince Nicolaus after complaints from the Kapellmeister, Gregor Werner.

1766 Haydn promoted to Kapellmeister after Werner's death, 3 March. Buys his own house in Eisenstadt. Composes Kyrie and Gloria (possibly the other movements too) of his first *Missa Cellensis*.

1767 Composes *Stabat mater*, destined to be one of his greatest international successes. Symphony No. 35.

1768 Opera house at Eszterháza, Prince Nicolaus's summer palace, inaugurated with Haydn's *Lo speziale*. Symphony No. 49, 'La Passione', *Applausus* cantata.

1769 Symphony No. 48, 'Maria Theresa'. String Quartets Op. 9.

1770 Comic opera *Le pescatrici*. Haydn suffers feverish illness during the winter of 1770–1.

1771 Keyboard Sonata in C minor, No. 20. String Quartets Op. 17.

1772 Symphonies Nos. 45 ('Farewell'), 46 and 47. String Quartets Op. 20. *Missa Sancti Nicolai*.

1773 Comic opera *L'infedeltà delusa* and marionette opera *Philemon und Baucis* performed in honour of Empress Maria Theresa in September.

1774 Symphonies Nos. 54–7, and Symphony No. 60 ('Il distratto').

1775 Successful premiere of oratorio *Il ritorno di Tobia* at the Tonkünstler-Societät in Vienna, 2 April. Comic opera *L'incontro improvviso*.

1776 Symphony No. 61. Regular opera seasons inaugurated at Eszterháza.

1777 Comic opera *Il mondo della luna*.

1779 Operas *La vera costanza* and *L'isola disabitata*. Opera house at Eszterháza destroyed by fire. Haydn composes

Symphony No. 70 to mark rebuilding. Signs new Esterházy contract allowing him to publish without the prince's consent. Soprano Luigia Polzelli and her husband engaged by Prince Nicolaus. Shortly afterwards Luigia becomes Haydn's mistress.

1781 Haydn's *La fedeltà premiata* inaugurates rebuilt Eszterháza opera house. String Quartets Op. 33.

1782 Symphonies Nos. 76–8 composed for a planned visit to London. Composes 'Mariazellermesse' and his last comic opera, *Orlando paladino*.

1783 Possible first meeting with Mozart in Vienna.

1784 Completes set of three symphonies, Nos. 79–81, and his final Eszterháza opera, *Armida*.

1785 Composes Symphonies Nos. 83 and 87, possibly No. 85, for the Concert de la Loge Olympique in Paris. At Mozart's apartment Haydn hears three of the six quartets subsequently dedicated to him.

1786 Composes remaining 'Paris' Symphonies, Nos. 82, 84 and 86, and *The Seven Last Words* to a commission from Cádiz.

1787 Symphonies Nos. 88 and 89. String Quartets Op. 50, dedicated to King Friedrich Wilhelm II of Prussia.

1788 Composes Symphonies Nos. 90 and 91 for Paris. Six String Quartets Opp. 54 and 55.

1789 Haydn meets Maria Anna von Genzinger, wife of Prince Nicolaus Esterházy's physician. She becomes his close confidante. Composes Symphony No. 92, later nicknamed 'Oxford'.

1790 Death of Prince Nicolaus, 28 September. Haydn immediately leaves Eisenstadt for Vienna. Composes String Quartets Op. 64. Signs a contract with the violinist-impresario Johann Peter Salomon and departs for London on 15 December.

1791 Arrives in England on New Year's Day. Composes opera *L'anima del filosofo* (never performed), and Symphonies Nos. 95 and 96 for Salomon's 1791 concert season. Receives honorary doctorate at Oxford University. Composes Symphonies Nos. 93 and 94 for 1792 season.

1792 Composes Symphonies Nos. 97 and 98, and *Sinfonia Concertante*. Returns to Vienna in July. Beethoven arrives in Vienna in November and becomes Haydn's pupil.

1793 In Vienna he composes Symphony No. 99, parts of Nos. 100 and 101 and String Quartets Opp. 71 and 74 in preparation for second London visit. Death of Maria Anna von Genzinger, 20 January.

1794 Leaves for second visit to London in January. Completes Symphonies Nos. 100 and 101 and composes Symphony No. 102, piano trios and Piano Sonatas Nos. 50–2. Visits Bath, where he stays with the famous castrato Rauzzini. Prince Anton Esterházy dies and is succeeded by his son, Nicolaus II.

1795 Composes piano trios, the *Scena di Berenice* and his last two symphonies, Nos. 103 and 104. Returns to Vienna in August.

1796 Composes 'Heiligmesse', *Missa in tempore belli* and Trumpet Concerto. Makes choral arrangement of *The Seven Last Words*.

1797 Composes *The Creation*, the 'Emperor's Hymn' and the String Quartets Op. 76.

1798 First, semi-private, performance of *The Creation* at Prince Schwarzenberg's palace. 'Nelson' Mass performed in Eisenstadt in September.

1799 Triumphant public premiere of *The Creation* in the Burgtheater, 19 March. Composes 'Theresienmesse' and last two complete String Quartets, Op. 77.

1800 Composes his second *Te Deum* and most of *The Seasons*. Meets Nelson and Lady Hamilton at Eisenstadt in September. Death of Haydn's wife, 20 March.

1801 Completes *The Seasons*, which receives its public premiere in the Redoutensaal on 29 May, after semi-private performances at Prince Schwarzenberg's. Composes 'Schöpfungsmesse' for Princess Esterházy's name-day celebrations.

1802 Composes the 'Harmoniemesse', his last mass for the princess and his last major work.

1803 Completes two movements of a string quartet, published as Op. 103. In December appears for the last time as conductor. Retires as Esterházy Kapellmeister.

1806 Death of Haydn's brother Michael in Salzburg, 10 August.

1808 In failing health Haydn makes his last public appearance, at a performance of *The Creation*.

1809 Dies at his home in Vienna on 31 May.

Friends, patrons and colleagues

ABINGDON, WILLOUGHBY BERTIE (1740–99)
A notorious political maverick who in 1795 served a jail sentence for libel, the Earl of Abingdon was a keen amateur flautist and composer, and a passionate lover of Haydn's music. He made several unsuccessful attempts to lure Haydn to England in the 1780s. Haydn seems to have been particularly friendly with Abingdon during 1794, when he stayed with him on his country estate and incorporated one of the earl's songs in his second 'London' trio for flutes and cello.

BANTI, BRIGIDA GIORGI (c.1756–1806)
Reputed to be the daughter of a Venetian gondolier, Banti was a star prima donna of the 1780s and 1790s, famed both for the sweetness, agility and 'taste' of her singing and for her dissolute lifestyle (she was reported to drink at least a bottle of wine a day). She caused a sensation in London in 1794–5. For her Haydn wrote his great *Scena di Berenice*, though a comment in his notebook ('She song very scanty') suggests that she may have been off-form at the premiere.

BURNEY, CHARLES (1726–1814)
As a young man the English composer, teacher and music historian had played the violin in Handel's oratorio orchestra. Some forty years later he came to revere Haydn, and immediately befriended him in London, writing that '[I] think him as *good* a creature as *great* a Musician'. It was at Burney's behest that Haydn received his honorary doctorate at Oxford. An indefatigable champion of Haydn's symphonies, quartets and oratorios, he arranged for the publication, by subscription, of *The Creation* in England. His daughter was the novelist and diarist Fanny Burney (1752–1840).

DICHTLER, LEOPOLD (d.1799)
An Esterházy stalwart and long-time friend of Haydn's,

Leopold Dichtler was an accomplished comic tenor who after he retired from singing in 1788 became a double-bass player. In 1790 he was granted an annual pension of four hundred gulden by Prince Anton Esterházy. Haydn's many operatic roles for Dichtler range from Apollonia in *La canterina* (played in drag and probably sung in falsetto) to Clotarco in *Armida*. His first wife, soprano Barbara Dichtler, dropped dead during an Eszterháza performance of Sacchini's *L'isola d'amore* in 1776.

ELSSLER, JOHANN (1769–1843)

Son of the Esterházy music copyist Joseph Elssler (d.1782), Johann Elssler became Haydn's main copyist in the late 1780s, and accompanied the composer on his second London visit in 1794. From 1796 he and his wife lived in Haydn's house in the Viennese suburb of Gumpendorf, where he also acted as the composer's general factotum. In 1805 Elssler prepared the *Haydn Verzeichnis*, a comprehensive catalogue of his works. His daughter Fanny (1810–84) became a famous dancer.

ERDÖDY, JOSEPH (1754–1824)

A member of a Hungarian noble family renowned for their musical patronage, Count Joseph Erdödy maintained his own string quartet and in 1796 commissioned a set of six quartets from Haydn. Sometimes known as the 'Erdödy' quartets, these were published in 1799 as Op. 76, with a dedication to the count.

ESTERHÁZY FAMILY

The Esterházys, the wealthiest and most influential dynasty in the Austro-Hungarian monarchy bar the Habsburgs themselves, were Haydn's employers from 1761 until his death in 1809. His first two Esterházy patrons, Prince Paul Anton (1711–62) and, especially, his younger brother Prince Nicolaus I, nicknamed 'The Lover of Magnificence' (1714–90), were cultivated musicians who spent lavishly on music and the other arts. They had palaces in Vienna, Eisenstadt and Kittsee, to which Nicolaus added Eszterháza, the 'Hungarian Versailles' he created from a hunting lodge in reclaimed swampland. On his death Nicolaus was succeeded by his son, Prince Anton (1738–94), who in economically straitened times dismissed the musicians and theatrical troupe, leaving Haydn free to travel to London. The musical establishment was revived in a much more modest form under Anton's son, Prince Nicolaus II (1765–1833), whose prime interests were the visual arts and women. For his wife, Princess Marie Hermenegild (1768–1845), Haydn composed most of his late masses.

FERDINAND IV, KING OF NAPLES (1751–1825)

The notoriously coarse and unpredictable King of Naples was a passionate exponent of that curious, and quickly obsolete, instrument, the *lira organnizata*, commissioning *lira* works from Haydn and other composers. An avid admirer of Haydn's symphonies, he tried unsuccessfully to entice the composer to Naples in 1790 and again in 1795.

FRIBERTH, CARL (1736–1816)

A member of the Esterházy company from 1759 to 1776, Carl Friberth was, with Leopold Dichtler, one of Haydn's two star tenors. Like Dichtler, he was a gifted comedian with an unusually wide vocal range and an agile coloratura technique. Friberth also prepared the libretto (from a French original) of *L'incontro improvviso*, in which he sang the role of Prince Ali, and adapted other operas for Haydn. He left to become a Kapellmeister at two Viennese churches, for which he composed masses and other works. In 1769 he married the soprano Magdalena Spangler (b.1750), who had joined the Esterházy opera troupe the previous year.

GENZINGER, MARIA ANNA VON (1750–93)

Wife of the surgeon Peter von Genzinger, Maria Anna (or Marianne) was Haydn's close friend and confidante for four years from 1789 until her early death in January 1793. His letters to her from Eszterháza and London – the most unguarded he ever wrote – hint at a deeper attachment on his side, though there is no evidence that their relationship was other than platonic. Haydn's feelings for Maria Anna can perhaps be gauged from the beautiful Adagio of the E flat Sonata, No. 49, written expressly for her.

GEORGE AUGUSTUS FREDERICK, PRINCE OF WALES (1762–1830)

The debauched but musically cultured future George IV (he was an enthusiastic cellist) was the composer's most avid supporter among the English royal family. Haydn often took part, as keyboard player or conductor, in the Prince of Wales's concerts at Carlton House, and in 1792 he composed a march for wind band for the prince's regiment. To Maria Anna von Genzinger he wrote that the prince, then just twenty-eight, was 'the most handsome man on God's earth; he has an extraordinary love of music and much feeling, but little money'. After his return to Vienna in 1795, Haydn sent a bill for £100 to the Commissioner of Parliament for fees owed him by the prince. It was promptly paid, although according to Griesinger Haydn's claim was 'ill received and attributed to greed'.

HUNTER, ANNE (1742–1821)

Haydn got to know the famous Scottish surgeon Dr John Hunter (1728–93) and his wife Anne (née Home), poet and salon hostess, during his first visit to London. When he returned in 1794 the now widowed Anne provided texts for several of his English canzonettas, the first six of which are dedicated to her.

JANSEN(-BARTOLOZZI), THERESE (c.1770–1843)

Haydn first heard the gifted Clementi pupil 'Miss Janson', as he called her, during his first London sojourn. On his return visit in 1794–5 he wrote for her his grandest keyboard sonatas, Nos. 50 and 52 (possibly also the more modest D major Sonata, No. 51), and three of his greatest piano trios, Nos. 27–29. In May 1795 he was a witness at her wedding, in St James's Piccadilly, to the picture dealer Gaetano Bartolozzi, son of the famous Francesco Bartolozzi who had engraved Haydn's portrait on his first London visit. Possibly the trios were intended as a wedding present.

KRAFFT ERNST, PRINCE OF OETTINGEN-WALLERSTEIN (1748–1802)

A fervent devotee and collector of Haydn's music, Prince Krafft employed one of the finest orchestras in Germany at his two Bavarian palaces. He was a subscriber to the Op. 33 Quartets; and he seems to have quickly forgiven Haydn for less than scrupulous dealings over Symphonies Nos. 90–2, of which he received only the orchestral parts rather than the promised autograph scores (these were with the Comte d'Ogny in Paris). Haydn stayed with the prince en route to London in December 1790.

LATROBE, CHRISTIAN IGNATIUS (1758–1836)

It was through Charles Burney that Haydn met this minister of the Moravian Brethren and amateur composer in London. The two men seem to have struck up a warm friendship, enhanced by their shared interest in religion. Latrobe had revered Haydn's music since encountering the *Stabat mater* in 1779, and helped propagate his masses in England. Haydn for his part encouraged the minister to publish his own works.

MORZIN FAMILY

Griesinger states that 'in 1759 Haydn was appointed music director in Vienna to Count Morzin'. The appointment – Haydn's first full-time post – almost certainly took place one or two years earlier; and no one can be sure whether the count in question was Franz Ferdinand Maximilian von Morzin (1693–1763) or his son Carl Joseph Franz (1717–83). The Morzins divided their time between Vienna and their summer palace at Lukavec in Bohemia. During his three or four years as Morzin Kapellmeister (the small orchestra was disbanded early in 1761) Haydn composed some twenty symphonies and assorted chamber works.

OGNY, COUNT CLAUDE-FRANÇOIS-MARIE RIGOLEY D' (1757–90)

Capitalising on the huge popularity of Haydn's quartets and symphonies in France, in the winter of 1784–5 the count commissioned the six 'Paris' symphonies on behalf of the Masonic Concert de la Loge Olympique, in which he played the cello. These led in turn to three more commissions, Nos. 90–2, the first two of which carry autograph dedications to D'Ogny.

POLZELLI, LUIGIA (1750–1831)

The Italian soprano (née Moreschi) and her violinist husband Antonio were engaged at the Esterházy court in 1779. Luigia quickly became the composer's mistress, and would remain so until the musical establishment was disbanded in 1790. From the 'insertion arias' Haydn wrote for her to sing in other composers' operas, we can infer that Luigia was a light soubrette with a limited range, probably making up in vivacity what she lacked in vocal allure. They corresponded during Haydn's London visits (she was engaged at the opera house in Piacenza after Prince Anton disbanded the Eszterháza opera troupe). After Antonio's death Luigia even secured a promise of marriage should Haydn become free. But she was happy not to hold the aged composer to his pledge after his wife's death in 1800, and soon married a singer by the name of Luigi Franchi. Haydn left Luigia an annuity of 150 gulden in his will. Luigia believed that her younger son Antonio (1783–1855), a violinist, was Haydn's.

ROSENBAUM, JOSEPH CARL (1770–1829)

Rosenbaum was an administrator in the service of the Esterházys and the husband of Therese Gassmann (1774–1837), who sang the soprano solos in the premieres of *The Seven Last Words* and most of Haydn's late masses. His diaries are revealing on the composer's last years and Viennese cultural life generally. Rosenbaum subsequently became infamous as the man who arranged to have Haydn's corpse decapitated and the head taken to hospital in Vienna in the name of phrenological research. After rather a murky history, Haydn's skull was finally reunited with his trunk in the crypt of the Bergkirche, Eisenstadt, in 1954.

SALOMON, JOHANN PETER (1745–1815)

Born in Bonn, the violinist and composer made his reputation as a virtuoso and orchestral leader in Germany before settling in London in 1781. He is remembered primarily as the man who netted Haydn for his London concert series in the Hanover Square Rooms (owned by Sir John Gallini) after Prince Nicolaus Esterházy's death in September 1790. Several of Haydn's 'London' symphonies contain solos for Salomon. He also played the solo violin part in Haydn's 1792 Sinfonia Concertante (calculated, according to the *Oracle*, 'to 'shew the brilliancy of Salomon's, and the sweetness of his tone'), and led his ad hoc string quartet in public performances of the Opp. 71 and 74 Quartets. Finding it increasingly difficult to recruit star singers from the Continent, Salomon merged for the 1795 season with his former rivals, the Professional Concert.

SCHROETER, REBECCA (1751–1826)

The Scottish-born widow (née Scott) of the composer Samuel Schroeter (1750–88) was Haydn's piano pupil during his first visit to London. From her increasingly ardent letters to him (his letters to her are not preserved) we can infer that they became lovers. Haydn later told Dies that he would happily have married Rebecca had he been free. In 1795 he dedicated to her three of his finest piano trios, Nos. 24–6.

SWIETEN, BARON GOTTFRIED VAN (1733–1803)

Closely associated with both Mozart and Haydn, the director of the Imperial Library in Vienna was a musical patron and connoisseur who in the 1780s set up the Gesellschaft der Associierten Cavaliers to promote the music of Handel and, to a lesser degree, J. S. and C. P. E. Bach. Swieten also had ambitions as a composer, though Haydn allegedly dubbed his symphonic efforts 'as stiff as the Baron himself'. He is best known as the man who fashioned the bilingual librettos of *The Creation* and *The Seasons*. Although Swieten's manner could be overbearing, Haydn valued him as a collaborator, and relied on him for advice on non-musical matters.

TOMASINI, ALOISIO LUIGI (1741–1808)

The Pesaro-born violinist entered the service of Prince Paul

Anton Esterházy as a page around 1753, honed his skill on the violin with Leopold Mozart and became leader of the Esterházy orchestra about the time of Haydn's appointment in 1761. With tenor Leopold Dichtler and, in the early years, cellist Joseph Weigl, Tomasini was Haydn's closest friend among the court musicians. For Tomasini he wrote the violin concertos in C major and A major (the C major is inscribed 'fatto per il luigi'), the violin solos in the 'times of day' symphonies, Nos. 6–8 and, almost certainly, the often florid first violin parts in the Op. 9 Quartets. Pensioned off by Prince Anton Esterházy in 1790, he was re-employed as concertmaster by Nicolaus II, and after Haydn's retirement became director of instrumental music at the Esterházy court.

TOST, JOHANN (1759–1831)

Tost already harboured entrepreneurial ambitions, sometimes of a dubious nature, while leader of the second violins in the Esterházy orchestra. His name is associated with Haydn's Quartets Opp. 54 and 55, which he sold on the composer's behalf to a Parisian publisher, and Op. 64, of which he is the dedicatee – though there is no foundation for the popular belief that they were written expressly for Tost. After inheriting money following the death of his wife Maria Anna Jerlischek (a former housekeeper to Prince Nicolaus Esterházy) in 1796, Tost flourished for a time as a businessman. Among other ventures, he opened a cloth factory in Bohemia and obtained a contract to supply equipment to the Austrian army.

WEIGL, JOSEPH (1740–1820)

Joining the Esterházy establishment in 1761 at exactly the same time as Haydn, Weigl was the orchestra's leading cellist until 1769, when he left to join the orchestra of the Kärntnerthor Theatre in Vienna. In 1764 he married soprano Anna Maria Scheffstoss who, inter alia, created the role of Gasparina in *La canterina* (1766). Haydn was godfather to two of their children. For Weigl he wrote concerto-like solos in several early symphonies and, probably, the C major Cello Concerto.

Haydn's composer contemporaries

ALBRECHTSBERGER, JOHANN GEORG (1736–1809)
Organist, composer and renowned pedagogue who became St Stephen's Kapellmeister in 1793. Haydn had known him since the 1750s, and passed Beethoven on to him for contrapuntal studies when he left for London in 1794.

ANFOSSI, PASQUALE (1727–97)
Popular Italian opera composer who trained under Sacchini and Piccinni and worked first in Rome and subsequently in London. Haydn performed eleven of his operas at Eszterháza and wrote 'insertion arias' for several of them. He also lifted a scene from Anfossi's *La vera costanza* (1776) for his own setting of the same libretto.

BACH, CARL PHILIPP EMANUEL (1714–88)
The second, and most famous, of Johann Sebastian Bach's sons, greatly admired by Haydn, Mozart and Beethoven. Griesinger quotes Haydn as saying: 'Whoever knows me thoroughly must discover that I owe a great deal to Emanuel Bach, that I understood him and studied him with diligence.' The impact of Bach's impassioned, improvisatory style is most strongly felt in the keyboard music Haydn composed between 1765 and 1771. *Pace* Griesinger, Haydn is unlikely to have known much, if any, of Bach's music during his 'galley years' of the early 1750s.

BEETHOVEN, LUDWIG VAN (1770–1827)
Haydn's sometimes difficult relationship with his most famous pupil is extensively chronicled in the literature, though stories of Beethoven's resentment of Haydn's supposedly lax teaching during 1793, and his sideswipes at Haydn's music, are not always reliable. In 1795 Beethoven apparently took umbrage when Haydn expressed misgivings about the C minor Piano Trio, Op. 1 No. 3. After about 1798 the two men had virtually no contact in Vienna. Yet whatever Beethoven liked to

maintain, Haydn was by far the most potent influence on his music, especially the symphonies and string quartets.

CHERUBINI, LUIGI (1760–1842)

The Italian-born honorary Frenchman, best known today as the composer of *Médée* (1797), was a great Haydn admirer. In Paris early in 1805 he composed a memorial cantata, *Chant sur la Mort de Joseph Haydn*, though it quickly emerged that reports of the master's death were greatly exaggerated. After Cherubini visited Haydn in 1805, the old man described him as 'an attractive little man [*Mandl*] with charming manners'.

CLEMENTI, MUZIO (1752–1832)

Famously denounced by Mozart as 'a mere *mechanicus*', with 'not an ounce of taste or feeling', Clementi moved from Rome to England in 1767 and made his reputation first as a composer and keyboard virtuoso, latterly as a music publisher and piano manufacturer. He met Haydn in London, and invited him to his country house in Evesham. The influence of Clementi's virtuoso keyboard style, inspired by the sonorous new Broadwood pianos in London, can be heard in several late Haydn sonatas, especially the finale of No. 48 and the first movements of Nos. 50 and 52. Clementi's four surviving symphonies from the first two decades of the nineteenth century tend to sound like Haydn's 'London' symphonies grown slightly bloated.

DITTERSDORF, CARL DITTERS VON (1739–99)

Haydn and the ennobled Viennese-born violinist and composer became friends in their street-serenading days in the mid-1750s, when the teenaged Dittersdorf was plain Carl Ditters. Haydn performed four of his comic operas at Eszterháza. According to the tenor Michael Kelly, the two men played quartets together at Stephen Storace's Viennese home in 1784, with Mozart on viola and Vanhal on cello.

GASSMANN, FLORIAN LEOPOLD (1729–74)

Gassmann was one of Vienna's most successful composers of symphonies, operas and string quartets (several with fugal finales, like three of Haydn's Op. 20) from the early 1760s until his premature death. Haydn conducted one of Gassmann's most popular operas, *L'amore artigiano*, at Eszterháza.

GLUCK, CHRISTOPH WILLIBALD (1714–87)

Though we have no precise documentation, Haydn apparently first met Gluck, probably through Metastasio or Porpora, in Vienna in the early/mid-1750s. He evidently admired Gluck's works, not just *Orfeo* (which he performed at Eszterháza in 1776) but also the revolutionary 1761 ballet *Don Juan*, a likely influence on Haydn's turbulent *Sturm und Drang* symphonies.

GYROWETZ, ADALBERT (1763–1850)

The popular Bohemian-born composer left Paris for London in 1789 and two years later befriended Haydn there. In his autobiography he claimed to have smoothed Haydn's path in London society, though corroborative evidence is lacking. On his own admission Gyrowetz modelled his style closely on Haydn's, making it easy for the violinist-entrepreneur Johann Tost to sell one of his symphonies to a Parisian publisher under Haydn's name.

HASSE, JOHANN ADOLF (1699–1783)

Born in Hamburg and active first in Dresden, then in Italy, Hasse was the most famous exponent of Italian *opera seria* from the 1730s to the 1760s. In 1767 Haydn sent a copy of his new *Stabat mater* to Hasse. The older composer's praise for the work (in a letter that has not survived) was cherished by Haydn, who wrote in his Autobiographical Sketch: 'I shall treasure this testimonial all my life as if it were gold.'

HAYDN, JOHANN MICHAEL (1737–1806)

A star treble in St Stephen's choir school, like his older brother before him, Michael Haydn was a gifted but unambitious composer who, in contrast to Mozart, was happy to spend most of his working life (from 1763) in the service of the Prince-Archbishops of Salzburg. Mozart father and son both remarked on Michael's drinking, Leopold with stern disapproval, Wolfgang with amusement. The Haydn brothers probably did not meet between the 1760s and 1798, when Michael spent some time in Vienna. During another visit in 1801 Michael, renowned above all for his church music, was offered the post of Esterházy vice-Kapellmeister but eventually refused.

HOFMANN, LEOPOLD (1738–93)

Unlike Haydn, the violinist and composer Leopold Hofmann was a favourite at the Habsburg court, holding the posts of *Hofklaviermeister* and (from 1772) St Stephen's Kapellmeister. His privileged status evidently rankled with Haydn, who, in one of his rare vitriolic attacks, called him (in a letter to the publisher Artaria) 'a braggart who thinks he alone has ascended the heights of Parnassus', and dubbed his Lieder 'street songs'.

HUMMEL, JOHANN NEPOMUK (1778–1837)

A child prodigy pianist, who lived with Mozart as his pupil in 1786–8, Hummel performed at several of the same London concerts as Haydn in 1791–2. In 1804 he became Esterházy Konzertmeister, and continued the tradition initiated by Haydn of composing masses for Princess Marie Hermenegild's name-day. Hummel's forthright personality and distaste for routine administration ensured frequent brushes with Prince Nicolaus.

KOZELUCH, LEOPOLD (1747–1818)

Admired by Mozart (whose moral character he allegedly slandered), the Bohemian-born Kozeluch was a successful composer, pianist and, from 1785, publisher in Vienna. He published the first edition of Haydn's Op. 64 Quartets, and from 1804 continued Haydn's profitable line of arranging folk songs for the Edinburgh publisher George Thomson.

MOZART, WOLFGANG AMADEUS (1756–91)

The two greatest composers of the day formed a famous friendship and mutual admiration society, though their meetings were confined to Haydn's brief sojourns in Vienna between the winter of 1783–4 and his departure for London in December 1790. In 1785 Haydn uttered his much-quoted encomium of his younger contemporary after hearing three of the quartets which Mozart dedicated to his musical 'father'. While the powerful impact of Haydn's music on Mozart can be heard in his quartets and, more obliquely, his symphonies, reciprocal influence is much harder to identify, at least until *The Creation* and *The Seasons*.

ORDOÑEZ, CARLO D' (1734–86)

A Viennese of Spanish ancestry who worked as a civil servant, d'Ordoñez was a prolific composer of symphonies – including several stormy minor-key works – and string quartets. Many of his instrumental works were published under Haydn's name. Haydn performed his marionette opera *Alceste* at Eszterháza in 1775.

PLEYEL, IGNAZ (1757–1831)

Pleyel was Haydn's pupil for several years from about 1772, and in 1792 was set up by the Professional Concert as Haydn's rival in London. Their friendship survived. His symphonies and chamber music often sound like slick Haydn imitations. They were hugely popular, especially in France, where he opened a music publishing business and a piano factory, and, in 1830, gave his name to the Salle Pleyel in Paris.

PORPORA, NICOLA (1686–1768)

Haydn met the venerable opera composer (he was a rival of Handel's in London between 1733 and 1736) and singing teacher through Metastasio in 1752–3, and for a time was employed as his valet-cum-accompanist. Through his contact with Porpora he honed his knowledge of the Italian language and Italian word-setting. The irascible old Neapolitan may also have informally supervised Haydn's study of Fux's counterpoint treatise *Gradus ad Parnassum*.

REUTTER, GEORG (1708–72)

Reutter was Haydn's teacher at St Stephen's in Vienna, where he succeeded his father as Kapellmeister in 1738, and a prolific composer of sacred music. Burney dismissed him curtly as 'an old German composer without taste or invention'. Although Haydn recalled receiving only two formal lessons from Reutter, his own masses were strongly influenced by those of his teacher, with their characteristic '*rauschende* [= rushing] *Violinen*'.

VANHAL, JOHANN BAPTIST (1739–1813)

Haydn had spasmodic contact with the gifted Bohemian composer in Vienna during the 1780s. According to Michael Kelly, he played the cello at a famous quartet party of 1784 that also included Haydn, Mozart and Dittersdorf. Vanhal's symphonies of the late 1760s and early 1770s include, like Haydn's, several agitated or melancholy works in the minor mode.

WAGENSEIL, GEORG CHRISTOPH (1715–77)

The prolific Viennese court composer, music master to Maria Theresa and her daughters (including Marie Antoinette), was a prime influence on Haydn's early symphonies, concertos and keyboard works. Wagenseil's *galant* harpsichord sonatas also provided a model for the young Mozart's keyboard music.

WERNER, GREGOR JOSEPH (1693–1766)

Appointed in 1728, Haydn's predecessor as Esterházy Kapellmeister composed vast quantities of church music in the late Baroque contrapuntal style. Old and infirm by the time of Haydn's appointment in 1761, and aware that his music was falling out of fashion, he evidently resented his brilliant young subordinate, dubbing him (as reported by Pohl) a blind follower of fashion ('*Modehansl*') and a cheap tunesmith ('*G'sanglmacher*').

HAYDN: THE MUSIC

Symphonies

Haydn is still routinely dubbed 'the father of the symphony'. Taken literally, this is manifestly absurd. The symphony had evolved out of the three-movement Italian opera overture in the first decades of the eighteenth century. From the 1730s composers such as Giovanni Battista Sammartini in Milan, Johann Stamitz, Ignaz Holzbauer and Franz Xaver Richter in Mannheim, and Matthias Georg Monn and Georg Christoph Wagenseil in Vienna turned out a regular supply of bright, extrovert 'sinfonias' and 'overtures' (the terms were inter-changeable) as concert openers and/or finales. The first four-movement symphony, a D major work by Monn, dates from as early as 1740, though four movements, including a minuet, would not become the norm until much later. Haydn would have heard, played and studied symphonies by Monn, Wagenseil et al. before he wrote his own earliest symphonies in the late 1750s. By then the symphony was bidding to eclipse the concerto in popularity in Austria, southern Germany, France and England.

Yet Haydn *can* legitimately be regarded as the father of the symphony in that he was the first fully to realise the genre's expressive and dramatic potential. For all their slightness, his earliest symphonies already reveal a taut logic, a sense that each phrase implies its successor, unequalled by his older con-temporaries. During the 1760s his symphonies grew in scale and individuality; and the finest works of the years around 1770 combine inspired eccentricity, impassioned rhetoric and a hitherto unmatched structural sophistication. By the 1790s Haydn's own late symphonies, together with the last six symphonies of Mozart, had made the genre the supreme touchstone of instrumental composition, and an ineluctable challenge for any aspiring composer. Small wonder, then, that the young Beethoven, conscious of Haydn's mighty example, did not complete a symphony until the winter of 1799–1800, long after he had achieved fame with his brilliant compositions for the piano.

Such was Haydn's international popularity by the 1770s that, in an age before copyright laws, nearly a hundred and fifty spurious symphonies circulated under his name. Some genuine early works may be lost. But the only subsequent additions to the list of 104 symphonies drawn up by Eusebius Mandyczewski in 1907 are two early works, Hob. I: 107, and Hob. I: 108.

Pre-1761

Symphony No. 1 in D
Symphony No. 2 in C
Symphony No. 3 in G
Symphony No. 4 in D
Symphony No. 5 in A
Symphony No. 10 in D
Symphony No. 11 in E flat
Symphony No. 15 in D
Symphony No. 18 in G
Symphony No. 19 in D
Symphony No. 20 in C
Symphony No. 25 in C
Symphony No. 27 in G
Symphony No. 32 in C
Symphony No. 33 in C
Symphony No. 37 in C
Symphony 'A', Hob. I: 107

Haydn told Griesinger that he composed his first symphony for Count Morzin in 1759, identifying the work as the D major, No. 1. As we know, at more than four decades' distance his memory was not always spot-on. Two other symphonies, Nos. 18 and 37, are also possible candidates (with the first forty symphonies, especially, Mandyczewski's numbering is often wildly askew); and as a copy of No. 37 exists dated 1758, Haydn was one, maybe two, years out.

With assorted works of the divertimento type under his belt, Haydn was already an experienced instrumental composer by 1757. Long patronised as crude and 'immature', these Morzin symphonies reveal him as a master of the contemporary Italianate lingua franca, rooted in *opera buffa* and staking almost everything on surface brightness and bustle. Haydn added to this his own brand of nervous energy and a taste, more pronounced than that of his contemporaries, for the comic and the wayward.

Though their instrumentation, determined by Morzin's small band, is more or less stereotyped (oboes, horns and strings, with trumpets and timpani in three of the C major symphonies, Nos. 20, 32 and 33), the early works are far more varied than the later ones in their number and ordering of movements. Several, including No. 1 and its three D major successors, Nos. 4, 10 and 19, adopt the fast-slow-fast pattern of the Italian opera overture favoured by most symphony composers around 1760. No. 1 opens with Haydn's tightly compressed take on the popular 'Mannheim crescendo' (actually of Italian rather than Mannheim origin) over a throbbing repeated bass. This launches a movement of typical pulsing energy, with rapid changes of texture and a multiplicity of brief motifs, including a distinct 'second subject' in the minor key – a common feature of Austrian symphonies of the 1750s and 1760s, including many of Haydn's own. The innocuous *galanterie* of the Andante is ruffled by abrupt dynamic contrasts. In the recapitulation, Haydn adopts a pattern common in the 1750s, omitting the first phrase of the theme and opening with the second phrase transposed into the minor key. Less conventionally, he then expands the phrase from five to six bars. Asymmetrical phrasing also enlivens the final Presto, in a leaping 3/8 metre found in so many symphonies and *opera buffa* finales of the 1750s and early 1760s.

No. 19, another D major symphony for Morzin's in-house band, has a propulsive triple-time opening movement launched by a rocketing trumpet-style fanfare – a cliché that Haydn would put to more far-reaching use in Symphony No. 82. The D minor Andante exudes an austere melancholy characteristic of so many minor-key Haydn slow movements. By contrast, the Andante of No. 4, likewise in D minor, is an evocative 'night piece'. Opening with a long-sustained *messa di voce* – a typical feature of slow *opera seria* arias – muted first violins spin an almost improvisatory line against syncopations in second violins and a 'walking' staccato bass. The finale is a stately Tempo di Menuetto rather than the usual Presto. The amiable G major Andante of No. 10 also begins with a sustained *messa di voce*. Here, though, the most memorable movement is the finale, a 3/8 romp as in No. 1, but with a more substantial central section that turns to D minor for a contrapuntal expansion of a brief phrase heard near the opening.

Of the other three-movement Morzin works, No. 2 has something of the ceremonial swagger characteristic of Austrian symphonies in C major, though without the peal and clatter of trumpets and drums. Its first movement is more 'learned' in cast than those of the D major symphonies, with the opening theme – a rising scale in pompous dotted rhythm – used in ever-changing combinations. The attractive Symphony No. 27 begins with another 'trumpet' fanfare whose rhythm also initiates the lyrical second theme. For the slow movement Haydn writes a serenade in siciliano rhythm, with muted violins and pizzicato basses, though the lopsided phrasing gives the music a slightly quirky air. Symphony 'A', No. 107, was long wrongly identified as a string quartet, Op. 1 No. 5. In the bouncy finale the recapitulation enters casually, before we realise it: an early instance of a ploy Haydn will use with increasing subtlety and wit right through to the finale of No. 104.

Three of the Morzin symphonies adopt the 'sonata da chiesa' form, with an opening slow movement, derived from the old Italian church sonata – though there is no evidence that such symphonies by Haydn and his contemporaries were actually played in church. The earliest, No. 18 in G, is in three movements only: a quasi-Baroque Andante moderato with occasional theatrical outbursts; a pounding Allegro molto; and a minuet finale, with a pensive trio in G minor. The other two weightier 'da chiesa' symphonies from these years, Nos. 5 and

11, both have four movements, deploying a slow-fast-minuet-fast plan. Like No. 18, No. 11 begins in the style of a Corelli trio sonata, with second violins answered by firsts; and the whole movement is built on the alternation and contrapuntal interplay of the two violin sections. The following Allegro – one of the rare monothematic movements in these early symphonies – is just as striking. Its theme, a variant of the old *cantus firmus* familiar from Mozart's 'Jupiter', invites polyphonic treatment, and duly gets it, firstly in the sinuous two-part counterpoint when the theme turns up as 'second subject', and then in the little three-part canon that launches the recapitulation.

Whereas the wind (oboes and horns) barely register in the opening movements of Nos. 11 and 18, in the Adagio, ma non troppo, of No. 5 the horns have a starring role from the moment they add their fanfare-like commentary to the strings' opening phrase. The stratospheric writing, here and in the bucolic trio of the minuet, speaks volumes for the virtuosity of Morzin's horn players. The spiky rhythms and wide leaps of the Allegro second movement may remind listeners of Mozart's C minor Piano Concerto, K491.

No. 37, Haydn's earliest symphony in four movements – perhaps his earliest *tout court* – falls within an Austrian tradition of festive C major works, though its trumpet and timpani parts are later additions, probably by another hand. Offsetting the lean brilliance of the outer movements, both the trio of the minuet (placed second) and the Andante are in C minor, with a distinct Baroque flavour. Nos. 20, 32 and 33 are Haydn's first symphonies with authentic parts for trumpets and timpani. Like No. 37, No. 32 has an old-fashioned trio in C minor for strings alone. The development of the first movement is Haydn's most powerful to date. The concentration on the minor-key second subject here means that Haydn can omit it from the recapitulation without any sense of imbalance. Sonority apart, Nos. 20 and 33 are less interesting, though the opening Vivace of No. 33 has an unusually long, irregularly phrased second theme, and No. 20 an Andante that, as in No. 27, suggests a parody of an Italian serenade.

Finer than any of these C major symphonies is the G major, No. 3. In all three quick movements Haydn uses counterpoint to enrich the symphonic fabric, as he would often do in the future. The opening theme – a chant-like motif in long notes against a running accompaniment – acquires new countersubjects in the development, and reaches its apotheosis in a passage of majestic polyphony near the start of the recapitulation. The robust third movement is in a Viennese tradition of canonic minuets that stretches, via Haydn's symphonies Nos. 23 and 44 and Mozart's Wind Serenade K388, to Schubert (the E flat Piano Trio, D929) and Brahms; and the finale exuberantly juxtaposes strict fugal writing and looser contrapuntal textures within a sonata-form design. For his 'second subject' Haydn puts the main theme in the cellos against a new countersubject in violins and violas, while the recapitulation begins as a tense *stretto*, with entries of the theme piling in on each other.

In the two remaining Morzin symphonies, No. 15 in D and No. 25 in C (though the latter, like No. 3, may have been composed after his Esterházy appointment), the first movements play tricks with the listener's expectations. The opening Adagio of No. 15, with its tootling horns, suggests a fully fledged slow movement. But the anticipated move to the dominant key, A major, never quite happens. Instead, the music swerves to D minor, then breaks off for a frenetic sonata-form Presto, before an abridged return of the Adagio: an echo here of the Baroque French overture, and a distant anticipation of the finale of the String Quartet Op. 54 No. 2. The stately opening of No. 25 also seems to herald a complete slow movement, but turns out instead to be an extended introduction to the following Allegro molto. There is no 'real' slow movement. The second movement is a minuet, with a serenading trio for oboes and horns over pizzicato strings, the third a Presto that begins with a four-note chant motif like that in No. 3 but only realises its contrapuntal implications in the recapitulation.

1761: the 'times of day' symphonies

Symphony No. 6 in D, 'Le matin'
Symphony No. 7 in C, 'Le midi'
Symphony No. 8 in G, 'Le soir'

Haydn's first Esterházy patron, Prince Paul Anton, had a passion for Italian Baroque music, with Vivaldi's *Four Seasons* a particular favourite. According to Dies, he immediately encouraged his vice-Kapellmeister to compose a comparable series of four quartets illustrating the times of day. Haydn took up the idea, though in his hands four quartets became three symphonies depicting morning, noon and evening. These colourful 'times of day' symphonies are, with the C major Cello Concerto, Haydn's most popular early works. With their pictorial touches and concerto-grosso-like solos for almost every instrument, right down to the lowly violone (precursor of the double bass) in the trios of the minuets, they simultaneously flattered the prince's taste and showed off his crack little orchestra, led by virtuoso violinist Luigi Tomasini.

Though Haydn's trilogy is not a scene-by-scene chronicle à la Vivaldi, it does open with a sunrise and close with an evening storm, modest precursors of the sunrise and storm in *The Creation* and *The Seasons*. As in *The Creation*, the sunrise in 'Le matin', No. 6, is evoked in a slow crescendo and an ascending scale, beginning with unaccompanied first violins. Then the Allegro gets under way with a chirruping flute tune. There is a witty touch at the end of the development, where a solo horn prematurely tootles the opening of the flute theme – a gambit that Beethoven was to use in an epic context in the 'Eroica'.

The slow movement begins with a comic send-up of a music lesson (the solo violin showing his incompetent 'pupils' how to play a simple rising scale), continues with a *galant* duet for violin and cello, and ends with a solemn peroration that could have come straight from a Corelli concerto grosso. The D minor trio of the minuet is a mock-lugubrious solo for bassoon, while the finale's development features a brilliant toccata-style episode: another glance back to the Italian Baroque, and a tribute to Tomasini's prowess.

There is no obvious 'event' in 'Le midi', No. 7. But we might hear the slow movement's duetting violin and cello and amorously warbling flutes as a languorous pastoral amid the shimmering midday heat. As in 'Le matin', Haydn prefaces the slow movement proper with a tongue-in-cheek introduction, with the solo violin parodying a sobbing tragic heroine. In the rollicking finale the opening theme neatly doubles as a closing gesture: an early example of a gambit that Beethoven would also exploit, most famously in the first movement of the Eighth Symphony.

For early listeners the tripping 3/8 rhythms of No. 8's opening Allegro molto – more typical of a finale than a first movement – may have evoked an evening dance on the village green. Haydn constructs the whole movement out of a catchy aria about snuff from Gluck's 1759 *opéra comique*, *Le diable à quatre*; as the American musicologist Daniel Heartz has pointed out, the melody closely resembles a popular Viennese street song. The fast-paced minuet also uses a popular-style tune. More than any other minuet in these early symphonies, the music suggests a rustic waltz rather than a dance for periwigged aristocrats. As the Esterházy band had no trumpets and timpani in 1761, the final *Tempesta* simulates thunder with growling violin tremolos. This is a pretty genial, unthreatening affair by comparison with Haydn's later storms. Yet forty years later, in *The Seasons*, he was to use an almost identical forking flute figure to evoke lightning.

The early Esterházy symphonies, 1761–1763

Symphony No. 9 in C
Symphony No. 12 in E
Symphony No. 13 in D
Symphony No. 14 in A
Symphony No. 16 in B flat

Symphony No. 17 in F
Symphony No. 36 in E flat
Symphony No. 40 in F
Symphony No. 72 in D
Symphony 'B', Hob. I: 108

Of the symphonies in this motley group, only No. 9 (1762) and Nos. 12, 13 and 40 (1763) can be dated confidently. No. 72 must belong either to 1763 or, less probably, 1765–6, the only periods when Haydn had four horns at his disposal. While a few of these works may date from Haydn's last months in Morzin's service, the slow movement of No. 36 in E flat, an ornate double concerto for violin and cello, à la Nos. 6 and 7, suggests that this symphony, at least, was composed for the Esterházy court.

Robbins Landon has speculated that No. 9, in three brief movements, may have originated as an overture to a lost *opera buffa* or celebratory cantata. The dashing opening movement is all gesture, with no theme to speak of. Oboes are replaced by pastoral flutes in the Andante, but come into their own in the trio of the minuet finale, a *Ländler* singled out for its charm in an early review. Symphony 'B', No. 108 in B flat, originally published, like Symphony 'A', as a string quartet, contains a gravely contrapuntal G minor Andante, again with a nod to the Baroque trio sonata, and a minuet with solos for oboes, horns and (in the trio) bassoon, here in the guise of courtier rather than clown.

No. 17 is memorable for the vigorous development of its triple-time first movement, with striding sequences punctuated by a plaintive fragment of the second subject. In Nos. 14 and 16 the slow movements deploy Haydn's characteristic bare two-part texture, though with a difference. In No. 14 violins are doubled an octave below by cellos, violas by basses (which in the early Esterházy years meant a single violone). No. 16 adds a refining gloss by muting the violins and doubling them with a solo cello – a tinkling harpsichord continuo, heard on some recordings, ruins the effect of this original sonority. No. 16's first movement, one of Haydn's hyper-economical monothematic structures, begins with a stretch of so-called double counterpoint. At the first *forte* the upper and lower lines are reversed, while the development and recapitulation enrich the contrapuntal fabric with new countermelodies. The skipping finale has a nice joke in the recapitulation, where the once-boisterous theme returns in a tentative *piano*, unharmonised and fragmented between first and second violins.

The sheer diversity of Haydn's early symphonies is epitomised by the three works of 1763, Nos. 12, 13 and 40. Opening with a quiet theme in balanced four-bar phrases, the first movement of No. 12 has a new poise and lyrical suavity, together with a radiance of sonority characteristic of the key of E major. This three-movement work, with its quasi-operatic siciliano in the minor and its prompt, pithy finale, is a delightful example of the intimate Austrian chamber symphony. No. 40 in F, much earlier than its numbering suggests, culminates in a more or less strict fugue that combines traditional 'species counterpoint' with a typically Haydnesque rhythmic drive. The faintly conspiratorial Andante più tosto Allegretto, with its dainty two-part texture (*sempre staccato e piano*) and odd phrase lengths, looks ahead to the not-so-slow second movement of the String Quartet Op. 50 No. 3, and, beyond that, to the Allegretto of Beethoven's Eighth Symphony.

Grandest of Haydn's symphonies to date is No. 13 in D, exploiting the four horns available in 1763. In contrast to No. 72, probably written the same year, the horns are not used soloistically but integrated into the orchestral texture, often as a massive, organ-like backdrop to the strings. In the resonant hall of the Eisenstadt palace the effect must have been sensational. The florid Adagio cantabile could have strayed from a cello concerto, the flute performs pirouettes in the trio of the minuet, while the finale, like that of No. 3, weaves fugal textures (using the 'Credo' chant famous from Mozart's 'Jupiter') and *buffo*-style figuration into an exhilarating sonata-form movement.

No. 72, extravagantly misplaced in Mandyczewski's number-ing, sounds like a dry run for the more inventive 'Hornsignal', No. 31. There are pyrotechnics for the four horns in the first movement, and Baroque-style echo effects in the minuet. Surprisingly, though, the horns sit out most of the finale, the earliest theme-and-variation movement in a Haydn symphony. The prettily decorative variations spotlight in turn solo flute, cello, violin, violone and a pair of oboes, with discreet horn backing, before the full orchestra enters for a final variation and a hunting-style send-off.

1764

Symphony No. 21 in A
Symphony No. 22 in E flat, 'The Philosopher'
Symphony No. 23 in G
Symphony No. 24 in D

By now four movements were becoming the norm in Austrian symphonies, despite mutterings that the minuet had no place in the concert hall. (The German composer Johann Adam Hiller likened the effect of a minuet in a symphony to 'a fashionable beauty spot on a man's face'.) Haydn's order of movements, though, is still unpredictable; and two of the symphonies dated 1764, Nos. 21 and 22, follow the 'sonata da chiesa' pattern. Nicknamed 'The Philosopher' within Haydn's lifetime, No. 22 is a favourite among these early symphonies. Its title was doubt-less prompted by the opening Adagio, a kind of chorale prelude in sonata form, with a sacerdotal chant intoned *fortissimo* against the strings' stalking quavers – a foretaste of the music for the two Armed Men in *Die Zauberflöte*. The movement's gravitas is enhanced by its unique instrumentation, with oboes replaced by deep-toned, faintly doleful cors anglais. Haydn told Dies that in one of his early symphonies – he couldn't remember which – he had portrayed a dialogue between God and a repentant sinner. This movement seems the most likely candidate. There is, though, nothing remotely philosophical or penitential about the rest of the symphony: a compact, racy Presto, a minuet enclosing a wind-serenade trio, and a bounding 6/8 finale with antiphonal fanfares for horns and cors anglais.

Just as original as the chorale movement of 'The Philosopher' is the Adagio of No. 21. Though it has the vague outlines of sonata form, this lovely movement sounds like a free fantasia on its gracious opening theme, shared between strings and wind (oboes and horns). The following Presto and the finale, linked by similar rhythmic figures, are Haydn at his most peremptory and hyperactive, while the opening of the minuet, with its blunt two-part writing, unmissably anticipates Mozart's *Eine kleine Nachtmusik*.

The minuet of No. 23, like those of Nos. 3 and 44, is in canon throughout, with violas and basses tracking violins and oboes at a bar's distance. Its trio intensifies the canonic texture by working a motif from the minuet in smooth three-part imitation. The slow movement's naive folk-like theme is increasingly disrupted by fidgety scales in the bass (is there a hidden programme here?), while the moto perpetuo jig finale stutters to a *pianissimo* close but then, just as the audience prepares to applaud, adds a rogue pizzicato chord – the kind of comic deception that Haydn would carry to extremes in the 'Joke' Quartet, Op. 33 No. 2. The outer movements of No. 24 in D infuse the bustle and brio of *opera buffa* with extraordinary nervous intensity. As if in awed reaction to the *fortissimo* climax of the first-movement development, the recapitulation enters *piano* and in D *minor*, with a plaintive variant of the once-assertive main theme. The Adagio is another of Haydn's ornate concerto-style movements, this time for solo flute, which also ousts the oboes in the minuet's trio.

1765

Symphony No. 28 in A
Symphony No. 29 in E

Symphony No. 30 in C, 'Alleluja'
Symphony No. 31 in D, 'Hornsignal'

Haydn's prolific production of symphonies continued with four sharply characterised works. The first movement of No. 28 is a claustrophobically concentrated piece, permeated by a four-note 'hammering' motif that initially keeps us guessing as to whether it is in 3/4 or 6/8 time. Bricks from little straw indeed. The Allegro molto minuet, with its bariolage effects (quickfire repetitions of the same note across different strings) and glumly obsessive A minor trio – dubbed 'silly' by a contemporary Leipzig reviewer – is the first instance of gypsy influence in Haydn's symphonies. No. 29 has an even stranger minor-key trio that sounds like a disconsolate accompaniment in search of a tune. The opening Allegro di molto shares the lyrical grace of its E major predecessor, No. 12, with an added breadth and mellowness. The rather dour Andante plays a whimsical joke by chopping the tune up between first and second violins, while the finale, with its brusque unison opening and ferociously pounding rhythms, is a major-key counterpart to the finales of the so-called *Sturm und Drang* symphonies.

Alone among the symphonies of 1764–5, No. 30 reverts to a three-movement plan, with a finale in the form of a minuet with two trios. The first movement's jubilant textures incorporate part of a Gregorian Easter chant, hence the work's nickname of 'Alleluja'. The tuttis are excitingly coloured by the pealing, slightly acidulous sound of C *alto* horns, used as surrogate trumpets in many of Haydn's C major symphonies of the 1760s and 1770s.

No. 31, the 'Hornsignal', is the last and most flamboyant in a series of works (the 'times of day' trilogy and No. 72) that cross the symphony with the Baroque concerto grosso, and also look ahead to the twentieth-century concerto for orchestra. Its nickname derives from the opening Allegro's horn calls, the first a military fanfare, the second a well-known posthorn signal. While the horn quartet holds extravagant sway in the first movement, the siciliano-style Adagio is a duet for solo violin and cello, interrupted by brief sallies from the horns playing in complementary pairs. The concerto-for-orchestra associations are most obvious in the variation finale, a more inspired rerun of the finale of No. 72. The theme itself has more character, and there is a gloriously showy variation for the horn quartet. After a brief turn to D minor (recalling the end of the first-movement development), a rambunctious Presto coda brings back the first movement's fanfares – the most overt instance to date of thematic cross-reference in Haydn's symphonies.

c.1765–1768

Symphony No. 26 in D minor, 'Lamentatione'
Symphony No. 34 in D minor
Symphony No. 35 in B flat
Symphony No. 38 in C
Symphony No. 39 in G minor
Symphony No. 49 in F minor, 'La Passione'
Symphony No. 58 in F
Symphony No. 59 in A, 'Fire'

The second half of the 1760s saw the first stirrings of what is often dubbed Haydn's *Sturm und Drang* style. The term, apparently coined in 1909 by the French musicologist Théodore de Wyzewa, invokes the slightly later German literary movement, named after Maximilian von Klinger's 1776 blood-and-thunder drama on the American Revolution, *Wirrwarr, oder Sturm und Drang* (Turmoil, or Storm and Stress). Taking their cue from Wyzewa, some commentators have attributed this outbreak of minor-key angst to a 'romantic crisis'. But there is no shred of evidence for this. In any case, Haydn was the least confessional of composers. Far more convincing is the notion that, like other Austrian composers, notably J. B. Vanhal, Carlo d'Ordoñez (Austrian despite his name) and the teenaged Mozart (in the 'little' G minor Symphony, K183), he was eager to explore the symphony's potential for sorrowful and turbulent expression.

Specific influences on these minor-mode symphonies include Gluck's revolutionary 1761 ballet *Don Juan*, the unbridled Berlin symphonies and keyboard works of C. P. E. Bach, and tempestuous opera arias, typically on the metaphor of a storm-tossed ship. This new proto-Romantic musical sensibility has also been linked to the fashion for the sombre and the terrifying in European literature from the 1760s, epitomised by works like James Macpherson's pseudo-bardic 'Ossian' poems (the century's greatest literary fraud) and Horace Walpole's nightmarish fantasy *The Castle of Otranto*.

Turbulence can also invade the major-key works of these years, which typically use the language of *opera buffa* with a new rhetorical force and – as in the limping (*alla zoppa*) minuet and zanily disjointed finale of the otherwise unadventurous No. 58 in F – comic eccentricity. Yet the eccentricity is always allied to a tight logic. Stormy, festive or playful, virtually every work of this period is intensely individual, and reflects Haydn's restless exploration of the symphony's potential, whether in heightened theatrical contrasts, increased rhythmic and harmonic complexity or a more far-reaching approach to thematic development.

Most theatrical of all the major-key symphonies here is No. 59 in A (placed, like No. 58, much too late by Mandyczewski), whose crackling opening theme spawned the nickname 'Feuer Sinfonia' (Fire Symphony) in one source. Scholars have speculated that the first two movements began life as music for the stage. One eccentric feature of the opening Presto is the 'fire' theme's tendency to peter out inconsequentially. Haydn duly expands and intensifies this effect both at the end of the exposition and in the recapitulation. The smartly paced 'slow' movement (Andante più tosto Allegretto) trades on the contrast between a stark A minor theme and a cantabile melody in C major, unfolded at extraordinary and, again, eccentric length. When the cantabile returns, oboes and horns make a surprise first appearance. Another ruder surprise quickly follows, when a fragment of the A minor theme provokes a raucous retort from the horns. The minuet is a major-key variant of the Andante's opening theme, while the finale foreshadows the 'Drumroll', No. 103, by fashioning an eventful and exciting movement entirely from a horn call and an answering melodic tag.

No. 35 in B flat, dated 1 December 1767, opens innocently enough. But the development is fiercely argumentative, working the once-demure main theme and a vigorous 'galloping' motif in combative counterpoint. The witty finale delights in sly rhythmic displacements, and ends laconically with its opening 'hammer blows' – the kind of beginning-as-ending joke Haydn would often exploit in his later works. No. 38 is in the line of ceremonial C major works with high horns and, in some sources, trumpet and drums. The second movement indulges in charming Baroque-style echo effects, enhanced by the colour contrast between muted second violins and non-muted firsts. The jaunty minuet features an oboe solo with vertiginous leaps, probably written for the virtuoso Vittorino Colombazzo, who joined the Esterházy establishment for a few months in 1768. In the finale Haydn distantly anticipates the finale of Mozart's Piano Concerto No. 19, K459, by combining footling *buffo* themes, concerto-like display (oboe again to the fore) and bouts of strict 'species' counterpoint.

Dating from *c.*1765, No. 34 in D minor is probably the first of Haydn's minor-mode symphonies. The opening movement, an elegiac Adagio with grimly sustained horn pedals and abrupt dynamic contrasts, foreshadows 'La Passione', No. 49. But alone among the minor-key symphonies of the 1760s and 1770s, No. 34 turns to the major for the last three movements: an Allegro of quivering brilliance, with a main theme built on huge vaulting intervals (a strong whiff of *opera seria* here); a minuet with a tangy *Ländler* trio for oboes underpinned by syncopated horns; and a moto perpetuo finale that sounds like an English country dance.

Arguably the weirdest movement in all Haydn's minor-key symphonies is the fretful, fanatically monothematic opening Allegro assai of No. 39, probably composed in 1767, when four horns were again briefly available. So often Haydn exploits silence to comic ends. Here, though, the sudden hiatuses create a sense of eerie unease. The E flat Andante is a light-weight affair, apparently incongruous in its dainty *galanterie*, though with a surprisingly expressive little coda. Back in G minor, the minuet uses stark, two-part textures and chromaticism with oddly perturbing effect; and the finale is the epitome of *Sturm und Drang* in its extravagant leaps, tremolos, rocketing scales and implacable rhythmic drive.

'La Passione', No. 49, of 1768 is the last Haydn symphony in the old 'da chiesa' form. But whereas its predecessor, No. 34, juxtaposes D minor threnody and D major merriment, 'La Passione' sets each of its movements in F minor. The upshot is a work of almost unremitting bleakness. As so often, the nickname's origins are obscure, though one story has it that the symphony was first performed on Good Friday in the Esterházys' Eisenstadt palace. Certainly, the title fits the opening Adagio, with its mournful, burdened tread suggestive of the *via crucis*. Its initial motif (C–D flat–B flat–C) pervades each of the four movements. The unexpected entry of the first-movement recapitulation, quietly reasserting F minor when the preceding bar led us to expect a chord of C minor, is paralleled by the abrupt, 'under-prepared' recapitulations in the second movement, a hectic, angular Allegro di molto, and the finale: all instances of Haydn's increasingly subtle play with the listener's expectations. The minuet has its own formal surprise in the unexpected twelve-bar coda, which introduces a new 'sighing' motif that deepens the mood of resignation. Its F major trio, with gleaming high horns, is the symphony's sole moment of repose. The driving, desperate finale revives the second movement's *Sturm und Drang* with a new terseness and explosiveness.

Composed in 1768 or 1769, probably for performance during Holy Week, the 'Lamentatione' symphony, No. 26, is a minor-key counterpart to No. 30: in three movements only, with a minuet finale, and incorporating medieval plainchant. The first movement begins with lashing syncopations (evoking Christ's scourging?), then, after a plunge into F major, introduces the

Gregorian Passion chant *fortissimo* on oboe and second violins. Its three phrases correspond respectively to the words of the Evangelist, Christ (the quiet response in long notes) and the baying crowd of Jews. In the recapitulation the first horn adds a gaunt majesty to the chant. The mysteriously serene Adagio in F – remote-sounding after the D *major* close of the first movement – introduces another liturgical chant, this time from the Lamentations of Jeremiah. There may be further Passion associations in the finale, the least *galant* of minuets, harmonically restless and replete with disquieting pauses and truculent canonic imitations.

c.1769–1771

Symphony No. 41 in C
Symphony No. 42 in D
Symphony No. 43 in E flat, 'Mercury'
Symphony No. 44 in E minor, 'Mourning'
Symphony No. 48 in C, 'Maria Theresa'
Symphony No. 65 in A

The striking intensification in Haydn's symphonies around 1770 goes hand in hand with a broadening of scale. The ample, stately unfolding of the first movement of No. 41 is a long way from the nervy brilliance of its C major predecessor, No. 38. In the slow movement Haydn counterpoints an expressive oboe melody, sustained notes for horns and dancing flute arabesques – an enchanting rococo tapestry that may have been inspired by the scena 'Che puro ciel' in Gluck's *Orfeo*.

Grandest and most expansive of these C major ceremonial works, though, is No. 48, long thought to have been composed for Maria Theresa's visit to Eszterháza in 1773. While the symphony seems to have been played in honour of the Empress, a contemporary set of manuscript parts bears the pencilled date '1769'. From its initial blazing horn fanfares, there is no more elementally exciting Haydn symphony movement than the opening Allegro. Balancing the majestic scale of the first theme, which sets off the prevailing pomp with a quiet deflection towards C minor, the second-subject group contains two distinct lyrical ideas. In the development Haydn screws up the tension with thrilling modulating sequences on a striding 'transition' theme. As has often been noted, the violins' flashing rapier thrusts at the climax surely influenced Mozart at the corresponding point of the 'Jupiter'. The equally expansive, siciliano-style Adagio, with muted violins (a delicate, silvery colour characteristic of Haydn slow movements around 1770), far transcends mere pastoral prettiness. The thunderous minuet, enclosing a half-menacing, half-mysterious C minor trio, evokes the military parade ground rather than the ballroom, while the moto perpetuo finale crosses C major pageantry with the explosiveness of Haydn's contemporary minor-mode symphonies.

The opening movement of No. 42 in D (1771), significantly marked 'Moderato e maestoso', is also laid out on the broadest scale. Again, the exposition contains two distinct second-subject themes, the first modulating as far afield as B major, the second a fragile wisp of a tune, like a charming afterthought. The sonorous massiveness of the orchestral writing, including at one point a slow-burn 'Mannheim crescendo', suggests that Haydn may here be deliberately emulating the style of the so-called Mannheim school of composers, perhaps even with a touch of parody in the rhetorical repetitions and emphatically prepared cadences. In the Andantino e cantabile Haydn writes, for the first time in his symphonies, a gravely flowing, hymn-like melody, of a type often found in Gluck (say, in the Elysian chorus 'Vieni ai regni del riposo' from *Orfeo*). The movement's harmonic range is typical of the symphonies around 1770, though in a sketch Haydn crossed out one particularly abstruse passage with the comment 'Dies war vor gar zu gelehrte Ohren' – 'this was for far too learned ears'. The finale is a witty amalgam of rondo and variations, complete with wind-band episode: the prototype of a 'popular' form that Haydn would often cultivate during the 1770s and 1780s.

No one knows how No. 43, composed in 1770 or 1771, acquired its nickname 'Mercury'. In contrast to No. 42, this delightful symphony is in the 'chamber' rather than the 'grand' style, with a monothematic first movement that mingles relaxed lyricism (the leisurely opening theme returns, compressed, as the second subject) with fiery tuttis. The rapt Adagio becomes strangely mesmerised by a five-note rhythmic figure; and the trio of the minuet, far from being a relaxation, is tonally unsettled, promising a tune that never quite burgeons. But the most extraordinary movement is the finale, with its hesitant opening theme teased out in five-bar phrases, its deadpan 'second subject' – a pair of cadences framed and punctured by silence – and its extended coda that draws out both the first theme and the cadences to bizarre lengths.

No. 65, another work numbered far too high by Mandyczewski, is one of Haydn's quirkiest symphonies. The *galant* obeisance that opens the Andante could not be more deceptive. This is music that wrong-foots the listener at every turn with its incongruous juxtaposition of disparate ideas – shades here of C. P. E. Bach at his most wayward. Robbins Landon has plausibly suggested a theatrical origin for this music of 'almost lunatic irrationality'. The minuet is hardly less eccentric, creating rhythmic mayhem with its constant clashes of 3/4 and 4/4 time.

The one minor-key symphony in this group is the famous No. 44 in E minor – known as 'Trauer' (Mourning) because its seraphic Adagio was performed at a Berlin memorial concert in 1809, though the story that Haydn wanted it played at his funeral is almost certainly apocryphal. Its first movement, saturated by its powerful unison 'motto', is more broadly laid out than those of its minor-key predecessors, Nos. 39 and 49, and encompasses lyrical pathos as well as agitation. The development has a magnificent, unrelenting impetus. But the expressive climax is reserved for the coda, which works the ubiquitous motto in a passage of chromatic canonic imitation. This subtly prepares the listener for the contrapuntal tour de force of the minuet, a stark canon at the octave between violins and bass. Harmonic balm comes with the glowing E major trio, whose dipping violin melody is answered by a stratospheric ascent for first horn. As the first movement's coda prepared for the minuet, so the key and mood of the trio foreshadow the Adagio, the essence of vocal *bel canto* translated into instrumental terms. This is the first Haydn symphonic slow movement that, to quote Maynard Solomon apropos Mozart, 'transforms loveliness into ecstasy, grace into sublimity'. The finale, fiercely contrapuntal in texture, resumes and intensifies the agitation of the first movement. In the development a relentless rising sequence on the opening motif ratchets up the tension to near breaking point.

1772

Symphony No. 45 in F sharp minor, 'Farewell'
Symphony No. 46 in B
Symphony No. 47 in G

The problem with the 'Farewell', No. 45, is that the finale's charming disappearing act – Haydn's players literally voting with their feet – has obscured the symphony's iconoclastic originality. Its key, F sharp minor, is unique in eighteenth-century symphonies; and the extreme tonality prompts extreme emotional states and a revolutionary structure. The opening Allegro assai is Haydn's most violent and unstable symphonic movement, with a startling contrast in the lyrical, minuet-like D major episode that interrupts the development. This vanishes enigmatically into thin air; then, after a pause, the recapitulation storms in with renewed vehemence.

The tender yet ascetic A major Adagio brings a degree of repose. Even here, though, there is a lingering unease, with oscillations between major and minor and, in the recapitulation, a passage where the music hovers hypnotically on the brink of strange harmonic regions. In the minuet – surprisingly, in F sharp *major* – stability is immediately threatened by the rude, dissonant D natural in the third bar and further undermined by the whimsical cadential phrase. Resolution of a kind comes only with the finale, whose two contrasting sections (Presto–Adagio) sum up the key sequence of the first three movements. The F sharp minor Presto, in Haydn's most searing *Sturm und Drang* vein, breaks off abruptly. Then, doubtless to the prince's astonishment, the symphony continues with a tranquil Adagio in A major (the key of the second movement) which then drifts magically to F sharp major (the key of the minuet). One by one, the players snuff out their candles and slip off-stage until only two solo violins are left. As James Webster – who has devoted the substantial part of a book to the 'Farewell' – has noted, the dreamlike close recalls both the 'unreal' D major episode in the first movement and the whimsical ending of the minuet.

The other two symphonies of 1772 are hardly less original. No. 46 is in the outré key of B major, found in only one other eighteenth-century symphony, by Monn. Again, extremes of key yield extremes of expression. Belying its major mode, the first movement is astonishingly tense and troubled, with its ferocious outbursts in the minor and obsessive concentration on a four-note unison 'motto' akin to that in No. 44. In the B minor Poco adagio, pastoral melancholy is immediately undercut by a spiky staccato scale, wryly echoed by cellos and basses. This ubiquitous staccato figure gives the whole movement a faintly furtive air. The minuet's proud, *galant* theme is freely inverted in the second half, with the rising pairs of notes now falling in a sighing *piano*; the enigmatic trio, again in B minor, seems to blur ecclesiastical chant and a half-remembered Balkan folk tune. The opening of the capricious finale echoes the falling contour of the inverted minuet theme. Near the end Haydn underlines the resemblance by breaking off and bringing back part of the minuet, beginning with the 'sighing' inversion – a dramatic stroke that has provoked inevitable comparisons with Beethoven's use of the same device in a very different context in the Fifth Symphony.

James Webster has argued that Haydn may have conceived Nos. 45 and 46 as a pair. Certainly, in their subversion of symphonic norms and their degree of 'through composition', with the finales referring back to features from earlier movements, they stand apart from the other works of this period. The final 1772 symphony, No. 47 in G, is one of three works, with Nos. 62 and 75, whose openings Mozart jotted down, perhaps with his Viennese subscription concerts in mind. Mozart would surely have relished the first movement's horn fanfares, in the march rhythm he used in so many piano concertos. In the recapitulation the fanfares erupt in G minor rather than G major, a dramatic recreation of a ploy often found in earlier Austrian symphonies, including Haydn's own No. 24.

Haydn follows this with his first symphonic slow movement (as opposed to finale) cast as a theme and variations, perhaps the earliest variation slow movement in any symphony. If the form is 'popular', the theme itself is in learned two-part counterpoint, designed so that its top and bottom lines can be inverted. There is contrapuntal legerdemain, too, in the palindromic 'Menuet al roverso': in both sections of the minuet and the trio the orchestra plays the music twice forwards and twice backwards to arrive at the beginning. In the reversal process, Haydn's original first-beat *forte* accents are now displaced to the third beat, turning, in Charles Rosen's words, 'an academic exercise into a witty and intellectual effect'. The tearing finale evokes the exotic Hungarian gypsy style in its syncopations, stinging grace notes and lightning major-minor alternations, and makes comic-dramatic capital of the triple 'hammer-blow' cliché at the start of the development.

c.1772–1773

Symphony No. 50 in C
Symphony No. 51 in B flat
Symphony No. 52 in C minor
Symphony No. 64 in A

After 1772, opera began to dominate Haydn's creative life; and at least one symphony in this group has theatrical connections. The first two movements of No. 50 were recycled from the overture to the lost marionette opera *Der Götterrath* (The council of the gods), performed as a prologue to *Philemon und Baucis* in September 1773. Shortly afterwards Haydn added trumpets and drums to the terse, dashing Allegro di molto (prefaced by a slow introduction), and appended an imposing minuet, in miniature sonata form, and a powerful monothematic finale that reserves a bold harmonic surprise for the coda. The result, uniquely in this period, is a work that concentrates its symphonic weight in the last two movements.

Like the Andante of No. 65, the Largo of No. 64 is extraordinarily eccentric, prompting speculation that it may have started life as incidental music. It begins with a promise of an eloquent hymn-like melody. But from bar 7 onwards expectations are constantly derailed, with fragmentary phrases left hanging in the air. Even the normal rules of musical grammar are subverted. Unlike in No. 65, though, there is no suggestion of comedy. This is music of mysterious power that prefigures the Capriccio of Symphony No. 86. The first movement and rondo finale also have a wayward streak. In the opening Allegro con spirito, for instance, the second-subject group contains a strangely haunting theme that hovers between C major and E minor. The symphony's enigmatic nickname 'Tempora mutantur', probably inspired by the Largo, refers to an epigram by the Welsh Elizabethan poet John Owen, later translated as 'The times are Chang'd, and in them Chang'd are we; How? Man, as Times grow worse, grows worse, we see.'

Eccentric, too, is the slow movement of No. 51, where Haydn showcases the phenomenal powers of his horn players. In the *bel canto* opening melody the first horn rises into the stratosphere, only for the mood to be punctured by the second horn's faintly grotesque descent to the underworld. There are more horn antics in the second of the minuet's two trios, while the waggish finale mixes rondo and variations, à la Symphony No. 42.

As with Nos. 51 and 64, the dating of No. 52 in C minor is speculative. One feature that suggests it may be slightly later than Haydn's other minor-mode *Sturm und Drang* symphonies is the emancipation of the bassoon in all four movements. Except for a few bars in the finale of the 'Farewell', all the other works of 1768–72 use the bassoon *col basso*, tied to the cellos and basses. No. 52's outer movements recall Nos. 44 and 45 in their ferocious drive, though in the opening Allegro con brio there is a skipping major-key second subject for contrast, presented twice but never allowed to develop into a fully rounded melody. This tune takes on a more sober cast in the development and, even more, in the recapitulation, where its final bars are poignantly drawn out before the brutally abrupt close. After a C major Andante of slightly capricious balletic grace, periodically disturbed by laconic outbursts, the minuet echoes the starkness of its predecessor in No. 44. Here, though, the trio turns out to be a smoother, major-key variant of the minuet itself. This overt thematic link between minuet and trio looks ahead to Symphony No. 57 of 1774 and, beyond that, to several of the later string quartets, especially the Op. 50 set.

1774

Symphony No. 54 in G
Symphony No. 55 in E flat, 'Schoolmaster'
Symphony No. 56 in C
Symphony No. 57 in D
Symphony No. 60 in C, 'Il distratto'

Three of the symphonies dated 1774, Nos. 55, 57 and 60, are more popular in tone than most of their predecessors – a foretaste of the lighter, theatrically influenced works of the later 1770s. Indeed, No. 60, 'Il distratto', scored for a festive C major orchestra, is the most overtly theatrical of all Haydn's symphonies: a dizzy six-movement concoction that originated as incidental music to a German version of Jean François Regnard's comedy *Le distrait* (literally, the absent-minded man).

Haydn has plenty of fun evoking absent-mindedness. In the opening movement, the second theme goes into a daydream before a rude awakening from the full orchestra, while the development plunges into the 'Farewell' – Haydn pretending to forget which symphony he is writing. Near the start of the finale there is a moment of slapstick when, in a variant of the old 'wrong note' joke, the violins break off to retune, raucously, their lowest string from F to G. Elsewhere Haydn hurls French, Hungarian and Balkan folk tunes into the mix. The frenetic C minor fourth movement is an East European folk-song pot-pourri, while the following Adagio di Lamentatione uses what sounds like an ancient Gregorian chant. 'Il distratto' was a runaway success, though late in life, after the Empress expressed a wish to hear the symphony again, Haydn dismissed it as *'den alten Schmarrn'* – 'that old tosh'.

The nickname 'Schoolmaster' (*Der Schulmeister*) that attached itself to No. 55, prompted by the pawky opening of the slow movement, has made it one of his best-known symphonies of the 1770s. Haydn's new popular idiom is exemplified by this Adagio, ma semplicemente (his studied 'simplicity', as so often, is deceptive) and the finale. Both use droll, ear-tickling themes as a basis for variations, though as in Nos. 42 and 51 the finale melds variation and rondo form, and even includes a modulating episode that sounds like a sonata development. The *Musikalischer Almanach für Deutschland* of 1782 noted, perhaps with the 'schoolmaster' movement in mind, that Haydn Adagios 'during which people are properly supposed to weep' produce instead an 'elevated comical' effect. The first movement is a masterpiece of urbane wit. Several symphonies from the early 1770s had included a 'false reprise' early in the development – too early to fool any half-awake listener. Here, though, Haydn artfully places the fake recapitulation just late enough to con his audience before swerving off into intensive further development that delays the real homecoming for nearly fifty bars. In the process, a development that had initially seemed slightly short in relation to the exposition becomes eccentrically long.

No. 57 opens with Haydn's weightiest slow introduction to date. It is also subtly linked to the Allegro, which recalls the *buffo* bustle of the early symphonies with an added grace and sophistication. As in 'The Schoolmaster', Haydn writes a *faux-naïf* variation slow movement, here built on a charming alternation of pizzicato and bowed phrases. The third movement is a rumbustious *Ländler*, with a trio that appropriates the minuet's final phrase for its own whimsical ends, while the tarantella finale, based on a comic scrap of melody derived from an old 'Capriccio on the clucking of a hen', provides a serious test of an orchestra's precision at speed.

Like No. 57, No. 54 has an imposing slow introduction (added as an afterthought) leading to a movement with a strong whiff of *opera buffa*, and a rollicking *Ländler*-style minuet. But the slow movement – a rarefied sarabande, with dreamy filigree figuration for muted violins – and the powerfully developed finale give the symphony a much higher specific gravity. Haydn originally composed No. 54 for the basic 1774 orchestra of oboes, horns, bassoon and strings. Much later, probably for performance in England, he enriched the orchestration with two flutes, a second bassoon, trumpets and timpani, making this the most massively scored of all the pre-'London' symphonies.

The other work of 1774, No. 56, stands in the regal line of Haydn C major symphonies. As in No. 60, the orchestra includes high horns, trumpets and timpani, deployed with barbaric splendour in the outer movements and minuet. In the thrilling opening Allegro di molto Haydn ingeniously explores and expands an apparently incidental figure (the little oscillating motif first heard in bars 7 and 8) both in the development and in an expressive modulating sequence near the start of the recapitulation. The Adagio is a movement of extreme, disconcerting contrasts, opening as ethereally as that in No. 54, continuing with a jaunty bassoon solo and then darkening for a romantically brooding, almost Schumannesque passage. The symphony's success in France was not lost on Haydn when he came to write his C major 'Paris' symphony, No. 82.

c.1775–1776

Symphony No. 61 in D
Symphony No. 66 in B flat
Symphony No. 67 in F
Symphony No. 68 in B flat
Symphony No. 69 in C, 'Laudon'

The symphonies of the mid- and late 1770s have commonly been regarded as inferior to their predecessors, especially the minor-key *Sturm und Drang* works. But as James Webster and others have argued, their aesthetic of 'entertainment' is just as valid as the more forceful or impassioned idiom of the symphonies of a few years earlier. If the dominant spirit is now one of comic opera – reflecting Haydn's prime preoccupation during these years – there is no falling off in craftsmanship and inventiveness in symphonies designed with an eye to international consumption. In any case, it was only in the twentieth century that entertainment and great art came to be considered as mutually exclusive.

The only symphony in this group whose autograph survives is No. 61 of 1776. Its first movement has a very Haydnish mix of grandeur, burlesque and lyrical charm. The second subject begins as a comically banal accompaniment for quacking oboes and bassoons (in the recapitulation subterranean stopped horn notes add a touch of grotesquerie) before flowering into a melody that may remind listeners of Elvira's aria 'Mi tradì' in *Don Giovanni*. The A major Adagio is one of Haydn's loveliest pastoral idylls, clouded briefly by a second theme that begins in E minor and then floats magically back to the major. For the finale Haydn writes a 6/8 rondo, somewhere between a hornpipe and a jig, that specialises in trailing off abstractedly just when we expect the return of the bouncy main theme.

The other stand-out symphony in this group, No. 67, may have a theatrical connection. The first movement, with its conspiratorial *pianissimo* opening, is, unusually, in 6/8, a metre far more characteristic of finales. This tuneful, vivacious music breathes the spirit of *opera buffa*, though as ever Haydn ensures that there is also a serious symphonic purpose at work. The Adagio has that mingled tenderness and austerity found in so many Haydn slow movements of the 1770s. There may be a reference to some clandestine stage action in the development's hypnotic canon between the two violins, and in the coda, where the strings play a variant of the main theme *col legno d'arco* (i.e., with the wooden backs of their bows) – a dry, nasal sonority that seems to mock the theme's innate poise. The minuet's trio, a duet for two solo violins, is Haydn in gypsy mode, with the second violin tuning its G-string down to F and imitating a hurdy-gurdy. In the finale, just as we expect a vigorous development, the music breaks off for a ravishing Adagio initiated by two solo violins and solo cello. Another 'Farewell' ending? Haydn has other ideas. The main Allegro returns as a recapitulation, followed by a miniature coda, where the violins play a prolonged trill against comically hesitant wind chords.

There is nothing quite as striking in Nos. 66, 68 and 69, which are all in Haydn's most uncomplicated, extrovert vein. Indeed, the so-called 'Laudon', No. 69 – (mis)named after Field Marshal Ernst Gideon von Loudon, a military hero of the Seven Years War – is as superficial as a Haydn symphony of this period can get. The first movement sounds like a decorous rewrite of the 'Maria Theresa': the C major trappings remain, but none of the flaming brilliance or dynamism. Only the rondo finale, with its fierce C minor episode, rises above routine.

The two B flat symphonies, Nos. 66 and 68, contain far more surprises. Highlights of No. 66 are the sinuous trio of the minuet (with bassoon shadowing the violins an octave lower), which Mozart may have remembered when he wrote the 'Linz' Symphony, and a comic rondo-variation finale on a lopsided theme in five-bar phrases. The coda is pure farce, dismembering the tune and then drawing it out with cod solemnity before a vulgarly whooping send-off.

No. 68's finale has an even crazier coda. After the music stutters to a halt, assorted solo instruments in turn mindlessly chortle out a snatch of the theme, before an emphatic tutti gets things moving again. The unusually long Adagio – placed, for the last time in a Haydn symphony, after the minuet – is in the same 'elevated comical' vein as that of 'The Schoolmaster'. The comedy lies in Haydn's treatment of a simple 'ticking' figure. Heard initially as an unassuming accompaniment to the courtly main theme, this soon asserts itself in an incongruous *forte* fanfare, and is then always likely to crop up as a thematic element in its own right. Nearly two decades later, Haydn would play even more sophisticated games with a banal ticktock accompaniment in the Andante of the 'Clock' Symphony.

*c.*1778–1779

Symphony No. 53 in D, 'L'Impériale'
Symphony No. 63 in C, 'La Roxelane'
Symphony No. 70 in D
Symphony No. 71 in B flat
Symphony No. 75 in D

With his immersion in opera, Haydn's production of symphonies slowed right down after 1776. Not surprisingly, given the pressures he was under, he often resorted to recycling in these years. Both No. 63 and the obscurely nicknamed 'L'Impériale', No. 53, are pasticcios, concocted partly from pre-existing music. Both, too, exist in alternative versions. The opening Allegro of No. 63 is a newly orchestrated rerun of the overture to *Il mondo della luna*, while the second movement pilfers a charming tune from the incidental music to an adaptation of Favart's comedy *Les trois sultanes* performed at Eszterháza in 1777. Haydn uses the melody – entitled 'La Roxelane', after the play's heroine – as a basis for a set of variations on two closely related themes, the first in C minor, the second in C major. No. 53's Andante adopts a similar design, with the minor-major order reversed. Haydn may well have got this 'double variation' plan from the C minor Sonata, Wq. 50 No. 6, from C. P. E.

Bach's set of *Sonaten mit veränderten Reprisen*. It was a form he would often cultivate in the 1780s and 1790s.

No. 53 has the most bewildering history of any Haydn symphony, circulating in assorted versions with or without the slow introduction and with no fewer than three different finales. One of these (printed as 'C' in the Philharmonia-Universal critical edition) is almost certainly spurious, and another, a distinctly uncapricious 'Capriccio' (version 'A'), sounds suspiciously un-Haydnesque. The one indubitably authentic finale was probably filched from an overture to a lost marionette opera, which in turn was recycled as the opening movement of Symphony No. 62. The stately elegance of No. 53's first movement and the ear-tickling, quasi-folk melodies of the Andante and the minuet's trio made it a smash hit in London and Paris during the 1780s. But even in this calculatedly 'easy' symphony there are moments 'for the connoisseur', as Robbins Landon put it. In the first movement Haydn prepares for the recapitulation via a leisurely chromatic sequence over sustained pedal points, with the wind adding a beautiful wash of colour: a magical passage that Mozart, who liked to 'glide' with smooth inevitability into his recapitulations, surely enjoyed.

No. 71 likewise sets a premium on elegance and poise. It opens with a brief slow introduction that subtly prefigures the main theme of the Allegro. Other felicities include the quizzical, tonally blurred passage leading to the second subject, and the beautifully scored cadenza in the theme-and-variation Adagio. The most memorable movement, though, is the finale, a strongly developed sonata form with a second subject evoking a rustic wind band. At the start of the development Haydn dips from F major to a *pianissimo* D flat, with comic-mysterious effect – the kind of tonal juxtaposition he would often exploit in the following two decades.

In No. 75 Haydn infuses his popular style with a new sinewy strength. We know that this symphony appealed to Mozart, who noted the theme of the Presto first movement and half-remembered it in the *Don Giovanni* overture. Mozart was surely struck, too, by the grandeur and gravitas of the slow introduction, with its arresting plunge from D major to D minor. In the Presto Haydn dramatically exploits the main theme's dissonant, 'tensing' D sharp, right through to the recapitulation, which omits the syncopated second subject in favour of a thrilling canonic elaboration of the opening theme. The Poco Adagio is a set of variations on a tender, hymn-like melody, of a type often found in late Haydn (did Mozart recall it when he composed the Andante of his B flat major Piano Concerto, K450?), while the finale is an idiosyncratic rondo design that constantly draws strength from Haydn's lightly worn contrapuntal mastery.

Counterpoint is more ostentatiously on display in another outstanding D major symphony, No. 70, premiered on 18 December 1779 at a ceremony to mark the rebuilding of the opera house after the Eszterháza fire. A 'fire' programme has even been posited for the extraordinary D *minor* finale, whose sputtering high repeated Ds ignite a ferocious triple fugue. Haydn brings back the soft repeated Ds as a 'framing' device in the D major coda, teasing them out with pauses: an effect at once jokey and disquieting. The Andante, a set of double variations à la Nos. 53 and 63 – albeit with none of their perkiness – likewise trades on minor-major contrasts, and on strict contrapuntal techniques: the march-like D minor theme is constructed in two-part double counterpoint (shades of Symphony No. 47), with the top and bottom lines inverted in the theme's second half. Though less obviously 'learned', the peremptory opening movement also has its contrapuntal leanings. In the development the first two notes of the main theme are worked into a canon of Beethovenian trenchancy.

c.1780–1781

Symphony No. 62 in D
Symphony No. 73 in D, 'La chasse'
Symphony No. 74 in E flat

Like Nos. 53 and 63, both the little-known No. 62 and the relatively familiar 'La chasse' are in part pasticcios. The first movement of No. 62 adapts the bustling Italianate overture that had already cropped up as a finale to No. 53. No. 73, composed in 1781, flatters Prince Nicolaus's passion for the chase by recycling as its finale the overture to Haydn's newest opera, *La fedeltà premiata*. This gloriously exuberant music quotes a traditional hunting call known as *l'ancienne vue* (i.e., the initial sighting of the stag), and uniquely among Haydn's later symphonies fades away *pianissimo*, perhaps to signify the expiring beast. For the Andante Haydn uses his recent song 'Gegenliebe' (Mutual love) as the basis for a rondo-cum-variations structure that incorporates two 'developing' episodes. The monothematic first movement treats its ubiquitous repeated four-note motif – carefully 'flagged' in the slow introduction – with astonishing resourcefulness. As Charles Rosen has observed, once the first violins have played those four repeated quavers, the accompaniment in the next bar immediately sounds 'thematic', audibly derived from the main motif. The whole movement is as intently argued as the first movements of the contemporary Op. 33 String Quartets.

Whereas No. 73 concentrates its weight at the beginning, the most impressive movement in No. 62 is the finale. Here Haydn momentarily, and mysteriously, withholds a definite sense of key, a favourite trick of C. P. E. Bach's. At the start of the recapitulation the texture is enriched and the tonality further blurred. No. 62 was one of the three symphonies that caught the fancy of Mozart, who seems to have remembered the finale's ringing 'Hallelujahs' in the first movement of his 'Linz' Symphony. One reason why Haydn began his finale off-key is that the Allegretto second movement is set, exceptionally, in the symphony's tonic key, D major. This is music of strange, trance-like delicacy, fashioned entirely from an unpromising, minimalist 'theme' that consists of just two notes plus a routine accompaniment.

The minuet and sportive 6/8 finale of No. 74 in E flat are in Haydn's most undemanding popular vein. But the first movement belies its formal opening with a far-reaching development that leads a fragment of the main theme through an astonishing harmonic labyrinth. The opening of the Adagio – a refined rococo melody on muted violins over a ticking accompaniment – recalls the slow movement of No. 68, though without the comic disruptions. This is another of Haydn's rondo-variations, with a delightful cadenza-cum-coda where woodwind and then strings weave the theme in half-playful, half-tender contrapuntal imitation.

1782

Symphony No. 76 in E flat
Symphony No. 77 in B flat
Symphony No. 78 in C minor

'Last year I composed three beautiful, elegant and by no means over-long symphonies . . . they are all very easy, without too much concertante for the English gentlemen, and I intended to bring them over myself and produce them there.' So wrote Haydn to his new Parisian publisher Boyer in 1783, introducing Nos. 76–8, designed as a set for an aborted visit to London. Few would contest their beauty and elegance; and while the wind writing (for the now standard solo flute plus pairs of oboes, bassoons and horns) is rich and inventive, the instruments do indeed have few unaccompanied (i.e., 'concertante') passages – though in stressing this, Haydn underestimated the prowess of the London wind players.

In places the two major-key works in the trilogy sound to us more suavely Mozartian than almost any other Haydn symphonies, though in 1782 he can have known very little of Mozart's music. But in essence they continue the trend of the late 1770s and early 1780s (especially the Op. 33 Quartets), combining an easy tunefulness with fastidious craftsmanship: a fusion of popular and learned styles that would reach its apogee in the 'London' symphonies. No. 77 in B flat has long been a favourite of Haydn-lovers: for the melodic charm and insouciant contrapuntal mastery of its outer movements, the delicately sensuous Andante sostenuto, scored with exquisite, chamber-music refinement, and the stomping, fast-paced minuet, more a lusty *Deutsche* than an aristocratic dance.

A deft detail in the triple-time opening Allegro of the E flat Symphony, No. 76, is the way the lyrical second subject grows from an apparently incidental phrase heard near the start of the movement. The development contains one quietly audacious harmonic stroke, settling on the brink of D flat, only for Haydn to pull the rug from under his listeners' feet and pivot the music towards E flat. Like No. 77's slow movement, the B flat Adagio, ma non troppo, is an individual fusion of rondo and variations. Here, though, the structure is more clear-cut, with increasingly embellished appearances of a dainty string melody alternating with two minor-key episodes. The first, in B flat minor, is haunting both in its wind colouring and its dusky modulations, while the second prefigures the G minor storms in the Andantes of the 'Clock' and 'London' symphonies. Nearly two centuries later, Robert Simpson quoted a fragment from No. 76's opening Allegro in the scherzo of his Fourth Symphony. 'The innocence of Haydn is confronted by us with a problem,' he wrote. 'Haydn is not disturbed, but we are.'

As in his sets of quartets, Haydn included one minor-mode work in the 1782 trilogy, No. 78 – his first symphony in the minor for a decade. The driving, angular first movement (definitely not 'easy') powerfully exploits the dramatic and contrapuntal potential of a 'pregnant' unison motif akin to the opening of Mozart's C minor Piano Concerto, K491. Whereas most of the *Sturm und Drang* symphonies had ended in the minor, No. 78 replicates the key relationships of the 'Farewell', with a slow movement in the relative major, E flat, a C major minuet and a finale that begins in a tense C minor but ends merrily in C major – too merrily for some ears accustomed to Mozart's minor-saturated fatalism and the grimness of Haydn's own 'Trauer' and 'La Passione' symphonies. But only in a helter-skelter performance need No. 78's finale – part sonata rondo, part 'double variations' – sound unduly frivolous. In any case,

Haydn's method, here and in most of his other later instrumental works, is in accord with the Classical ideal of resolution.

1783–1784

Symphony No. 79 in F
Symphony No. 80 in D minor
Symphony No. 81 in G

Mozart's famous description of his piano concertos, K413–15, could stand equally well as an epigraph to Haydn's symphonies Nos. 76 and 77, and to the two major-key works from the trilogy completed in 1784:

> They are . . . easy on the ear and natural, without being vapid. Here and there there are passages from which connoisseurs [*Kenner*] alone will derive satisfaction, but they are written in such a way that the less learned [*Liebhaber*] cannot fail to be pleased, without knowing why.

No. 79 in F is the most uncomplicated of a set designed, like Nos. 76–8, for international consumption. Even here, though, there is plenty for the connoisseur to relish. After a comparatively bland first-movement development, for instance, the recapitulation slips via F minor to A flat, seizes on a chattering 'transition' theme and subjects it to contrapuntal elaboration. The second movement is surprising, too, beginning as an ornate, courtly Adagio and then breaking off in mid-flow for a skittish, Hungarian-flavoured dance.

The beguiling Andante of No. 81 is a set of four variations on a graceful siciliano theme, of a kind Haydn often favoured in his later works: famous examples are the Andante of the Trumpet Concerto and 'With verdure clad' in *The Creation*. For the first time in his major-key strophic variation movements, Haydn includes one variation in the minor. Characteristically, too, this D minor variation is by far the freest of the four, sounding more like a contrasting episode or even a miniature sonata development. With its mingled urbanity and subtle symphonic thinking, the opening Vivace is a perfect example of a movement designed to appeal equally to *Kenner* and *Liebhaber*. After a prompt G major call to attention, a soft, long-held F natural tilts the music mysteriously towards C major: a harmonic ambiguity that Haydn further exploits near the start of the development, and, even more breathtakingly, in the hushed, oblique opening of the recapitulation. Having deprived us of the complete main theme here, Haydn creates a 'mirror' structure by bringing it back in the final bars, before the music fades away *pianissimo*.

No Haydn symphony movement juxtaposes the vehement and the flippant as bluntly as the initial Allegro spiritoso of No. 80 in D minor. For most of its course, the exposition lives up to the expectations aroused by its turbulent opening. Then, at the last moment, Haydn introduces a trivial *Ländler* tune that, but for its irregular phrasing (four plus three bars), could have drifted in from a Viennese beer garden. Despite a ferocious burst of activity from the main theme, the *Ländler* dominates the development, turning up in various remote keys separated by silences. In the recapitulation Haydn quickly switches from D minor to D major, and gives the *Ländler* the last word, its phrasing now 'normalised' into four plus four bars. As Dean Sutcliffe put it, a movement that began in *Sturm und Drang* mode becomes progressively 'hijacked by a Pythonesque tune'. The noble serenity of the sonata-form Adagio is ruffled by sudden impassioned outbursts, while the minuet, back in a stern D minor, encloses a beautiful D major trio that sets an ancient Gregorian chant against an agitated accompaniment. If these two movements are wholly serious, Haydn the humorist takes immediate control of the D major finale. The syncopated opening, fashioned so that we do not initially hear it as syncopated, is one of his funniest rhythmic jokes.

1785–1786: the 'Paris' symphonies

Symphony No. 82 in C, 'L'ours'
Symphony No. 83 in G minor, 'La poule'

Symphony No. 84 in E flat
Symphony No. 85 in B flat, 'La reine'
Symphony No. 86 in D
Symphony No. 87 in A

After the relative lull of the late 1770s, Haydn's symphonic production had been gathering pace with the two sets Nos. 76–8 and 79–81. Now, with the six works for Paris, the symphony again assumed the dominant position it had occupied a decade and more earlier. Haydn's symphonies were as popular in the French capital as they were in London; and in the winter of 1784–5 a commission for six symphonies arrived from a young French aristocrat, Claude-François-Marie Rigoley, Comte d'Ogny, a prime mover in the Masonic concert organisation Le Concert de La Loge Olympique. For each work Haydn was to receive the colossal fee of twenty-five louis d'or – five times the sum Mozart had been paid for his 'Paris' Symphony in 1778! He composed Nos. 83, 87 and (probably) 85 in 1785, and the remaining three symphonies in 1786. They caused a sensation when they were performed in the guard-room of the Tuileries Palace by the sixty-strong orchestra (more than double the size of the Esterházy band), ostentatiously attired in sky-blue dress coats.

Though Haydn never visited Paris, he wrote these symphonies with an eye to local taste and the prowess of the large Parisian orchestra. As Mozart reported to his father, the French relished sonorous splendour and bold, assertive gestures in their symphonies. Haydn took this into account, above all in the two works with trumpets and drums, No. 86, and No. 82, whose piping finale theme over a drone bass reminded contemporary listeners of the music that accompanied dancing bears. No. 82's opening Vivace assai is the apogee of Haydn's martial C major style, and one of the most dynamic, explosive movements he ever wrote. Amid the brass- and timpani-dominated aggression, the second theme comes as an oasis of bucolic calm, though it later plays a crucial role in the symphonic argument.

Capitalising, perhaps, on the popularity of Symphony No. 53, the Allegretto second movement is a set of double variations on two closely related themes, one in F major, the other in F minor. Unlike in No. 53, though, Haydn adds a substantial coda that destabilises the hitherto regular phrasing and introduces a new rustic dance tune. More than any other minuet in the 'Paris' symphonies, the third movement seems to epitomise the red-and-gold pomp of the *ancien régime*. The picturesquely scored trio, by contrast, is an idealised Austrian *Ländler*. Fusing the symphony's two dominant modes of C major ceremony and bucolic naivety, the finale is a movement of intoxicating verve and invention. The drones that underpin the ubiquitous 'bear' tune are liable to invade the texture at any point, reaching extremes of rebarbative splendour at the start of the development and in the thunderous coda.

The first movement of No. 83 in G minor equals its minor-key predecessor, No. 80, in *bizarrerie* and surpasses it in rhetorical force. The opening theme's dissonant, accented C sharp sets up a grating harmonic tension which Haydn exploits both in the exposition and in the vehement contrapuntal development, dominated by the theme's initial four-note 'motto'. Only towards the end of the recapitulation, now in G major, does the theme attain consonance. In extreme, comical contrast is the mincing second subject, whose 'clucking' oboe accompaniment spawned the nickname 'La poule'. While the contrasts are never fully resolved, the clucking figure clearly derives from the opening theme's repeated dotted notes. This eccentric yet oddly powerful movement could hardly be further removed from the lyrical pathos characteristic of Mozart's G minor works. The main theme of the Andante, in E flat, promises repose. (Commentators have noted its resemblance to the Andante of Mozart's Symphony No. 40, in the same key.) But eccentricity returns with two frantic eruptions, separated by several bars of mesmerised stasis. Haydn intensifies this effect in the development, and then writes a yearning lead-back to the recapitulation over a sustained horn pedal. The pastoral minuet and 12/8 finale, both in G major, are more 'normal', though the accentuation of the minuet's theme gives it a faintly queasy feel, while the finale's development hurtles through a dizzying range of keys.

Reviewing some of the 'Paris' symphonies, a writer in the *Mercure de France* of 12 April 1788 praised 'the work of this great genius, who in each of his pieces knows how to draw such rich and varied developments from a single subject'. While Haydn's famed monothematicism is more typical of his quartets than his symphonies, the first and last movements of two of the 'Paris' set, Nos. 84 and 85, do indeed generate all their symphonic energy 'from a single subject'. No. 84 is, with No. 87, the most overtly 'popular' of the six. But it has its own distinctive beauties and characteristic harmonic surprises. In the first movement's development, for instance, the music hovers tentatively around A flat and D flat before the dapper main theme enters *forte* in a brilliant burst of F major. The symphony's jewel is the Andante, a set of variations on a 6/8 melody foreshadowed in the first movement's slow introduction. Its climax comes in an exquisitely wrought contrapuntal cadenza that pays tribute to the Parisian taste for colourful wind writing. There are shades here, too, of the 'Et incarnatus est' from Mozart's unfinished C minor Mass, whose manuscript Haydn just might have seen on one of his trips to Vienna.

As the alleged favourite of Marie Antoinette, No. 85 quickly acquired the nickname 'La reine'. A prime attraction for the Queen, famous for her back-to-nature play-acting at Versailles, was doubtless the *faux-naïf* second movement that presents an old French folk song, 'La gentille et jeune Lisette', in varied pastel colourings. (Legend has it that Marie Antoinette would console herself in her final imprisonment by playing this movement on the harpsichord.) We may guess, too, that the Austrian-born queen relished the trio of the minuet, a yodelling *Ländler* for bassoon doubled an octave higher by violins – a sonority Haydn would exploit in the trio of No. 86 and in many of the 'London' symphonies. In 'La reine', the second half of the trio is expanded at improbable lengths as woodwind muse on a fragment of the theme over a horn drone. This is another of those Haydn moments that transmutes whimsical eccentricity into poetry. With its pompous dotted rhythms and sweeping scales, the symphony's slow introduction sounds like an updated Baroque French overture. We can imagine Paris audiences nodding with approval. The scale flourishes also recur in the triple-time Vivace, a movement saturated by its graceful, gliding theme, first heard in a lean, two-part texture and then wonderfully expanded and enriched. In the exposition Haydn swerves into F minor for a virtual quotation of the opening of the 'Farewell' Symphony, a work introduced to Paris in 1784. Connoisseurs in the audience doubtless got the joke.

Together with No. 82, No. 86 is the most resplendent of the 'Paris' set. After an ample slow introduction, with rich wind scoring, the Allegro spiritoso initially feints at E minor before D major is rammed home in a pounding *fortissimo* tutti. The whole movement trades on the extreme contrasts between the fragile, halting principal themes (unlike in Nos. 84 and 85, there is a distinct second subject) and the brazen power of the full orchestra. So, too, does the finale, one of those pieces that reminds us that Rossini was a great Haydn enthusiast. After a main theme initiated by stuttering repeated quavers, the first tutti crashes in far earlier than expected, no doubt to the startled delight of the Parisians. In the recapitulation he then caps this *coup* with a spectacular *fortissimo* swerve from D major to B flat. The minuet is the grandest in the 'Paris' symphonies, recalling that of No. 50 both in its pomp and its miniature sonata-form design, with the main theme developed in yearning sequences. The waltz-like trio shares the idealised rusticity, though not the eccentricity, of No. 85's trio.

Uniquely in the 'Paris' set, No. 86's slow movement lacks any singable melody. Here Haydn challenges rather than charms his French audience in an extraordinary Capriccio, full of strange tonal excursions, with the main theme – a bare rising arpeggio and a sustained note that swells and fades – given a new harmonic twist each time it appears. 'Brooding' and 'smouldering' are the epithets commentators habitually reach for when describing this powerful, emotionally ambivalent music. While ostensibly free in design, it combines the outline of a sonata with rondo-like recurrences of the theme. Nikolaus Harnoncourt, though, evidently hears it differently, writing in the notes to his recording that 'the composer follows his droll (*skurrilen*) ideas without concern for form'.

If the main theme of No. 87 – based, like the finale of No. 86, on a volley of repeated notes – could have come from a symphony of the 1760s, its treatment has all the power and resourcefulness of the mature Haydn. The theme becomes surprisingly strenuous in the development, and the recapitulation contains more fresh adventures than anything else in the 'Paris' set. For the slow movement Haydn writes a beautiful, hymnic Adagio with elaborate woodwind writing that, as in No. 84, pays tribute to the favourite Parisian form of the *sinfonia concertante*. The second theme, wonderfully expanded in the recapitulation, is an expressive cadenza for flute, oboe and bassoon. The oboe solo in the minuet's trio ascends into the stratosphere, while the monothematic finale gets so engrossed in its contrapuntal play that the development gobbles up most of the recapitulation. When the theme finally reappears, just before the end, Haydn colours it with wistful subdominant harmony.

1787–1789

Symphony No. 88 in G, 'Letter V'
Symphony No. 89 in F
Symphony No. 90 in C
Symphony No. 91 in E flat
Symphony No. 92 in G, 'Oxford'

After the huge success of the 'Paris' set Haydn lost no time composing another two symphonies for the Parisian market. He entrusted them, together with the Quartets Opp. 54 and 55, to the entrepreneurial violinist Johann Tost, who agreed to sell the works to a French publisher. When Tost arrived in Paris he duly struck a deal with the firm of Sieber. True to form, though, he sold a third symphony, by Adalbert Gyrowetz, under Haydn's name, and then conveniently forgot to forward the payment to Haydn! In the meantime, Symphonies Nos. 88 and 89 had been published by Forster in London, and formed the last two in a series identified by letters of the alphabet: No. 88 is still sometimes called 'Letter V' in the English-speaking world.

Nickname apart, No. 88 owes its perennial popularity to its combination of tunefulness, intellectual power and sheer elan, and to the melody of the Largo, so admired by Brahms. As in all but two of his symphonies from now onwards, Haydn prefaces the opening Allegro with a slow introduction, here terse and formal rather than, as so often, mysterious and speculative. The Allegro itself is a movement of immense dramatic power and harmonic daring that grows entirely from a wisp of a theme and a wriggling semiquaver figure that accompanies the tune on its repetition. Though often described as a theme and variations, the Largo is really a free fantasy on the long-arched melody, first heard on solo oboe and solo cello (a beautiful and original sonority) and later enhanced by ever more elaborate accompanying figuration. Midway through the movement a thunderous tutti introduces trumpets and timpani for the first time in the symphony – a sensational *coup de théâtre* singled out in contemporary reports.

The minuet, drawing maximum capital from its initial five-note figure, has an irresistible bucolic swing; even more rustic is the trio, with its drowsy musette drones on violas and bassoons. The finale matches the opening movement's brilliant fusion of the popular and learned styles. In the central development the ubiquitous theme is put through its paces in an exciting *fortissimo* canon between lower and upper strings, and is then reduced to its first two notes as Haydn leaves us guessing as to the exact moment of the theme's return.

No. 89 has always been overshadowed by the more obvious attractions of No 88. Haydn was evidently even more pressed for time than usual, pilfering both the slow movement and the finale from one of his recent concertos for *lire organizzate*. The concerto's Andante con moto, a siciliano with a contrasting minor-key episode, was recycled intact except for its delectable new wind scoring. But Haydn spiced up the breezy rondo finale with a syncopated, Hungarian-style section in F minor, and added gleefully vulgar downward swoops (marked *strascinando* – 'dragging') to the return of the main theme. The first movement begins with cool formality but has plenty of surprises up its sleeve, above all in the recapitulation, which contains far more intensive development than the development proper.

In one of his more flagrant acts of deception, Haydn managed to persuade two noblemen, the Comte d'Ogny and Prince Krafft Ernst of Oettingen-Wallerstein, that he was writing Symphonies Nos. 90–2 exclusively for them. In 1789 he sent the autographs to the count in Paris, and the orchestral parts to Prince Krafft Ernst, appeasing him with the wafer-thin excuse that due to his poor eyesight the autograph scores were almost indecipherable!

No. 90 trades on the success of its C major Parisian predecessor, No. 82. Except for No. 90's introduction, which announces the main theme of the Allegro in slow motion, the two symphonies share a similar formal pattern: a triple-time first movement that mingles the ceremonial and the pastoral – though No. 90's is more gracious than its aggressive counterpart in No. 82; a not-so-slow second movement cast as a set of major-minor variations; a spacious minuet replete with the pomp of the dying *ancien régime*; and a racing finale that turns drollery into high art. Drollest of all is Haydn's trickery in the second half of the movement. After a suspiciously short recapitulation, an ultra-emphatic C major cadence invites applause – and sometimes gets it, especially if the conductor mischievously broadens the tempo here, as happens in Simon Rattle's Berlin Philharmonic recording. But after four bars of rest Haydn resumes in a furtive *pianissimo* D flat, initiating the longest coda in all his symphonies. There is further 'false ending' confusion when the second half of the movement is repeated.

No. 91, Haydn's last symphony without trumpets and drums, is a more intimate work, bathed in the glowing warmth of E flat major. More subtly than in No. 90, the slow introduction prefigures the main theme of the Allegro, constructed in 'invertible counterpoint' – i.e., with inter-changeable top and bottom lines. Haydn later enriches the weave with new countermelodies, culminating in a noncha-lant display of four-part polyphony in the coda. Another delight is the Schubertian sideslip to a remote D flat major for the lilting second theme, which then glides back, via E flat minor, to the 'proper' key of B flat. The dancing theme of the Andante also includes a striking, more aggressive deflection from B flat to D flat. This is a set of variations, with the (by now) usual free variation in the minor and a raucous trilling coda that seems to proclaim, with Verdi's Falstaff, 'Il trillo invade il mondo'. After a minuet poised between suavity and earthiness and another of Haydn's captivating *Ländler* trios (with that favourite violin/bassoon doubling), the finale tempers high spirits with a certain autumnal mellowness.

Most celebrated of the 1788–9 trilogy is the 'Oxford' Symphony, No. 92, so called because it was played when Haydn received his honorary doctorate at Oxford University in July 1791. This magnificent work is one of Haydn's greatest achievements in any genre. Its slow introduction, with its harmonically ambiguous close, again adumbrates the tiny, inconclusive main theme of the Allegro, essentially a decorated five-finger exercise and a final upward leap. Equally slender is the chirpy second subject, sailing in as an afterthought to round off the exposition. But from these slight materials Haydn fash-ions a thrilling, tightly woven movement, with a sinewy contra-puntal development and a recapitulation that creates a sense of continuous expansion as Haydn continues to explore the dramatic potential of that upward leap. The Adagio rivals the Largo of No. 88 in melodic sublimity. Its serenity is tinged with nostalgia, above all in the poignant coda, where woodwind ruminate on a cadential phrase first heard in the minor-key central episode. The minuet is grandly symphonic, with a syn-copated trio that constantly fools the listener as to where the main beat is, while the finale fully equals No. 88's in wit and contrapuntal brio. Here, though, Haydn introduces a clear melodic contrast, courtesy of what Donald Tovey dubbed 'a daddy-long-legs of a second subject'.

1791–1792: the first set of 'London' symphonies

No. 93 in D
No. 94 in G, 'Surprise'
No. 95 in C minor
No. 96 in D, 'Miracle'
No. 97 in C
No. 98 in B flat

The twelve symphonies Haydn composed for London build on the fusion of easy memorability and intellectual rigour found in the works of the 1780s. While there is now less bizarre eccentricity of detail, his melodies become more spacious and more popular-sounding, his forms still freer, his modulations even bolder. Inspired, too, by the substantial London forces (numbering around forty in 1791–2 and 1794, and over sixty in 1795), Haydn's treatment of the orchestra outdoes even the works written for Paris in colour and panache. These are his most glittering, worldly symphonies, reflecting the exhilarating milieu in which they were written and Haydn's determination to impress a broad public. Yet, except for Nos. 95 and 96, they are more searchingly argued than all but a handful of his earlier works. More, perhaps, than any instrumental music before or since, the 'London' symphonies encapsulated and flattered their listeners' 'taste' (eighteenth-century buzzword) and understanding, while increasingly expanding and challenging them. Together with the greatest symphonies of the 1780s, they are the consummation of what Charles Rosen has called 'heroic pastoral': not only for their rustic trios and quasi-folk melodies, but for 'that combination of sophisticated irony and surface innocence that is so much part of the pastoral genre'.

Fine as they are, Nos. 95 and 96, premiered in the spring of 1791, are on the whole 'safer', less innovative than the ten symphonies that followed, and, indeed, than earlier works like No. 88 and the 'Oxford'. No. 96 is still nicknamed 'The Miracle', though the 'miracle' in question – a chandelier crashing down without seriously injuring anyone – actually occurred during a performance of No. 102. After a slow introduction that turns to D minor for its final bars, the Allegro recalls the 'Oxford' in its fleeting, fragmentary opening theme – the mainspring of the whole movement – and propulsive rhythmic energy. Here, though, the recapitulation bluntly compresses the events of the exposition, with a climax on a 'shock' *fortissimo* D minor chord that echoes the move to D minor in the slow introduction.

The G major Andante contrasts transfigured rococo pastoral with a stormy 'developing' fugato episode in G minor that caps any previous Haydn symphony slow movement in physical power. An extended cadenza-coda for two solo violins and wind contains a gorgeous sideslipping modulation from G to E flat. The swaggering minuet is another of Haydn's miniature sonata-form structures, the trio a delicious *Ländler* for solo oboe. With a nod, perhaps, to Symphony No. 75 in the same key (a popular work in London), the finale is a quicksilver rondo fertilised by a single theme, with a mock-heroic D minor episode and a wind-band solo near the end. Writing to Maria Anna von Genzinger apropos a planned performance in Vienna, Haydn stressed the movement's delicacy and the need for 'the softest *piano* and a very quick tempo'.

No. 95 is the only 'London' symphony in the minor, and the only one without a slow introduction. For late eighteenth-century listeners the minor mode already implied a gravitas that made a solemn or dramatic preamble superfluous. No. 95's stark unison 'motto' recalls Haydn's previous C minor Symphony, No. 78, published in London in 1784. As in the earlier work, the motto promises, and duly receives, vigorous contrapuntal treatment, though in No. 95 Haydn contrasts C minor severity with a demurely charming second theme, adorned in the recapitulation with a violin solo for Salomon. The triumphant C major close sweeps away rather than truly resolves earlier harmonic tensions.

After a theme-and-variations Andante in E flat that includes an expressive cello solo and the now customary free *minore* episode, the minuet again juxtaposes C minor and C major. The main section is restless and chromatically troubled, while the C major trio features another, more extended, solo for cello. The frequent solo passages, here and elsewhere in the first six 'London' symphonies, were calculated to please both Haydn's audience and his orchestral principals. As in his two previous minor-mode symphonies, Nos. 80 and 83, No. 95's sonata-rondo finale is entirely in the major. No Haydn symphony finale to date had begun with such a broad, serene melody. But initial impressions are deceptive. Haydn proceeds to work the theme's first five notes in an intricate display of counterpoint that has a distinctly Handelian ring. With its polyphonic virtuosity and C major splendour, the movement has provoked inevitable comparisons with the 'Jupiter' Symphony, beginning with a review in the *Allgemeine musikalische Zeitung* in 1798 that praised Haydn's finale while chiding Mozart's for 'pushing things a bit too far'!

By the time Haydn wrote Symphonies Nos. 93 and 94 in the summer and autumn of 1791 he had had more time to study English taste. Both works are broader in scale and bolder in their arguments than Nos. 95 and 96. No. 93 has a new grandeur and melodic allure. Even more than the two earlier works, both symphonies were designed to appeal to his London audience's penchant for spectacular, sometimes ironic contrasts between the comical and/or naive and what the political philosopher and aesthetician Edmund Burke called 'the sublime'. The American musicologist David Schroeder has proposed that these and the later 'London' symphonies take the audience on a journey of enlightenment, with a final resolution of conflicting or refractory forces. In Symphonies Nos. 93–4 and 97–8 Haydn guides the listener carefully through complex compositional strategies across four movements. In

Nos. 99–104 he often trusts his audience's capacity for sophisticated reflective listening without the need for overt signposts.

'Novelty of idea, agreeable caprice, and whim combined with all *Haydn's* sublime and wonten grandeur, gave additional consequence to the *soul* and feelings of every individual present,' enthused *The Times* after the premiere of No. 93, on 17 February 1792. Haydn immediately evokes 'the sublime' in the slow introduction, when the music slips from a proud *fortissimo* D major to a soft and strange E flat major. This 'flatward' tendency finds an echo in deflections to flat keys in each of the following movements. The Allegro assai is built on two symmetrical cantabile melodies of great charm, the first tender, the second – a fragment of which fuels the strenuous contrapuntal development – a roguish waltz. The minuet is one of Haydn's most muscular and theatrical, while its trio sets aggressive military tattoos on wind and brass against the strings' speculative excursions into distant keys: no trace here of the pastoral topos found in most Haydn trios.

After the first performance Haydn told Frau von Genzinger that the finale was 'too weak' in relation to the opening movement and needed altering. We don't know whether he did in fact revise it. But the finale as we know it is one of the wittiest and most powerful he ever wrote, culminating in a coda of rowdy hilarity. With an outrageous display of rhythmic and harmonic trickery, Haydn continually foils his listeners' expectation of a full recapitulation. He also plays his characteristic games with the main theme's upbeat quavers, at one point setting the thunderous power of the full orchestra against a lone cello. The Largo cantabile, a fusion of sonata, rondo and variations, is just as original. It begins with a delicately soulful theme on solo strings (corrupt later editions stipulated full orchestra here) and continues with a parody of a Handelian French overture. Towards the end, after an oboe solo of piercing beauty, the music becomes becalmed, only for the mood to be punctured by a gigantic bassoon fart – a joke whose *Till Eulenspiegel* crudeness more than matches the 'surprise' in No. 94. With its mingled sentiment, parody and comedy, the movement made an instant appeal, and was duly encored.

The premiere of No. 94 on 23 March capped even No. 93's triumph. Reports inevitably seized on the *fortissimo* chord that disrupts the exaggeratedly naive theme of the Andante, added by Haydn as an afterthought. He allegedly remarked to the composer Adalbert Gyrowetz that 'there the [sleeping] ladies will jump', though he later told Griesinger that he had not intended to waken anyone nodding off in the audience (Salomon's concerts often went on beyond midnight), but rather to surprise them with something new, 'in order to prevent my rank from being usurped by Pleyel, my pupil'. *The Oracle* put it rather more poetically: 'The surprise might not unaptly be likened to the situation of a beautiful Shepherdess who, lulled to slumber by the murmur of a distant Waterfall, starts alarmed by the unexpected firing of a fowling-piece.' However you hear this big bang, the variations that Haydn weaves on his nursery tune are delightfully colourful, encompassing a thunderous 'developing' variation in C minor, barnyard jollity from the oboe, and a coda that transfigures the theme with twilit harmonies over a sustained horn pedal.

In the eighteenth century G major was the pastoral key *par excellence*. And from the slow introduction's radiant aubade (oboes and bassoons over another horn pedal), both the first movement and the lusty Allegro molto minuet share the Andante's bucolic associations. Typically, though, alfresco vigour is allied to a complexity of argument that encouraged concentrated, 'philosophical' listening. In the first movement the floating repeated notes and rising chromatic lines that blur a sense of key become vital ingredients in the bouncy 6/8 Vivace assai. This initially pretends it is in A minor rather than G major, an ambiguity that Haydn slyly exploits throughout the movement. (He had done something similar in the first movement of No. 86.) Only at the end of the recapitulation, after another grand expansion, is the fragile main theme allowed to reach a rounded conclusion. Launched by one of Haydn's catchiest tunes, the last movement arguably surpasses all his symphonic finales to date in harmonic drama, comic brio and sheer flamboyance, not least the thunderous timpani roll that batters the music into an alien key in the coda: a far more potent surprise than the Andante's famous *Paukenschlag*, and the kind of *coup de théâtre* that left its mark on the young Beethoven.

Composed early in 1792 and premiered on 2 March, three weeks before the 'Surprise', No. 98 in B flat is a more serious, inward-looking work, at least in its first two movements. 'The new Symphony in B flat was given, and its first and last Allegros encored,' noted the composer laconically. The success of the opening movement testifies to the sophistication of Haydn's audience, for this intently argued music demands the most concentrated philosophical listening. The fertile main theme, prefigured in a stark B flat *minor* in the slow introduction, dominates much of the movement, though this is not one of Haydn's obsessive monothematic structures. Near the end of the exposition, a sustained, chromatic oboe melody over a pedal point makes, in Tovey's phrase, 'an exquisite appeal to finer sensibilities'. The development works the main theme's separate components in a tense imbroglio; and the recapitulation continues to explore the theme's contrapuntal potential before finally presenting it in its bluntest, most elemental form.

The Adagio is traditionally supposed to be Haydn's requiem for Mozart. Certainly there are unmissable echoes of the 'Jupiter' Symphony's Andante in this sublime movement, in full sonata form, with a development by turns turbulent and gently elegiac. In the recapitulation, the hymn-like main theme (which initially suggests 'God Save the King') is wonderfully intensified, first with a sinuous counterpoint for solo cello, then in woodwind imitation, and finally in an aching new chromatic harmonisation. Even the minuet, another miniature sonata design, is less flamboyant than those in Nos. 93, 94 and 96. The 6/8 finale, though, is Haydn at his most irrepressible. Its cheeky second theme belongs to the world of Rossini's Figaro; and the comedy continues in the development, with its series of violin solos for Salomon in wildly contrasting keys, and the huge coda. In what sounds initially like a cadenza, Haydn slows down the main theme with mock solemnity, and then decorates it with a 'cembalo [i.e., fortepiano] solo' for himself, an effect that must have brought the house down in 1792.

Haydn closed the 1792 season on 3 (or possibly 4) May with the most forceful of the first 'London' set, No. 97, last in a proud line of festive C major symphonies. The first movement's martial swagger – offset, as in No. 82, by a pastoral second theme – goes hand in hand with one of Haydn's subtlest designs. The unusually subdued slow introduction is framed by a haunting cadence on a diminished seventh chord – another of the composer's endings-as-beginnings. Haydn binds the introduction closely to the main Vivace by bringing back the expressive cadence at the very end of the exposition. Then, after a violently compressed recapitulation, the ambiguous diminished seventh becomes a pivot to remote flat keys, necessitating a long coda that gradually pulls the music back to C major.

Capitalising on the success of No. 94, Haydn writes a variation slow movement that subjects a graceful, instantly appealing melody to dramatic transformations, most spectacularly in the third variation, where the violins create a whining, metallic sonority by playing *al ponticello* (on the bridge). Extraordinary, too, is the coda, with its keening flute and oboe above unquiet string tremolos. Uniquely in these symphonies, the ceremonial minuet and rustic-dance trio both have fully written-out repeats that present their themes in ever new orchestral guises. The trio culminates in a delicious passage, like a transfigured village band, with Salomon ('*solo ma piano*') playing the melody an octave above the orchestral violins. Haydn's public were by now prepared for the inspired theatricality of his sonata-rondo finales. No. 97's adds an aggressive brilliance and harmonic and contrapuntal dexterity of its own, culminating in a coda that comically stutters to a halt before erupting in a final, flamboyant peal of C major.

1793–1795: the second set of 'London' symphonies

No. 99 in E flat
No. 100 in G, 'Military'
No. 101 in D, 'Clock'
No. 102 in B flat
No. 103 in E flat, 'Drumroll'
No. 104 in D, 'London'

When Haydn arrived in London for his second visit on 4 February 1794 he brought with him one newly completed symphony, No. 99, plus two works in progress, Nos. 100 and 101. After No. 99's premiere on 10 February, the *Morning Chronicle* wrote that 'it rouses and affects every emotion of the soul. – It was received with rapturous applause.' For the first time in a symphony Haydn was able to call on clarinets, whose presence is immediately felt in the slow introduction's majestically sonorous opening chord. This is the E flat of the *Zauberflöte* Overture and Beethoven's 'Emperor' Concerto. Then, as the chord dies away, Haydn tellingly exploits the clarinet's deep, chalumeau register as a sustained bass to strings and bassoon. The introduction is Haydn's most harmonically adventurous to date, with an emphasis on mediant, or third-related, keys that will have repercussions later in the symphony. After a dramatic pause on a unison C flat, this note is enharmonically reinterpreted as B natural, heralding a brief excursion to the exotically remote key of E minor; at the end of the introduction Haydn then prepares obliquely rather than directly for the E flat of the Vivace assai, stressing the chords of C minor and its dominant, G major.

Repeated emphasis on the introduction's alien C flat gives a tangy, chromatic flavour to the Vivace assai's sweeping tuttis. But the most striking feature of this densely argued movement is the way the raffish second subject, appearing like a casual afterthought, gradually usurps the musical narrative. After dominating the development, it virtually crowds out the main theme from the recapitulation, generating another of those amazing expansions that led Tovey, rather misleadingly, to equate Haydn's recapitulations with Beethoven's codas.

'The effect of the wind instruments in the second movement was enchanting,' wrote the *Morning Chronicle*, a reference to the beautiful contrapuntal elaboration of the opening theme by flute, oboes and bassoon. If I could take just one Haydn symphony movement to a desert island, it would be No. 99's Adagio, in the third-related key of G major. This is music at once tender and exalted, with a dramatic development and a recapitulation that works the serene second theme to a disturbing climax replete with military-style fanfares. Perhaps, as Robbins Landon has suggested, Haydn composed this Adagio in memory of Maria Anna von Genzinger, who had died in January 1793.

The powerfully symphonic minuet continues the work's 'mediant' tendency by setting its wistful *Ländler* trio in C major, while the finale is a tour de force of kaleidoscopic instrumental colouring (the tootling second theme is a comical mini-concerto for orchestra) and contrapuntal brilliance. The young Beethoven was so impressed with the scintillating fugato at the centre of the movement that he copied it out for study.

In No. 100, premiered on 31 March 1794, Haydn set out to match the sensational success of the 'Surprise' two years earlier. He triumphantly succeeded, thanks to the 'military' effects in the Allegretto second movement, which reworks and enriches a march-like *Romanze* from one of the *lire* concertos for the King of Naples. The C major opening is all pastoral innocence, with picturesque scoring for woodwind, including clarinets, which Haydn omits from the other movements; and even the battery of 'Turkish' instruments (triangle, cymbals and bass drum) that reinforce the C minor central episode is initially more exotic than menacing. But the *éclat terrible* of war gradually infiltrates the music, culminating in a trumpet fanfare that quotes the Austrian General Salute, and a *fortissimo* crash in the remote key of A flat – 'a climax of horrid sublimity', according to the *Morning Chronicle*, and a reminder that in 1794 England was at war with Revolutionary France.

Another reviewer, in the *Allgemeine musikalische Zeitung*, wrote that the symphony was 'rather less learned and easier to take in than some other recent works of his, yet equally rich in new ideas'. One inspired novelty is the 'fairy' scoring for flute and oboes of the Allegro's chirruping first theme, whose outline had been prefigured in the slow introduction. This turns up in the key of the dominant, D major, before Haydn introduces an even catchier melody, the inspiration for Johann Strauss the Elder's famous Radetzky March. Like the equivalent popular-style tune in No. 99, this late-arriving theme then proceeds to hijack the musical argument, through the explosive development (presages here of the Allegretto's 'military' topos) and the truncated recapitulation, to the most flamboyant coda of Haydn's symphonic career.

In a rare instance of negative criticism, an early reviewer found the return of the 'Turkish' battery at the end of the finale 'discordant, grating and offensive'. To modern ears it raucously caps a sonata-form movement of coruscating energy that develops its 'kittenish' (Tovey's word) main theme and a comically sparring second subject with fantastic intricacy. Even today the music's rhythmic and harmonic adventures – which include a mysterious mock fugato in the far-flung key of C sharp minor – still produce a sense of pleasurable shock.

No. 101, completed after the 'Military' but premiered four weeks earlier, on 3 March, also contains a 'characteristic' slow movement that guaranteed the symphony's popular appeal. 'The Clock' was a nickname waiting to happen. Typically, though, the Andante is not all naive horological charm. The tune's dotted rhythms generate an awesome power in the tumultuous G minor central episode, reinforced at the climax by battering horns and trumpets – more 'horrid sublimity' here. When G major tranquillity returns, Haydn wittily reassigns the pendulum's ticking to flute and bassoon, above and below the violin melody, and then, after a bar's rest, dips to the unscripted key of E flat major.

'Nothing can be more original than the subject of the first movement', enthused the *Morning Chronicle* after No. 101's premiere; 'and having found a happy subject, no man knows like HAYDN how to produce incessant variety without once departing from it.' As usual in the 'London' symphonies, the motivic seeds are sown in the slow introduction, which prefigures the 6/8 Presto's 'happy' (and pointedly irregular) subject in a veiled D minor. Again, though, it is the second subject – a playful, sinuous tune, closely derived from the first – that controls the plot, both in the development and in another of Haydn's unpredictable, expanding recapitulations.

Such is the symphonic weight and grandeur of the minuet, the longest in any Haydn symphony, that it comes as a surprise to learn that it was originally composed for mechanical organ. The trio's pointedly naive flute solo is accompanied by a notorious 'wrong harmony' joke which the strings then put right on the repeat. Nineteenth-century editors with a musical humour bypass thought the joke must be a misprint and duly 'corrected' it. Haydn may have intended the mellow opening theme of the finale, beginning with a decorated rising scale, to link back to the first movement, though the connection is more evident to the eye than in performance. More crucially, this is one of the most powerful finales in the whole set, a sonata rondo at once intensely concentrated (much of the action is fuelled by its first three notes) and gloriously free in design. As Robbins Landon put it, here is a movement 'with everything in it', from a ferocious episode in D minor, the key of the symphony's slow introduction, via a shimmering *pianissimo* fugato that Mendelssohn surely remembered in his Octet, to a final, 'sunset' reminiscence of the theme.

At the end of the 1794 season Salomon was forced to suspend his concerts because the war with Revolutionary France was making it increasingly difficult to engage 'vocal performers of the first talents from abroad'. For the time being he merged with the new Opera Concert under the direction of violinist-composer Giovanni Battista Viotti at the King's Theatre Haymarket. Haydn agreed to write three more symphonies for Viotti's 1795 concert series, the first of which, No. 102 in B flat, was premiered on 2 February. This was the concert where a great chandelier crashed to the floor, though since the audience in the parterre had crowded forward to see Haydn at close range, no one suffered more than minor bruises. According to Dies, 'Many people showed their state of mind by shouting loudly: "miracle, miracle!"' The nickname stuck, and still sticks, to the wrong symphony, No. 96.

In the second set of 'London' symphonies, Haydn's arguments become even more intricate and engrossing. And the first movement of No. 102 – like No. 99, a favourite work of Haydn aficionados – is arguably the most challenging of all. It begins with a rarefied slow introduction whose initial five-note phrase (following a long-held unison B flat) will play a crucial role in the main Vivace. From its explosive opening, this is Haydn at his most truculent and Beethovenian. The drive and intensity of the music, peppered with violent offbeat accents, never abate; and even the main theme of the second group, heralded by a disruptive unison, is tense and restless where Haydn's audience had come to expect a popular-style tune. The development ratchets up the tension even further: first in a rebarbative three-part canon, then, after a solo flute optimistically proposes the main theme in the alien key of C major, in a stupendous *fortissimo* build-up to the recapitulation.

Haydn follows this high-pressure symphonic drama with one of his loveliest meditations, an arrangement of the rhapsodic Adagio from his recent Piano Trio in F sharp minor. It is just possible that the symphony movement came first, though the evidence of the autograph, and the music's delicately ornamental style – typical of his late keyboard slow movements – point the other way. When the exposition is repeated, Haydn rescores it with almost impressionistic subtlety, enhancing its misty colourings with muted trumpets and muffled drums. This was surely a movement in Rimsky-Korsakov's mind when he pronounced Haydn the greatest of all orchestrators. The stomping minuet restores us to a world of robust normality, making bellicose play with a three-note figure that invades all sections of the orchestra. Haydn spices the inspired comic antics of the finale with a streak of cussedness that brings it into line with the opening Vivace. An early reviewer commented admiringly on the lightning tonal shifts within the main theme. This is another movement that influenced Beethoven, not least the coda, where the main theme disintegrates and stammers to a halt before the madcap final send-off – an idea Haydn's erstwhile pupil took up in the finale of his own B flat symphony, No. 4.

'The introduction excited deepest attention,' wrote the *Morning Chronicle* after No. 103's premiere on 2 March, as Haydn surely calculated it would. With its initial drumroll and its sepulchral theme in the bowels of the orchestra that evokes the *Dies irae* chant, this is the most mysterious, ominous symphonic opening before Schubert's 'Unfinished' and Beethoven's Ninth. Haydn then proceeds to integrate the introduction systematically into the 6/8 Allegro con spirito. A fragment of the *Dies irae* theme flits by, speeded up and transmuted into a blithe dance, just before the *Ländler*-ish second subject. At the heart of the development, after a grand pause, it makes a more theatrical appearance in its original deep bass register, like a spectre at the feast. Then, near the end of the movement, a series of seismic orchestral shocks heralds another dramatic pause and a return of the lugubrious introduction, complete with drumroll, in its original Adagio tempo. This is finally banished in a peal of laughter, courtesy of the *Dies irae* theme in its dance transformation: at once a gleeful parody and a reinforcement of the symbiotic link between introduction and Allegro. Haydn probably got the idea of bringing back the slow introduction at the end from Mozart's String Quintet, K593, which he had played with the composer in December 1790. Beethoven was to follow suit, most famously in the 'Pathétique' Sonata, but also in the E flat Piano Trio, Op. 70 No. 2, a work that pays tribute to the 'Drumroll' Symphony on several levels, including the use of double variation form, with one theme in the minor, the other in the major, in its second movement.

In the 'Drumroll' variations, both the C minor melody and its C major relative are Croatian folk melodies. Haydn gave the C major tune a more exotic gypsy flavour by raising its F naturals to F sharps, in the process aligning it more closely with the C minor tune. After the second major-key variation, beginning as delectable 'toy soldier' music and ending as an imperious march, a nostalgic reminiscence of the C major theme suggests a final *envoi*. Haydn, though, slews round into E flat – a reminder of the main key of the symphony – for a dramatic, modulating coda that draws new shades of meaning from the C major tune.

The minuet, with its yodelling 'Scotch snaps' (wonderfully transformed when the second section dips to a secretive G flat major), encloses a particularly beguiling trio, with liquid arabesques for clarinets doubled by violins. Like the last movement of Mozart's 'Jupiter', the finale is designed as a true symphonic apotheosis. This is one of Haydn's supreme monothematic triumphs, a thrilling and decidedly un-comic movement that generates all its harmonic and contrapuntal drama from a traditional horn call and a snatch of Croatian folk song.

Haydn's last symphony, No. 104, was premiered at his benefit concert on 4 May 1795. The response, as usual, was ecstatic. The *Morning Chronicle* wrote that 'for fullness, richness, and majesty in all its parts, [the Symphony] is thought by some of the best judges to surpass all his other compositions'. Whether or not Haydn intended No. 104 as his symphonic testament, its mingled grandeur and earthy vigour, argumentative power and visionary poetry make it a glorious final summation. If there is one symphony that encapsulates the essence of Haydn, this is it.

No one can say for sure why this, of all the last twelve symphonies, has attracted the nickname 'London'. One possible explanation is that the main theme of the finale reminded listeners of a London street cry to the words 'Live cod!' or 'Hot cross buns!' The slow introduction of the 'Drumroll' might have seemed an impossible act to follow. Yet No. 104's D minor opening fully equals it in mystery, evoking vast, strange expanses within its two-minute time frame. The Allegro resolves minor into major with a heart-easing melody, quintessentially Haydnesque in its blend of affability and sublimity.

This tune returns, varied, as a 'second subject'; and there is another delightful variation, airily scored for flute and oboes, at the beginning of the recapitulation. The development is the most powerful and rigorous in all Haydn's symphonies, worrying obsessively at a six-note fragment of the theme and building inexorably to a climax of white-hot intensity.

The G major slow movement is the consummation of Haydn's ostensibly easy-going symphonic Andantes. Its tranquil opening, as so often, is deceptive. The second half of the melody expands with an unsuspected breadth and profundity, while the ferocity of the G minor central episode eclipses even the comparable outburst in the 'Clock'. But the apotheosis comes after the varied reprise of the opening tune, where the music floats towards unearthly tonal regions before slipping gently back to the home key.

The minuet is one of the most boisterous (it is tempting to add 'Beethovenian') in these late symphonies, trading on aggressive offbeat accents and rude dynamic contrasts. There is a typical Haydnesque joke when the laughing trill that ends the first half later breaks off for two bars of silence and then re-enters in a conspiratorial *piano*. After all this fooling Haydn begins the idyllic trio with a more subtle joke, feinting at D minor before opting for a more remote key, B flat major. The finale's main theme, announced over a rustic drone, may have evoked 'Live cod!' to early London audiences. But its origin has also been traced to a Croatian folk tune. To set off the swashbuckling energy there is a yearning second theme in sustained notes, of a kind unique in Haydn's finales. This melody reappears near the end of the development, where it seems to become hypnotised. Then, with a breathtaking harmonic sideslip, the recapitulation takes us unawares – perhaps the subtlest transition in all Haydn, at once witty and poignant. True to form, the composer continues to exploit the rich potential of the opening folk tune, right through to an incandescent coda which Brahms was to remember in the finale of his own D major symphony, No. 2.

Concertos

Haydn wrote some forty concertos, many of them lost, for instruments ranging from the flute and oboe to the baryton, bassoon and violone. Yet the concerto never played the central role in his creative life that it did in Mozart's. One obvious reason is that, although more than competent on the keyboard and the violin, he was by his own admission 'no wizard on any instrument', and except for the early organ concertos he did not write concertos specifically for his own use. Another is that from around 1750, the symphony gradually usurped the concerto in popularity and prestige in the Austro-Hungarian lands – a situation briefly, and locally, challenged with the great series of piano concertos Mozart wrote in his Viennese heyday between 1782 and 1786.

In any case, Haydn's characteristic strengths – concision, tight thematic unity, intensive dialectical argument – found only limited scope in the concerto genre, at least until the D major Keyboard Concerto (*c.*1780) and the Trumpet Concerto of 1796. In the 1750s and 1760s, when he wrote most of his works in the form, concerto first movements were, typically, ungainly affairs, with their ponderous ritornello structures, old-fashioned Baroque sequences and reams of freewheeling virtuosity. Haydn's early concertos, essentially modelled on those of Wagenseil and the Venetian Baldassare Galuppi, often share this diffuseness, though one or two succeed in injecting the form with something of the dynamic energy of his contemporary symphonies. It was Mozart's achievement two decades later to bring the Classical concerto to its apogee, integrating soloist and orchestra in a comprehensive symphonic design, and manipulating his vocally inspired themes like characters in an opera.

Keyboard concertos

Organ concertos

Haydn's earliest concertos are the six cheery works he composed for organ in Vienna in the mid-1750s. Two of his reliable sources of income at this time were leading the orchestra in the church of the Barmherzige Brüder and playing the organ in the chapel of Count Haugwitz in the Bohemian Court Chancellery. Haydn probably wrote his organ concertos for these establishments, performing them between the Sanctus and Benedictus sections of the mass. Churchgoers in Maria Theresa's Austria liked their Sunday services as long and as jolly as possible.

All the concertos were conceived for a so-called *Positiv* organ, without pedals and with an upper range limited to C above the treble clef; and, as early sources confirm, they were designed to be equally playable on the harpsichord. Three of them, all in C major (Hob. XVIII: 5, 8, and 10), cannot be authenticated, though the balance of evidence suggests they are by Haydn. XVIII: 10 is probably the best, certainly the least prolix. The F major, Hob. XVIII: 7, is almost certainly spurious.

Haydn entered the D major concerto, XVIII: 2, in his *Entwurf-Katalog* around 1766, though it must be from at least a decade earlier. The first movement, as in so many concertos of this period, unalluringly combines short-breathed early Classical phrasing and rambling Baroque sequences. One of the organ concertos, XVIII: 6 in F, also includes a modest obbligato part for violin. After the amiable trickle of the first two movements, the finale features some spirited raillery for the two soloists.

Most popular of the concertos is the C major, XVIII: 1, composed in 1756, perhaps for the ceremony in which Haydn's first love Therese Keller took the veil. The autograph score obviously had sentimental value for the composer, who preserved it to the end of his life. There is, though, no hint of regret in the music, whose festive spirit is enhanced in some contemporary sources by trumpets and drums. The

most memorable – and least discursive – movement is the last,
a jolly jig in the style of Haydn's early symphony finales.

Harpsichord concertos

Apart from a clutch of featherweight concertinos and divertimenti for harpsichord and strings from the late 1750s and
early 1760s (Hob. XIV: 1, 3–4, 7–11; XIV: 2, with an additional part for baryton, is lost), only three of the many harpsichord concertos attributed to Haydn are authentic. Two, both
scored for strings only, probably date from the late 1760s: the
F major, Hob. XVIII: 3, and the G major, Hob. XVIII: 4,
which may have been composed for the blind pianist Maria
Theresa von Paradis, for whom Mozart wrote his B flat concerto, K456, in 1784. That same year Paradis introduced
Haydn's G major concerto to Paris. Both the F major and the
G major sound old-fashioned alongside Haydn's contemporary symphonies, though their first movements are more harmonically venturesome than the earlier concertos, and the
aria slow movements have a touching purity. Typically, the
finales are the most appealing, especially the one in the G
major, a popular-style contredanse with a faint gypsy tang.

Though its main tune has been identified as a dance from
Bosnia or Croatia, the *Rondo all'Ungarese* of Haydn's last keyboard concerto, in D major, Hob: XVIII: 11, mines this
Tokay-flavoured Hungarian gypsy style with unprecedented
bravado. Written around 1780 'for the harpsichord or fortepiano', with an orchestra of oboes, horns and strings, this
compact work became by far Haydn's best-known concerto in
his lifetime. Here, for the first time, he infuses the Baroque-
derived ritornello design with the dynamic, dramatic spirit of
sonata form, as Mozart had already done in his 'Jeunehomme'
Concerto, K271, of 1777. Except in the exotic finale, Haydn
does not work with Mozart's profusion of themes. But the
opening Vivace has just enough melodic contrast to offset the
crisp, clear-cut main theme that galvanises the whole movement. In the rhapsodically ornamented Adagio, which cries

out for the dynamic shadings possible on the fortepiano, Haydn draws the tenderest poetry from the simplest material. The central episode expands a little triplet figure heard near the start of the movement into an exquisite modulating dialogue between keyboard and strings.

String concertos

Violin concertos

Of Haydn's four violin concertos, dating from the late 1750s and 1760s, one, in D major (Hob. VIIa: 2) is lost. The others are all slender pieces of modest charm. Slenderest of all is the G major, Hob. VIIa: 4, probably the earliest and by far the easiest technically. Robbins Landon has proposed that it may have been intended for the leader of Count Morzin's orchestra, or for one of Fürnberg's music parties. The relatively familiar C major concerto, Hob. VIIa: 1, was composed some time in the early 1760s for Esterházy concertmaster Luigi Tomasini. The first movement, as so often in these early concertos, meanders and frolics to no great purpose; the Adagio is a guileless serenade, fashioned to display Tomasini's sweet tone; while the finale puts his virtuoso technique through its paces with vertiginous leaps, rapid spiccato bowing, double-stopping and flashy *brisé* arpeggios.

The A major, Hob. VIIa: 3, sometimes known as the 'Melk' concerto, may also have been written for Tomasini. The first movement goes through the same motions as the C major, at more tedious length, and the Adagio is humdrum. The exhilarating finale, though, is one of the best in these early concertos, enlivened by some wiry contrapuntal writing and quickfire exchanges between violin and orchestra.

Cello concertos

Among these early concertos, the C major Cello Concerto, Hob. VIIb: 1, stands out for its freshness and vigour. Haydn composed it some time between 1761 and 1765, probably (that word again) for his close friend Joseph Weigl, virtuoso principal cellist in the Esterházy orchestra. Though now one of his most popular works, the concerto was presumed lost until a set of manuscript parts – the sole surviving source – was discovered in Prague in 1962. The noble, sturdy opening Moderato, with its purposeful central 'development', has none of the longueurs of comparable movements in the other early concertos. In the courtly Adagio, the cellist appropriates a typical vocal technique known as *messa di voce*, in which singers would display their breath control and 'taste' with a long-held note that slowly swells and ebbs. Haydn uses this same gambit, now with gleeful exuberance, in the finale. Virtually a moto perpetuo, this headlong movement showcases Weigl's virtuosity with dizzying pyrotechnics that make comic capital from quickfire changes of register.

The equally famous D major Cello Concerto also has a che-quered history. Haydn composed it in 1783 for Esterházy court cellist Anton Kraft. After the composer's death the auto-graph disappeared for over a century, leading many to suspect that the concerto was in fact by Kraft. This myth was demol-ished only when Haydn's autograph turned up in 1951. The work's popularity with cellists and audiences is not matched by its reputation among scholars. They have a point. For a Haydn work of this date (compare the bright-eyed D major key-board concerto), the first movement is uncharacteristically static and discursive, and its cello acrobatics (on which Kraft may have collaborated) tend to sound fussy and vapid. But the Adagio is a lovely piece of tranquil lyricism. The 6/8 rondo, too, is attractive 'easy listening'. As Tovey pointed out, the main theme sounds like the folk song 'Here we go gathering nuts in May', while the long central episode introduces a perky little tune with a distinct whiff of Sullivan.

Wind and brass concertos

Haydn's concertos for wind and brass have suffered a particu-larly high casualty rate, with works for flute, bassoon, horn and two horns lost. Three other concertos, long ascribed to Haydn and still occasionally aired, are spurious: an oboe concerto, grandly scored with trumpets and drums; a horn concerto (Haydn's 'No. 2') with a gently plaintive slow movement in the minor key; and an instantly forgettable flute concerto, now known to be the work of Leopold Hofmann.

Horn Concerto in D, Hob. VIId: 3

We cannot be sure for whom Haydn wrote this lively and fetching concerto dated 1762. But Robbins Landon has suggested that it was a present for Joseph Leutgeb (1732–1811), the future recipient of Mozart's horn concertos (and the butt of his most dotty humour), on the birth of his daughter, to whom Haydn's wife was godmother. For the first time in his concertos Haydn composed a brisk Allegro first movement; and while there are no tunes worth the name, the music is spirited and attractive, with none of the otiose triplet sequences that dog most of the other concertos. Here and in the dashing sonata-form finale, with its comically spluttering repeated notes, Haydn exploits Leutgeb's famed virtuosity over the instrument's whole range, including his expertise in 'hand-stopping'. In the lovely Adagio Haydn pays tribute to the cantabile eloquence of Leutgeb's playing, if the concerto was indeed composed for him. While finishing the work, perhaps in the early hours, Haydn mixed up the oboe and violin staves. He corrected his mistake with the wry comment '*In Schlaff geschrieben*' – written in my sleep.

Trumpet Concerto in E flat, Hob. VIIe: 1

Haydn composed his last and best-loved concerto in 1796 for his friend, the Viennese court trumpeter Anton Weidinger. Weidinger had recently evolved a new *Klappentrompete* (keyed trumpet), which could play chromatic notes throughout its range, though its tone was softer than the natural valveless trumpet (contemporary writers likened it to an oboe) and there was a marked difference between the quality of different individual notes. It took several more years for Weidinger to develop the instrument to his satisfaction; and it was not until March 1800 that he finally premiered both his new invention and Haydn's concerto in Vienna's Burgtheater.

Haydn seized on the opportunities offered by Weidinger's new (and, as it turned out, short-lived) instrument and wrote a work that vastly expands the trumpet's expressive range. Traditional martial brilliance is not neglected. But much of the concerto, scored for large orchestra, with trumpets and drums, is mellow, even veiled in colouring, exactly the opposite of what an eighteenth-century audience might have expected from the trumpet. The first movement, with its delicate interplay between soloist and orchestra, immediately establishes the autumnal mood. At its centre, just before the recapitulation, is a haunting passage of hushed expectancy, with the trumpet descending to its lowest register beneath a series of brooding chromatic phrases in the orchestra. The tender siciliano-style Andante, in the outré key (for the trumpet) of A flat, is a simple three-part structure, with a middle section that dips mysteriously to C flat major. Even in the extrovert sonata-rondo finale Haydn offsets the trumpet's flamboyant sallies with closely woven contrapuntal textures and moments of reflective poetry, above all in the soft chromatic harmonisation of the theme near the close.

Sinfonia Concertante in B flat, Hob. 1: 105

'A new concertante from Haydn combined with all the excellencies of music; it was profound, airy, affecting and original, and the performance was in unison with the merit of the composition. Salomon particularly exerted himself on this occasion, in doing justice to the music of his friend HAYDN.' So wrote the *Morning Herald* after the premiere of the *Sinfonia Concertante* for violin (a starring role for Salomon), oboe, cello and bassoon on 9 March 1792. Haydn composed the work in a spirit of rivalry with the Professional Concert directed by Ignaz Pleyel, a hugely successful composer of *sinfonie concertanti* both in France and England. Needless to say, Haydn outdid Pleyel at his own game. This tuneful and urbanely inventive multiple concerto uses the four solo instruments in ever-changing permutations: the wind pair pitted against the strings, the two higher instruments against the two lower, violin and bassoon against oboe and cello (as at the beginning of the slow movement), or simply as a quartet of contrasting timbres.

The gracious first movement has a particularly inspired development, initiated by the main theme in the shadowy key of D flat major and evolving into a beautiful contrapuntal dialogue. The Andante, in Haydn's favourite 6/8 pastoral metre, is a piece of relaxed chamber music for the soloists, briefly interrupted by an unexpected appearance of the main theme in the orchestra. Delighting in 'sudden surprises of abrupt rests', as the *Oracle* put it, and mock-portentous recitatives for Salomon, the finale matches those of the first six 'London' symphonies in ebullience and contrapuntal resource.

The Seven Last Words of Our Saviour on the Cross

It was probably the success of Haydn's *Stabat mater* in Spain that led to a request from Cádiz in 1785 or 1786 for a series of orchestral reflections on The Seven Last Words of Christ, as recorded in the gospels of Matthew, Luke and John. The composer himself left a famous account of the work's origin in the preface to the choral version, published in 1801.

> About fifteen years ago I was asked by a canon of Cádiz to compose instrumental music on The Seven Last Words of Our Saviour on the Cross. It was customary at Cádiz Cathedral to produce an oratorio every year during Lent, the effect of the performance being greatly enhanced by the following circumstances. The walls, windows and pillars of the church were hung with black cloth, and only one large lamp hanging from the centre of the roof broke the solemn darkness. At midday the doors were closed and the ceremony began. After a short service the bishop ascended the pulpit, pronounced the first of the seven words (or sentences) and delivered a discourse on it. When this had finished he left the pulpit and prostrated himself before the altar. The interval was filled by music. The bishop then in similar manner pronounced the second word, then the third, and so on, the orchestra following on the conclusion of each discourse. My composition was subject to these conditions, and it was no easy task to compose seven adagios lasting ten minutes each, one after the other, without tiring the listeners; indeed, I found it quite impossible to keep to the prescribed duration.

Haydn finished *The Seven Last Words* in time for performances during Lent 1787, both in Cádiz (though probably in the Grotto San Cueva rather than the cathedral) and at the

Schlosskirche in Vienna, and the same year he made an arrangement of the piece for string quartet. (He also authorised a keyboard arrangement.) Haydn pronounced it one of his most successful works, writing to the publisher William Forster (8 April 1787) that the music was 'of a kind to arouse the deepest impression on the soul of even the most naive person'. He performed the orchestral and quartet versions during his visits to England, where Charles Burney deemed the work 'perhaps the most sublime composition without words to point out its meaning that has ever been composed'. In 1794 or 1795, stopping in Passau on his journey to or from London (reports are contradictory), Haydn heard a choral arrangement of *The Seven Last Words* by the local Kapellmeister and felt that he could have done the thing better. He proved his point the following year (see p. 284).

Eschewing naively explicit descriptive writing, Haydn avoids any danger of monotony in a sequence of sonata-form slow movements through carefully planned contrasts of tonality, texture and orchestral colour. At the same time he binds them together by recurrent rhythmic and melodic figures, especially the falling thirds, symbolising supplication or resignation, that saturate the first, third, fifth and sixth Words.

The D minor *Introduzione*, with its pervasive dotted rhythms (another of the work's unifying features), graphically evokes the pity and anguish of the scene, transmuting its implacable opening into a tender 'second subject'. There is another telling thematic transformation in the second Word, where the C minor funeral march (reminiscent of the mourning chorus that opens Gluck's *Orfeo*) turns to E flat major for a vision of Paradise. ('He lifts us suddenly from the vale of tears into the Elysian Fields,' was Dies's description.) The doubling of the violins by a solo cello an octave lower is one of many inspired touches of orchestration that are inevitably lost in the quartet arrangement. No. 3, 'Mother, behold thy son', in the luminous key of E major and coloured by the lambent sonority of a single flute, mingles gentle lyricism with an almost mystic ecstasy. The majestic progression to a remote key in the recapitulation is paralleled by equally awesome distant modulations in the fourth and fifth Words.

Haydn calculated his sequence of tonalities for maximum dramatic contrast. And the F minor opening of No. 4, 'My God, my God, why hast thou forsaken me?', sounds all the more stark after the quiet E major close of No. 3. Reflecting the despair of the biblical text, this is music of shocking dissonant harshness; there is also a graphic sense of abandonment in the mournful unaccompanied violin figures. The fifth Word ('I thirst'), in A major, contrasts a lone oboe solo above 'desiccated' pizzicato strings (another beautiful effect lost in the quartet version) with violent, jagged music for full orchestra.

The catharsis comes with No. 6, 'It is finished', in G minor. Haydn makes inspired use of the opening 'motto', based on descending thirds: as an underlay to the consolatory B flat melody – one of the work's most sublime moments – and as the mainspring of the central development. After a climax of excruciating intensity the development elides with the recapitulation, which slips almost at once to G major; and the movement ends in a spirit of hope and reconciliation. The final Word, 'Father, into thy hands I commend my spirit', in the warm key of E flat, consolidates this newly won acceptance with the most serenely diatonic music in the work. Towards the end the textures grow more fragmentary, culminating in a haunting evocation of ebbing life. The mood is then shattered by the final earthquake (*Il terremoto*), marked *Presto e con tutta la forza* (with, for the first time, trumpets and timpani) and depicting in a series of savage orchestral shocks how 'the earth did quake; the rocks were rent; the graves opened'.

Dances and marches

Haydn's occasional dance music, most of it virtually unknown, ranges from the so-called 'Seitenstetten' minuets of the 1750s, probably composed for balls at the Viennese Imperial Court, via two sets of minuets from the 1770s and 1780s, to the orchestrally splendid minuets and *Deutsche* of the 1790s. In the autumn of 1792 Haydn composed, without fee, twelve minuets (Hob. IX: 11) and twelve *Deutsche Tänze* (Hob. IX: 12) for a charity masked ball of the Gesellschaft bildender Künstler at the Redoutensaal in Vienna. (The *Deutsche*, or German dance, was a bucolic cousin of the minuet, and a prototype of the waltz. The social distinctions are graphically illustrated in the famous 'multi-dance' scene in *Don Giovanni*, where Donna Anna and Don Ottavio dance a minuet while Leporello and Masetto lurch through a *Deutsche*.) Like Mozart's late dance music for the Redoutensaal, these dances pack a surprising variety of colour and expression into their brief, formalised spans. The wind writing, especially in the trio sections of the minuets, matches that of the first set of 'London' symphonies in charm and sophistication, though the Redoutensaal dances also include clarinets (there is a beguiling clarinet solo in the trio of minuet No. 11) and, in the trio of No. 7, a piccolo.

Even more colourfully scored are the twenty-four minuets Hob. IX: 16, composed, we may guess, in 1795 or 1796 (only a set of undated manuscript parts survives). One pointer to their late date is that the clarinet writing is more adventurous than in the Redoutensaal dances: the delicious duet in the trio of No. 9, with the second clarinet gurgling in its chalumeau register, recalls Mozart's writing for the instrument, and may even have been composed for Anton Stadler (recipient of Mozart's quintet and concerto) and his brother Johann. Throughout the set Haydn specialises in extreme contrasts between minuets and their trios. No. 12 in G, for instance, sets its exquisitely bred outer sections against a battering *fortissimo* G minor trio; the A minor trio of No. 19 is in the fashionable 'Turkish' style, with piccolo and optional assorted percussion, while No. 22 juxtaposes a splenetic D minor minuet and the most dulcet of major-key trios.

We can assume that Haydn provided several marches for Prince Nicolaus Esterházy's private regimental band of clarinets, bassoons and horns, though only one, Hob. VIII: 6, survives. Marches are not normally noted for their subtlety. But in 1792 Haydn wrote the remarkably unbellicose 'March for the Prince of Wales', Hob. VIII: 3, scored with fastidious refinement for trumpet, clarinets, bassoons, horns and serpent. The delicate use of trumpet and horns in the trio is especially striking. In 1795, with England now at war with France, he composed two brief, stirring marches, Hob. VIII: 1–2, for the Derbyshire Voluntary Cavalry, raised at the behest of Sir Henry Harpur, Sheriff of Derbyshire. Haydn's last march, and the last instrumental work he completed, is the Hungarian National March, Hob. VIII: 4, written in the autumn of 1802 for the Esterházy wind band of oboes, clarinets, bassoons and horns, with the addition of a trumpet. Orchestrated with all the old composer's panache, the music has a splendid abrasive swagger, spiced by touches of Hungarian gypsy colour.

Other orchestral works

The so-called Scherzandi, Hob. II: 33–8, probably composed in the early 1760s, are in effect miniature lightweight symphonies for oboes, horns and strings (minus violas). Their first movements and the tiny jig-like finales have all the young Haydn's teeming high spirits. The slow movements, all but one in the minor key, are pleasantly melancholy serenades, while the minuets infuse the aristocratic dance with a dash of rustic vigour, and feature a capering flute solo in each of their trios.

In 1786 Artaria published six of Haydn's opera overtures, adapted for concert use. Another overture, a bristling D major movement, Hob. Ia: 7, probably derives from a lost marionette opera. It was twice recycled, as finale 'B' of Symphony No. 53, and as the first movement of Symphony No. 62. A laconic entry in Haydn's London catalogue, 'Overtura Conventgarden', evidently refers to the overture he provided for Salomon's 'grand masque' *Windsor Castle*, performed at Covent Garden in April 1795 in celebration of the wedding of the Prince of Wales and Princess of Brunswick. While the work in question may just have been lost, it is probable that this was the belated first outing of the overture to Haydn's unperformed London opera *L'anima del filosofo*, consisting of a portentous C minor Largo and a wiry, monothematic C major Presto. Reviewing the performance of *Windsor Castle*, *The Oracle* noted that the overture 'bespoke the style and fancy of HAYDN in notes, which no other genius could ever so combine'.

Early chamber music

Divertimenti for strings and/or wind

Late in life Haydn told his biographers how, as a young man, he and his friends would often perform his works 'gassatim' (i.e., in street serenade parties) in Vienna. He specifically remembered writing a string quintet for this purpose in 1753. The piece in question may well have been the G major Divertimento, or Cassation (the word derives from 'gassatim'), for two violins, two violas and double bass, Hob. II: 2 (for obvious reasons the cello was ill suited to peripatetic alfresco serenades). With its cheeky, quick-witted fast movements and its pair of sturdy minuets enfolding an aria-like Adagio, this delightful six-movement work – perhaps Haydn's first surviving instrumental composition – is far more individual than his early keyboard music. There are occasional 'grammatical errors' of part-writing. But in style and spirit the quintet is close to the divertimenti for string quartet of Opp. 1 and 2.

Between the early 1750s and his Esterházy appointment in 1761 Haydn composed some twenty-five pieces (several of them lost), variously titled 'Divertimento', 'Cassation' or 'Parthia', for wind band or wind and strings. We can guess that most of the pieces for mixed ensemble were intended for alfresco performance in the streets and courtyards of Vienna. Like the earliest string quartets, these artless works are usually in five short movements, with two minuets. In several Haydn deploys unusual instrumental forces. Hob. II: 16 in F major, for instance, calls for the rare (unique?) combination of two cors anglais, two horns, two violins and bassoons. Hob. II: 11, one of two cassations for flute, oboe, two violins, cello (seating was evidently available) and double bass, was evidently prompted by a birthday celebration and duly nicknamed 'Der Geburtstag'. The work was made popular by its slow movement, a set of variations on a rather gruff tune entitled 'Mann und Weib' (Man and Wife) that sounds like a folk song and may actually be one.

Around 1759–60 Haydn wrote a clutch of 'parthias', or 'Feld-partien', for the standard wind sextet of oboes, horns and bassoons, perhaps as dinner entertainment (*Tafelmusik*) at Count Morzin's Bohemian summer palace (the F major Parthia, Hob. II: 15, bears the autograph date 1760). These cheery wind-band pieces tend to be even briefer than those for mixed ensemble. Their prime interest comes from Haydn's deftly varied sonorities, and his colourful exploitation of the Bohemian horns, famed throughout Europe for their virtuosity.

At the Esterházy court Haydn was rarely called upon to provide alfresco music for the prince's wind band. During the early 1760s he composed four divertimenti with parts for clarinets, only one of which, for pairs of clarinets and horns (Hob. II: 14), survives. Haydn may have intended this work for a Polish count and dilettante clarinettist, Michael Casimir Oginski, and his travelling companion. He would barely use clarinets again until the London period. Most entertaining of all these works is the Cassation in D for four horns, violin, viola and bass, Hob. II: D22, dating from either 1763 or 1765, when a quartet of horns was temporarily available in Eisenstadt. In the trios of the two minuets, especially, the horn writing has the flamboyant swagger of the contemporary 'four-horn' symphonies, Nos. 72 and 31.

String duos and trios

Among nearly eighty string trios attributed to Haydn, twenty-one (Hob. V: 1–21) have been authenticated (three of these are lost), and a further dozen or so may be genuine. Trios for two violins and either violone or cello were popular in Austria years before the string quartet came into vogue; and Haydn's first trios may date from as early as 1752–3, before his Op. 1 and Op. 2 String Quartets. According to the less than reliable

Carpani, Haydn's early patron Baron Fürnberg was so delighted by daily performances of his string trios that he asked the young composer to go one better and write a *quartetto*. Whatever the circumstances that prompted this series of trios, we can guess that Haydn, who by his own testimony 'could play a concerto on the violin', would often have taken one of the violin parts himself.

All but two of the trios (Nos. 7 and 11) are in three movements. Many begin with an Adagio, and most have a minuet in second or third place, as in many of the early keyboard divertimenti. While the first violin parts are often florid, the second violin and, especially, the bass instrument usually do little more than provide harmonic support, with a consequent monotony of texture. There are spasmodic exceptions, above all in some of the minor-key trios of the minuets: the one in No. 15, for instance, unfolds as an imitative dialogue between the three instruments. James Webster, in *The New Grove Haydn*, has called the trios 'works for connoisseurs, in "high style", difficult for player and listener alike'. They are essentially 'private' music: sober, carefully wrought, with little of the popular melodic appeal of Haydn's early symphonies and quartets. Like the equally private baryton trios, they can strike the modern listener as arid, though there are some fetching movements threaded through them, including (to pick just two at random) the coltish Scherzo that opens No. 6, and the gracefully gliding siciliano in No. 21.

Monotony of texture also afflicts the violin and viola duos, Hob. VI: 1–6, composed around 1766–8, probably for Tomasini. As their original designation as '6 Violin Solo mit Begleitung einer Viola' indicates, these are violin sonatas rather than democratic partnerships in the manner of Mozart's duos for violin and viola, K423 and K424. Routinely accompanied violin melody is the norm. Except for No. 3, which opens with variations on a homely Andante theme, the first movements are in the ornate, leisurely style found, on a higher creative level, in the slightly later Op. 9 String Quartets. All the finales are minuets with perfunctory decorative variations.

The slow movements, four of them in the minor mode, leave a more enduring impression, especially the Adagio of No. 4, whose grave, processional tread and touches of contrapuntal imitation – rare in these duos – give it a distinctly Baroque flavour.

String quartets

String Quartet in E flat, Op. 0
String Quartet in B flat, Op. 1 No. 1, 'La chasse'
String Quartet in E flat, Op. 1 No. 2
String Quartet in D, Op. 1 No. 3
String Quartet in G, Op. 1 No. 4
String Quartet in C, Op. 1 No. 6
String Quartet in A, Op. 2 No. 1
String Quartet in E, Op. 2 No. 2
String Quartet in F, Op. 2 No. 4
String Quartet in B flat, Op. 2 No. 6

If the nineteenth-century notion of Haydn as 'the father of the symphony' needs serious qualification, his status as the father of the string quartet remains unchallenged. Not that he composed the first quartet of all. Before Haydn alighted on the genre, there had been spasmodic examples of divertimenti for two solo violins, viola and cello by Viennese composers such as Wagenseil and Holzbauer; and there had long existed a tradition of performing orchestral works with one instrument to a part. But these older composers showed no interest in exploring the potential of the string quartet as a medium. It fell to Haydn who, by his own admission, stumbled on the form 'by accident', to raise the string quartet from its humble beginnings in the outdoor serenade to a vehicle for the most sophisticated and challenging musical discourse.

Griesinger describes the circumstances that led him to try his hand at quartets.

A Baron Fürnberg had an estate in Weinzierl, several staging posts from Vienna; and from time to time he invited his parish priest, his estates manager, Haydn and Albrechtsberger, brother of the famous contrapuntist, in order to have a little music. Fürnberg asked Haydn to write something for these four friends of the art. Haydn, who was then eighteen years old, accepted this proposal, and originated his first quartet, which was praised immediately after its appearance. This encouraged him to produce more works in this field.

Griesinger, relying on Haydn's memory nearly half a century after the event, almost certainly got the date wrong: Fürnberg's quartet parties on his summer estate at Weinzierl, near Melk, probably took place some time between *c.*1754, when Haydn was twenty-two, and 1757. One or two of the early string quartets – the works bundled together in the mid-1760s and published as Op. 1 and Op. 2, plus the E flat quartet known as Op. 0, which went missing until the 1930s – may even have been written after Haydn's Esterházy appointment.

'The less said about the early "divertimento" quartets the better', was agent provocateur Hans Keller's sweeping dismissal in *The Great Haydn Quartets* of the ten works of Opp. 0, 1 and 2 (Op. 1 No. 5 and Op. 2 Nos. 3 and 5 are not quartets at all, but adapted from works for larger ensemble). Others may feel that these little *divertimenti a quattro*, as the composer dubbed them, well deserved their early popularity. Their succession of five compact movements, including two minuets, is typical of mid-eighteenth-century Austrian serenade music. But their exuberance and melodic freshness, exemplified in the 6/8 'hunting' opening movement of Op. 1 No. 1 (hence the nickname), already mark out the young composer as someone special; so, too, do their fondness for irregular phrase-lengths, as at the start of Op. 2 No. 1, and their lively sense of ensemble: these are emphatically chamber works, not orchestral-style music that happens to be written for single players. Especially delightful is the scherzo-like Presto in Op. 1 No. 3, with its impish repartee between first violin and viola on the one hand, and second violin and cello on the other: just the kind of piece that prompted po-faced Berlin critics to accuse Haydn of 'debasing the art with comic fooling'.

The Adagios are serenades or quasi-operatic arias for the first violin. That of Op. 1 No. 4, with its shy, *con sordino* echoes from the second violin, is particularly charming, while the F minor Adagio non troppo from Op. 2 No. 4 – the only minor-key movement in all these quartets – has a delicate pathos. Framing the slow movements (except in Op. 1 No. 3 and Op. 2 No. 6, which open with an Adagio) are two distinctive minuets, the first a courtly *minuetto galante*, the second brisker and earthier – sometimes, as in Op. 1 No. 1, with the bald two-part counterpoint and octave doublings found intermittently in Haydn's minuets right through to Op. 76. One otherwise appreciative Hamburg review of 1766 likened this deliberately harsh texture to 'a father and son going begging: and that is a bad subject for music to imitate'.

String Quartet in C, Op. 9 No. 1
String Quartet in E flat, Op. 9 No. 2
String Quartet in G, Op. 9 No. 3
String Quartet in D minor, Op. 9 No. 4
String Quartet in B flat, Op. 9 No. 5
String Quartet in A, Op. 9 No. 6

It was long assumed that the six quartets of 'Op. 3', including the one (No. 5 in F) with the famous 'Serenade', were genuine Haydn. But all that changed in 1964, when the name of Roman Hofstetter, a Benedictine monk, was discovered hidden behind Haydn's on eighteenth-century prints of two of the quartets. The case for Haydn's authorship was always flimsy; and Hofstetter is now accepted as the most likely composer of all six works.

The disappearance of Op. 3 leaves a gap of nearly a decade between the 'Fürnberg' quartets and Op. 9. These were Haydn's first years at the Esterházy court, dominated by the intensive production of symphonies and, later, sacred works and music for the baryton. But when Haydn returned to the quartet medium, he did so with a vengeance, producing in quick succession the three sets of Op. 9 (*c.*1769), Op. 17 (1770–1) and Op. 20 (1772) which mark the string quartet's coming of age. Indeed, late in life he said he wanted his canon of quartets to begin only with Op. 9. Although still labelled *Divertimenti a quattro*, these works, written during the period when Haydn emerged as an incontestably great composer, have a seriousness of intent and an increasing mastery of rhetoric that are a world away from the breezy little divertimento-quartets of the 1750s.

We can only guess what prompted this sudden effusion of quartet writing. Perhaps Haydn's experience of writing baryton trios by the bushel for Prince Nicolaus from 1765 onwards had made him eager to explore, in a less limited medium, the possibilities afforded by solo strings, with the cello emancipated from its traditional continuo role. Significant, too, was the presence of Luigi Tomasini, leader of the Esterházy orchestra and, we may infer, of the ad hoc court string quartet, with Haydn as second violinist. Tomasini was renowned for his pure, sweet tone and virtuoso panache. In the Op. 9 quartets, especially, the often florid first violin parts were surely calculated to show off the fire, agility and 'taste' of his playing.

Whereas the Op. 1 and Op. 2 quartets had comprised five brief movements, the quartets of Op. 9 proclaim their more serious, symphonic purpose in weighty four-movement structures. Nos. 1–4 have an identical ground plan. Their monothematic opening movements are spacious and dignified, with a leisurely basic pulse to allow room for elaborate figuration for all the instruments, especially the first violin. Those in Nos. 1 and 3 sometimes threaten to turn into miniature concertos, and sound more like Boccherini than almost any other music by Haydn. Minuets invariably come second, slow movements, like those in the earliest quartets, are accompanied arias, ending with an improvised cadenza for Tomasini. Finales are terse (disconcertingly so in the case of No. 6) and spirited, and typically contain more democratic interplay than the earlier movements. The last two quartets have first movements in lighter, popular vein. No. 5 begins with decorative variations on a homely Poco adagio theme, while hunting calls and musette drones give a bracing alfresco flavour to the opening Presto of No. 6.

The most famous – or better, least neglected – of the Op. 9 set is No. 4 in D minor, Haydn's first minor-key quartet. In the Classical period the minor mode was associated with a special rhetorical intensity and the expression of sorrowful or turbulent emotion. With its disquieting pauses, 'pathetic' sighing appoggiaturas and extreme dynamic contrasts, the first movement of No. 4 evokes the *empfindsamer Stil* of C. P. E. Bach. But this music is also more tautly argued than the other opening movements in Op. 9. Equally powerful is the minuet, which the teenaged Mozart used as a model for his own D minor quartet, K173. As so often in Haydn's minuets from this period onwards, this is pointedly written against the grain of the courtly dance. The phrase structure is asymmetrical, the tonality restless, with cadences asking new questions rather than resolving. After a relaxing aria-serenade for Tomasini, the 6/8 finale begins as if it were a fugue (the minor mode was closely associated with counterpoint in the 1760s and 1770s) and continues with bantering scherzando textures. But levity is banished from the development, with its grimly striding arpeggios, and the recapitulation, even more violently compressed than that in the first movement and reaffirming D minor right to the close.

If none of the major-key quartets is as consistently gripping, this unfancied set has its share of memorable movements. The finale of No. 3 in G is perhaps Haydn's wittiest to date. He manipulates the two limbs of the folk-like main theme in all sorts of unexpected ways, and then starts the recapitulation in the 'wrong' key of E minor before slipping to G major as if nothing had happened. The varied minuets range from the bucolic No. 5 (with Haydn's favourite 'raw' octave doublings) to the suave, chromatically inflected No. 2, which Haydn later used as a basis for keyboard variations. No. 2 also has an eloquent C minor Adagio. The rhapsodic opening sounds like a keyboard improvisation transcribed for strings. Then, with a change to triple metre, the first violin spins a sorrowful, rather Gluckian aria, with an expressively embellished repeat of the exposition – a technique

Haydn borrowed from the 'varied reprises' of C. P. E. Bach's keyboard sonatas.

String Quartet in E, Op. 17 No. 1
String Quartet in F, Op. 17 No. 2
String Quartet in E flat, Op. 17 No. 3
String Quartet in C minor, Op. 17 No. 4
String Quartet in G, Op. 17 No. 5
String Quartet in D, Op. 17 No. 6

Op. 17 has also had a raw deal from commentators and players, for whom the real business of Haydn quartets only begins with Op. 20. As a set the quartets closely follow the pattern of Op. 9. Four of their first movements are in spacious Moderato tempo, one (No. 3) is a slowish theme and variations, and one (No. 6) a bounding 6/8 Presto. Slow movements, again, are in essence wordless arias. But though there are passages in Nos. 2 and 5, especially, that showcase Tomasini's virtuosity, their first movements are on the whole less luxuriant than those in Op. 9.

True to its vernal key of E major, No. 1, opening with a 'grass-green theme' (Tovey), is tender rather than brilliant in style, with more varied and inventive textures than in any of the Op. 9 first movements. The beautiful E minor trio of the minuet is a piece of flowing, quasi-vocal polyphony, perhaps a distant echo, as Rosemary Hughes suggests, of a motet that Haydn had sung as a choirboy at St Stephen's; and the Adagio, also in E minor, is a siciliano with dreamy suspensions. The finale mingles quirky exuberance (its main theme consists of five-bar phrases plus a bar's rest) and a touch of Balkan folk melancholy. No. 2 in F is melodically less attractive, though the finale is typically gamesome and the trio foreshadows later Haydn in reinterpreting and developing motifs from the minuet. The vapid variations that open No. 3 find the composer on autopilot. But he makes amends with the minuet's picturesque trio, evocative of pealing bells, and the entertaining, contrapuntally inclined finale.

As in Op. 9, it is the minor-mode quartet, No. 4, that leaves the deepest impression. The opening Moderato, broader and more ardent than its counterpart in Op. 9 No. 4, grows from a rising three-note motif that fleetingly suggests the movement will be in E flat major rather than C minor. Each time it recurs the motif pivots the music in unexpected directions. Haydn twice delays the anticipated start of the recapitulation, initially in an ethereal canon, and needs a separate coda, with a last-minute gleam of C major, to resolve the accrued harmonic tension. The sonorous C major minuet encloses a wailing, syncopated trio in C minor (Haydn would do something similar in a later quartet in C, Op. 54 No. 2), while the intensity of the first movement is matched by the blunt, strenuously contrapuntal finale.

Op. 17 No. 5 has a tangy minuet, full of metrically disruptive canonic imitations, and a theatrical G minor Adagio alternating arioso and recitative, with Tomasini impersonating a forlorn *opera seria* heroine. Conversely, the outstanding movements in No. 6 in D are the first and last. The opening Presto, like its predecessor in Op. 9 No. 6, conjures up the chase, though with an added breadth and harmonic adventurousness. Of all the movements in Op. 17, the finale, with its chuckling, quickfire exchanges, is the most effortlessly democratic in texture, and could fit easily into the Op. 20 quartets. The *pianissimo* close is an early example of a sly, throwaway ending, a Haydn speciality in his later quartets. There is also a foretaste of the famous 'Frog' Quartet, Op. 50 No. 6, in the first violin's gypsy-flavoured *bariolage* – rapid repetitions of the same note played alternately on open and fingered strings.

'Sun' Quartets, Op. 20

String Quartet in E flat, Op. 20 No. 1
String Quartet in C, Op. 20 No. 2
String Quartet in G minor, Op. 20 No. 3
String Quartet in D, Op. 20 No. 4

String Quartet in F minor, Op. 20 No. 5
String Quartet in A, Op. 20 No. 6

The promise of Op. 9 and, especially, Op. 17 is richly fulfilled in the Op. 20 quartets of 1772, an *annus mirabilis* which also saw the production of three magnificent symphonies, Nos. 45–7. These great works are as much a watershed in the development of the quartet as is Mozart's E flat Piano Concerto, K271, in the evolution of the Classical concerto. From every standpoint – technical, formal, expressive – the Op. 20 quartets display a mastery only intermittently glimpsed in Op. 9 and Op. 17. Far more than in the earlier works, the form of each movement is dictated by the material, with the recapitulations both resolving and reinterpreting, often radically, earlier events. Op. 20 left a profound impression on Mozart, and on Beethoven, who copied out No. 1 in 1794. Brahms owned the autograph manuscripts until he bequeathed them to the Viennese Gesellschaft der Musikfreunde. When Op. 20 was published by the firm of Hummel, the title page carried an emblem of a rising sun – hence the sobriquet 'Sun' Quartets.

Unprecedented is the variety of texture and colour in Op. 20. Whereas the first violin had ruled over long stretches of Opp. 9 and 17, Haydn here often cultivates the spirit of flexible give-and-take that lies at the heart of the Classical string quartet, with each player accorded a vital, distinct identity. Much of the writing in Op. 20 suggests 'a conversation between four intelligent people', as Goethe pithily characterised the string quartet – a reminder that the art of civilised, witty conversation was avidly cultivated in eighteenth-century salons. The finale of No. 3, for instance, distributes its theme between first and second violins, and later between cello and first violin, while No. 2 begins in three-part counterpoint, with the cello taking the lead, and then immediately reassigns the cello tune to the first violin. These equal-opportunity tendencies culminate in the fugues that crown Nos. 2, 5 and 6. During the 1760s composers such as Florian Gassmann, Carlo D'Ordoñez and Franz Xaver Richter had written fugues in their quartets, a sign that the string quartet was increasingly acknowledged as a 'learned' genre. But whereas their fugues are exercises in a venerable ecclesiastical style, Haydn's, especially those in Nos. 2 and 6, have a spontaneous freshness and urgency. The contrapuntal mastery honed in his early symphonies and his sacred music of the late 1760s is coloured here by the drama and wit of his sonata style.

No less striking is Op. 20's vast range of expression, from the sorrowful No. 5 in F minor, through the gypsy pungency and inspired foolery of No. 4's minuet and finale, to the rapt, mesmeric beauty of No. 1's Affetuoso e sostenuto. Far more than in Opp. 9 and 17, each work has a sharply individual profile. It is as if Haydn conceived the set as a showcase for his technical and expressive virtuosity. The six quartets that Mozart dedicated to Haydn in 1785 leave a similar impression.

Reflecting the preoccupation with the minor mode in Haydn's symphonies *c.*1770, the Op. 20 set, uniquely, contains two minor-key quartets. They could hardly be more strongly contrasted. The outer movements of No. 3 in G minor are astringent, nervy, sometimes bizarrely elliptical. C. P. E. Bach's spirit is distantly felt. In the opening Allegro con spirito Haydn switches abruptly between earnestness and *buffo* frivolity, with an apparently incongruous little unison figure, like a stage aside, adding a touch of grotesquerie. The music's unnerving waywardness reaches its climax in the recapitulation, which expands a brief snatch of violin recitative from the exposition into an almost hysterical *cri de coeur*. The desolate minuet, trading in five-bar phrases, is relieved by its exquisite, lulling E flat major trio. Both minuet and trio fade away strangely and inconclusively on the brink of C minor, an effect that Haydn replicates in the *pianissimo* close of the finale. Though written against the background of sonata form, the Poco adagio, in G major, is essentially a fantasy on a single ardent melody. Each of its reappearances is characterised by an evocative new sonority, typical of Haydn's heightened sensitivity to tone colour in Op. 20.

While the G minor is still relatively neglected, the F minor, No. 5, has long been a favourite. Its elegiac first movement culminates in an astonishing coda. Here Haydn wonderfully expands a moment of harmonic mystification in the exposition and then works a fragment of the second theme to an impassioned, even tragic, climax. The minuet contrasts a strenuous *forte* statement with a plaintive *piano* answer which Mozart perhaps remembered in the minuet of his G minor String Quintet. After this almost unrelieved emphasis on F minor, the F major trio, gliding in without a break, brings harmonic repose, though with its irregular phrase lengths it is not quite so innocent as it seems. F major returns in the limpid Adagio, whose guileless siciliano theme is freely varied with quasi-improvisatory arabesques from the first violin. The closing fugue, initiated by a common tag used by Handel in *Messiah* ('And with His stripes') and Mozart in the Kyrie of the Requiem, is the most austerely Baroque of the Op. 20 fugues, though a Baroque composer would not have modulated as far afield as A flat minor, as Haydn does. The two subjects are elaborated with every contrapuntal trick of the trade: inversion, *stretto* (i.e. with thematic entries piling in on top of each other) and, near the end, a climactic *fortissimo* canon between first violin and cello, all the more dramatic after so much tense *sotto voce*.

Lightest of the four major-key quartets is No. 6 in A, opening with a hunting-style movement that outdoes its predecessors in Opp. 9 and 17 in wit and harmonic sleight of hand. Haydn marks it 'scherzando', as he might well have done the dancing final fugue, on three subjects. The music's comic verve – matched among fugues only by the finale of Verdi's *Falstaff* – reaches its acme when Haydn exuberantly turns the principal theme on its head: the technique is 'learned', the effect anything but.

No. 1 in E flat is a more reticent work, well described by Rosemary Hughes as springing from 'that central core of tranquillity that lies at the heart of Haydn's music'. The easy instrumental interplay in the opening Allegro moderato is a world away from the violin-dominated first movements in Opp. 9 and 17. Virtually every commentator has singled out the A flat *affetuoso e sostenuto* (tender and sustained) third movement, music of self-communing inwardness that unfolds throughout in a hushed, rich four-part chorale texture, with no discernible 'theme' and minimal articulation. There is something strangely elusive about this movement, with, to quote Robin Holloway, its 'perverse interlocking and crossing of parts, arbitrary doublings, [and] passing chords that if lingered on would be solecisms, even Stravinskyisms'. Mozart would remember it in the A flat Andante of his third 'Haydn' quartet, K428.

Like Beethoven's first 'Razumovsky' Quartet, the C major Quartet, No. 2, is a favourite of cellists, who have glorious solo opportunities in the first three movements. Of all the works in Op. 20, this is the one that most ostentatiously proclaims Haydn's delight in his new-found freedom of texture. The sonorities in the first movement, founded on the cello's deep C-string, have a wonderful sensuous richness. The C minor Adagio, labelled 'Capriccio', is the consummation of the Baroque-flavoured operatic scenas found in Op. 9 No. 2 and Op. 17 No. 5. After a recitative, with cello and first violin in turn pleading with an implacable 'orchestra' (some performances stress parody here, others tragedy), the first violin spins a heart-easing E flat cantabile. The unsettled mood of the opening returns; and resolution comes only with the gliding, syncopated minuet, an ethereal musette written pointedly *against* the rhythm of the courtly dance. The closing fugue, on four subjects and in a jig-like 6/8 metre, is the most contrapuntally virtuosic in Op. 20. More than anywhere else in the set, Haydn here designs his finale as the work's intellectual climax. Yet, as in No. 6, he displays his learning with a light, scherzando touch, using fugue as an opportunity for witty banter, and delightedly exploiting the principal subject's octave leap. After pages of unbroken *sotto voce*, the music erupts in an assertive *forte* that transforms the close fugal texture into free imitation, typical of Haydn's 'normal' mature quartet style.

Haydn punningly encapsulated the mercurial spirit of this finale when he wrote at the end of the score: 'Laus omnip: Deo / Sic fugit amicus amicum' (Praise to Almighty God / thus one friend escapes another).

No. 4 in D is the most obviously tuneful of Op. 20, and the most forward-looking in its incorporation of popular-style melodies. The expansive yet sinewy opening Allegro di molto, making ingenious capital of its initial three-note 'drum tap', is a counterpart to the triple-time first movement of the 'Mercury' Symphony, No. 43. In the *Menuet alla Zingarese*, with its collision between gavotte and minuet rhythms, and the Presto scherzando finale, Haydn gleefully mines his favourite gypsy vein. The poignant D minor Adagio is Haydn's only variation movement cast entirely in the minor key. After three variations (the first fashioned as a dialogue between second violin and viola, the second spotlighting the cello and the third the first violin) and a return to the original theme, Haydn expands the scale in an impassioned fantasia-cum-coda that explores the implications of the dissonances within the theme: one of the supreme moments in this ever-astonishing set of quartets.

'Russian' Quartets, Op. 33

String Quartet in B minor, Op. 33 No. 1
String Quartet in E flat, Op. 33 No. 2, 'Joke'
String Quartet in C, Op. 33 No. 3, 'Bird'
String Quartet in B flat, Op. 33 No. 4
String Quartet in G, Op. 33 No. 5, 'How-do-you-do?'
String Quartet in D, Op. 33 No. 6

After the monumental achievement of Op. 20, Haydn again wrote no string quartets for nearly a decade, during which his energies were overwhelmingly absorbed by opera. When he did produce another set, published by Artaria in 1782 as Op. 33, he wooed potential subscribers with the announcement that they were composed 'in a completely new and special way'. The first 'official' performance of at least some of the quartets took place on Christmas Day 1781 in the Viennese apartment of the visiting Russian Grand Duke Paul (the future Tsar Paul II). Haydn subsequently dedicated the set – sometimes known as the 'Russian Quartets' – to the Grand Duke.

The composer's 'new and special way' has often been dismissed as a sales gimmick. But there *are* new features in Op. 33. Compared with Op. 20, the quartets are altogether more 'popular' in tone (Haydn now had his eye on the international market), with a livelier, more fluent sense of rhythm that Haydn had honed in his comic operas. Ideas seem to grow effortlessly and inevitably out of each other, in a spirit we might describe as 'monothematic plurality'. Crucial, too, as Rosen and others have observed, is the ease with which the instruments change roles in Op. 33, moving almost imperceptibly between background and foreground, theme and accompaniment. David Schroeder sets this in a wider social and philosophical context:

> In a heightened way with Op. 33, the music places four intelligent people in a 'harmonious' setting, sharing both intellectual and heartfelt experience. The ability to share and exchange the important material offers a strong sense of unified purpose, one in which the player is both aware of his individual importance and the role he plays in creating the whole. In a very real way, then, the quartet became a realization of one of the highest goals of the Enlightenment. With accompaniments that can be transformed to melodies and vice versa, there is apparent recognition of a higher social truth, which is that differences do not preclude equality.

Op. 33 circulated rapidly throughout Europe, exactly as Haydn planned; and with their sophisticated conversational textures, they were a prime influence on the six quartets Mozart dedicated to Haydn in 1785.

Unbridled jocularity rules in several of the scherzos, as Haydn labelled the minuets – hence the nickname 'Gli

Scherzi' sometimes attached to Op. 33 – and in the finales, all of which except No. 1 adopt the 'popular' forms of rondo or variations. Yet playfulness and charm are far from the whole picture. No. 1 in B minor is a highly unsettling piece, a compound of pathos, truculence and mordant humour. In the first movement Haydn exhaustively investigates the consequences of the tonal ambiguity set up at the opening, where we initially seem to be in D major rather than B minor. This is followed by a stinging, contrapuntal scherzo (marked Allegro di molto) with an emollient B major trio. In the sonata-form Andante Haydn contrasts the tripping grace of its opening with a chromatically piquant second theme, played in bare octaves by viola and cello and repeated by the two violins. This leads to a melting cadence over a cello pedal that Mendelssohn virtually quoted in the minuet of his 'Italian' Symphony. The finale has an almost fevered brilliance, with gypsy-style virtuoso flights for the first violin.

The comic disintegration of the theme in No. 2's bubbly rondo, repeatedly fooling the listener as to whether the piece has ended or not, has spawned the quartet's English nickname 'The Joke'. The story goes that Haydn wrote the ending in order to win a bet that 'the ladies will always begin talking' before the music stops. His outrageous deception can still throw listeners of both sexes. The relaxed first movement encapsulates Op. 33's prevailing spirit of easy, conversational give-and-take, with virtually everything growing from its genial opening phrase: this is a *locus classicus* of Haydn's famed monothematicism, where a single theme suffices for a varied and inventive movement. The stomping scherzo was the model for Mozart in his own E flat Quartet, K428. In the trio the first violin gives a graphic imitation of an Austrian village fiddler, complete with deliciously vulgar glissandi (slides) between notes that were eschewed by squeamish nineteenth-century editors. Amid all this frivolity, the Largo e sostenuto, initiated by a solemn duet for viola and cello (a novel colour in the quartets), introduces a note of gentle gravity, ruffled by sudden rhetorical outbursts.

The glorious first movement of No. 3, beginning, after a bar of pulsing accompaniment, with a suggestion of birdsong, matches that of No. 1 in its large-scale exploration of harmonic ambiguity. Haydn subtly exploits the implications of the unstable opening in the development, culminating in one of his oblique, off-key recapitulations; and the coda subjects the main theme to further harmonic questioning. Contradicting its title of 'scherzo' – and the usually bright, 'open' key of C major – the tenderly veiled second movement transmutes a dance into a hymn, with the four instruments playing *sotto voce* on their lowest strings. In comic contrast, the trio resumes the first movement's avian associations with a twittering violin duet. The serene, warmly textured Andante surely left its mark on the slow movement of Mozart's 'Dissonance' Quartet, K465, in the same key, while the finale contrasts a chattering refrain that may derive from a Slavonic folk dance with an episode in the fashionable 'Turkish' style. The two elements are fused in the second episode, while the coda fragments the refrain in a passage of pure slapstick – a game Haydn had previously played in the codas of Symphonies Nos. 66 and 68.

No. 4 in B flat has always been the least favoured of the Op. 33 quartets, banished by Hans Keller from *The Great Haydn Quartets* on account of its 'textural shortcomings' and 'surprisingly unoriginal' melodic invention. True, the perky first movement has few surprises and devotes most of its development to routine sequences for the first violin. But the rapt Largo is perhaps the most elevated of all the Op. 33 slow movements, looking ahead to the profound meditations in the Op. 76 Quartets. The rondo finale again ends in slapstick. After a distended, spidery version of its contredanse theme and a failed attempt to 'normalise' it, Haydn cuts his losses and exits with a comical simplification of the tune, played pizzicato.

The G major, No. 5, was probably the first of the Op. 33 set to be composed. It opens *pianissimo* with a *galant* cadence – the musical equivalent of a bow or curtsey – that duly prompted the nineteenth-century nicknames 'How-do you-do?' and 'Compliments'. This is Haydn's ending-as-beginning joke at its most basic, initiating a movement of almost symphonic drive and panache, with, uniquely in Op. 33, a clear-cut lyrical second theme. The G minor Largo e cantabile is an old-fashioned *opera seria* aria for the first violin that could fit easily into the Op. 9 Quartets. But at the last second Haydn undercuts the mood with a single pizzicato twang. As Dean Sutcliffe nicely put it, 'having poured out his heart, so to speak, the composer now pokes out his tongue'. He sticks it out even further in the scherzo, fazing the listener with displaced accents, and then inserting a malicious pause just when we seem to have found our feet. The finale – three variations plus coda on a guileless siciliano tune – can seem an anticlimax, though the second variation has a luminous grace, with that easy fluidity of texture typical of Op. 33. Mozart took up Haydn's idea of a variation finale in siciliano rhythm and gave it a far more troubled cast in his D minor Quartet, K421.

The opening Vivace assai of No. 6 also evidently appealed to Mozart, who echoed its mingled al fresco exuberance and quicksilver motivic development in his 'Hunt' Quartet, K458. This is the most puckishly inventive of all Haydn's hunting movements, with an implausibly premature recapitulation that turns out to be the real thing after all – an inversion of the favourite 'false recapitulation' strategy in the symphonies of the 1770s. The gravely absorbed Andante is again in the tonic minor key, with echoes of a Baroque aria, though this time there is no final ironic deflation. Subversive comedy returns in the scherzo, with its slightly crazy imitative entries that result in the viola being left stranded at the very end. The finale is a mix of rondo and variations, with alternating major and minor sections. The D minor theme is a classic instance of that free, informal counterpoint so characteristic of Op. 33, with instruments shifting imperceptibly between foreground and accompaniment.

String Quartet in D minor, Op. 42

'Prussian' Quartets, Op. 50

String Quartet in B flat, Op. 50 No. 1
String Quartet in C, Op. 50 No. 2
String Quartet in E flat, Op. 50 No. 3
String Quartet in F sharp minor, Op. 50 No. 4
String Quartet in F, Op. 50 No. 5, 'Ein Traum'
String Quartet in D, Op. 50 No. 6, 'Frog'

In a letter of 5 April 1784 to the Viennese publisher Artaria, Haydn wrote that he was working on three 'very short' quartets, in three movements only, for a Spanish patron. Either the commission was aborted, or the quartets are lost. But it may be that the lone Op. 42 quartet – short and relatively easy, though in four rather than three movements – contains music from the Spanish project. Its surface simplicity, epitomised by the first movement's marking Andante ed innocentemente, belies its subtle mastery. The serene Adagio is a richly scored meditation on its tranquil opening phrase, while the finale, like that of Mozart's G major Quartet, K387, mingles 'learned' fugato textures with the spirit of *opera buffa*.

In that same letter to Artaria Haydn accepted the publisher's offer of three hundred florins for a set of six new quartets, and promised to complete them by July. As it turned out, he became sidetracked by other projects; and the first two quartets were not ready until February 1787. There is no evidence that at this stage Haydn was intending to dedicate them to the cello-playing King Friedrich Wilhelm II of Prussia, who in 1789 may (or may not) have commissioned Mozart's 'Prussian' quartets, K575, K589 and K590. Then, in April, the King wrote to Haydn thanking him for copies of the 'Paris' symphonies and enclosing a gold ring. This mark of royal favour clinched the matter. In December 1787 Artaria duly published the set as Op. 50 with a dedication to 'Sa Majesté FREDERIC GUILLAUME II, ROI DE PRUSSE'. By then, though, Haydn had already sold 'exclusive rights' to Forster in London. The autographs were long lost until four of the quartets (Nos. 3–6) improbably turned up in Melbourne in 1982, having arrived there via an English colonel who had acquired the manuscripts in London before emigrating first to New Zealand and then to Australia.

The 'Prussian' quartets have sometimes been seen as a response to the six quartets that Mozart dedicated to Haydn. Perhaps the unusual weight and chromatic intensity of some of the minuets are Haydn's answer to the astonishing, subversive minuet in the younger composer's G major Quartet, K387. But there is little of Mozart's lyricism and harmonic sensuousness in Op. 50, which in its musical procedures is arguably Haydn's most ascetic and rigorously argued set of quartets.

No movement in Op. 50 is more self-denying than the first of No. 1. Here Haydn sets himself the problem of how to construct a complex, challenging argument from a stark minimum of material. In a tour de force of economy and logic, the whole movement grows from the opening four bars: a repeated 'drum' figure on the cello and a six-note cadential phrase featuring a gentle discord and the interval E flat–D which is to play a crucial role in the movement. The theme-and-variations Adagio is a relaxing interlude between the obsessive first movement and the dense, contrapuntal minuet. It quickly became something of a popular hit; and its shapely, siciliano-style melody was engraved on the monument erected in 1793 in Haydn's native village of Rohrau. The square, jolly tune of the finale promises a rondo. Instead, it turns out to be an unpredictable monothematic sonata movement that derails expectations right through to a coda that repeatedly keeps us guessing as to when the music has actually finished – a more sophisticated counterpart to the finale of the 'Joke' Quartet.

In contrast to the almost minimalist No. 1, the first movement of No. 2 in C is Haydn is at his most expansive and harmonically adventurous. Uniquely in Op. 50 there is a clear, almost exaggerated contrast between 'first' and 'second' subjects, the one irregular and chromatically inflected (and destined for intricate contrapuntal treatment), the other a blithe *Ländler* tune. As in No. 1, the Adagio is more relaxing than searching. Its plain theme over a strumming accompaniment uses stock *galant* formulae to gently ironic effect. The music then swoops into the minor key for what sounds like a melodramatic parody of the 'pathetic' operatic style. The toughly argued minuet, restlessly probing the implications of the cello's dissonant C sharp in bar 2, again leaves its dance model far in the background. In the finale Haydn once more launches a resourceful sonata movement with a catchy rondo-style theme. But, mirroring the opening movement, there is also a contrasting subject whose 'Mozartian' chromaticisms accord with the chromatic pungency of the whole quartet.

Beginning with a teasing take on Haydn's familiar 6/8 'hunting' mode, No. 3 in E flat returns to the monothematic economy of No. 1, with a new terseness of its own. The briskly paced second movement, in B flat, opens with one of Haydn's 'walking' themes in a spare two-part texture, with the cello taking the lead over a viola line that is somewhere between an accompaniment and a counterpoint – an ambiguity characteristic of the Classical style. The whole wonderful movement evolves as a synthesis of variation, ternary and rondo form, with even a hint of sonata development in the B flat minor variation that follows the theme. Thematic interconnections between movements are found in many Haydn symphonies and quartets. Here the links are more overt than usual, with the minuet, its trio and the finale all audibly derived from the fertile theme of the first movement.

Nothing could be further from the voluptuous pathos typical of Mozart's minor-key music than the acerbic F sharp minor Quartet, No. 4, with its harsh sonorities and bleak, restive final fugue. The outré key, found in only two other Haydn works (the 'Farewell' Symphony and the Piano Trio No. 26), promises, and yields, something exceptional. The opening movement, in extreme contrast to the melodically lavish Mozart, draws all its energy from the angular contours and driving rhythms of the opening theme, launched by a unison 'motto'. Though the unusually regular recapitulation turns to F sharp major, the conclusion is too terse and blunt to constitute a 'happy ending'.

The gracious A major theme of the Andante provides welcome respite. But a subterranean growl from the cello introduces a contrasting A minor section, whose dissonant harmonies and contrapuntal textures look back to the first movement. The minuet replicates the Andante's major-minor contrasts. Its main section, in F sharp major, worries insistently at its opening figure, while the F sharp minor trio, far from easing the tension, is a single-minded contrapuntal development of the minuet itself. As in three of the Op. 20 quartets, Haydn closes with a fugue, coloured by the drama of his sonata style. For Tovey this was the 'quietest and deepest of all instrumental fugues since Bach'. Very few of Haydn's later minor-mode works end in the minor, and none does so as enigmatically as this.

No. 5 in F could hardly be more different. In its outer movements this is the lightest of the Op. 50 set. But Haydn being Haydn, the serenade-like tone does not preclude rigorous motivic development. Both the first movement and the prancing finale, with its charming *una corda* effects (controlled slides between notes, using a single string), are as determinedly monothematic as most of the rest of Op. 50. In the easy-paced opening movement Haydn makes the disruptive C sharps on viola and cello in bar 5 the mainspring of the musical action. Beethoven was to do something similar, albeit on a much grander scale, with the 'rogue' C sharps in the finale of the Eighth Symphony. Uniquely in Op. 50, the centre of gravity here lies in the two middle movements. The serene, lulling motion of the Poco adagio, with its undulating chords below a rhapsodic violin line and gentle (occasionally not so gentle) dissonances, has spawned the nickname in German-speaking countries 'Ein Traum' (A dream). The minuet is sinewy and tonally restless; and as in the F sharp minor Quartet, the trio increases rather than decreases the tension with a development of motifs from the minuet itself.

Like Op. 50 No. 1, No. 6 opens with a Haydnesque pun, turning a closing formula into an unstable opening whose implications Haydn works out during the course of the movement. Compared with its counterpart in No. 1, though, this is an altogether more complex, assertive piece, highly chromatic, often contrapuntal in texture, and exploiting the sonorous warmth of the key of D major. Surprisingly for such a forth-right movement, Haydn ends in a shadowy *pianissimo* that prepares us for the D minor beginning of the second movement. Just as the opening Allegro was the most imposing of the Op. 50 set, so this expressively ornamented Poco adagio is the most far-reaching of the six slow movements. The proudly striding minuet, with its flicking Scotch snap figures, is the shortest in Op. 50. But the trio again challenges convention by turning out to be nearly twice as long as the main section. The finale is Haydn at his most antic, with a touch of grotesquerie in its pervasive *bariolage* – a quavering effect created by the quickfire repetition of the same note on open and fingered strings. Someone in the mid-nineteenth century thought this sounded like a croaking frog, and the nickname stuck.

String Quartets Op. 51, 'The Seven Last Words'

These are not true string quartets at all, but Haydn's own arrangement of the orchestral meditations composed for Cádiz in 1786–7 (see p. 165). Haydn also authorised a keyboard arrangement by another hand. Doubtless for economic reasons, the quartet version still receives many more performances than the orchestral original. Whatever the gains in intimacy, the arrangement inevitably mutes the music's colour, sense of awe and – especially in the final Earthquake – sheer physical power. The textures, too, with long stretches of theme-plus-chordal-accompaniment, are often uncharacteristic of Haydn's mature quartet style. Still, if the quartet version remains something of a makeshift, few would go as far as to echo Hans Keller's *ex cathedra* dismissal: 'It cannot be too decidedly maintained that the passion certain ensembles show for the work is an indisputable sign that they have not even begun to understand the true nature of the string quartet and its textures.'

String Quartet in G, Op. 54 No. 1
String Quartet in C, Op. 54 No. 2
String Quartet in E, Op. 54 No. 3
String Quartet in A, Op. 55 No. 1
String Quartet in F minor, Op. 55 No. 2, 'Razor'
String Quartet in B flat, Op. 55 No. 3

Hot on the heels of Op. 50 came another dozen quartets: six in 1788, published in two sets of three as Opp. 54 and 55, and six more (Op. 64) in 1790. All these are associated with Johann Tost, a slightly shady character who was given to dreaming up various scams (including an illegal outfit to market stolen copies of works that had entered Prince Nicolaus's domain!) while employed as leader of the second violins in the Esterházy orchestra. The brilliant, high-lying first violin parts in many of these quartets, especially Op. 54 Nos. 1 and 2 and Op. 55 No. 1, have led commentators to assume that they were fashioned explicitly for Tost. But this is only speculation. Tost's only known connection with Opp. 54 and 55 is that Haydn gave them to him, along with Symphonies Nos. 88 and 89, to sell to a Parisian publisher. They were duly issued by the firm of Sieber in June 1789.

Whether or not they were a tribute to Tost's own prowess, Opp. 54 and 55 tend to be much more assertive than Op. 50. These are Haydn's most 'public' string quartets to date. Indeed, the flamboyant violin writing in Op. 54 Nos. 1 and 2 suggests that he may have tailored them not so much for Tost as for Paris, where the flashy, first-violin-dominated *quatuor brillant* was immensely popular. Unlike some of his French contemporaries, though, Haydn never allows brilliance to become an end in itself.

In the most famous of these quartets, the C major, Op. 54 No. 2, virtuosity is a key element in music of extraordinary force and rhetorical boldness: in the spacious, muscular opening movement, with its wide tonal reach (the second paragraph erupts, after a long pause, in A flat major, an effect at once eccentric and dramatic); and in the C minor Adagio, where the leader weaves deliriously impassioned *Zigeuner* fantasies above the brooding chorale theme in the lower voices. Did Brahms remember this music when he came to write the gypsy episode in the Adagio of his Clarinet Quintet?

Haydn's Adagio leads without a break into the minuet, which, hesitantly at first, returns us to C major. But the C minor trio, with its wailing dissonances, at once recalls the feverish Adagio and presents a distorted parody of the minuet itself. The quartet's accumulated tensions – way beyond the norm in a Classical work – are then resolved in the revolutionary finale. This opens not with the expected Presto but with an Adagio of sublime simplicity and calm, juxtaposing a chaste song for first violin with a soaring cello line. Then a racy Presto intrudes. Was the Adagio only an extended slow introduction after all? But no: the Presto turns out to be only an interlude before the Adagio returns to provide a touching, and unprecedented, close to one of Haydn's most original quartets.

Though more 'normal' – inasmuch as the epithet can be applied to any mature Haydn quartet – in design and expression, Op. 54 Nos. 1 and 3 are both thoroughly absorbing, inventive works. At times the driving first movement of No. 1 in G sounds like a scaled-down double concerto for jousting violins, though the hitherto subordinate viola and cello come to the fore in the combative development. In the following Allegretto Haydn pointedly contrasts an insouciant serenade with nebulous, groping harmonies that recall the (by 1788) notorious slow introduction to Mozart's 'Dissonance' Quartet, K465. The minuet trips up the unwary with its five-bar phrases, while the finale is an exuberant rondo that comes to a comically stuttering end, with the theme's two-note upbeat sounded *pianissimo* by the four instruments in their highest register: a novel version of Haydn's favourite beginning-ending pun.

Despite bouts of first violin brilliance, No. 3 is a gentler, more lyrical work, as you would expect from Haydn in E major, with frequent 'relaxing' pedal points in both outer movements. The (sole) theme of the first movement, initiated by second violin and viola and seamlessly continued by first violin, is a delightful example of Haydn's 'conversational' thinking in the quartets. The second violin also takes the lead at the start of the finale before the first chimes in with a chuckling counterpoint. In the Largo cantabile Haydn writes an increasingly florid rhapsody for solo violin that encloses another wild, gypsy-flavoured minor-key episode. The minuet, with its pervasive Scotch snap rhythms, fruitfully revives the bare two-part octave textures of the earliest quartets.

In a story told by Pohl, Haydn, unable to get a decent shave at Eszterháza, offered 'his best quartet' to the visiting music publisher John Bland in November 1789 in exchange for a pair of English razors. These were duly supplied, and the jokey nickname 'Rasierquartett', or 'Razor' Quartet, somehow attached itself to Op. 55 No. 2, even though the Opp. 54 and 55 works were never published by Bland. In any case, there is nothing jokey about the music, at least until the bouncy 6/8 finale. The whole quartet charts the gradual ascendancy of F major over F minor. For the first time since Op. 17 No. 3, Haydn begins with a variation slow movement: here a set of 'double variations' on two related themes, the second a radiant major-key transformation of the astringent F minor opening. The first violin holds absolute sway until the cello soars into its plangent tenor register in the final F major variation.

F minor returns with a vengeance in the Allegro second movement, a spiky, rebarbative piece, rigorously monothematic and twice making disquieting capital from lengthy silences followed by a shift to the key a semitone higher. After the theme has been obsessively scrutinised in the contrapuntal development, the compressed recapitulation plunges immediately into F major and stays there. F major is confirmed in the extraordinary third movement, a minuet for philosophers that begins as a grave colloquy for first violin and viola and gradually flowers into four parts. (Could Haydn have been thinking of the introspective, intently polyphonic minuet in Mozart's A major Quartet, K464?) The trio reintroduces F minor for one last time before the finale's runaway triumph of F major.

Of Op. 55's two major-key quartets, No. 1 has a bold and brilliant first movement that gives plenty of scope to the leader's creative virtuosity, and a rondo finale that, like that of the slightly later 'Lark' Quartet, suddenly breaks into an elaborate fugato, with the skittering opening motif set against a sustained, *cantus firmus*-type theme. Opening as a string trio (i.e. minus the first violin), the noble Adagio cantabile, with its vocally inspired contrapuntal episode and written-out cadenzas for all four instruments, prefigures the great hymnic Adagios in the Op. 76 Quartets. In the trio of the minuet Haydn counterpoints the second violin's convivial *Ländler* tune with a stratospheric descant for the leader.

No. 3 in B flat is a more inward-looking work, with a pervasive (to some ears Mozartian) chromatic flavour. The ostensibly easy-going triple-time first movement – as monothematic as that in Op. 55 No. 2 – draws its tonal drama from the piquant clash between E flat and E natural in the opening bars. In the recapitulation the theme becomes even more chromatically unstable, and is then turned upside down in its reincarnation as 'second subject'. The Adagio ma non troppo – characterised, in Rosemary Hughes's words, by its 'grave and candid sweetness and underlying march-like tread' – consists of an unusually extended theme and two variations, the first decorative, the second conceived as a free canon. Nearly a decade later Haydn would provide an even more elaborate contrapuntal climax to a variation movement in the E flat Quartet, Op. 76 No. 6.

String Quartet in C, Op. 64 No. 1
String Quartet in B minor, Op. 64 No. 2
String Quartet in B flat, Op. 64 No. 3
String Quartet in G, Op. 64 No. 4
String Quartet in D, Op. 64 No. 5, 'Lark'
String Quartet in E flat, Op. 64 No. 6

With time on his hands in Vienna after the death of Prince Nicolaus Esterházy in September 1790, Haydn completed a new set of string quartets, published as Op. 64 and dedicated to Johann Tost. Again, there is no evidence that the first violin parts were conceived with Tost in mind, as has often been claimed. But we do know that Haydn took copies with him to England, and that three of the quartets, including, we may guess, Nos. 5 and 6 – the most 'public' of the six – were performed at Salomon's concerts in 1791.

The first, and least familiar, of the Op. 64 set opens with a leisurely Allegro moderato, written against the background of a march and exploiting the rich resonance of the cello's low C string. Though the movement is not strictly mono-thematic, the narrative is dominated by the sturdy opening theme, beginning as a trio before solidifying into a sonorous quartet texture. After an abbreviated recapitulation, the coda marvellously expands the music's scale and harmonic reach, pivoting to D flat major and then, after C major is regained, treating the theme in close canon. The upwardly mobile cello arpeggio that opens the minuet also fertilises the C minor trio, in essence a quizzical commentary on the minuet itself. For his skittish, not-so-slow movement (Allegretto scherzando) Haydn writes two variations on a popular-style theme (compare the Allegretto of Symphony No. 82) that includes an expressive deflection to A flat major. A flat also makes a surprise appearance at the centre of the scintillating finale, in a comically conspiratorial passage of tight canonic imitation. Like Nos. 2, 3 and 4, the quartet ends with a whisper.

Haydn's first B minor quartet, Op. 33 No. 1, had begun as if it were in D major. Op. 64 No. 2 follows suit, establishing B minor only at the end of the second bar, with an effect at once witty and disturbing. This initiates a movement that juxtaposes furious *Sturm und Drang* rhetoric and footling *buffo* tunes – though the closing theme, with its comic pizzicato twangs, acquires a more edgy cast when it recurs in B minor near the end, now shorn of its pizzicato. After this hyperactivity, the B major Adagio ma non troppo is a movement of seraphic calm, cast as a continuous series of ornamental variations on a sustained, four-note scale figure, like an ancient *cantus firmus*. In another extreme contrast, the mordant, naggingly asymmetrical minuet encloses a regularly phrased B major trio of Schubertian sweetness. The gypsy-influenced finale, growing entirely from its opening theme, plays with phrase structure and silence to unsettling effect. Midway through the recapitulation Haydn brings back the theme in an unsullied B major before the movement evaporates in a whimsical *pianissimo*.

Where the humour of No. 2 has a sardonic edge, the outer movements and minuet of No. 3 can approach slapstick. In the first movement the promise of Mozartian elegance is faintly undermined by the theme's irregular structure, and totally destroyed by a zany, galloping ostinato announced on the cello and enthusiastically taken up by the whole quartet. Suavity returns briefly with a cantabile 'second subject', which reappears in B flat minor in the development but is excised from the compressed recapitulation. The E flat Adagio is a solemn, gracious march in Haydn's favourite 'ternary variation' form, used also in the slow movements of Nos. 4, 5 and 6. Its rhetorical central section in E flat minor functions as both variation and development of the opening theme. The trio of the minuet, like its counterpart in the 'Oxford' Symphony, makes comic play with syncopation; and the finale is a riot of rhythmic fooling and gleefully thwarted expectations, its animation momentarily stilled by recurrent passages of hushed reflection, harmonised differently each time.

Haydn the subversive is also immediately at work in the G major Quartet, No. 4, deflating the dignity of the sweeping opening phrase with a little dactylic motif. This is a movement unusually rich in contrasting ideas, including a series of jagged syncopations and, as a resolving 'closing' theme, a tender, folk-like melody coloured by the violin's G-string. Even by late-Haydn standards, the recapitulation is an astonishing, radical reinterpretation of the events of the exposition. The minuet, with its yodelling, pizzicato-accompanied trio, is a bucolic *Ländler* transplanted into the drawing room, while the Adagio has that melodic purity and unsentimental sweetness so typical of Haydn's late slow movements. Characteristically, too, Haydn subjects the artless opening theme of the finale – little more than a Viennese street tune – to some artful polyphonic elaboration, both in the mercurial development (where it is combined with a slithering chromatic countermelody) and in the extended coda.

Most popular of the Op. 64 quartets is, of course, No. 5, 'The Lark'. The nickname comes from the first movement's unforgettable, winged melody high on the violin's E-string, played as a soaring descant to the pawky, staccato march for the lower three instruments that had opened proceedings. This Allegro moderato is as intently argued as any movement in Op. 64, yet creates an impression of marvellous spacious-ness thanks to the strategic recurrences of the complete 'lark' theme. After a recapitulation that develops as much as it resolves, the glorious melody makes a final, surprise appear-ance, initiating a long closing section that can be construed either as a coda or as a second, more orthodox recapitulation. The A major Adagio cantabile is a glowing meditation, with a central A minor section that draws poignant new meanings from the theme. As so often in Haydn, the minuet combines a peasant earthiness with witty and sophisticated motivic devel-opment. Its pervasive rising scale is taken up in the furtive D minor trio, initially in counterpoint to a traditional chromatic descending 'ground bass'. Haydn's irreverent use of a Baroque technique finds an echo in the fleeting fugato, likewise in

D minor, at the centre of the finale. This gossamer moto perpetuo – a favourite encore piece – was surely the prototype for Mendelssohn's 'fairy scherzos'.

Haydn may well have calculated the effect of this breathtaking finale, with its vote-catching *forte* ending, on his future English audiences. The finale of the E flat quartet, No. 6 – the model for the finale of Mozart's string quintet in the same key, K614 – is another tour de force, anticipating the 'London' symphonies in its wit and contrapuntal virtuosity. Just before the end, the scampering theme becomes comically hesitant, a ploy found elsewhere in Haydn's late works. By contrast, the monothematic first movement is quiet and inward-looking, with a widely modulating development that seems mesmerised by an apparently insignificant cadential figure. The minuet is sturdily symphonic, with a *Ländler* trio featuring peasant-style slides, as in Op. 33 No. 2. But the heart of the quartet is the B flat Andante. The outer sections, with their exquisitely interwoven lines and gently piercing dissonances, enfold a B flat minor episode in which the first violin weaves wild gypsy arabesques above a throbbing accompaniment.

String Quartet in B flat, Op. 71 No. 1
String Quartet in D, Op. 71 No. 2
String Quartet in E flat, Op. 71 No. 3
String Quartet in C, Op. 74 No. 1
String Quartet in F, Op. 74 No. 2
String Quartet in G minor, Op. 74 No. 3, 'Rider'

The long-standing tradition of public quartet performances in London – in this respect far ahead of Vienna – prompted Haydn to compose six new string quartets during 1793 for his forthcoming second visit to England. Two of them (it is not known which) were introduced at Salomon's concerts in 1794, though plans to perform the other four were aborted after the concerts came under new management. The six works, published in two groups of three, were dedicated to (and may have been commissioned by) Count Anton Georg Apponyi, who had sponsored Haydn's initiation into the Masonic brotherhood in 1785.

Though they never overstep the bounds of true chamber music, Opp. 71 and 74 are clearly designed for the concert hall rather than the salon. All six quartets feature powerful, sometimes quasi-orchestral sonorities, virtuoso writing for all four instruments, especially the first violin (a tribute to Salomon's prowess), and extreme contrasts of texture, register and dynamics. Allegros are urgent and strenuously argued, reflecting the proximity of the 'London' symphonies; and in both fast and slow movements Haydn favoured clearly defined melodies that could be easily assimilated by his audience. These extrovert tendencies were in part a response to the showy *quatuors concertants* by, inter alia, Adalbert Gyrowetz and Haydn's former pupil Ignaz Pleyel that were so popular in London – though unlike Pleyel and Gyrowetz, Haydn the architect never allows virtuosity to run amok. Another tendency of these quartets, characteristic of late Haydn, is their highly adventurous sense of tonality, manifested both in remote modulations within movements, and by the choice of a key a third away from the tonic for the trios of Op. 74 Nos. 1 and 2, and the Largo assai of Op. 74 No. 3.

Whereas most of Haydn's earlier quartets open quietly, those of Opp. 71 and 74 all begin with a forceful introductory gesture, a cue for any audience chattering to cease. In Op. 71 No. 1, this consists of five brisk cadential chords, another ending-as-beginning pun. The first movement gives the quartet ample opportunity to display its collective virtuosity. But this is one of Haydn's tightly argued monothematic structures, permeated by variants of the arpeggio figure in the theme's first bar. The beautiful F major Adagio, with its gently pungent chromaticism, is written against the background of the siciliano. After a central section that slips from F major via F minor to D flat, the return of the main theme is rescored with grace notes in all four parts, as if the whole quartet has been transformed into a harp. In the minuet Haydn has fun undermining the sturdiness of the main tune with quizzical little echoes and new chromatic harmonisations. Like the finales of many of the 'London' symphonies, the last movement combines racy tunes (including a rustic bagpipe melody), brilliant instrumental effects and intricate motivic development. It ends *pianissimo* with fragments of the bagpipe theme – the only one of these 'London' quartets to go out with a whisper.

Uniquely, Op. 71 No. 2 expands its initial gesture into a rhetorical four-bar slow introduction. Then the Allegro bursts in with a plunging octave figure that Haydn exploits with truculent energy, nowhere more than in the astringent modulations of the recapitulation and coda. The Adagio is one of those broad, majestic slow movements, part-aria, part-hymn, so characteristic of Haydn's late music. Though the outlines of sonata form are discernible, the movement is in essence a meditation on the spacious opening theme, unfolding with a sensuous richness of texture and gorgeous deep modulations. Conversely, the minuet is Haydn at his most laconic, teasingly irregular in phrase structure and worrying obsessively at the arpeggio figure proposed by the cello in the first bar. The trio, counterpointing chorale-like phrases with an insistent two-note figure, seems to remember the equally inscrutable trio of Symphony No. 46. The 6/8 finale is not quite the easy-going rondo it first appears. A minor-key episode takes up and develops the hints of counterpoint in the opening section; then, after an embellished return of the opening, the tempo increases from Allegretto to Allegro for a rousing send-off. Haydn would closely replicate this movement in the opening Allegretto of his last D major Quartet, Op. 76 No. 5.

The opening gesture of Op. 71 No. 3 is simply a grandly spaced E flat chord followed by a pregnant pause – a foretaste here of Beethoven's 'Eroica'. This is another of Haydn's intently monothematic movements, fertilised by the theme's first four bars. There is a touch of slapstick in the way the three repeated quavers of bar 4 are immediately echoed in hushed, conspiratorial tones (compare the opening of Op. 64 No. 4); and the whole restless movement is an absorbing mixture of the genial, the bizarre and (in the coda's shift to E flat minor, echoing the start of the development) the disturbing. The Andante is a blend of rondo and variations, built on the alternation of major and minor and on vivid contrasts of sonority. The most extreme contrast comes towards the end, as the sombrely contrapuntal second B flat minor episode yields to gossamer fairy music conjured by the three upper instruments, *staccato assai e piano*, in their highest register. Like the first movement, the minuet and the finale both concentrate fanatically on their opening phrases. The finale's 'oom-pah' accompaniment initially suggests a Viennese waltz. But soon Haydn is working his tune polyphonically, first in a 'rough' two-part octave texture (shades here of the earliest quartets), then in a sinewy fugato.

The laconic introductory gesture in the C major Quartet, Op. 74 No. 1 – a pair of massive, widely spaced chords – immediately proclaims the work's trademark sonorous richness and outlines the interval of a rising semitone that pervades the thematic material. Despite important subsidiary ideas, including a gypsy-style tune that appears as a belated 'second subject', virtually the whole movement is saturated by the chromatically rising opening theme. The recapitulation continues to excavate the theme's potential, first in a powerful passage of canonic imitation, then in a dramatic deflection to A flat that heralds perhaps the most incandescent climax in all Haydn's quartets.

The Andantino, opening with two-part octave writing, is a foil to all this brilliance and intensity. Yet despite its easy charm, this is fastidiously wrought music, with subtly irregular phrase lengths, fluid textures and, in the coda, a nonchalant shift from G major to its polar opposite, C sharp. The forthright minuet is a miniature sonata structure, even including a 'second development' after the theme's reprise. Emphasis on the flat side of the spectrum here makes the turn to A major for the trio (a lyrical variant of the minuet's theme) all the more radiant. The finale again epitomises Haydn's popular style, combining contredanse tunes and bucolic bagpipe effects with dazzling virtuosity.

Op. 74 No. 2 opens with peremptory, fanfare-like unisons that turn out to be a skeletal outline of the main (and virtually only) theme. For all the tune's comic opera flavour, this is a grand and complex symphonic structure, with an exciting contrapuntal imbroglio in the central development. Even more than in Op. 74 No. 1, the writing is palpably orchestrally influenced, with its assertive unisons, massed trills, broken-octave basses and rhetorical pauses. There is a strong family likeness between the melody of the B flat Andante grazioso and the 'clock' theme of Symphony No. 101. The three variations on this skittish tune show a delicate sense of colour, highlighting each of the instruments at one point or another. In the central one, a free meditation on the theme in B flat minor, first and second violins swap their usual roles. As in several of the 'London' symphonies, the minuet is more than halfway to a scherzo. The trio dips romantically into the dusky key of D flat major. Not surprisingly, the impish melody of the finale was an instant hit, and soon appeared in keyboard arrangements. Its riotous progress is several times interrupted by an enigmatic, faintly oriental-sounding tune in long note values. The finale of Op. 64 No. 3 had traded on a similar contrast.

While No. 95 in C minor was probably the least popular of the 'London' symphonies, the obligatory minor-key work in the Opp. 71/74 quartets, Op. 74 No. 3, became a special favourite. Its nickname, 'The Rider', prompted by the galloping rhythms of the finale, further reinforced its popularity. Like Op. 74 No. 2, it begins with eight bars of arresting in-tempo introduction; and even more than in No. 2, this introductory material is closely integrated into the main body of the movement. Its repeated pairs of notes influence both the tense, fragmentary first theme and the second subject, a blithe *Ländler* that later initiates the mysterious chromatic journey back to the recapitulation.

Whereas the Andantes of Op. 74 Nos. 1 and 2 were points of relaxation, No. 3's slow movement is one of Haydn's most searching. Its key, E major, is a glowing contrast with the G major close of the Allegro; its tempo, Largo assai, the slowest known to the eighteenth century. The whole sublime movement is built on a grave melody that becomes more and more boldly rhetorical as it proceeds, with startling plunges to remote chords. When the main section returns, after the central E minor episode, Haydn intensifies the rhetoric with flamboyant decorations for the leader, and an awed *pianissimo* tremolo for all four instruments – a recreation of orchestral technique that was not lost on nineteenth-century composers.

After the Largo's hushed close, the G major minuet at first tactfully avoids the boisterous rhythms and forceful emphasis on the home key that marked the minuets of Nos. 1 and 2. The leader's repeated high Ds in the second half provide the cue for the edgily chromatic G minor trio, which confounds expectations by heightening rather than relaxing the tension. The finale sets the agitated 'riding' theme against high-lying bravura for the leader and an airborne second subject. Haydn fuses elements of both themes in the explosive development and in the coda, which finally resolves the movement's contrasts in a joyous burst of G major.

String Quartet in G, Op. 76 No. 1
String Quartet in D minor, Op. 76 No. 2, 'Fifths'
String Quartet in C, Op. 76 No. 3, 'Emperor'
String Quartet in B flat, Op. 76 No. 4, 'Sunrise'
String Quartet in D, Op. 76 No. 5
String Quartet in E flat, Op. 76 No. 6

The quartets published as Op. 76 by Longman & Broderip in 1799 are contemporaneous with *The Creation*. Commissioned by, and dedicated to, Haydn's friend Count Joseph Erdődy, they were begun in the autumn of 1796 and finished the following summer. These, his last completed set of six, share the combination of popular appeal and profundity of thought found in the 'London' symphonies and the Opp. 71 and 74 quartets. Like Opp. 71 and 74 they were designed as much for the concert hall as for the salon. But their arguments are still more unpredictable, sometimes to the point of magisterial eccentricity, their contrasts – not least their lurches from sophisticated salon to village green – still more extreme. No set of eighteenth-century string quartets is so diverse, or so heedless of the norms of the time. After hearing them in London, Haydn's friend Charles Burney wrote to say that he 'never received more pleasure from instrumental music: they are full of invention, fire, good taste and new effects, and seem the product, not of a sublime genius who has written so much and so well already, but one of highly-cultivated talents, who had expended none of his fire before'.

After three introductory chords – shades here of the calls to attention in Opp. 71 and 74 – No. 1 in G begins with an almost absurdly naive tune on solo cello (could this be an irreverent fugue subject, we fleetingly wonder), and continued by the viola. Then, in no time, the tune is being put through its paces, repeated in two-part counterpoint and developed in a full, sonorous quartet texture. The whole movement is a supreme example of Haydn's popular style, in which square-cut, quasi-folk melodies are treated with exhilarating freedom. Next comes one of those hymn-like Adagios that are among the glories of late Haydn. The noble, assuaging theme, wonderfully varied on its reappearances, alternates with minor-key episodes featuring sorrowful or agitated dialogue between cello, in its deepest register, and first violin.

Late in life, when he was obviously feeling minueted-out, Haydn exclaimed that he wished someone would write a really *new* minuet. He answered his own call in spades with Op. 76. The laconic so-called 'minuet' of No. 1, with its tiptoeing staccato and tactless *forte* outbursts, is no minuet at all, but Haydn's first Presto scherzo. Perhaps, as Robbins Landon has suggested, he was influenced here by the scherzos in Beethoven's recently published Op. 1 Piano Trios. The tempo slows right down for the trio, a yodelling serenade, with a suggestion of comic parody.

After this foolery the finale, marked Allegro ma non troppo (many quartets ignore the 'non troppo' and turn the movement into a hectic tarantella), opens in a strenuous G *minor*: a startling move in a work that had begun in the major, and something Haydn had done only once before, in Symphony No. 70. Mendelssohn, in the 'Italian' Symphony, and Brahms, in works including the G major Violin Sonata and Third Symphony, would follow suit. Here, for the first time in his quartets (with the partial exceptions of the fugal finales of Op. 20 and Op. 50 No. 4), Haydn writes a finale that far surpasses the first movement in weight and expressive scope. The development explores the mysterious extremes of the harmonic universe; then, in the recapitulation, the driving main theme emerges, as if in a daze, into the light of G major. Finally, the coda turns the theme into a flippant polka, cocking a snook at the drama and turbulence that have gone before: the kind of ironic dissociation that calls to mind the throwaway ending of Beethoven's F minor Quartet, Op. 95.

In contrast to the blithe first movement of No. 1, the opening Allegro of the D minor Quartet, No. 2, is the composer at his grimmest and most obsessive: yet again, there is no hint of Mozartian pathos in Haydn's use of the minor mode. The initial falling fifths motif that spawned the work's nickname is developed with fanatical concentration and ingenuity, right through to the ferocious coda. The serenade-like D major Andante, o più tosto Allegretto, a typical amalgam of variation, ternary and sonata form, is a relaxing interlude between the argumentative rigour of the first movement and the extraordinary so-called 'witches' minuet'. This carries the archaic-sounding, two-part canonic writing of Haydn's earliest quartets to rebarbative and, as some have heard, sinister extremes. The trio, with its head-on collisions of D minor and D major, is just as brutally eccentric, looking forward through late Beethoven to the scherzo of Bruckner's Ninth Symphony. Sharpened fourths and violin glissandi give the main theme of the finale an exotic, Hungarian flavour. The rustic atmosphere is later enhanced by musette drones and braying donkey imitations – Mendelssohn's *Midsummer Night's Dream* Overture *avant la lettre*. Near the start of the recapitulation D minor yields to D major with a magical, *pianissimo* transformation of the main theme.

The famous 'Emperor', Op. 76 No. 3, follows the broad structural pattern of No. 1, with an Adagio of particular beauty and intensity, and a powerful finale that begins in the minor. The opening Allegro, built entirely from a single blunt, compact theme, is the culmination of Haydn's sonorous symphonic style in his late quartets, with the four players often doing a fair imitation of a string orchestra. At the centre of the development the protean theme morphs spectacularly into a peasant dance in the bright, distant key of E major: perhaps Haydn's most raucous rustic outburst (and there is plenty of competition) before the whooping wine chorus in *The Seasons*.

After this unbridled extroversion, the Poco adagio, variations on Haydn's 'Emperor's Hymn', is a miraculous fusion of the popular and the elevated. Sounded in turn by second violin, cello and viola, the great melody is treated as a *cantus firmus* against countermelodies of growing chromatic and polyphonic complexity. In the fourth and final variation the tune is subtly reharmonised in a full four-part texture to create a quiet apotheosis. The minuet, aggressively asymmetrical in phrasing, develops its first three notes with nagging insistence; its pensive A minor trio, enclosing a beautiful turn to A major, surely struck a chord with Schubert. As in Op. 76 No. 1, the hurtling Presto finale defies convention by beginning in the minor key and remaining there for most of its impassioned, densely argued course. Only at the very end does C major shyly emerge, with an ethereal lightening of the hitherto massive textures.

No. 4's sobriquet 'The Sunrise' comes from its poetic opening, unprecedented in Haydn's, or anyone else's, quartets: over soft, sustained chords that seem to steal in from nowhere, the first violin spins a rapt, upward-curling melody. Characteristically, though, this air of improvisatory freedom goes hand in hand with taut monothematic argument. The 'London' legacy is again felt in a brilliant 'tutti' passage, based on a speeded-up version of a four-note figure from the theme; then, when the 'second subject' arrives, it turns out to be a free, condensed inversion of the first, with the theme now curving downwards in the cello. True to form, Haydn continues to draw new meanings from this unforgettable theme in the recapitulation, and in the coda, where a variant of the opening sounds hauntingly in the viola's husky lowest register.

The E flat major Adagio is one of Haydn's profound meditations, strangely ambivalent in mood. Though it has the outlines of sonata form, with a recapitulation beginning in E flat *minor* and continuing with a sequence of closely overlapping imitative entries, the movement sounds like a series of free variations on the theme's first five notes. The *sans-culotte* minuet typically combines unkempt earthiness with a sophisticated elaboration of its pounding theme. There is an exotic, Balkan flavour to the trio, with its drones and strange equivocations between major and minor. Whereas the other Op. 76 quartets end with movements in full sonata form, the finale here begins as if it is to be a rondo on a country-dance theme (some have heard an English accent here). But after a B flat minor episode and a varied reprise of the main theme, Haydn writes a crazy, gradually accelerating coda that fragments the theme between the four instruments – a ploy Beethoven was to pick up in his late string quartets.

In the last two works of Op. 76, Haydn abandons the traditional sonata-form opening movement for variation-based structures that serve as preludes to their profound slow movements. The D major, No. 5, begins with an ingenuous-sounding melody, first cousin to 'With verdure clad' in *The Creation*. But pastoral innocence is belied by the central section in D minor, which develops the melody in austere contrapuntal textures before launching into an energetic new theme. After a return of the opening, Haydn ratchets up the tempo for an exhilarating coda that is both a culmination and a further development.

The quartet's centre of gravity is the celebrated Largo ma non troppo, *cantabile e mesto*, in the remote, luminous key of F sharp major. Nowadays we tend to hear this fathomless music as serenely contemplative rather than sorrowful (*mesto*), touched with a visionary strangeness in the labyrinthine harmonic explorations at the centre of the movement. The minuet takes the theme of the Largo and transmutes it into something altogether more robust and convivial; in extreme contrast, the D minor trio is an edgy piece, counterpointing an obsessive two-note cadential figure with a scurrying cello part. This same cadential figure launches the finale, an irresistible movement that works the scrapings and skirlings of a village band into a sonata structure of coruscating verve and endless surprises.

The final quartet of the set is the most elusive, with little of the mellow lyricism usually associated in Haydn and Mozart with the key of E flat. Its first movement begins as a set of variations on a dry, skeletal theme – hardly a tune – treated, like the 'Emperor's Hymn' in Op. 76 No. 3, as a kind of *cantus firmus*. After three variations Haydn quickens the tempo and works the theme in an extended fugato: the upshot is the first great example of the variation-and-fugue form that was to have such an influence on Beethoven and later nineteenth-century composers.

Marked 'Fantasia', the Adagio, astonishingly original even by the standards of Op. 76, takes its theme through such a maze of tonalities, linked by winding solos for first violin or cello, that the music initially has no key signature. After eventually settling in B major, the key in which it had begun, it flowers into tranquil, rarefied polyphony that simultaneously looks far into the past and forward to the late Beethoven quartets. The manic Presto scherzo contains a trio (or, as Haydn dubs it, 'Alternativo') that repeats a simple E flat scale, first descending then ascending, in kaleidoscopically varied textures and harmonies. The effect is both witty and mesmerising. Descending scales also saturate the boisterous yet laconic finale, another movement without a tune worth the name. But this is thoroughly engrossing music, forever deceiving the listener as to where the main beat comes, and reaching unruly extremes of rhythmic anarchy in the development.

String Quartet in G, Op. 77 No. 1
String Quartet in F, Op. 77 No. 2
Quartet Fragment, Op. 103

In 1799, two years after completing Op. 76, Haydn was commissioned to write six more quartets by Prince Lobkowitz, best known as one of Beethoven's most generous patrons. But with his physical strength gradually sapped by *The Seasons*, he could only complete a brace of quartets, published as Op. 77. Though less inclined to eccentricity than Op. 76, the two works make a glorious culmination. They have all the nonchalant mastery of technique acquired over five decades of quartet writing; and they encompass with ease a vast range of experience, from rustic revelry, through sociable wit and lyrical tenderness to Wordsworthian voyages through 'strange seas of thought, alone'.

The crisp opening Allegro moderato of the G major, No. 1, has a suggestion of Schubert's 'wandering' movements in its tramping rhythms. Haydn makes great play with chirpy dialogues; and characteristically, the 'second subject' begins as a reinterpretation of the first (with a new violin/cello dialogue), before the brief appearance of a new, soaring cantabile theme. The development's emphasis on sharp keys makes the E flat of the Adagio sound even richer and deeper. Haydn again emphasises violin/cello dialogue in a movement that mingles sonata form, variation and passacaglia (the initial unison motif is present virtually throughout). Traversing realms of dazzling darkness, it majestically crowns the series of exalted Haydn Adagios that left such a profound effect on Beethoven.

The so-called minuet, like those of Op. 76 Nos. 1 and 6, has all the Presto pace, aggressive offbeat accents and uncombed energy of a Beethovenian scherzo; the trio, diving abruptly into E flat (the key of the Adagio), suggests a frenzied peasant dance. Could Beethoven have remembered it when he came to write the trio of his final quartet, Op. 135? The bucolic spirit spills over into the finale, full of rhythmic quirks and subtleties, and making much of quickfire antiphonal exchanges between the upper and lower pairs of instruments. Typically, too, the whole movement grows ingeniously from its opening bars.

Compared with the breezy first movement of the G major quartet, the Allegro moderato that opens Op. 77 No. 2 is an altogether grander, more densely worked affair. The main theme here is an ample, lyrical melody, immediately repeated and varied in an enriched texture. Its opening phrase pervades the second-subject group, initially as a shadowy counterpoint to a sinuous new tune. But it is an apparently incidental, 'transitional' figure of repeated quavers that dominates the development, taking the music, via a series of mysterious, gliding modulations (including an 'enharmonic' shift from E flat to D sharp), deep into abstruse tonal regions. The Menuetto, placed second for the first time since the minuet of Op. 64 No. 4, is as much a one-in-the-bar scherzo as its counterpart in the G major quartet. It is even more zany in spirit, with a half-comic, half-truculent conflict between triple and duple metre and an ongoing identity crisis for the cello, which persists in imitating a drum. As in Op. 77 No. 1, the trio dips to the key of the flat submediant (here D flat), though in this quartet the tone is one of lyrical warmth, with deep, glowing textures.

The move to the 'flat' side of the spectrum for the trio is balanced by the choice of the bright, 'sharp' key of D major for the slow movement. This opens with an oddly haunting duet for violin and cello memorably described by Robin Holloway as ' "three blind mice" with twiddles'. But, as so often in Haydn, initial simplicity is deceptive; and from the moment second violin and viola add their voices for a gravely sonorous four-part harmonisation, the music suggests an altogether more complex experience. The whole movement, a synthesis of rondo and variations (the 'three blind mice' theme, illuminated by ever-changing harmonies and textures, is omnipresent), is a quiet and sublime apotheosis of the characteristic Haydn 'walking' Andante. The scherzo's tugs between duple and triple time are resumed in the finale, music of unflagging rhythmic and contrapuntal energy that juxtaposes and transfigures polonaise and Slavonic folk-dance. 'Grant me an old man's frenzy,' implored Yeats in his poem 'An Acre of Grass.' It was granted to Haydn.

This irrepressible movement rounds off Haydn's last completed quartet. In 1803 he composed the slow movement and minuet of a projected quartet in D minor, intended to supplement the two works of Op. 77. By this time the seventy-one-year-old composer could not muster the sustained concentration needed for what were traditionally the most intellectually demanding movements, the first (from which a sketch for a bass line survives), and the last, which, we may guess, would have ended in the major key. The two movements, 'Haydn's swansong' (Griesinger), were published as Op. 103.

The B flat Andante grazioso, true to its marking, opens with one of Haydn's most gracious, friendly tunes, though its innocence is compromised by the touches of chromatic harmony and refined, semi-contrapuntal textures. It is typical of late Haydn that the middle section plunges to G flat and modulates as far afield as C sharp minor and E major. The drooping chromaticisms of the coda exude a valedictory melancholy. The D minor minuet (this time definitely not a scherzo) is equally chromatic, a cussed, angular piece briefly relieved by a nostalgic D major trio: 'the last incandescence of the flame now held captive within the failing body' (Rosemary Hughes's words), and testimony to the old composer's undimmed inventiveness in the medium which, almost single-handedly, he took to supreme heights of expressiveness, textural subtlety and intellectual power.

Keyboard trios

In the late eighteenth century the combination of keyboard (usually played by a woman), violin and cello (traditional male preserves) was a popular one in aristocratic and bourgeois homes, and a highly lucrative one for publishers, especially in England. It was primarily to satisfy this flourishing market that Haydn composed twenty-eight keyboard trios (Nos. 5–32 in Hoboken's catalogue) between 1784 and 1796. While the 'Gypsy Rondo' has long been a popular hit, the other trios are still among Haydn's least-known masterpieces, mainly because of their supposed lack of interest for violinists and, especially, cellists. 'Only pianists will ever want to play them,' opined Charles Rosen in a superb chapter on the trios in *The Classical Style*. Haydn followed eighteenth-century convention in describing the trios as for harpsichord or fortepiano, with violin and violoncello. Yet while the keyboard remains pre-eminent, their textures are far more varied than is often assumed, as string players who have actually bothered with the trios will vouch.

Far from being a dispensable supporting act in the mature trios, the cello adds crucial timbral and harmonic colour, rhythmic definition and sustaining power to the keyboard bass, which on the fortepiano had nothing like the sonority of the modern Steinway. Beyond that, as Dean Sutcliffe has argued in a challenging article in *Music Analysis* (6/3, 1987, subsequently expanded in *Haydn Studies* (CUP)), the textures frequently raise the question, 'Who is doubling whom?' Certainly, Haydn's eloquent, wide-ranging bass lines, especially in the slow movements, arise directly from the presence of the cello. There are also many instances where the not-so-subservient cello provides the true bass, often in the form of pedal points, while the keyboard is otherwise occupied.

What all commentators agree on is the glorious quality of Haydn's trios. In Tovey's words, they are 'far richer than the quartets in fine specimens of his smaller forms, such as alternating variations, sectional rondos, lyric "A, B, A" slow movements, and, above all, movements breaking off and leading into finales'. More intimate than the contemporary string quartets, less concerned with intensive motivic development, the trios mingle relaxed lyricism, a spacious freedom of design, and a tonal adventurousness astonishing even by late-Haydn standards. Like the part-songs he wrote after his second London visit, they give the impression of being written 'in happy hours, *con amore*'.

Note: Various numbering systems exist for the trios, most recently those devised by H. C. Robbins Landon (Doblinger) and Wolfgang Stockmeier (in the complete Haydn edition published by the Joseph Haydn Institut, Cologne). For simplicity's sake, the traditional Hoboken numberings, still the most commonly used, are given here.

Early trios

Partita in E, Hob. XV: 34
Divertimento in A, Hob. XV: 35
Partita in E flat, Hob. XV: 36
Divertimento in F, Hob. XV: 37
Divertimento in B flat, Hob. XV: 38
Divertimento in F, Hob. XV: 40
Divertimento in G, Hob. XV: 41
Partita in F minor, Hob. XV: f1
Partita in G minor, Hob. XV: 1
Divertimento in F, Hob. XV: 2

A quarter of a century and more before the great keyboard trios of the 1780s and 1790s, Haydn composed a dozen or so trios, dubbed 'divertimento' or 'partita', that look back to the Baroque trio sonata. Melodies are usually proposed by the keyboard's right hand and answered by the violin, while the keyboard bass, faithfully shadowed by the cello, performs a *basso continuo* function. Like the sonatas, these early trios are a minefield for the scholar. Some works are lost, others were attributed to Haydn but not verified by him, while several are arrangements, probably by another hand, of keyboard sonatas. Of the ten listed above, the F major, Hoboken No. 2 – beginning, unusually, with a violin solo, and ending with a set of variations on a typically asymmetrical theme – reworks movements from baryton pieces composed around 1770. The others probably date from 1755–60, and were composed either for pupils or for musical parties at the country residences of Haydn's two earliest patrons, Fürnberg and Count Morzin.

All the early trios except the four-movement No. 41 have three movements, including a minuet (replaced in No. 36 by a lusty polonaise). One of the most attractive is No. 37 in F, on the old *sonata da chiesa* pattern (i.e. with an opening slow movement) found in several early Haydn symphonies. The second movement is a scherzando frolic, the finale an urbane, leisurely minuet that could have come from the pen of Bach's youngest son, Johann Christian. There is nothing very capricious about the so-called Capriccio that opens No. 35 in A; and both Nos. 38 and 41 trip by uneventfully. The minuet of No. 34 in E contains a dusky syncopated trio in E minor. Most memorable are the F minor, No. f1, and the G minor, No. 1, probably Haydn's earliest works in the minor key. The G minor is especially striking, with its austere, Baroque-style first movement, its laconic minuet enfolding a *galant*, violin-dominated trio, and a finale that infuses the capering 3/8 metre of Haydn's early symphonies with a spiky abrasiveness.

Mature trios
1784–1785

Trio in G, Hob. XV: 5
Trio in F, Hob. XV: 6

Trio in D, Hob. XV: 7
Trio in B flat, Hob. XV: 8
Trio in A, Hob. XV: 9
Trio in E flat, Hob. XV: 10

Inundated by requests from publishers in the 1780s, Haydn was not averse to taking the odd short cut. When asked by the London firm of William Forster for three new keyboard trios (or 'sonatas', as they were routinely called), he duly supplied a recent one of his own, No. 5. But to save time he pilfered the other two, Nos. 3 and 4 in Hoboken's catalogue, from his former pupil Ignaz Pleyel. The 'stolen' trios still appear in some editions, though it is amazing that their cliché-ridden banality could ever have fooled anyone. By contrast, the genuine Haydn trios from the mid-1780s – the period of the 'Paris' symphonies – are subtly inventive works, with close collusion between fortepiano and violin and a crucial, and varied, role for the cello. All except Nos. 5 and 7 are in the fashionable two-movement form. No. 6 in F and No. 8 in B flat both end with a meditative minuet that, as in several of Mozart's violin sonatas and Haydn's own keyboard sonatas, transmutes aristocratic *galanterie* into something more personal. In their central minor-key episodes, beginning as free variants of the main sections, Haydn exploits the violin's capacity for plangent lyricism, supported by the sustaining power of the cello.

In a review of trios Nos. 2 (composed much earlier), 9 and 10, the writer in Cramer's *Magazin der Musik* of 1786 noted the 'inexpressible charm' of No. 9's initial Adagio. Uniquely, Haydn here abandons close, small-scale dialogue in favour of a broad opposition of keyboard and strings. The quasi-Baroque formality of the opening melts into pure Romanticism as the strings, playing in sonorous tenths, spin their succulent lyrical lines over gently rippling piano sextuplets: a thoroughly 'modern' trio texture that to our ears evokes Schubert and Mendelssohn. At the climax of this ravishing movement is a written-out cadenza for the three instruments. For the *Magazin der Musik*, the E flat Trio, No. 10, was the work 'in which Haydn's genius soars to its greatest heights'. The opening Allegro moderato, launched by an arresting unison 'motto', veers between the 'learned' style (the motto is tightly worked in overlapping imitations) and the free-flowing, improvisatory manner characteristic of these trios. Haydn follows this with a mercurial rondo in tarantella rhythm in which everything derives from the darting main theme.

Of the two trios in three movements, No. 5 in G is notable for its opening Adagio non tanto, a mix of rhetorical grandeur and poetic fantasy. The D major, No. 7, has two undemanding movements followed by a rondo in contredanse style that indulges in some comically outlandish harmonic adventures. After finding himself in the unscripted key of E flat, Haydn uses the theme's teasing two-note upbeat figure to pivot the music enharmonically into B major. Then, almost before we realise it, we are back in the home key of D major. A surviving sketch shows the care with which Haydn worked out this elaborate modulatory strategy.

1788–1790

Trio in E flat, Hob. XV: 11
Trio in E minor, Hob. XV: 12
Trio in C minor, Hob. XV: 13
Trio in A flat, Hob. XV: 14

Nos. 11–13 were published as a set by Artaria in 1789, while No. 14 was finished in January 1790 and issued separately. Though Nos. 11 and 13 are in the fashionable two-movement form favoured in the trios of 1784–5, all four trios are more ambitious and, on the whole, more serious. Parts of No. 11 in E flat and No. 12 in E minor sound distinctly Mozartian to us. The unhurried procession of themes in No. 11's expansive first movement, the peculiar tenderness of its minuet finale (shades here of Mozart's F major Violin Sonata, K377), and the mingled breadth, brilliance and passion of No. 12's opening Allegro, which has little of the nervy abruptness typical of

Haydn in the minor key: all might be mistaken for Mozart on a casual hearing. Characteristic of Haydn, though, are the remote modulations in No. 11's first movement, including the most fake of fake recapitulations in the key of F major, a ploy Haydn had recently used in another E flat work, Symphony No. 84. It was doubtless a movement like this that prompted a contemporary reviewer of Nos. 11–13 to alert prospective purchasers of their 'frequent excursions into distant keys – which often require many accidentals, even double ones'.

Typically Haydnesque, too, is the way No. 12's vehement opening theme saturates the texture, often in contrapuntal combinations. In the coda, set implacably in E minor, the three instruments in unison hurl out a fiercely compressed version of the theme, a thrilling climax to one of the most powerful movements in all Haydn's chamber music. Though the Andante, in the composer's lilting 6/8 pastoral vein, and the finale are in a relaxing E major, they are comparably sophisticated in workmanship. In the second episode of the finale – a sonata rondo that often treats the trio as a surrogate orchestra – Haydn plays all sorts of impish games with the theme, including a passage of quicksilver canonic imitation where the cello has its own independent voice.

For whatever reason, Artaria asked Haydn to recompose the first movement of No. 13. He duly obliged, writing to the publisher on 29 March 1789, 'I am sending the third sonata [i.e. trio], which according to your taste, I have newly rewritten, with variations.' As in the near-contemporary 'Razor' Quartet, Op. 55 No. 2, the movement is in Haydn's (by 1789) favourite minor-major 'double variation' form. While the sober C minor opening is largely the piano's property, its radiant C major transformation is always associated with the violin. Another telling transformation comes in the finale, where at the very end of the exposition the military-style main theme morphs into a songful tune in the piano's warm tenor register.

Haydn obviously had a special regard for the A flat Trio, No. 14, presenting it at a London concert on 20 April 1792 with the thirteen-year-old Hummel at the fortepiano. Like its closest counterpart among the solo sonatas, No. 52 in E flat, this glorious work has a symphonic amplitude and grandeur that make it well suited to public performance. Even by late-Haydn standards, the first movement is breathtaking in its tonal reach. A 'rogue' B natural near the end of the exposition presages a whole section in the development in the key of B major (in technical terms, the enharmonic equivalent of the flat mediant, C flat major). As in Sonata No. 52, this enharmonic excursion has repercussions in the choice of E major (= F flat) for the Adagio, whose serene outer sections enfold an impassioned, gypsy-style episode in E minor. This is the earliest of Haydn's works to set its slow movement in a 'third-related' key: a practice unknown in Mozart's instrumental works, but eagerly taken up by the young Beethoven. The Adagio leads without a break, via further enharmonic sleight of hand, into a sonata-form finale that exploits its repeated-note upbeat with gleeful inventiveness, throwing the listener with clownish contrasts of register and sly chromatic dislocations.

1790

Trio in G, Hob. XV: 15
Trio in D, Hob. XV: 16
Trio in F, Hob. XV: 17

Though they work well as 'normal' piano trios, Haydn wrote these three works for flute – the favourite instrument of the eighteenth-century gentleman amateur – rather than violin. As Dean Sutcliffe has remarked, their airy, 'open' quality, akin to Mozart's flute concertos, derives from the presence of the wind instrument. Textures tend to be looser and simpler than in the conventionally scored trios, with long stretches for keyboard alone, less complex part-writing and relatively little intimate dialogue between the instruments. Far lighter than Nos. 11–14, the flute trios set a premium on tunefulness and charm. But for all their amiability, they share with

Haydn's other works of the period a taste for harmonic adventure. In Nos. 15 and 16, particularly, the first movements specialise in leisurely, pre-Schubertian digressions to distant keys. The opening Allegro of No. 16 in D has such a lengthy and widely modulating development that Haydn needs to balance it, à la Beethoven, with a substantial coda, initiated by the Papageno-ish second subject in the remote key of E flat. Both these trios have comically exuberant rondo finales (No. 15's takes Haydn's favourite teasing upbeat ploy to outlandish lengths), while the two-movement No. 17 ends with a *galant* minuet in fully developed sonata form.

c.1792–1794

Trio in G, Hob. XV: 32
Trio in A, Hob. XV: 18
Trio in G minor, Hob. XV: 19
Trio in B flat, Hob. XV: 20

With the probable exception of the innocuous two-movement Trio No. 32, published in 1794, there are no keyboard trios from Haydn's first London sojourn. But on his second visit and in the months after his final return to Vienna in the autumn of 1795, he produced no fewer than fourteen trios. Though written in response to the popular demand for accompanied keyboard music in general, and Haydn's in particular, these late trios enshrine some of the composer's most personal music. As David Wyn Jones has suggested, during the 1790s, as the string quartet moved from the chamber to the concert hall, the piano trio in some respects assumed the role of musical initiate and confidant.

Nos. 18–20 appeared as a set in 1794 with a dedication to the Dowager Princess Maria Anna, widow of Prince Anton Esterházy. Like all but two of the late trios, they are in three movements. Most immediately striking is No. 18 in A, with its lyrically expansive yet tightly monothematic first movement, its pensive A minor Andante enclosing a heart-easing episode in A major, and its syncopated finale, a sort of polonaise in the Hungarian gypsy style. At the centre of the opening Allegro moderato Haydn indulges in one of his most audacious volte-faces: after hovering on the edge of F sharp minor, he pauses briefly and then plunges us somewhere in the region of E flat, initiating a kaleidoscopic sequence of modulations underpinned by the first three notes of the theme.

The G minor Trio, No. 19, opens with a set of alternating major-minor variations, but with an original twist. The major-key melody grows smoothly out of the chromatic clos-ing phrase of the marchlike minor-key tune. After varying each melody once, Haydn ups the tempo to a gigue-like Presto and cunningly expands the G major tune into a minia-ture sonata movement. The Adagio ma non troppo has the dreamy, improvisatory quality so characteristic of the late trios (compare, say, the slow movements of Nos. 22 and 26), while the finale is a brisk 6/8 canter that begins in G minor but brightens to G major for the homecoming.

With its rich chordal writing and exploitation of the keyboard's extremes, the monothematic opening Allegro of No. 20 in B flat is Haydn's most pianistically virtuosic trio movement so far. The Andante is a curiously haunting piece, a set of variations whose theme is presented in an austere two-part texture for piano left hand, like a duet for viola and cello. For his finale Haydn writes a minuet, faster and earthier than in the trios of the 1780s, with a *zingarese*-flavoured violin solo in the central B flat minor episode.

1794–1795

Trio in C, Hob. XV: 21
Trio in E flat, Hob. XV: 22
Trio in D minor, Hob. XV: 23
Trio in E flat minor, Hob. XV: 31

Haydn dedicated trios 21–3 to Princess Marie Hermenegild Esterházy, for whom he would compose most of his late masses. No. 21, which uniquely in the trios opens with a brief slow introduction, is an outgoing piece that trades on broad, quasi-symphonic effects. Bucolic bagpipes are evoked in the 6/8 opening movement, where Haydn atones for a relatively brief, uneventful development with a vastly elaborated recapitulation. The Andante is built on a *Romanze*-style melody (shades here of Symphony No. 85), while the darting final Presto is a more compact counterpart to the finales of the 'London' symphonies. No. 23 begins with another set of minor-major double variations, a form that had delighted English music-lovers since the success of Symphony No. 53 in the 1780s. After a richly ornamented Adagio non troppo comes a catchy German dance finale – a typical feature of the late trios – opening in sinuous two-part counterpoint and spiced by disruptive cross-rhythms.

Finest of the set, though, is the E flat, No. 22, all of whose movements show Haydn's harmonic thinking at its most exploratory. The opening Allegro moderato is at once majestic and intimate, with what Charles Rosen has called a 'feeling of spacious, relaxed, almost improvised expansion' so characteristic of the late trios. The musing Poco adagio, in the bright, 'third-related' key of G major, sublimates rococo sentiment into Romantic poetry: as so often in the late trios, Schubert is on the horizon. Haydn ends with another fetching triple-time dance movement, here somewhere between a *Deutsche* and a polonaise. Eighteenth-century connoisseurs will have relished the spectacular modulating sequence at the start of the development, moving to a far-flung A major, the polar opposite of E flat.

Published on its own as late as 1803, No. 31 began life in 1794 as a single-movement trio for Therese Jansen, for whom Haydn also wrote the trios Nos. 27–9 and at least two of the last three piano sonatas. The following year Haydn created a two-movement trio by prefacing this Allegro ben moderato with an Andante cantabile in E flat minor, his only movement in this 'extreme' key. This is one of Haydn's individual rondo-variation designs. The first episode, in E flat major, turns the austere, march-like E flat minor theme upside down, while the second introduces a soaring violin tune in the distant, 'enharmonic' key of B major. Haydn also alights in B major at the centre of the finale, another sophisticated take on a German dance, with a specially close and animated collusion between keyboard and violin. According to Dies, the rapid violin scales at several points were intended to depict 'the heavenly ladder that Jacob saw in his dream' – hence the movement's original title 'Jacob's Dream', which Haydn suppressed when he added the opening Andante. In 1803, asked to supply a new sonata for the wife of General Victor Moreau, the now frail composer omitted the cello part and offered the work as a sonata for piano and violin.

1795–1796

Trio in D, Hob. XV: 24
Trio in G, Hob. XV: 25 'Gypsy Rondo'
Trio in F sharp minor, Hob. XV: 26
Trio in C, Hob. XV: 27
Trio in E, Hob. XV: 28
Trio in E flat, Hob. XV: 29
Trio in E flat, Hob. XV: 30

Completed in the summer of 1795, Nos. 24–6 were dedicated to Haydn's lover Rebecca Schroeter. The most famous by far is the G major, No. 25, with the rondo 'in the Gypsies style', as Haydn called it in the Longman & Broderip print. This begins innocently enough, with a typically sparkling Haydn rondo tune. But we are soon whisked to the Hungarian *puszta* with a riot of authentic *verbunkos* melodies, each one more delirious than the last, with the cello giving a lusty kick to the rhythms. It is revealing of Haydn's relaxed conception of the trio medium that none of the three movements is in sonata form. The sprightly opening Andante is another rondo-variations design, the reflective E major Adagio a simple ternary (ABA) form, with a romantic violin solo in the middle.

Of the other two trios dedicated to Schroeter, No. 24 has lyrical outer movements, with little of the extrovert brilliance habitually associated with D major. Rosemary Hughes, in her Master Musicians *Haydn*, well describes the trio as 'irradiated by that sunset calm that is so peculiarly his'. The spacious first movement makes a special feature of quizzical (rather than comic) pauses, while the finale is the tenderest of Haydn's many sublimated German dance movements. No. 26, in the rare key of F sharp minor (shared with the 'Farewell' Symphony and the String Quartet Op. 50 No. 4), is a very different affair: tense, disquieting, almost tragic in tone. Even the beautiful F sharp major Adagio cantabile, which Haydn shortly afterwards transposed into F major as the slow movement of Symphony No. 102, has an underlying brooding unease. The first movement is a complex, emotionally ambivalent Allegro, veering into the mysterious enharmonic region of E flat minor in the development. Contrary to Haydn's usual practice in his late works, the recapitulation stays in the minor throughout, giving a troubled cast to the popular-style tune in the second-subject group. The third movement is the last and most gravely introspective of Haydn's minuet finales, harmonically unsettled (the first full cadence is delayed until the latest possible moment) and returning fatalistically to F sharp minor after its major-key central section.

Nos. 27–9 were written, either in London or shortly after Haydn's return to Vienna in September 1795, for the professional pianist Therese Jansen-Bartolozzi, a star pupil of Clementi. In the extrovert C major, No. 27, especially, Haydn exploits Jansen-Bartolozzi's virtuoso technique. The first movement combines vaulting, muscular energy with the relaxed, improvisatory feel typical of the late trios. The development opens with a passage of intricate neo-Baroque polyphony, continues with a grand statement of the theme in A flat (another of Haydn's favourite 'third' relationships), and then approaches the recapitulation via a startling last-minute deflection to B minor, of all keys, with a kind of inspired casualness that could only happen in these trios. After a pastoral A major Andante, disrupted by a violent, Hungarian-tinged episode, the finale matches the drama and comic virtuosity of late symphonies like the 'Military' and No. 102. Its manipulation of the first three notes, always liable to appear in unexpected registers, constantly duping us as to the exact moment of the theme's return, carries Haydn's favourite 'upbeat joke' to crazy new extremes. Here is the musical equivalent of the lightning word games in a Tom Stoppard play. Remembering, perhaps, the first movement's brief glimmer of B minor, the coda dives into that outrageously remote key, the kind of ploy we also find in Beethoven's recently completed Op. 1 Piano Trios. Could the pupil have influenced the master here?

No. 28 is a much more inward-looking work, characteristic of Haydn's music in E major. From its exotically scored opening, where the strings play pizzicato and the keyboard evokes a harp, the radiant opening movement explores fanciful new keyboard sonorities. As in Nos. 14 and 27, the climax comes in the development with a statement of the main theme in a distant, third-related key, A flat, here richly harmonised in full, sustained textures. Though in triple time, the finale is neither a minuet nor a German dance, but a movement of sinuous, slightly whimsical lyricism, with an impassioned violin solo in its minor-mode episode. Echoing the Sonata No. 31 of two decades earlier, the central E minor Allegretto weaves gaunt counterpoints above and below a passacaglia-style running bass, gradually rising in intensity until the music disintegrates in a series of wild keyboard flourishes. As Charles Rosen observed in *The Classical Style*, this astonishing, eccentric music is Baroque in its formal character, Classical in its firmly established movement to the relative major key and its plethora of dynamic accents, and finally, 'Romantic in its tension, keyed to a steadily higher pitch than most eighteenth-century works could bear'.

The third of the Jansen-Bartolozzi set, No. 29, is far lighter in tone. Its Poco allegretto first movement, on a laconic march tune akin to the opening of the E flat String Quartet, Op. 76 No. 6, is a typical mix of ternary and variation form, with the E flat minor central section also functioning as a development. The Andantino, in B major, is marked *innocentemente*, though characteristically, the nursery-tune innocence of the opening is belied when it slips towards the remote regions of E flat major-minor in preparation for the finale. Despite its nonchalant canonic writing, this is the beeriest and most unbuttoned of all Haydn's German dance movements. Its evocations of a village band tuning up prefigure the rowdy wine harvest in *The Seasons*.

Composed in 1796 and published on its own, No. 30 in E flat is Haydn's final trio and the last major work he composed for keyboard. It makes a magnificent culmination. The unhurried first movement is the most ample in all Haydn's chamber music, with a lavish procession of cantabile melodies that, in Rosen's words, 'seem to well from one source in a fusion of power, lyricism and logic'. Not for the only time in Haydn's late works, the cut of the themes and the harmonic colouring can seem distinctly Schubertian. The second movement, once more in a 'third-related' key, C major, is a deep-toned, often richly chromatic Andante con moto, a Romantic transformation of a slow minuet. Again, the music leads, after a mysterious change of key, directly into the finale. This is another of Haydn's German dances, a quasi-scherzo that mingles bucolic boisterousness, drama, keyboard virtuosity and contrapuntal sleight of hand. The quickfire imitations between violin and cello, with the piano in support, once more attest to the cello's indispensable role in these trios.

Other chamber music

Trios for wind and strings

In 1784 Haydn responded to the ready market for amateur flute music by hastily concocting six trios, Hob. IV: 6–11, for flute (or violin), violin and cello. Five of these appealing miniatures adapt one or more movements from the opera *Il mondo della luna* – Haydn's most fruitful source of self-borrowing – while the other (in G major, Hob. IV: 9) recycles three movements, including the tiny fugato finale, from the baryton trio No. 97.

As Robbins Landon has suggested, it was probably the success of these trios that prompted two flute-playing aristocrats, Lord Abingdon and Baron Aston, to commission the four so-called 'London' trios, Hob. IV: 1–4, during Haydn's second visit to England. Nos. 1 and 3 are in three movements, while Nos. 2 and 4 consist of a single movement. No. 2 is a set of variations on the little round by Lord Abingdon that Haydn used in the song 'The Lady's Looking Glass' (early editions created a two-movement trio by appending the finale of No. 3). Even these pastoral trifles proclaim late Haydn in their subtleties of form and harmony. Given the limitations of the medium, the textures are cunningly varied, with the two flutes carolling in thirds and sixths, vying with each other in playful imitation, or – especially in the strutting opening movement of No. 3 – discoursing with the cello in elegant three-part counterpoint.

Music for baryton

In his oft-quoted edict of November 1765, Prince Nicolaus enjoined his vice-Kapellmeister to 'apply himself to composition more diligently than hitherto, and to write such pieces as can be played on the gamba [i.e. baryton], of which we have seen very few up to now'. Haydn jumped to, and over the next decade or so produced nearly two hundred works for the instrument that had become an obsession for the prince. The chastened composer even taught himself to play it, though his zeal seems to have backfired. As Griesinger tells it, 'one evening Haydn quite unexpectedly gave a concert on it. The prince was rather offended, saying that Haydn wanted to usurp his position with regard to the instrument; and from that hour Haydn never touched the baryton again.'

Cultivated from the early seventeenth century to the early nineteenth, the baryton was a kind of bass viol with a harp extension: behind the fretted fingerboard, with its six bowed strings of gut, were up to twenty (but more usually nine or ten) harp-like metal strings, which vibrated in sympathy with the bowed strings and could also be plucked by the left thumb through the open back of the neck. (In the works composed after about 1767 Haydn sometimes required the bowed and plucked strings to be played simultaneously.) Plucked strings were indicated by numbers above and below the notated pitch.

Haydn's baryton music, not all of which has survived, includes duets for two barytons, trios for two barytons and cello, quintets for baryton, viola, cello and horns, and three lost concertos. By far the largest group of works are the trios, Hob. XI: 1–126, all with viola and cello except Nos. 89–91, which substitute violin for viola. A few of the trios predate the princely rap on the knuckles, but most were composed between late 1765 and about 1775. Of all Haydn's instrumental works, those involving the baryton were the least known outside the Esterházy court, and remain the hardest to 'sell' today, with good reason. In the trios the rather dour, husky sonorities created by three instruments in the alto and tenor range are an acquired taste. Beyond this, Haydn obviously tossed off many of these miniature three-movement pieces with minimal effort, hampered by the baryton's limitations and, at least in the earliest works, the prince's restricted technique. The vast majority of the trios, including the first seventy-five, are in the keys of A (the easiest key of all for the baryton), D and G, with a correspondingly narrow modulatory range within movements. Nowhere do we find the formal breadth and adventurousness or the expressive intensity of the contemporary symphonies, sonatas and quartets.

Yet amid countless workaday minuets and crochet-your-own variations are a fair number of absorbing movements, especially in the later works. The subdued instrumental palette lends itself well to stately slow movements, something of a speciality in these trios. Several rise well above dignified routine, including the touching 'Pastorello' in No. 36, the doleful Largo of No. 96 in B minor – one of only two minor-key trios – and the opening Adagio of No. 97 in D, a unique seven-movement work (including a mildly exotic polonaise) designed for the prince's birthday celebrations. Intriguing, too, are the Balkan-flavoured minor-key trios of many minuets: Nos. 5, 35 and 109 are three cases in point, counterparts to the enigmatic A minor trio of Symphony No. 28. While simple melody-dominated textures are the norm, occasionally enlivened by baryton/viola dialogues, eleven of the finales, including that of No. 97, are fugal in texture. The most elaborately worked is the finale of No. 101, a fugue 'on three subjects in double counterpoint', and a more modest counterpart to the fugal finales of the Op. 20 Quartets. All these contrapuntal movements are testimony to Haydn's renewed interest in the so-called *stylus antiquus* that he had studied assiduously in Fux's *Gradus ad Parnassum*.

Threading through these trios are self-borrowings from recent works, doubtless acknowledged with a knowing smile by the prince. No. 52, for instance, adapts the 'limping' *alla zoppa* minuet from Symphony No. 58, while No. 29 recycles Apollonia's breezy aria from *La canterina*. In No. 5 Haydn even quotes the aria 'Che faro senza Euridice?' from Gluck's *Orfeo*, evidently a favourite opera of Prince Nicolaus.

Most attractive of the baryton works are the seven *Divertimenti a otti voci* of 1775, Hob. X: 1–6 and 12. The prince's instrument plays only a modest role in the octet ensemble (string quartet, double bass, baryton and a pair of horns), often merely doubling the first violin at the octave and adding its distinctive buzzy resonance to the textures. As in the trios, sonata-form Allegros tend to be cheerful and compact, with minimal thematic development. Here and in the many rondo and variation movements the ear is intrigued by the varied tone colours, and the antics of the horns at both extremes of their compass (the horn fireworks in the finales of Nos. 1 and 3 are particularly spectacular). But the real glory of these works lies in their intense, introspective Adagios, five of them in the minor key. Artaria gave six of the octets wider currency by publishing them with the baryton parts transposed up an octave for flute or oboe.

Music for lira organizzata

Haydn's patrons certainly had their offbeat tastes in instruments. In 1785 or early 1786, a decade after Prince Nicolaus had 'retired' from the baryton, he received a handsome commission from the Bourbon King of Naples and the Two Sicilies, Ferdinand IV, to compose chamber concertos (probably six, one of which is lost) for a not dissimilar oddball instrument: the *lira organizzata*, a high-tech hurdy-gurdy with sympathetic strings and an inbuilt miniature organ. Tutored by Norbert Hadrava, an Austrian official in Naples, Ferdinand became something of a *lira* virtuoso, and commissioned works not only from Haydn but also from Gyrowetz, Pleyel and others. Virtually no one outside France or Italy could ever play the *lira*, which in any case gradually became obsolete. Modern performances of the concertos (Hob. VIIh: 1–5) and the nine *notturni* of 1788–90, eight of which have survived (Hob. II: 25–32), use the revised versions Haydn made for his London concerts in 1791–2, with the two *lire* replaced by a flute and an oboe.

In writing for an instrument he almost certainly never heard, Haydn relied heavily on Hadrava's guidance. The *lira*, it seems, was only comfortable in the most 'elementary' keys.

With this in mind, Haydn set each of the concertos (and, later, the *notturni*) in C, G or F major, and reined in his adventurous sense of modulation. There was little to challenge his royal patron in these easy-going occasional works, in which the *lire* are accompanied by a string sextet and a pair of horns. Though each of the first movements opens with a miniature ritornello (No. 5 introduces the four-note 'Credo' chant familiar from Haydn's Symphony No. 13 and Mozart's 'Jupiter'), the alternation between 'solo' and 'tutti' sections is more fluid, less formal, than in the full-blown Classical concerto: the two *lire* now disport themselves in mellifluous thirds and sixths or, in airy imitation, now blend easily into the instrumental texture.

Three of the slow movements (Nos. 1, 4 and 5) are graceful siciliano serenades – very apt for the King of Naples and the Two Sicilies – while one (in No. 2) transcribes a courtly 'insertion aria' Haydn had composed for Gazzaniga's opera *L'isola d'Alcina*. Except for the minuet finale of No. 3, the last movements are sectional rondos in contredanse style, with none of the developmental tension of the contemporary symphonies and string quartets. With Haydn reluctant to waste good music of limited currency, the *lire* concertos became a fruitful source of self-borrowing: the Andante and finale of No. 5 were quarried for Symphony No. 89, while No. 3's Romanze, a march for toy soldiers, was sensationally dressed up as the Allegretto of the 'Military' Symphony.

In the *notturni* Haydn complemented the two *lire* with clarinets, horns, violas, cello and double bass, substituting violins for clarinets in Nos. 27 and 28. All except No. 25, which has a spruce little introductory march, are in three brief movements (the finale of No. 30 is lost). Even more than the concertos, the *notturni* are composed *con amore*, with exquisite touches of chromatic harmony and kaleidoscopically varied tone colours that recall Mozart's wind serenades. Most of the finales are ebullient rondos, full of quickfire badinage; the exception is that in No. 29, an amalgam of fugal textures and sonata form. The slow movements are in the same pastoral vein as those of the *lira* concertos, though the brooding, dark-coloured Adagio of No. 27 goes deeper. Perhaps, as Robbins Landon has suggested, this beautiful movement reflects Haydn's melancholy and loneliness in that final Eszterháza summer of 1790.

Solo keyboard music

Haydn's name is far less closely associated with the keyboard sonata than with the string quartet or symphony. Though a more than competent player (the English composer Samuel Wesley described his execution of the brilliant fortepiano solo in the finale of Symphony No. 98 as 'neat and distinct'), he never sought to promote himself as a virtuoso. Yet the keyboard remained central to Haydn's creative process. His morning routine would invariably begin, after prayers and breakfast, with him trying out new ideas on the clavichord or, from the 1780s, the fortepiano. He told Dies, 'My imagination plays on me as if I were a Keyboard . . . I really am just a living keyboard.' Dies also relates how Haydn's 'worm-eaten clavichord' was a profound solace to the young composer in his Viennese garret in the early 1750s.

Haydn wrote prolifically for keyboard throughout most of his career. Yet apart from a few favourites, his solo sonatas are still habitually relegated to teaching fare, ignored by all but a handful of leading pianists. Far more than Mozart's much slenderer body of sonatas, they chart and epitomise the evolution of the Classical sonata: from the jejune early divertimenti and partitas, modelled, like Mozart's early sonatas, on the harpsichord style of the Viennese master of *galanterie* Georg Christoph Wagenseil, especially his influential *Six Divertimenti for Harpsichord*, Op. 1; through the more individual sonatas of the late 1760s, several touched by the *Empfindsamkeit* of C. P. E. Bach, and the 'popular' idiom of the 1770s and 1780s, to the magnificent works written for the new, sonorous Broadwood instruments Haydn encountered in London.

Note: The traditional Hoboken numberings, still commonly used for recital programmes and recordings, are given first, followed by the revised numberings in Christa Landon's Wiener Urtext edition, published by Universal.

Early sonatas

Partita in C, Hob. XVI: 1 (10)
Partita in B flat, Hob. XVI: 2 (11)
Divertimento in C, Hob. XVI: 3 (14)
Divertimento in D, Hob. XVI: 4 (9)
Partita in G, Hob. XVI: 6 (13)
Partita in C, Hob. XVI: 7 (2)
Partita in G, Hob. XVI: 8 (1)
Divertimento in F, Hob. XVI: 9 (3)
Divertimento in C, Hob. XVI: 10 (6)
Divertimento in G, Hob. XVI: 11 (5)
Divertimento in E, Hob. XVI: 13 (15)
Divertimento in D, Hob. XVI: 14 (16)
Divertimento in G, Hob. XVI: G1 (4)

More than any area of his output, Haydn's earliest harpsi-chord partitas and divertimenti (he never used the term 'sonata' until around 1770) are fraught with problems of authentication. As with so much eighteenth-century music that speaks the prevailing lingua franca with fluency but no real individuality, it is precarious to judge from internal evidence alone. Only the autograph for one, in G major, Hob. XVI: 6, survives, and even here the finale is missing. The consensus is that the thirteen listed above are genuine Haydn, though doubts have been raised about Hob. XVI: 1 and 11. Several other doubtful works have found their way into modern complete editions of the sonatas.

Dating, too, is speculative. All we can say with fair certainty is that these partitas and divertimenti (as with the early keyboard trios, the titles are interchangeable) were composed at various times between the early 1750s and the early 1760s. Many were probably designed for young pupils such as Marianne von Martínez, a Countess Thun, and Haydn's first love and future sister-in-law, Therese Keller. Griesinger gives us a charming glimpse of the young composer's naivety – a far cry from the shrewd negotiator of later years:

Many of his easy *Klavier* sonatas, trios and the like fall into this period . . . Only a few originals remained with him; he gave them away, and considered it an honour if people took them. He did not realise that music dealers did good business with them, and he used to enjoy stopping in front of shops where one or another of his works was displayed in print.

As the American musicologist A. Peter Brown observed in his study of the keyboard music, we should substitute 'handwritten copies' for 'print'. It was only in the 1760s that his sonatas and trios began to circulate in printed editions. Ironically, the first sonata of all to be published, No. 5 in Hoboken's catalogue, is probably not by Haydn at all.

The editor of the complete Henle Haydn edition, Georg Feder, divides these apprentice works into 'early sonatas' and 'short early sonatas'. Into the latter group, doubtless written as teaching pieces, fall Hob. XVI: 1, 3, 4, 7–10, and G1, whose finale also turns up as the first movement of No. 11, a work omitted from the Henle edition on grounds of authenticity. Except for the four-movement No. 8 and the two-movement No. 4, these inconsequential trifles are in three movements, with a minuet in second or third place. Just occasionally, Haydn hints at something more individual: in the opening Allegro of No. 9 in F, where octave doublings enrich the tinkling, *galant* textures, or in the gambolling finale of the same sonata, living up to its billing of Allegro scherzo.

Several works categorised as 'early sonatas' in the Henle edition are of dubious authorship. The four definitely, or very probably, by Haydn are Nos. 2, 6, 13 and 14, all of them technically and musically more ambitious than the 'short early sonatas'. One of the finest is No. 2 in B flat, with its crisp opening Moderato, its florid, chromatic G minor Largo and its elegantly proportioned minuet enclosing a syncopated trio in B flat minor. Trios in the tonic minor key were something of a convention in the keyboard music of Wagenseil and other Viennese composers. Haydn followed suit in each of these

four works, always with memorable results. The minuet of the
E major, No. 13, has a serene lyricism typical of Haydn's
music in this key; and the Presto finale, with its quickfire
major-minor contrasts, is rivalled in piquancy by the whimsical finale of No. 14. Largest in scale is the four-movement
G major, No. 6, with another expressive G minor slow
movement ('a Bachian arioso of great lyrical beauty,' as John
McCabe put it in his *BBC Music Guide* to the sonatas) and a
final Allegro molto in 3/8 time that shares the drive and dash
of Haydn's early symphony finales.

c.1765–1770

Divertimento in D, Hob. XVI: 19 (30)
Divertimento in E flat, Hob. XVI: 45 (29)
Divertimento in A flat, Hob. XVI: 46 (31)
Divertimento in E minor, Hob. XVI: 47 (19)

With these indubitably authentic works of the mid- to late
1760s, Haydn's keyboard music becomes more varied in texture and richer in expression. It is likely that Haydn immersed
himself in C. P. E. Bach's influential *Versuch über die wahre Art
das Clavier zu spielen* (Essay on the true art of keyboard playing) around 1765–6, and studied his *Sonaten mit veränderten
Reprisen* (Sonatas with varied repeats) when they became
available in Vienna in 1767. While the growing power and
individuality of the sonatas from this period parallel developments throughout Haydn's art, the influence of Emanuel
Bach is revealed in various ways: in their bold use of the whole
range of the keyboard, their tendency to vary rather than simply repeat material and, above all, in their intricate and
expressive ornamentation.

It is not too fanciful to hear the finest sonata of this group,
the A flat, No. 46, as a personal response to Bach's brand of
Empfindsamkeit, the language of heightened sensibility that
had its literary roots in the novels of Samuel Richardson and

the writings of Jean-Jacques Rousseau and the German poet Klopstock. The first movement of this beautiful work begins with a typically *empfindsam* theme, irregularly phrased and characterised by delicate ornaments and sighing appoggiaturas. With its leisurely unfolding and its rich fantasia-like episodes – another Emanuel Bach speciality – the movement leaves an impression of inspired improvisation. For the Adagio, Haydn moves to the subdominant, D flat major, a recherché key in the eighteenth century, and one never used by Mozart. With the extreme tonality goes a peculiar intimacy of expression. The polyphonic and chromatic enrichment of the main theme in the development suggests not so much C. P. E. as J. S. Bach at his most inward; and Haydn opens up wonderful new harmonic vistas (moving through D flat minor to B double-flat major!) in the coda. The compact finale provides a glorious physical release. Yet this is no mere frothy romp. The toccata-like passagework always has a strong sense of direction, above all in the powerful chromatic sequences just before the recapitulation.

Flashing toccata-style figuration, with more than a whiff of Domenico Scarlatti, also animates the finale of No. 45 (dated 1766). The lovely Andante often suggests a two-part invention, with the hands engaged in tender, musing colloquy. In contrast, the Andante of No. 19 sounds like (and perhaps was) a transcription from a cello or bassoon concerto. Quasi-orchestral 'tuttis' frame an eloquent 'solo' cantilena written largely in the bass clef. There are some vertiginous leaps between registers, and, at the end, a cue for an improvised cadenza. The sportive finale is an amalgam of rondo and variations, a form influenced by C. P. E. Bach's 'varied reprises' that Haydn often cultivated in his sonatas and symphonies of the 1770s.

The other sonata in this group, No. 47, was published in two versions. In the first, a plaintive E minor siciliano leads without a break to an E major Allegro, saturated by its opening theme. The finale is a lyrical minuet in condensed sonata form. Coincidentally or not, all three movements begin with the same descending scale motif. The second version (No. 57

in the Wiener Urtext edition), published by Artaria in 1788, jettisons the minuet, transposes the first two movements up from E to F, and prefaces them with a contrapuntal movement that sounds like a simplified rerun of the opening of J. S. Bach's Fourth English Suite. It certainly doesn't sound much like Haydn; and, not surprisingly, its authenticity has been contested.

Also from this period are seven lost sonatas, including two in the minor key (D and E) and one in B major. In 1993 a German piano teacher, Winfried Michel, claimed to have rediscovered six of them in an old lady's house in Münster. The event made front-page news, scholars gave their guarded assent, and a recording was hastily arranged. But before it could be issued the whole thing was exposed as a hoax: Michel had plausibly forged the sonatas from the incipits in Haydn's *Entwurf-Katalog*. Not quite on a par with the Hitler Diaries spoof, perhaps. But Michel's clever confidence trick left egg on several faces.

c.1770–c.1773

Sonata in B flat, Hob. XVI: 18 (20)
Sonata in G minor, Hob. XVI: 44 (32)
Sonata in C minor, Hob. XVI: 20 (33)
Sonata in D, Hob. XVI: 33 (34)
Sonata in A flat, Hob. XVI: 43 (35)

Roughly contemporary with the string quartets of Op. 17 and Op. 20, these were Haydn's first keyboard works designated as 'sonata' rather than 'divertimento'. Nos. 18 and 44, both from around 1770, share a near-identical two-movement design – a moderately paced first movement followed by an expressively ornamented minuet – and may have been conceived as a pair. The spirit of *Empfindsamkeit* is felt in both sonatas, especially the intimate, melancholy G minor, No. 44. Its opening movement, permeated by the main theme's initial triplet upbeat, rises to a magnificent, densely textured contrapuntal climax in the development, while the G minor-major minuet sublimates typical *galant* gestures into pure pathos. Haydn varies and embellishes the repeat of the G minor section, à la Emanuel Bach, and then introduces a truncated version of the G major trio (itself a variant of the G minor theme) as a coda.

Although the autograph bears the date 1771, Haydn withheld publication of the famous C minor Sonata, No. 20, until 1780, when it appeared as the last, and by far the most challenging, of the set dedicated to the Auenbrugger sisters. With its frequent abrupt dynamic contrasts, this is the first of Haydn's keyboard works conceived essentially in terms of a touch-sensitive instrument – either the clavichord or the new fortepiano – rather than the harpsichord. Its 'brilliance and massiveness' (Charles Rosen's words) are unique in the sonatas before the late 1780s, as is its tragic intensity. This is Haydn's 'Appassionata'. The first movement, whose yearning main theme Brahms perhaps subconsciously recalled in his song of a dying girl, 'Immer leiser wird mein Schlummer', combines rhapsodic *Empfindsamkeit*, *Sturm und Drang* turbulence and argumentative rigour. As in the C minor Andantino of Mozart's 'Jeunehomme' Piano Concerto, K271, Haydn enhances the music's poignancy with passages of 'speaking' recitative, like heartfelt oratory. The Andante con moto, unfolding over an expressive running bass line, shares the Baroque leanings and the soulful beauty of No. 46's Adagio. But its mood is more restless, rising to passion in the mounting sequences that sweep the music into the recapitulation. The finale, written against the background of a fast minuet, has a latent despairing fury that becomes manifest towards the end. Mingling violence and virtuosity, Haydn here expands a brief toccata-like sequence in an astounding crossed-hands passage, with the left hand touching the extremes of the contemporary five-octave keyboard.

Two much slighter sonatas, Nos. 33 and 43, were first published in London in the early 1780s, though both date from a decade or so earlier. With the autograph lost, some commentators have doubted No. 43's authenticity. If it is indeed by Haydn, it shows him at his most blithely *galant*. The otherwise lightweight No. 33 has a gravely expressive D minor slow movement, a condensed sonata-form design whose third section is both a recapitulation and a decorated variation.

1773

Sonata in C, Hob. XVI: 21 (36)
Sonata in E, Hob. XVI: 22 (37)
Sonata in F, Hob. XVI: 23 (38)
Sonata in D, Hob. XVI: 24 (39)
Sonata in E flat, Hob. XVI: 25 (40)
Sonata in A, Hob. XVI: 26 (41)

Issued in February 1774, with a judicious dedication to Prince Nicolaus Esterházy, this set of six harpsichord sonatas constitutes the first authorised publication of any of Haydn's works. Like the symphonies of 1773–4, they are on the whole lighter than the works of the late 1760s and early 1770s. Haydn was composing with one eye on the amateur market – and perhaps, too, in deference to the taste and technique of the prince. But polished *galanterie* by no means precludes Haydnesque inventiveness. The C major, No. 21, with its prompt, no-nonsense opening Allegro, does least to ruffle expectations, though even here the skipping finale indulges in some sly rhythmic and harmonic tricks. No. 22 in E is a richer, more varied work. The first movement has something of C. P. E. Bach's flamboyant, improvisatory manner, the E minor Andante is a wordless aria, and the minuet finale, like that in No. 44, varies two themes in turn, one in the major, one in the minor. The *European Magazine, and London Review* of October 1784 found the first movement and, even more surprisingly, the whole of No. 23, 'expressly composed in order to ridicule Bach of Hamburgh', a judgment that would surely have astonished Haydn: 'The stile of Bach is closely copied, without the passages being stolen, in which his capricious manner, odd breaks, whimsical modulations, and very often childish manner, mixed with an affectation of profound science, are finely hit off and burlesqued.'

No. 23's crisp opening Moderato trades mainly on scintillating toccata-style figuration. Its development is a free fantasia, brilliant in effect and flattering the amateur player's technique by sounding far more difficult than it actually is. Between this and the frolicsome finale comes a rhapsodic F minor siciliano: music that surely influenced Mozart in his F major sonata, K280, of 1775, though unlike Mozart's siciliano it lives less from melody than from dreamy figuration and expressive harmony. The triple-time first movement of No. 24 is an athletic, tautly developed piece, alternating wiry, two-part writing with toccata-style sequences. The D minor Adagio opens with a forlornly hesitant theme over a Baroque-style repeated-note accompaniment – a typically Haydnesque blend of pathos and austerity – before growing more floridly expressive. Following the example of many Emanuel Bach slow movements, Haydn then lets the music dissolve into the mercurial, syncopated Presto finale.

Alone among the 'Esterházy' sonatas, No. 25, in E flat, has two movements only: a Moderato, grand in aspiration but rather discursive in effect, and a sturdy *Tempo di menuet* written in canon throughout. For the minuet second movement of No. 26 Haydn appropriates the palindromic *Menuet al rovescio* from Symphony No. 47 and transposes it up a tone. The finale, curiously akin to the last movement of the A major quartet, Op. 9 No. 6, is a disconcertingly brief scamper. The expansive first movement offsets its mock-military opening theme (horns are evoked at the outset) with rhapsodic excursions into the minor key. In the development Haydn makes something romantically expressive out of an extended chain of Baroque-style sequences.

c.1774–1776

Sonata in G, Hob. XVI: 27 (42)
Sonata in E flat, Hob. XVI: 28 (43)
Sonata in F, Hob. XVI: 29 (44)
Sonata in A, Hob. XVI: 30 (45)
Sonata in E, Hob. XVI: 31 (46)
Sonata in B minor, Hob. XVI: 32 (47)

This heterogeneous bunch of sonatas was published privately in manuscript copies in 1776, though No. 29 had been composed in 1774, and the innocuous No. 27 may be earlier still. Haydn fights shy of writing a full slow movement in all except No. 29, whose ornate Adagio characteristically relies more on gesture and rhetorical flourishes than on lyrical melody. Three of the sonatas, Nos. 27, 28 and 32, include a leisurely minuet as a surrogate slow movement, while two others, Nos. 29 and 30, have minuet finales in variation form. More than anything in the 1773 sonatas, the first movement of No. 29, with its comic false starts and wildly disparate textures and rhythmic patterns, might be dubbed a 'burlesque' of C. P. E. Bach. Underlying its waywardness, though, is Haydn's mastery of long-range sonata strategy, right through to a recapitulation that further investigates the material of the exposition. Eccentric as the movement is, it never sounds like an agglomeration of random ideas, as superficially similar pieces by Emanuel Bach sometimes can. The minuet finale contains a haunting F minor trio, restlessly syncopated, freely polyphonic in texture.

Uniquely in Haydn's sonatas, No. 30 runs its three movements together. The first movement – in mock-military style, like its A major predecessor, No. 26 – breaks off just before the anticipated end and plunges into a brief, rhetorical F sharp minor Adagio, another recreation of Emanuel Bach's *Empfindsamkeit*. This in turn leads directly into the finale, a set of variations on a rather fragile minuet tune.

By far the most striking part of the E major, No. 31, is the second movement, a neo-Baroque E minor Allegretto that suggests both a chorale prelude and a three-part invention. Again, the finale – a dashing theme and variations, with a contrasting E minor episode – follows without a break. Haydn was to remember the beautiful Allegretto two decades later in the E major piano trio, No. 28.

The last and finest of the 1776 collection, No. 32, has the vehement astringency typical of Haydn's music in B minor (compare the String Quartets Op. 33 No. 1 and Op. 64 No. 2). In his later works Haydn preferred to end his minor-key movements cheerfully in the major. Here, though, the recapitulations of the outer movements remain grimly in the minor throughout; and what had seemed brilliant or even skittish in the exposition subsequently acquires a tense, anxious edge. The finale, with its obsessively pounding theme – the mainspring of the musical action – and disconcerting silences, culminates in a laconic coda that thunders out the theme in stark octave unison. Amid this turbulence, the long-spanned minuet-cum-slow-movement in B major provides harmonic balm, with the darkly agitated B minor trio aligned to the mood of the outer movements.

c.1776–1779: the 'Auenbrugger' sonatas

Sonata in C, Hob. XVI: 35 (48)
Sonata in C sharp minor, Hob. XVI: 36 (49)
Sonata in D, Hob. XVI: 37 (50)
Sonata in E flat, Hob. XVI: 38 (51)
Sonata in G, Hob. XVI: 39 (52)

Issued early in 1780 with the C minor, No. 20, these five sonatas inaugurated Haydn's long relationship with the publisher Artaria. They were dedicated to the talented sisters Franziska and Maria Katherina von Auenbrugger, whose playing drew the admiration of both Leopold Mozart, never one to dish out compliments lightly, and Haydn himself. As he wrote to Artaria, the sisters possessed 'true insight into music equal to that of the greatest masters'. Designated, for the first time, 'for harpsichord, or forte-piano', and often calling for the dynamic flexibility only possible on the newer instrument, these 'Auenbrugger' sonatas are as disparate in style as the 1776 set. No. 35 in C, Haydn's equivalent to Mozart's famous C major Sonata, K545, is a facile teaching piece – hardly a sonata to flatter the sisters' 'true insight into music'. Far more challenging is No. 36, in the rare key of C sharp minor, though unlike the C minor Sonata, No. 20, it juxtaposes serious and popular styles.

The first movement develops the two limbs of its sole theme – a brusque *forte* unison and a soft, 'pathetic' response – with a trenchancy that recalls the B minor, No. 32. Coming between this and the finale, a slow minuet of exquisite, refined melancholy with an assuaging C sharp major trio, the perky A major Scherzando seems like a facetious interloper.

Haydn reused the tune of this Scherzando more fruitfully in the variation-rondo first movement of No. 39. To deflect 'the criticism of various half-wits' (even as late as 1780 Haydn could be surprisingly touchy), he got Artaria to add a note on the reverse of the title page: 'Among these six sonatas are two movements that use the same idea for the first few bars . . . the composer wishes it to be known that he has done this on purpose to demonstrate different methods of treatment.' The Adagio is florid and ruminative, the finale a featherweight 6/8 Prestissimo with a strong whiff of Scarlatti. The E flat Sonata, No. 38, is a more sober work that may date back to the early 1770s. In the elegiac, siciliano-style C minor Adagio (which leads directly into the minuet finale), Haydn embellishes the repeats after the manner of C. P. E. Bach's 'varied reprises'.

With its chirruping main theme and quicksilver brilliance, the first movement of the popular D major, No. 37, again evokes the spirit of Scarlatti at his most dashing. The D minor Largo e sostenuto is especially striking: a sombre, sonorously scored sarabande, archaic in flavour, with a suggestion of a Baroque French overture in its dotted rhythms and contrapuntal textures. Like the Adagio of No. 38, it leads without a break into the finale, a catchy rondo that lives up to its marking *innocentemente*.

c.1780–1784

Sonata in E minor, Hob. XVI: 34 (53)
Sonata in G, Hob. XVI: 40 (54)
Sonata in B flat, Hob. XVI: 41 (55)
Sonata in D, Hob. XVI: 42 (56)

During the 1780s Haydn's production of solo keyboard music fell off sharply, partly because of foreign commissions, partly because of his renewed absorption in the string quartet and the piano trio. The E minor, No. 34, was one of three sonatas (with Nos. 33 and 43) published without Haydn's consent in London in 1783–4, though it probably dates from several years earlier. Its Adagio, overladen with fussy rococo arabesques, and double-variation finale are routine Haydn. But the 6/8 Presto first movement has a fierce nervous energy, rising to a splenetic climax in the coda before the curt opening phrase vanishes into thin air.

The same year, 1784, the firm of Bossler published a triptych of two-movement works, Nos. 40–2. They were dedicated, perhaps as a wedding gift, to the sixteen-year-old Princess Marie Hermenegild Esterházy, who the previous year had married the future Prince Nicolaus II. For all their surface lightness, all three sonatas – later published in arrangements (probably not by Haydn) for string trio – are sophisticated, subtly wrought works. Cramer's *Magazin der Musik* specially complimented the first movements of Nos. 40 and 42: 'In these variations, so well suited to the instrument, the composer is like an accomplished, tasteful singer when she repeats an aria.' With its rhetorical silences, No. 42's opening Andante con espressione suggests heightened speech. In contrast, the double-variation first movement of the G major, No. 40, grows from a beguiling song-like tune in a pastoral 6/8 metre.

Haydn marks it Allegretto innocente. But here, unlike in the finales of Nos. 34 and 37, innocence is not to be taken quite at face value. Even at the opening Haydn disturbs the idyll with offbeat *sforzando* accents, smoothed out in nineteenth-century editions; and there are further disruptive accents in the contrasting (but audibly related) G minor theme, with its broken phrases and tense harmonies. The finale likewise trades on variations and major-minor contrasts, now in a spirit of quixotic humour.

The assertive Allegro of No. 41 is the only movement in the Marie Esterházy sonatas in full sonata form. Its second group of themes begins with a reinterpretation of the first before moving to F minor for a new, restlessly modulating theme over an Alberti-style bass. As in the finale of No. 40, the development immediately dips a major third to a distant key (here D flat after F), a favourite ploy of Haydn's in the 1780s and 1790s. Before we have got our bearings, the music swerves abruptly to an equally surprising E flat major for a restatement of the main theme. The finale is a mercurial movement full of wiry two-part counterpoint. Its form (ABA, with the 'A' section playfully varied on its reprise) is akin to the finale of No. 40, though here the minor-key central section begins as a free paraphrase of the opening.

1789–1794

Sonata in C, Hob. XVI: 48 (58)
Sonata in E flat, Hob. XVI: 49 (59)
Sonata in C, Hob. XVI: 50 (60)
Sonata in D, Hob. XVI: 51 (61)
Sonata in E flat, Hob. XVI: 52 (62)

Early in 1789 the Leipzig publisher Breitkopf, not yet joined with Härtel, announced that Haydn was writing 'six Clavier sonatas' for publication by subscription. Breitkopf evidently failed to attract sufficient subscribers; and in the event only one sonata appeared, the C major, No. 48. Like the Marie Esterházy sonatas, it is in two movements only. There, though, any resemblance ends. Influenced by the virtuoso keyboard style of Clementi (decried by Mozart, but relished by Haydn), No. 48 is far grander in intent, and exploits the fortepiano's whole range with unprecedented power and flamboyance. Its plethora of dynamic markings makes it unrealisable on the harpsichord. In the sonata-rondo finale the keyboard even becomes a surrogate orchestra. The second half of the contredanse theme evokes bantering repartee between bassoons and oboes, while just before the end a rousing tutti, complete with timpani rolls, is comically deflated by timidly stuttering violins. Just as original in its sonorities is the opening Andante con espressione, music both elevated and capricious that crosses Haydn's favourite double variation form (the *minore* theme is both a variation and a development of the rhapsodic opening) with the spirit of a free fantasia. On a notorious Columbia recording, Glenn Gould makes this music sound like proto-jazz.

Also in 1789 Haydn composed an Allegro and minuet for keyboard, perhaps intending them to stand as another two-movement sonata. Then, in spring 1790, he added an Adagio e cantabile to create a three-movement work, No. 49. Although the autograph carries a dedication to Maria Anna Jerlischek, Esterházy housekeeper and future wife of violinist-entrepreneur Johann Tost, Haydn intended the sonata for Maria Anna von Genzinger. 'This sonata is in E flat, entirely new and forever meant only for Your Grace,' he wrote to her, adding that the Adagio was 'somewhat difficult, but full of feeling'. Though delighted with the sonata, she did indeed find the Adagio 'somewhat difficult', asking Haydn to simplify a passage involving crossed hands in the rolling, romantically impassioned B flat minor central episode. (Whether or not he obliged is unknown.) If Haydn was in love with Maria Anna – and we can guess that he was – his feelings might be divined from this sensitive, intimate music. Unlike in some of the earlier sonatas, the increasingly elaborate variations of the theme delicately enhance rather than dissipate the music's expressiveness.

Uniquely in the sonatas, each of the movements is in 3/4 time. Belying its nonchalant opening, the initial Allegro is a dramatic, closely wrought movement that evolves almost all its ideas from the main theme. The far-reaching development culminates in a tense modulating passage on a four-note 'drum' rhythm, with extreme contrasts of register. Remarkable, too, is the expansive coda, musing first on the gentle cadential theme and then on a lyrical 'transitional' idea that had immediately followed the opening. The minuet finale, a free rondo with two episodes, relaxes the tension after two such highly charged movements – though it is surely no coincidence that its first episode recalls the first movement's cadential theme.

In contrast with the crystalline, Mozartian keyboard style of No. 49 (the Adagio's B flat minor outburst excepted), the three London sonatas of 1794, Nos. 50–2, exploit the fuller sonorities of the new Broadwood instruments. As in the finale of No. 48, their piano writing at times suggests the influence of Clementi, who had settled in London and often performed in the same concerts as Haydn. But whereas Nos. 50 and 52 are quasi-symphonic sonatas, written for a professional pianist, No. 51 is an intimate, two-movement work. Perhaps Haydn intended it for Rebecca Schroeter. Yet for all its modest scale, No. 51 is as forward-looking as the two grander London sonatas. The first movement's relaxed stroll anticipates Schubert in its 'open-air' textures (right hand in octaves against rippling left-hand triplets) and piquant harmonic touches, while the syncopated scherzo-finale, with its continuous, restless chromaticism and disruptive offbeat accents, could easily have come from the pen of the young Beethoven.

Nos. 50 and 52 are both 'public' works, composed, like trios Nos. 27–9, for Therese Jansen. The first movement of the C major, No. 50 – probably Haydn's last sonata – is a *ne plus ultra* of thematic concentration, a brilliant, comedic counterpart to the 'Fifths' Quartet, Op. 76 No. 2. The whole movement grows from a bald staccato theme, a mischievously conjured vision of dry bones that Haydn proceeds to enrich and elaborate in a series of virtuosic compositional games. At the centre of the development is a famous 'open pedal' passage, where the once skeletal theme is transformed into something rich and strange. What Haydn seems to have envisaged here was not the sustaining pedal, as is sometimes assumed, but the *una corda* (i.e. soft) pedal available on the Broadwood fortepiano. In the recapitulation the theme attains its lyrical apotheosis with another, more extended 'open pedal' passage, now ethereal rather than darkly mysterious. Wagner once remarked that Beethoven could create whole worlds out of nothing. In a movement such as this, Haydn got there first.

After a rhapsodic, quasi-improvisatory Adagio, the finale is surely the most Monty-Pythonesque piece that Haydn ever wrote. A madcap scherzo, it continually baffles the ear with its lopsided phrases (the main theme consists of five plus two bars), outlandish silences and disorienting feints to the odd key of B major. In the words of Alfred Brendel – a pianist who thoroughly relishes Haydn's subversive mischief – 'These B major chords are arbitrary and unjustified, an insult veiled by apparent innocence, an act of splendid nonsense that is all the more delightful because it cannot be explained away.'

Remote tonal relationships are also a prime feature of the great E flat Sonata, No. 52, Haydn's noblest and most spacious work for the piano. Here, though, they are integrated into a boldly comprehensive design. Haydn sets the slow movement in the distant 'Neapolitan' key of E major. But he is careful to flag this during the massive opening Allegro moderato, as lavish in its themes as the C major's first movement was economical. At the heart of the development the music pauses rhetorically on a deep, full chord of G major, leading the ear to expect a resolution to C minor. Instead, the flippant second theme prances in in E major, of all unlikely keys. Having conjured this strangely unreal vision, Haydn then spirits the music back to E flat for the recapitulation via a wonderful sequence of floating chromatic harmonies.

Like the slow movement of No. 50, the Adagio suggests a fantasia in its richly ornamented style. But it is a more varied, far-reaching piece, more sonorously scored and more audacious in its harmony. Haydn has another tonal surprise up his sleeve at the start of the finale. After the E major Adagio, the unharmonised repeated Gs lead the ear to expect E minor; and when a sustained bass note in bar 2 establishes the key of E flat, we experience a sense of pleasurable shock (Beethoven would do something similar in the finale of his C minor Piano Concerto, No. 3). The whole movement is the consummation of Haydn's Scarlatti-influenced toccata style, developing its main theme with spellbinding verve and chromatic sleight of hand: a coruscating ending to a work that, if not quite his last sonata, gloriously crowns a genre that Haydn, more than anyone, had raised from lightweight, divertimento origins to a status comparable with the symphony and string quartet.

Miscellaneous keyboard works

As with the sonatas, numerous spurious shorter keyboard works appeared under Haydn's name during his lifetime. Variations were perennially popular with the amateur market; and as late as 1807, Artaria, happy to trade on the old composer's prestige, brought out a highly dubious 'Haydn' *Andante con variazioni*. Only four sets of keyboard variations, plus an arrangement of the 'Emperor's Hymn' variations from the String Quartet Op. 76 No. 3, can be reliably authenticated. Three of these are minor Haydn: the brilliant but rather mechanical *20 Variazioni per il cembalo solo* in G major of *c*.1765, Hob. XVII: 2, a compendium of mid-eighteenth-century keyboard technique (Artaria published an abridged version, transposed up to A major); the more appealing *Arietta con 12 Variazioni*, Hob. XVII: 3, from the early 1770s, on the lyrical minuet theme from the E flat Quartet, Op. 9 No. 2; and the C major Variations,

Hob. XVII: 5, of 1790, accurately described by Artaria as 'agréables et faciles'.

A world away from these trifles is the *Andante con variazioni* in F minor, Hob. XVII: 6, composed in Vienna in 1793 for Mozart's one-time pupil Barbara ('Babette') von Ployer, and described by Haydn, perhaps with a touch of irony, as 'Un piccolo Divertimento'. This vies with the Andante of the 'Drumroll' Symphony as his greatest set of alternating minor-major variations. After the stoic melancholy of the F minor opening, with its gently insistent dotted rhythms, the ornate F major theme exudes a kind of whimsical, abstracted playfulness. Haydn's original conception ended with the second F major variation and a few bars of coda. He subsequently appended a long, disturbingly chromatic coda that draws unsuspected force from the pervasive dotted rhythms before dissolving in a feverish swirl of arpeggios. After a measure of equilibrium is restored, the dotted rhythms toll deep in the bass, like a funeral knell. As Robbins Landon first suggested, the tragic intensity of the coda may have been prompted by Maria Anna von Genzinger's sudden death on 26 January 1793.

The shorter keyboard pieces also include two entertaining *jeux d'esprit*, one early, one late, both influenced by the rondos and fantasias of C. P. E. Bach. In the G major Capriccio, Hob. XVII: 1, of 1765, Haydn uses an Austrian folk song, 'Acht Sauschneider müssen seÿn' (It takes eight men to castrate a boar), as the basis for a free rondo that traverses a giddying range of keys. This is by far the most adventurous of his keyboard works to date. Nearly a quarter of a century later, in March 1789, Haydn wrote to Artaria: 'In a moment of great good humour I have completed a new Capriccio for fortepiano, whose taste, singularity and special construction cannot fail to receive approval from connoisseurs and amateurs alike. It is . . . rather long, but by no means too difficult.' The work in question – harder to play than Haydn implied – was the one we know as the C major Fantasia, Hob. XVII: 4. Based on another Austrian folk song, 'Do Bäuren hat d'Katz valor'n' (The farmer's wife has lost her cat), this 3/8 Presto is a work of scintillating virtuosity, full of quasi-orchestral effects that recall the contemporary C major Sonata, No. 48. It is also one of Haydn's craziest essays in comic deception, repeatedly leading us to expect one key and then darting or slinking off in a quite different direction.

Sacred music

Masses

Missa 'Rorate coeli desuper', in G, Hob. XXII: 3
Missa brevis in F, Hob. XXII: 1
Missa Cellensis in honorem BVM in C ('Cäcilienmesse'),
   Hob. XXII: 5
Missa sunt bona mixta malis in D minor, Hob. XXII: 2
Missa in honorem BVM in E flat ('Grosse
   Orgelsolomesse'), Hob. XXII: 4
Missa Sancti Nicolai in G ('Nikolaimesse'), Hob. XXII: 6
Missa brevis Sancti Johannis de Deo in B flat ('Kleine
   Orgelsolomesse'), Hob. XXII: 7
Missa Cellensis in C ('Mariazellermesse'), Hob. XXII: 8

Haydn was a man of devout, unquestioning religious faith. Yet
even in his lifetime, critics lambasted his masses for their supposed worldliness: too much of the ballroom and the opera
house, not enough of sobriety and penitential gloom. Salieri,
for one, accused Haydn of 'gross sins against the church style'.
To such criticisms the composer is supposed to have rejoined,
disarmingly, that whenever he thought of God, his heart would
'leap for joy'. (He told Dies that he always expressed the Deity
'by love and goodness'.) The truth is that Haydn's masses,
like Mozart's (dubbed by Stravinsky 'rococo-operatic sweets-
of-sin'), are rooted in the cheerful, Neapolitan-influenced idiom
prevalent in Austria and southern Germany, with what Charles
Burney disapprovingly called its 'light airs and turbulent accompaniments': the musical equivalent of the luminous rococo inte-
riors of churches like Ottobeuren, overlooking Lake Constance,
or St Peter's Abbey in Salzburg, built to inspire the faithful not
through fear but through grace and delight. We can guess that
Haydn would have enjoyed Francis Poulenc's vindication of his
Gloria: 'I had in mind those frescoes by Gozzoli where the

angels stick out their tongues, also some serious Benedictine monks I had once seen revelling in a game of football.'

There were two fundamental types of eighteenth-century Austrian mass: the *missa brevis*, designed for normal services, lightly scored and typically lasting between ten and twenty minutes; and the longer, more elaborately orchestrated *missa solemnis*, usually sung on festive occasions. Haydn's two earliest masses, composed around 1749, perhaps while he was still a chorister at St Stephen's, are extreme examples of the *brevis* type, with different clauses of the Gloria and Credo sung simultaneously, much to the displeasure of the ecclesiastical authorities. Stylistically, both the 'Rorate coeli desuper' Mass (the title comes from an Advent text, 'Drop down, ye heavens, from above') and the *Missa brevis* in F owe much to the masses of St Stephen's Kapellmeister Georg Reutter, especially in their routine chordal writing for chorus against busy violin writing. With no authentic sources, the eminently forgettable 'Rorate coeli desuper' Mass may even be at least partly Reutter's work.

Though hardly prophetic of future greatness, the F major *Missa brevis* – Haydn's earliest surviving authenticated work – has greater melodic and rhythmic vitality, and contrasts the choral textures with florid parts for two soprano soloists, one of them perhaps sung by Haydn's younger brother Michael. The Benedictus, often a highpoint in eighteenth-century Austrian masses, is a movement of unassuming lyrical charm. Haydn himself had a soft spot for the mass. On rediscovering it late in life, he looked indulgently on its errors of part-writing, telling Dies: 'What specially pleases me in this little work is the melody and a certain youthful fire.'

With the *Missa Cellensis in honorem Beatissimae Virginis Mariae*, we move forward to Haydn's first years as Esterházy Kapellmeister, when for the first time he was responsible for both instrumental and sacred music. This C major *missa solemnis*, for soloists, chorus and an orchestra including trumpets and drums, is by far the most grandly scaled of all his masses. Clocking in at some seventy minutes, it subdivides each of the main sections into independent solo and choral movements (seven in the Gloria alone), after the manner of the so-called Neapolitan 'cantata mass'.

It was long assumed that Haydn composed the mass in the early 1770s for a Viennese service in celebration of St Cecilia, hence the nicknames *Missa Sanctae Ceciliae* and 'Cäcilienmesse'. Then, in 1975, an autograph fragment was discovered with the date 1766 and the title *Missa Cellensis* – literally 'Mass for Zell', a reference to the famous pilgrimage church of Mariazell in the Styrian hills. As the church's musical resources were slender, the mass was probably composed not for Mariazell itself but for a service in one of the Viennese churches associated with the pilgrimages. There is also evidence that only the Kyrie and Gloria were heard in 1766, and that the remaining movements were added around 1772–3 for a service requiring a full setting of the Ordinary – perhaps one of the annual celebrations of the Viennese Cecilian Congregation.

Like Bach's B minor and Mozart's C minor masses, the *Missa Cellensis* embraces a heterogeneous array of styles, from florid operatic arias (most spectacularly, the soprano's 'Quoniam') to elaborate choral fugues, from the archaic to the fashionably up-to-date. Among no fewer than four full-dress fugues, the 'Et vitam venturi' stands out for its thrilling sustained impetus. To quote Robbins Landon, 'at the end, the first trumpet, rising to the highest *clarino* register, flashes like a shining sword across the horizon'. Some of the most memorable sections, though, are ones that set off the work's flaming C major splendour: the austerely beautiful 'Gratias', an inspired amalgam of fugal and chordal textures; the 'Et incarnatus–Crucifixus', introduced, as so often in Austrian masses, by the tenor soloist; or the extraordinarily sombre C minor Benedictus, with violins shadowed by an expressive bassoon line.

At the opposite extreme from this regally expansive *Missa Cellensis* is the D minor *Missa sunt bona mixta malis* of 1768. The title, also found in a mass by Haydn's Esterházy predecessor, Gregor Werner, comes from a classical proverb, 'The good mixed with the bad, the bad mixed with the good', though, as David Wyn Jones has suggested, it may also have been Haydn's ironic comment on his own efforts. The work was lost until an autograph fragment containing the Kyrie and the opening of the Gloria turned up, the way these things do, in a farmhouse in Northern Ireland in 1983. Scored for chorus and organ continuo, this is Haydn's sole mass setting in the ascetic, Palestrina-inspired *stylus a cappella* cultivated by several of his Austrian contemporaries. We can only speculate as to whether the work was ever completed. As an exercise in a hallowed style the fragment has its curiosity value, though it would not be surprising if Haydn did indeed lose interest midway through the Gloria.

Haydn's next mass, perhaps the first he composed expressly for Eisenstadt, was the *Missa honorem BVM* or 'Grosse Orgelsolomesse' (Great Organ Mass) of *c.*1768–9, so called because of its decorative organ solos, played by the composer himself – an aural counterpart to the scrolls, curlicues and putti in rococo churches. In its time span (around forty minutes) and its alternation of chorus and solo quartet, this *missa solemnis* looks ahead to the six late masses. But it is a more subdued work than any of them, scored without festive trumpets and drums. Its key, E flat, is unusual in eighteenth-century Austrian masses; and like the E flat sections of the *Stabat mater* composed a year or two earlier, it is coloured by the faintly melancholy sonority of two cors anglais. Again, the 'Et incarnatus–Crucifixus', beginning with the customary tenor solo, inspires music of intense chromatic eloquence. The organ is prominent in the gently syncopated Kyrie, and the idyllic Benedictus, where its concerto-like flights offset the serene music for solo quartet. It also chirps in, with delightful inconsequentiality, during the dancing 6/8 'Dona nobis pacem': just the sort of movement that put Haydn's masses beyond the pale for some critics.

If the 'Great Organ Mass' belongs to an Austrian lineage of masses with organ obbligato, the *Missa Sancti Nicolai*, composed in 1772, probably for Prince Nicolaus's name-day (6 December), falls within another established tradition: that of the pastoral mass, usually (as here) in G major, with prominent parts for high horns. Midway between a *missa brevis* and a *missa solemnis*, the 'St Nicholas' Mass draws on musical imagery associated with Advent and Christmas, most obviously in the swaying 6/4 metre and mellifluous parallel thirds of the Kyrie. Elsewhere Haydn, evidently pressed for time, can lapse into rococo auto-chug, though, typically, the mystery and drama of the 'Et incarnatus–Crucifixus' and the anguished supplication of the Agnus Dei (here heightened by contorted violin figuration) inspire a more heartfelt response. Memorable, too, is the Benedictus, a quintessentially Austrian movement for solo quartet that recalls the corresponding section of the 'Great Organ Mass'. Haydn reuses the assuaging music of the Kyrie for the Dona nobis pacem: a familiar, labour-saving ploy in eighteenth-century masses, yet here apt both to the meaning of the words and to the pastoral spirit of the whole mass.

After the regular production of sacred music between 1766 and 1772 (four masses, the *Stabat mater* and the *Salve regina*), Haydn composed just two masses during the next two decades, when his energies were absorbed first by opera for Eszterháza and then by instrumental music for the international market. The *Missa brevis Sancti Johannis de Deo*, or 'Kleine Orgelsolomesse' (Little Organ Mass), is the most modest of all Haydn's mature masses. It was composed some time between 1775 and 1778 for the chapel of the Barmherzige Brüder, who ran the hospital in Eisenstadt and whose patron saint was St John of God, hence the mass's dedication. The tiny orchestral forces (two violins, obbligato organ and bass continuo) were dictated by the chapel's organ loft, which barely had room for fifteen players and singers.

The Gloria – a mere thirty-one bars of polytextual bustle – and the outer sections of the Credo whip through the text in near-record time. Elsewhere, though, Haydn expands the scale: in the gravely tender Kyrie, the Benedictus, a graceful rococo duet for soprano solo and organ, and the Agnus Dei–Dona nobis pacem, which uniquely in these masses remains in Adagio tempo throughout. The gradual fade into silence in the final bars makes a haunting close to Haydn's quietest and gentlest setting of the Ordinary.

Haydn's final mass before his London visits is the so-called second *Missa Cellensis*, or 'Mariazellermesse', of 1782. Like its C major predecessor, Hob. XXII: 5, this has traditionally been associated with the Styrian pilgrimage church of Mariazell. All we know for certain, though, is that the mass was composed for the retired army officer and salon host, Anton Liebe von Kreutzner, who may have belonged to a Viennese brotherhood that supported pilgrimages to Mariazell. Although Haydn resorts to some time-saving polytextuality in the Credo, this is essentially a *missa solemnis*, prefiguring the six masses of Haydn's old age in its bold rhetoric and symphonic inclinations.

The most obviously forward-looking movement is the Kyrie, designed like the first movement of a symphony. A slow introduction, rising majestically *de profundis*, leads to a triple-time Vivace in sonata form: as in most of the late masses, supplication here quickly yields to celebration. Between the jubilant outer sections of the Gloria, with their C major trumpeting and drumming, Haydn sets the 'Gratias' as a soprano aria in lilting 3/8 time (a traditional metre for Austrian 'Gratias' settings), before the chorus enters dramatically in the minor key at 'Qui tollis peccata mundi'. Equally arresting is the 'Et incarnatus', which opens in A minor with the usual tenor solo but then moves via C minor to D flat for the 'Crucifixus' – testimony to Haydn's ever-growing sense of harmonic adventure. The fugues at 'Et vitam venturi' and 'Dona nobis pacem' also anticipate the late masses in their unabashed exuberance, the former bounding along in 6/8 time, the latter elaborately developed from a catchy, syncopated subject. While the Benedictus was often a cue for pastoral tranquillity in Austrian masses, there was also a tradition of stern, minor-key settings, exemplified by the earlier

Missa Cellensis, Mozart's last Salzburg mass, K337, and this 'Mariazellermesse'. (Haydn would later inject the tradition with unprecedented drama in the 'Nelson' Mass.) For the 'Mariazellermesse' Benedictus, Haydn adapted, with no sense of incongruity, an aria from his opera *Il mondo della luna*, contrasting the implacable, Baroque-style opening with a lyrically expansive second subject for the soloists.

Missa in tempore belli in C ('Paukenmesse'), Hob. XXII: 9
Missa Sancti Bernardi von Offida in B flat
    ('Heiligmesse'), Hob. XXII: 10
Missa in angustiis in D minor ('Nelsonmesse'), Hob.
    XXII: 11
Mass in B flat ('Theresienmesse'), Hob. XXII: 12
Mass in B flat ('Schöpfungsmesse'), Hob. XXII: 13
Mass in B flat ('Harmoniemesse'), Hob. XXII: 14

The six masses associated with the name-day of Princess Marie Hermenegild Esterházy surpass even the finest of the earlier works in drama and spiritual depth. They at once satisfy liturgical convention, engage in challenging argument, and give consummate expression to Haydn's reverent, life-affirming faith, described by Griesinger as 'not of the gloomy, tormented kind, but rather cheerful and reconciled'.

Though the chronology is not watertight, the first of the masses was probably the *Missa Sancti Bernardi von Offida*, performed in the Bergkirche in Eisenstadt on 11 September 1796, the first Sunday after the princess's name-day. That date is also the saint's day of Bernard of Offida (1604–94), a Capuchin monk who had devoted his life to caring for the poor. Haydn's mass is thus both a tribute to the princess and a commemoration of the monk who had been canonised by Pope Pius VI in 1795. The nickname 'Heiligmesse' (literally 'Sanctus Mass') comes from the use of an old German chorale, 'Heilig, Heilig', in the Sanctus.

In all these late masses Haydn at once crowns and transcends the eighteenth-century Austrian mass tradition with his own brand of symphonic drama, his contrapuntal mastery, and choral writing whose brilliance and flexibility reflect his encounter with Handel's oratorios in London. Alone among the six works, though, the 'Heiligmesse' does not integrate a solo quartet into the choral movements. The soloists appear only in the 'Gratias', and in the 'Et incarnatus–Crucifixus', where the quartet is expanded to a sextet.

The Kyrie follows the pattern of the 1782 *Missa Cellensis*: a solemn, supplicatory slow introduction, and an Allegro that welds folk-like melody and fugal textures into a powerful, quasi-symphonic design. In a familiar complaint, one early critic found the graceful main theme too redolent of the ballroom. The magnificent Gloria falls, as always in the late masses, into three main sections. The choral cries of 'Miserere' in the 'Qui tollis' (which grows out of the gravely polyphonic 'Gratias') have an almost Verdian theatricality. As usual, Haydn caps the Gloria with an exhilarating – and delightfully tuneful – double fugue that weds Handel's spirit to Haydn's own freedom of form.

After the confident, march-like opening of the Credo, the 'Et incarnatus est' is set as a gentle canon, or round, for three female soloists, ethereally accompanied by clarinets, bassoon and high pizzicato strings. Haydn here recycles a canon he had recently composed to a secular text 'Gott im Herzen, ein gut Weibchen im Arm' (God in your heart, a good little wife in your arms), though listening 'blind' to this celestial music, no one would guess. The 'Crucifixus' transmutes the melody of the canon in a shrouded E flat minor, with sepulchral textures created by three male soloists and low bowed strings.

In the Sanctus Haydn conceals the traditional 'Heilig' chorale in the alto and tenor parts; the exultation of 'Pleni sunt coeli' is curiously muted. The sonata-form Benedictus taps a characteristic vein of serene lyricism, though early listeners may have been surprised at the unusually full orchestration and the strangely withdrawn central development, where a solo viola adds its haunting voice to the contrapuntal weave. The Agnus Dei presents a moving contrast between the austere B flat minor opening and the more urgently expressive music at 'Miserere nobis'. Not for the first (or last) time in Haydn's masses, the 'Dona nobis pacem' is less a prayer for peace than a celebration of its imminence. Like the Kyrie, it drew criticism for its unseemly brilliance, though Haydn was careful to temper the jubilation with passages of quiet contemplation.

Alone among the late masses, the *Missa in tempore belli* ('Mass in time of war' – Haydn's own title) was not composed primarily for Princess Esterházy's name-day celebrations. Although Haydn directed an Eisenstadt performance in her honour in September 1797, the mass was first heard in the Piaristenkirche in Vienna on 26 December 1796, in a service marking the admission to holy orders of Joseph Franz von Hoffmann. Hoffmann's father was Imperial Paymaster for War, and probably commissioned the mass, perhaps even suggesting its 'war' theme. During the autumn of 1796 Napoleon's forces were already encamped in Styria; and the drum rolls and wind fanfares in the Agnus Dei (the German nickname is 'Paukenmesse' – 'Kettledrum Mass') are a graphic reference to the advancing French armies, 'as though one could already hear the enemy approaching in the distance' (Griesinger). Haydn's Agnus Dei would leave its mark on Beethoven's *Missa solemnis* a quarter of a century later.

The war topic colours other parts of the mass, especially the 'Pleni sunt coeli' of the Sanctus, and the Benedictus. This is a far more assertive, flamboyant work than the 'Heiligmesse', exploiting the martial associations of C major. The sonata-form Kyrie begins with a slow introduction whose quiet fervour is shattered first by pounding timpani and then by ominous trumpet fanfares. Insistent fanfares also permeate the outer sections of the Gloria. The central 'Qui tollis', opening as a mellifluous duet for bass and solo cello in the contrasting key of A major, is another movement in these masses to provoke critical head-shaking, not least from Charles Rosen ('to be accepted as an adequate setting of the *Qui tollis peccata mundi* it requires more tolerance than the most emotional religiosity of eighteenth-century painting . . .'). Over-sweet it may be to some ears. But with the choral entry, on a 'shock' chord, at 'Suscipe', the music develops a harmonic intensity that powerfully enhances the supplicatory anguish of the text.

Austrian composers, including on occasion Haydn himself, often lapsed into workaday bustle at the opening of the Credo. In the *Missa in tempore belli*, though, Haydn shouts his faith from the rooftops in combative contrapuntal textures. The C minor 'Et incarnatus est' is music of extraordinary spiritual depth, from the grave bass solo, through the mysterious ecstasy of the soprano's 'et homo factus est' to the hushed awe of the close. Following the theatrical upsurge of 'Et resurrexit', Haydn sets the long doctrinal clauses against a restless ostinato before the chorus celebrates the life to come in excited fugato textures.

After the delicate opening of the Sanctus, the 'Pleni sunt coeli' erupts violently in the minor key, with bellicose trumpets and timpani. The shadow of war also hovers over the C minor Benedictus, whose anxious unease is resolved only with the turn to C major at the recapitulation. The Agnus Dei sets the threefold choral prayer in a crescendo of intensity against the menacing soft drumbeats and strident fanfares. Its martial spirit carries over into the 'Dona nobis pacem', though the aggressive demands for peace are balanced by a pleading chromatic passage for soloists near the beginning (singled out by Griesinger for its pathos) and the sudden lulls near the close.

Explicit war references, with intimations of Beethovenian heroism, also permeate the famous *Missa in angustiis* (Haydn's title) or 'Nelson' Mass, composed in just fifty-three days during July and August 1798. Its first performance seems to have been planned for Sunday 9 September, the day after the princess's name-day, and that year the feast of the Most Holy Name of Mary, when Austrians celebrated the defeat of the Ottomans in 1683. In the event there was insufficient rehearsal time; and the new mass was not heard until 23 September, during a service in St Martin's Church (now Eisenstadt Cathedral). Haydn's own title – meaning 'Mass in straitened times' – seems to allude to the Napoleonic wars. As David Wyn Jones has suggested, it may also have been an ironic reference to the breakneck speed at which the mass was composed. In early August the British fleet under Nelson routed the French in the Battle of Aboukir, though as Vienna only heard of the victory after the score was finished, we must ditch the attractive idea that the trumpet fanfares to the Benedictus were Haydn's spontaneous response to the news. The Nelson association actually dates from two years later, when the Admiral was entertained by Prince Nicolaus Esterházy. Tradition has it that he attended a performance of the mass in his honour, though there is no firm evidence for this.

In 1798 Prince Nicolaus dismissed his wind players (the *in angustiis* title might even be a jokey allusion to the prince's cash-flow problems). But Haydn turned this restriction to inspired account, adding to the strings a prominent organ part (which he played himself), three trumpets – imported for the occasion – and timpani. This distinctly archaic instrumentation gives the 'Nelson' Mass a uniquely lean, acidic sonority, stark and minatory in the D minor Kyrie and Benedictus, fiercely exultant in the D major sections.

The sonata-form Kyrie, with its ominous trumpet fanfares, has a grim, austere power. After a tense central fugato, the recapitulation enhances the mood of urgent supplication with soaring coloratura for the solo soprano, who has a starring role in this mass. The Gloria is a masterpiece of large-scale design. The outer sections, with their terrific rhythmic impetus, are unified by recurrent ideas: the music first heard at 'Et in terra pax', for instance, returns in modified form at 'Domine Deus' and then, much later, as a coda to the whole Gloria, after one of Haydn's most euphoric fugues. Between the fast D major sections stands the 'Qui tollis' in B flat, where the noble declamation of the solo bass (Haydn's tribute to the 'Tuba mirum' from Mozart's Requiem?) and the solo soprano's entreaties are underpinned by soft choral chanting.

The Credo opens as a craggily energetic canon, with the sopranos singing in octaves with the tenors, the altos with the basses. After the exquisite G major 'Et incarnatus est', initiated, as so often in this mass, by the soprano soloist, and moving to a dramatic choral unison for 'Crucifixus', Haydn sets 'Et resurrexit' in B minor, reserving D major splendour for the Last Judgement ('judicare vivos'). The sudden soft radiance of the soprano's 'Et vitam venturi' against an eloquent high cello line is one of the great moments in these masses.

In the Sanctus the swell and ebb of voices and strings punctuated by trumpets and drums creates a profound sense of awe. The Benedictus returns to the mood and key of the Kyrie. Is there a more troubled setting of this comforting text? Near the close, the music swerves to B flat for the shattering trumpet fanfares, echoing (and capping) a similar dramatic moment in the Kyrie. The G major Agnus Dei has the same lyrical tenderness as the 'Et incarnatus', though the alto soloist and the chromatic harmonies give it an aptly darker colouring. The music swings dramatically into D major for the ebullient 'Dona nobis pacem', praised by the *Allgemeine musikalische Zeitung* as 'full of fugal imitations and beautiful harmonic passages and inversions'.

Haydn's next mass, probably performed in the Bergkirche, Eisenstadt, on 8 September 1799, has a very different character. Though the militant trumpet fanfares in, say, the Kyrie's slow introduction are a reminder that this, too, was composed *in tempore belli*, the 'Theresienmesse' is the most intimate and lyrical of all the late masses. Its restrained scoring – strings, two clarinets, two trumpets (which lose some of their strident brilliance in the key of B flat) and timpani – is complemented by the unusually full role for the soloists. The familiar nickname probably stuck after Empress Marie Therese took a particular liking to the work. There is, though, no substance in the tradition that the mass was composed originally for the Empress rather than Princess Esterházy.

The gentle, almost chamber-music spirit of much of the

'Theresienmesse' is immediately felt in the soloists' musing discourse near the start of the Kyrie. Formally this movement is an original take on the slow-fast-slow Baroque French overture, with the lively yet dignified central fugato and the 'Christe eleison' episode for soloists based on themes adumbrated in the initial Adagio. As usual, the Gloria falls into three extensive sections. After a blazing climax on 'Glorificamus te', the music swerves to a remote C major for the central 'Gratias'. This builds from its glowing opening for alto solo to the vehement C minor 'Qui tollis', which alternates strenuous imitative writing for chorus with solo interjections that further develop the music of the 'Gratias'. In the Gloria's final section ('Quoniam tu solus sanctus'), the crisp theme announced by the soloists spawns a choral fugato rather than the usual full fugue. The coda makes prominent play with a melting chromatic cadence, of a kind found at several other points in this mass.

At the centre of the Credo, the B flat minor 'Et incarnatus est', for soloists alone, is one of Haydn's profoundest meditations. Its unearthly tranquillity is carried through into the 'Crucifixus', which has none of the drama of the 'Nelson' Mass at this point, but quietly develops an expressive figure associated with the words 'Et homo factus est'. Haydn then dances into the life everlasting in a fugal jig, capped by a stunning theatrical climax. The songful Benedictus, in the brightly contrasting 'pastoral' key of G major, features ravishing ensemble writing for the four soloists. Remembering, perhaps, the dramatic *coup* in the Benedictus of the 'Nelson' Mass, Haydn engineers a majestic central climax in the work's home key of B flat.

After the stark choral unisons of the G minor Agnus Dei, the 'Dona nobis pacem' reasserts B flat major with the military fanfares heard at the same point in the *Missa in tempore belli*. Yet more than in any of the other late masses, Haydn here offsets martial aggression with the beseeching lyricism characteristic of the whole work.

For his two final masses, the 'Schöpfungsmesse' ('Creation'

Mass) and the 'Harmoniemesse' ('Wind-Band' Mass), Haydn could again call on a full complement of wind players. Both are scored for pairs of oboes, clarinets, bassoons, horns and trumpets, with timpani, organ and strings. In the 'Harmoniemesse' Haydn also takes advantage of the availability of a flute: and the upshot is the most richly scored of all the masses, reflected in the work's nickname.

Haydn finished the 'Schöpfungsmesse' in the nick of time for a performance in the Bergkirche on 13 September 1801. In the Gloria he mischievously set 'Qui tollis peccata mundi' to the contredanse melody of Adam and Eve's duet in *The Creation* – hence the mass's sobriquet. We may smile at this harmless joke. But one of Haydn's warmest admirers, the Empress Marie Therese, was apparently unamused; and at her behest he altered her printed score of the mass to eliminate the offending passage.

As in three of the other late masses, Haydn prefaces a lively setting of the Kyrie with a slow introduction, here of unusual breadth and intensity, and motivically linked to the fast section. After the resplendent opening section of the Gloria, Haydn quickly atones for the Adam and Eve quotation by plunging into a solemn Adagio at 'Miserere nobis' and continuing with imploring solos for alto and soprano. Typically, the rousing fugue at 'In Gloria Dei patris' is increasingly coloured by Haydn's symphonic-operatic thinking, with the soloists superimposing a graceful new 'Amen' theme over the chromatic fugue subject. Beethoven copied out two passages from the Gloria of the 'Schöpfungsmesse' while sketching his Mass in C in the spring of 1807.

In the Credo the flutey, rococo organ obbligato of 'Et incarnatus est' (symbolising the fluttering of doves, time-honoured symbol of the Holy Ghost) looks back to an earlier age. But decorative charm is banished with the tortuous bass solo at 'Crucifixus' and the awesome entry of the chorus, on a surprise chord, at 'Sub Pontio Pilato'. In the Credo's final section, after the solo soprano's frolicking F major 'Et iterum venturus est', chorus and orchestra erupt spectacularly in a far-flung D flat major for a swift and shattering evocation of the Last Judgement.

After the Sanctus, the Benedictus moves to the 'relaxing' subdominant, E flat, and an easeful 6/8 metre, though pastoral innocence is belied by the fervent, rapidly modulating central development: the whole movement is essentially symphonic in conception. The Agnus Dei, in G major, like the 'Et incarnatus est', has a profound supplicatory tenderness extraordinary even among Haydn's many settings of this text. Another abrupt tonal shift initiates the 'Dona nobis pacem', whose pounding diatonic energy is tempered by chromatic fugato writing (shades here of the 'In Gloria Dei patris'), and, near the end, by an ominous shift to B flat minor that lends a deeper perspective to the final jubilation.

Haydn's last mass, the 'Harmoniemesse', cost him more effort than any of the others. He began work on it early in 1802, and in June wrote to Prince Nicolaus Esterházy from Vienna that he was 'labouring wearily' on the mass. It was finally completed in August, and performed in the Bergkirche on 8 September. There is, though, no sign of weariness in the music. It is tempting to hear an autumnal serenity in the sonata-form Kyrie which, uniquely among the late masses, remains in Adagio tempo throughout. This is a great symphonic prayer, with none of the celebratory spirit of Haydn's other Kyrie settings. Yet the music's mellowness is tinged with a chromatic disquiet that colours the whole work. There is intense drama, too, in the initial entry of the chorus, which bursts in *fortissimo* on an unexpected discord, and at the start of the recapitulation, where the chorus reasserts the home key of B flat with shocking abruptness.

The Gloria and Credo are on the usual grand scale, with vigorous outer sections enclosing slower, more reflective music at 'Gratias' and 'Et incarnatus est'. In a structure of majestic breadth, the 'Gratias' begins as a serene alto solo and grows inexorably in intensity, culminating in the tremendous choral 'Qui tollis', Haydn's most turbulent and dramatic setting of this text. The solo soprano's 'Et incarnatus est' opens with a gentle solo for clarinet, that beautiful latecomer to the composer's orchestral palette. Like the 'In Gloria Dei patris' of the 'Schöpfungsmesse', the closing fugues of the Gloria and Credo have a pungent chromatic flavour. The one in the Credo also recalls the corresponding fugue of the 'Theresienmesse' in its jig-like (and to some ears, thoroughly profane) 6/8 metre.

Perhaps the most original movement of all is the Benedictus, marked Allegro molto (!), a kind of tense scherzo, half-awed, half-ecstatic, relaxing only in the soloists' playfully operatic second subject. The exquisitely scored Agnus Dei, set, like that of the 'Schöpfungsmesse', in the 'third-related' key of G major, is strongly reminiscent of the Adagio of Symphony No. 98 and the trio and chorus 'Sei nun gnädig' in *The Seasons*. But, as in the Kyrie, serenity is edged with chromatic unease as each of the theme's three statements modulates in an unexpected direction. Still more startling is the launch of the 'Dona nobis pacem'. Here the tonal wrench, from the dominant of G to B flat major, echoes the Kyrie. But the execution is uniquely apocalyptic, as brazen *fortissimo* fanfares leave the tonality ambiguously poised before a clinching thunderstroke on the timpani – one bar before the chorus enters – triumphantly confirms the home key.

Other sacred works

***Ave regina* in A, Hob. XXIIIb: 3**
***Salve regina* in E, Hob. XXIIIb: 1**
***Salve regina* in G minor, Hob. XXIIIb: 2**

Two of Haydn's three Marian antiphons, the A major *Ave regina* and the E major *Salve regina*, each scored for soprano, chorus, strings (minus violas) and organ, are early works from the mid-1750s. Both combine a guileless charm with an Italianate fluency that reflects his recent studies with Porpora. Taking his cue from Haydn's recollection late in life that he had composed the *Salve regina* in 1756, Robbins Landon has suggested that, like the C major Organ Concerto (Hob. XVIII: 1), it was written for a service at which his first love, Therese Keller, took the veil. While this touching story cannot be verified, the *Salve regina* is one of Haydn's most attractive works of the 1750s. The first section has a beguiling sweetness, while the third is a florid aria in *opera seria* style. Most memorable, though, is the second section, 'Ad te clamamus': a vigorous chorus that suddenly breaks off for a sorrowful minor-key soprano solo, with drooping chromaticisms to paint 'gementes et flentes' (groaning and weeping).

Haydn's second setting of the eleventh-century *Salve regina* antiphon, dated 1771, is a more intimate counterpart to the *Stabat mater*. Though it became popular in an edition for chorus and soloists, Haydn's autograph specifies a solo quartet throughout, with strings and a solo organ that features prominently in the first and last of the four interlinked sections. Nothing remains in this melancholy, introspective music of the ornate Italianate style of the E major *Salve regina*. After an expressive organ solo, the voices enter arrestingly on a discord in mid-phrase. Haydn repeats this dramatic ploy near the close of the third section, a poignant accompanied recitative for tenor. The overwhelming concentration on minor keys makes the gleam of G major in the *pianissimo* final bars all the more moving. In London in 1791 Haydn told his friend Christian Latrobe that he had vowed to compose a thanksgiving offering to the Virgin after recovering from a dangerous illness. Latrobe assumed that this was the *Stabat mater*. But the dates don't tally. We know now that *Stabat mater* was composed in 1767, and that Haydn was ill in 1770 or early 1771. Following Robbins Landon, commentators now agree that the token of thanksgiving was this beautiful G minor *Salve regina*.

Te Deum in C, Hob. XXIIIc. 1
Te Deum in C, Hob. XXIIIc. 2

Though similar in design (with a slow central section at 'Te ergo quaesumus' and a final fugue), Haydn's two settings of the *Te Deum* epitomise the immense distance he travelled during his long career. The earlier seems to have been composed either to mark Prince Nicolaus Esterházy's inauguration as Lord of Eisenstadt in May 1762, or for the celebrations surrounding the wedding of Count Anton Esterházy in January 1763. Its rococo exuberance and (in the fugal peroration) slightly stiff species counterpoint are a world away from the grandeur, sweep and massive, rough-hewn energy of the later *Te Deum*. Scored for large orchestra, including three trumpets and (in one source) three trombones, this was written in 1799 or early 1800, apparently at the request of the Empress Marie Therese. The opening Allegro incorporates the ancient Te Deum plainchant, partly concealed during the orchestral introduction but then boldly intoned by the chorus against a glittering, hard-edged instrumental background. After the mystery of the central C minor Adagio, the final section resumes the C major exultation of the opening, culminating in one of Haydn's most thrilling – and most Handelian – fugues. Near the close, disorientating chromatic syncopations introduce a brief moment of terror at the prospect of damnation before the work ends in a brazen peal of C major.

Stabat mater in G minor

Haydn's *Stabat mater* of 1767 was the only eighteenth-century setting of the anonymous medieval Passion poem to rival Pergolesi's in fame. Though probably composed for semi-private liturgical performance in the Esterházy chapel in Eisenstadt, it became one of his greatest successes in the concert halls of Paris and London. Newly promoted to Kapellmeister after the death of Gregor Werner in 1766, Haydn was eager to prove his credentials as a church composer; and as with the monumental *Missa Cellensis*, Hob. XXII: 5, he lavished immense care and craftsmanship on the *Stabat mater*. He must have known the celebrated Pergolesi setting. Indeed, three of the solo movements, the soprano's 'Quis non posset' and the tenor's 'Vidit suum dulcem natum' and 'Fac me cruce', with its tripping Scotch snap rhythms, could almost have come from the pen of the Italian.

More characteristic than this Neapolitan sweetness, though, is the power of numbers like the bass solo 'Flammis orci ne succendar' – an operatic 'rage' aria transplanted from stage to chapel – and the choruses, three of them in the minor key. In the opening movement, alternating solo tenor and chorus, Haydn indulged his love of word painting: falling, chromatically inflected lines for 'dolorosa'; harsh orchestral unisons at 'crucem'; an oscillating, wailing figure on 'lacrimosa'; syncopated suspensions for 'pendebat'. Yet the music is far more than a series of Baroque-style 'affects'. The soft entry of the choral basses over the solo tenor's final 'filius', and the sudden violent outburst at 'Dum pendebat', are thrilling dramatic strokes. 'Quis est homo', with its massive, rhetorical opening and majestically striding fugato, is equally powerful. The next chorus, 'Eja mater', is more lyrical and consolatory, as its text dictates, though its graceful lilt is tempered by the minor mode and a chromatic intensity typical of much of the *Stabat mater*.

In two movements, both in E flat – the alto aria 'O quam tristis' and the quartet with chorus 'Virgo virginum' – oboes are replaced by the dark, throaty timbre of cors anglais, used in several other Haydn works of the 1760s and 1770s. In its gait (triple time, moderate pacing) and serene, imitative textures, 'Virgo virginum' recalls the 'Gratias' sections of many Haydn masses.

The last movement opens with morbidly sinking chromaticisms before brightening to G major for the final vision of Paradise. In an extreme clash of styles roundly condemned by Pohl, a rather stiff choral fugue in strict 'species' counterpoint alternates with giddy roulades for solo soprano. Yet this (to our ears) incongruous juxtaposition would hardly have fazed eighteenth-century audiences familiar with the church works of Hasse (who wrote to Haydn expressing his admiration for the *Stabat mater*) and other composers of the so-called Neapolitan school.

Motets, offertories and psalms

During his freelance years in the early 1750s, Haydn composed four little *Motetti de Venerabili Sacramento* (Hob. XXIIIc: 5) for the Corpus Christi procession, always a lively and colourful affair in Austria. Scored for soloists, chorus and small orchestra (strings, oboes, trumpets and organ), these settings of verses from Thomas Aquinas's 'Lauda Sion', all in a minuet-like 3/4 metre, have an ingenuous, folk-like charm. The opening of the fourth motet, 'Bone pastor', is a rococo cliché that Haydn would put to exalted use at the climax of his 'Emperor's Hymn'. Around 1767–8 Haydn returned to Aquinas's hymn in the *Responsoria de Venerabili* (Hob. XXIIIc: 4). Gone is the jauntiness of the earlier settings. Horns replace trumpets in the orchestral palette, and the music exudes a quiet gravitas that suggests the proximity of the *Stabat mater*.

Among several offertories of dubious authenticity, including *Animae Deo gratae* (which may be by Haydn's brother Michael), is one incontestably genuine article: the D minor *Non nobis, Domine*, an austerely impressive essay in the *stylus a cappella* that may be contemporary with Haydn's other known work in the so-called 'Palestrina style', the *Missa sunt bona mixta malis* of 1768. Long presumed lost, it was rediscovered in the 1980s by David Wyn Jones, copied into a choirbook in the monastery of El Escorial near Madrid. Another offertory in the *stylus a cappella*, *Libera me, Domine*, unearthed by Robbins Landon in Eisenstadt in 1966, may well be spurious.

Probably dating from the late 1750s is the Christmas *pastorella* for solo soprano (singing in dialect), strings, horns and continuo 'Herst Nachbä, hä, sag mir was heut' (Hey, neighbour, tell me what's going on today; Hob. XXIIId: 3). Using traditional pastoral imagery – rustic fiddler tunes, drone basses and the like – the piece is a light-hearted dialogue between two shepherds as they prepare to visit the infant Jesus. In similar vein, though not reliably authenticated, is the *pastorella* 'Ey, wer hat ihm das Ding gedenkt' (Well I never, who'd have thought of such a thing; Hob. XXIIId: G1).

Haydn's six English Psalms of 1794 were a contribution to the Rev. William Dechair Tattersall's *Improved Psalmody*, dedicated to George III and intended to propagate a more refined type of congregational psalm-singing in Anglican parish churches. 'We are all perfectly agreed that plainness and simplicity are the grand criterion, that ought to guide us,' wrote Tattersall in his Preface. Haydn's tuneful, elegant settings for three voices (SAB) and organ or string accompaniment, most of them in minuet rhythm, broadly fulfil his expectations. Several sound like superior Ancient and Modern hymns. This being late Haydn, though, there are artful touches of harmonic colour, contrapuntal imitation and word painting, especially in the 'through-composed' 'Maker of all! be thou my guard', which prefigures the late part-songs. As Robbins Landon and others have noted, the sturdy, march-like 'The Lord, th'almighty monarch' (which sets verses from Psalm 50) anticipates the opening of 'The heavens are telling' in *The Creation*.

Cantatas and oratorios

Applausus

Haydn composed the congratulatory *Applausus* cantata (Hob. XXIVa: 6) in spring 1768 for the Cistercian Abbey of Zwettl in Lower Austria, as part of the celebrations surrounding the fiftieth anniversary of the Abbot's first vows. In the tradition of *applausus* works, the allegorical, moralising Latin text hymns the joys of the monastic life and the benevolence of the Abbot in a discourse between the four Cardinal Virtues – Temperance (soprano), Prudence (alto), Justice (tenor) and Fortitude (bass) – and the stern figure of Theologia (bass), symbolising the Christian Church. Haydn's duties in Eisenstadt prevented him from travelling to Zwettl to direct the cantata. But in a long letter to the monastery he gave instructions on matters such as tempo, dynamics ('there is a very great difference between *piano* and *pianissimo*, *forte* and *fortissimo*, crescendo and sforzando') and the correct execution of recitatives (to be taken slowly, 'so as to allow each word to make its effect'), on the importance of the viola line, and the need for a bassoon to double the bass.

The style of *Applausus* is essentially that of mid-eighteenth-century *opera seria* cultivated most famously by Hasse. Elaborate *da capo* arias hold sway. There are just two ensembles (a quartet and a duet), and a single chorus at the end. Most of the arias are laid out on a vast scale, none vaster than Justice's eighteen-minute 'O beatus incolatus!', with violin obbligato (one of several numbers to include a concertante solo part). Here and elsewhere, interminable roulades over harmonically static accompaniments can put serious strains on the modern listener's powers of attention. The most memorable numbers in a less than compelling work are Fortitude's tumultuous *Sturm und Drang* aria 'Si obtrudat ultimam', and Temperance's 'Rerum, quas perpendimus', with its warm textures (bassoons often doubling the first violins at the octave, a favourite sonority in later Haydn) and graceful melodic lines.

Il ritorno di Tobia

Haydn wrote his first oratorio, *Il ritorno di Tobia* (Tobias's Return), during the autumn and winter of 1774–5 for the Tonkünstler-Societät, the Viennese musical charity that mounted biannual oratorio performances for the widows and orphans of former members. The premiere on 2 April 1775, involving some 180 musicians, was a huge artistic and financial success. Nowadays, though, *Il ritorno di Tobia* is probably the least known of all Haydn's major works. It will certainly disappoint anyone expecting a prototype *Creation*. In the tradition of the fashionable Neapolitan oratorio, *Tobia* is in effect a sacred *opera seria*, powered by a succession of gargantuan bravura arias, with, in the original version, just three choruses for contrast. Mozart's early *La betulia liberata*, K118, is in similar vein.

A prime stumbling block is the hopelessly undramatic, sometimes muddled libretto by Giovanni Gastone Boccherini, brother of the composer Luigi. With its multiple murders and miracles, the story of Tobias from the apocryphal Book of Tobit could have been a composer's gift. Instead, Boccherini laboriously observes the Classical *bienséances* and sets Tobias's adventures in the past tense, telling us not only what actually happened but what might have happened if things had turned out differently. When Tobias finally appears with his new wife, the serially widowed Sara (husbands one to seven have all been despatched by the demon Asmodeus), the action grinds forward with stultifying slowness. 'Delay could prove fatal,' says Tobias to his mother Anna as he prepares to cure his father Tobit's cataract with the gall of a giant fish. He then launches into an eight-minute aria, to which his mother rejoinders, 'A just sense of urgency spurs him on.' Even the climax of the story – the restoration of Tobit's sight, symbolising the imminent liberation of the Jews from captivity – is botched by Boccherini.

While *Tobia* is a write-off dramatically, the music is much better than the oratorio's poor reputation would suggest. The many accompanied recitatives are skilfully composed and – especially the one preceding Anna's aria 'Come in sogno' – harmonically adventurous. The arias, most of them *da capo* (ABA) structures brought up to date under the influence of sonata form, are vastly challenging for the singers, but far more inventive than the interminable bravura arias in the *Applausus* cantata. Several, including Anna's opening 'Sudò il guerriero' and the (disguised) Archangel Raphael's apocalyptic prophecy 'Come se a voi parlasse', give Haydn scope for picturesque tone-painting. Equally memorable are Tobias's dulcet E major love song 'Quando mi dona un cenno', Anna's F minor 'nightmare' scene, 'Come in sogno', with its pulsing Gluckian ostinato, and – the jewel of the entire oratorio – Sara's aria of rapt contentment, 'Non parmi essere'. Haydn here enhances the tender vocal cantilena with luxurious concertante writing for the largest wind group (pairs of flutes, oboes, cors anglais, bassoons and horns) he had used to date.

Splendid, too, are the three choral numbers in the original 1775 version: the opening prayer, interleaved with solos for Anna and Tobit, and the powerful fugues that end each of the two parts. The shock switch from a blazing C major to a hushed, fearful C minor near the close of Part One is an unforgettable stroke. An early reviewer enthused that 'the choruses, especially, glowed with a fire otherwise found only in Handel'. In 1784 Haydn revived the oratorio for two Lenten concerts of the Tonkünstler-Societät, with a cast including Mozart's first Susanna, Nancy Storace, and the first Count Almaviva, Stefano Mandini, together with the singers who had created the roles of Konstanze, Blonde and Belmonte in the 1782 premiere of *Die Entführung aus dem Serail*. For the occasion he pruned many of the arias and added two choruses, each of which breaks in dramatically on the preceding aria. 'Gran Dio', in Part One, is a resplendent C major contrapuntal movement that would not be out of place in the late oratorios, while the stunning 'storm' chorus in Part Two, 'Svanisce in un momento', prefigures Haydn's 'madrigal' *The Storm* and the mighty tempest in *The Seasons*. Seething, convulsive D minor music alternates with a major-key vision of calm that picks up the final section of Anna's preceding aria, 'Come in sogno'. Sensing that here was music too good to waste, around 1797–8 Haydn adapted this chorus, with minimal musical changes, as a sacred motet, *Insanae et vanae curae*.

The Seven Last Words of our Saviour on the Cross (choral version)

The background to the composition of *The Seven Last Words* is given on pp. 165–7. After hearing a choral arrangement in Passau by the local Kapellmeister Joseph Friebert, Haydn expressed his approval but privately felt he could have written the vocal parts better. He persuaded Friebert to part with a copy of the score, and on his return to Vienna commissioned a revised text from Baron van Swieten. The Baron adapted the Passau text, pilfering K. W. Ramler's popular poem 'Der Tod Jesu' for the final *Il terremoto*, while Haydn reworked the vocal lines and amplified his original orchestration with pairs of clarinets and trombones and a second flute. But his most significant additions were the brief *a cappella* choral chants before each Word (except the fifth) and an extraordi-narily bleak, archaic-sounding A minor interlude for wind and brass, like a Renaissance *canzona* refracted through a late eighteenth-century prism. The choral arrangement was an immediate success on its premiere on 26 March 1796, and far eclipsed the magnificent orchestral original in popularity. It still does so today.

The Creation (Die Schöpfung)

The roots of Haydn's most famous masterpiece lie in his two visits to England. At the 1791 Handel Festival in Westminster Abbey he was overwhelmed by the gargantuan performances of, inter alia, *Messiah* and *Israel in Egypt*, and was fired by the idea of composing an oratorio of his own. Four years later, just before Haydn left London for the last time, Salomon handed him an anonymous English libretto on the theme of the Creation, allegedly compiled for Handel half a century earlier. Haydn later told Griesinger that the author was 'an Englishman by the name of Lidley'. No plausible candidate of that name has ever been identified; and it was long assumed that the author was in fact the composer/impresario Thomas Linley the Elder (1733–95). But though Linley may well have passed the libretto on to Salomon, he was a musician rather than a poet, and would in any case have been too young to have worked with Handel. With the original English text lost, the author's identity is destined to remain a mystery, although the tenor Neil Jenkins, in an article published in the *Journal of the Haydn Society of Great Britain* (No. 24/2, 2005), has made a plausible case for Charles Jennens, librettist of Handel's *Saul* and *Belshazzar*, and compiler of the *Messiah* texts.

Haydn found the text 'well chosen', and, once back in Vienna, asked Gottfried van Swieten for his opinion. In Swieten's words, 'I recognised at once that so elevated a subject would give Haydn the opportunity I had long desired . . . to express the full power of his inexhaustible genius; I therefore encouraged him to take the work in hand.'

The libretto's main sources were the Book of Genesis, Milton's *Paradise Lost* (for the accompanied recitatives and arias) and, for the choruses, the Book of Psalms. Swieten described his role as 'more than that of a mere translator; but not by any means so extensive that I could call the text my own'. After completing his German version, he provided his own frequently stilted 'back translation' that often fits poorly with the music. In 1804, the Scottish publisher George Thomson wrote to Haydn's friend Anne Hunter that it was 'lamentable to see such divine music joined with such miserable broken English'. There have been countless subsequent attempts to improve Swieten's English text, with its mistranslations and clumsy Teutonic word order ('The wonder of his works displays the firmament' is a prime example). Two of the most successful are by Neil Jenkins, in the new Novello edition of *The Creation*, and Paul McCreesh, on his 2007 Archiv recording.

The baron's libretto was ready towards the end of 1796, by which time Haydn had already begun to sketch the 'Representation of Chaos'. (More sketches survive for *The Creation* than for any other Haydn work.) Perhaps at the composer's request, Swieten annotated the manuscript with suggestions for musical setting, some of which were adopted (several were blindingly obvious), others rejected. He was, though, adamant that 'Let there be Light . . . And there was Light' should be sung only once, thereby claiming a small share in one of music's most elementally thrilling moments.

With its picture of a benevolent, rationally ordered universe and its essentially optimistic view of humanity – unlike in *Paradise Lost*, the Fall is touched on only *en passant* – *The Creation* accorded perfectly with the temper of the Enlightenment, unsullied by Romantic angst. Its theological content, minimising conflict, guilt and retribution, also chimed in with Haydn's own faith. Composing the oratorio was for him an act of religious devotion. It is ironic, then, that the Catholic church was quick to take offence at its non-moralistic tone and 'secularity' of expression, and banned it from places of worship.

But the church could not hinder the work's immediate, and enduring, success. Haydn had completed the score by the end of 1797; and the first, private, performance took place at the Schwarzenberg palace on 30 April 1798, preceded by an open rehearsal the previous day. The reception was ecstatic. Haydn, who conducted, was as moved as his listeners. Griesinger reported that the composer 'could not describe the feelings with which he was filled when the performance went just the way he wished, and the public listened in total silence. "Sometimes my whole body was ice-cold", he admitted, "sometimes a burning heat overcame me, and more than once I was afraid I would suddenly have a stroke." '

Further, semi-private performances were arranged in May. But it was not until the following year that the wider Viennese public was able to hear Haydn's *opus summum*. The grandly scaled performance, in the Burgtheater on 19 March 1799, caused a predictable sensation; and within a few years *The Creation*, so unlike any previous oratorio, was being acclaimed throughout Europe.

A prime factor in the libretto's appeal to Haydn was surely the simplicity and strength of its structure. In the first two parts the six days of creation are announced in 'dry' recitative by one of the archangels, Raphael (bass), Uriel (tenor) and Gabriel (soprano); after each act of creation the archangels expatiate on its wonders in accompanied recitative and aria; and each day after the first (which ends with the delightful, *faux-naif* chorus heralding the 'new created world') culminates in a hymn of praise by the heavenly hosts. Part Three, depicting the first morning in Eden, Adam and Eve's systematic praise of all creation (a kind of celestial Cook's Tour) and their mutual love, falls into two sections, each likewise climaxing in a jubilant chorus.

The arias and accompanied recitatives gave Haydn marvellous opportunities for instrumental tone-painting, using techniques honed in his operas and *Il ritorno di Tobia*. In the magnificent D minor bass aria, 'Rolling in foaming billows', tone-painting permeates the whole texture, beginning with the powerful evocation of the turbulent ocean. The jagged 'second subject' (like most of the solo numbers, the aria adapts sonata form to its own ends) portrays the mountains; and a modulating 'development', with oboes duetting against violin swirls, introduces the rivers' 'serpent error'. The final section functions as a recapitulation. Here Haydn poetically depicts the 'limpid brook' with a new lyrical D major melody that turns out to be a variant of the D minor opening. Another inspired moment for the bass is the creation of 'great whales and every living creature that moveth' in Part Two. Haydn originally set this as dry recitative. But as an afterthought, he added the solemn, shrouded accompaniment for divided violas and cellos to enhance the mysterious power of God's words.

Haydn's pictorialism is at its most naively charming in Gabriel's avian aria in Part Two, 'On mighty pens', where soprano and woodwind evoke each of the birds in turn: eagle, lark, dove (with delicate coloratura) and, finally, the nightingale's 'sweet notes'. Even more graphic is the famous zoological extravaganza in Part Two, where Haydn has a field day illustrating the 'creatures numberless, in perfect form and fully grown': the lion (with a gleeful, dissonant roar for trombones and contrabassoon), the 'flexible tiger', the noble steed, then, with a radiant turn from D flat to A major, the cattle and sheep. Lastly, in one of his most endearing strokes, he describes the worm's 'sinuous trace' in an absurdly solemn Adagio. There is more of his trademark humour in the majestic bass aria, 'Now Heav'n in fullest Glory shone', where the 'heavy beasts' make their appearance courtesy of rude belches from the contrabassoon.

At the opposite end of the spectrum is the introductory 'Representation of Chaos', a miraculously scored evocation of the primal void: here, in the most harmonically audacious music of the whole eighteenth century, vague thematic fragments grope and twist through tonal nebulae (Haydn's initial inspiration here was probably the notorious slow introduction of Mozart's 'Dissonance' Quartet, K465). In the spring of 1797 Haydn played through 'Chaos' to his Swedish friend Fredrik Silverstolpe, remarking: 'You have certainly noticed how I avoided the resolutions that you would most readily expect. The reason is, there is no form in anything yet.' Towards the end there is even an anticipation of Wagner's famously shocking 'Tristan' chord. The whole movement is the epitome of what Edmund Burke termed the 'sublime' in music, calculated to evoke astonishment, awe, wonder, even terror. Hardly less sublime are the first sunrise, as simple (a D major scale that slowly expands in height and depth) and as elementally moving as the choral explosion on 'Light', and the veiled shimmer of the moon.

In the celebratory choruses Haydn deploys his contrapuntal mastery with a freedom and brilliance of effect that reflect Handel's example. 'Awake the harp' is the most exciting chorus Handel never wrote. In several numbers, though, Haydn integrates choir and soloists, a favourite technique in the late masses but one rarely used by Handel: in, say, the famous chorus that ends Part One, 'The Heavens are telling', with its incandescent chromatic climax, all the more overwhelming after the preceding emphasis on a C major (Beethoven virtually cribbed this climax in the first movement of his Second Symphony); in the trio and chorus 'The Lord is great', where soprano and tenor spin coloratura cascades around the sustained choral lines; or in the great Hymn in Part Three, a free-ranging symphonic rondo in which Adam and Eve survey the whole of creation and enjoin each element in turn to praise God.

Adam and Eve's quasi-operatic love duet, 'Graceful consort', has been criticised as too demotic for such exalted surroundings. (Tovey even advocated that it should be jettisoned, along with the final chorus.) But as H. C. Robbins Landon and others have argued, the duet's contredanse rhythms, tootling woodwind and suggestions of Papageno and Papagena are entirely apt. Whereas in the Hymn Adam and Eve aligned themselves with the angels, here they appear as everyman and everywoman, in all their humanity and innocent sensuality.

The Seasons (Die Jahreszeiten)

After the phenomenal success of *The Creation*, Swieten lost no time in proposing another oratorio text to Haydn, again with a British source: his own drastically abridged adaptation of James Thomson's pastoral epic *The Seasons*, which since its publication in 1730 had become one of the most popular and influential of all eighteenth-century poems. Jettisoning most of Thomson's abstract moralising, Swieten shifted the scene to Haydn's native Austria, inserted a couple of popular poems to jolly up 'Winter', and in a spirit of Enlightenment optimism omitted tragic details such as the wanderer frozen to death in a snowstorm.

The baron was certainly no poet. (Griesinger wryly commented that 'the best in his poetry was not that which he actually wrote but that which he imagined'.) Time and again he dulled Thomson's brilliant imagery, compounding the problem with another, and even more inept, English retranslation of the German text (to maximise sales *The Seasons* was published trilingually, in German, English and French). But, working closely with the composer, he was shrewd in his choice of which details to omit and which to include. In many ways the finished libretto was right up Haydn's street: akin to *The Creation* in its celebration of a harmonious, divinely ordered world, yet embracing an even wider range, from the stag hunt and the wine harvest to paeans of praise to the Almighty.

Haydn, though, worked on *The Seasons* with increasing reluctance, protesting that he was too weary and that the libretto was banal by comparison with *The Creation*. He derided the croaking fogs and chirping crickets as *französicher Quark* – 'Frenchified trash' (i.e., the sort of thing favoured by *opéra-comique* composers); and when he came to set the words 'O Fleiss, o edler Fleiss' in 'Autumn', he muttered that while he had been an industrious man all his life, he would never have dreamed of setting 'industry' to music.

Nowadays, of course, few share Haydn's view that a less elevated subject inevitably means less inspired music. Whatever his misgivings, Swieten's text gave him plenty to fire his imagination; and he responded with music of unquenchable vitality and inventive richness. First heard by an invited audience in the Schwarzenberg palace on 24 April 1801, *The Seasons* is a joyous evocation of the world in which the composer had grown up. Though God is invoked directly in the fugal choruses that close 'Spring' and 'Winter', *The Seasons* is the most hedonistic of oratorios, and killed by an excess of solemnity in performance. Essentially a series of lovingly painted frescoes, it epitomises Haydn's final creative period in its juxtaposition and fusion of the 'popular' and the 'sublime', pastoral innocence and the most sophisticated orchestral and

harmonic language. Like *Die Zauberflöte*, Mozart's great celebration of Enlightenment values, *The Seasons* effortlessly
incorporates a diverse array of styles, from Viennese Singspiel
(in, say, the 'Autumn' love duet and Hanne's faintly risqué
tale in 'Winter') to noble fugal choruses that never sound
remotely stiff or academic.

Each of the four 'cantatas' that make up *The Seasons* opens
with an orchestral tone poem. As with *The Creation*, the
would-be composer in Swieten could not resist supplying
suggestions in the margin of the libretto. Haydn followed
or ignored these as he saw fit. The G minor introduction,
heralded by four hammer-blows, 'depicts the passage from
winter to spring', the former evoked in blustery, densely contrapuntal music coloured by rasping trombones, the latter in
the airy 'second subject'. In the recapitulation Haydn omits
this 'spring' tune and, following the baron's suggestion,
sweeps directly into the recitative for the three peasants:
Simon (bass), Lukas (tenor) and Simon's daughter Hanne
(soprano). Tonal resolution comes only with the lilting
G major chorus, 'Komm, holder Lenz', with its musette-like
drones, and its opposition of women's and men's voices – a
technique Haydn fruitfully uses elsewhere in *The Seasons*.

In the ploughman's song Haydn resisted Swieten's attempts
to get him to include a tune from a popular German opera
and instead had Simon whistle the famous melody from his
'Surprise' Symphony: the upshot was one of the oratorio's
instant hits, spiced by picturesque scoring for piccolo (its sole
appearance in all Haydn), oboes, bassoons and horns. Two
extended solo-choral complexes make up the second half of
'Spring'. The Prayer 'Sei nun gnädig' begins with a serene,
hymnic melody, akin to the Adagio of Symphony No. 98 and
the 'Agnus Dei' settings of the late masses, and ends with an
urgent fugue that virtually quotes the 'Quam olim Abrahae'
from Mozart's Requiem – the first of several, surely conscious,
Mozartian reminiscences in *The Seasons*. The popular and the
sublime are directly juxtaposed in the last number of 'Spring'.
This opens in A major with a 'Song of Joy', enlivened by

charming illustrative touches (gambolling lambs, swarming bees, etc.). After working its way to D major, the music seems to peter out. Then, after a pause, Haydn introduces a series of majestic fanfares in the remote-sounding key of B flat, with trumpets and timpani making their first appearance since the Overture. We owe this *coup de théâtre* to Swieten's annotation: 'At the entrance "Ewiger &c." I think that a key remarkably different from that of the preceding Song of Joy would greatly bring into prominence the solemn and devotional aspect of the chorus's cry.' After a solo trio with dramatic choral interjections, 'Spring' closes with a magnificent, intricately worked fugue that, as so often in Haydn, becomes more symphonic and less strictly contrapuntal as it proceeds.

'Summer' falls into two large, virtually continuous sections. The first moves from the atmospheric portrayal of 'the meek-eyed morn', via the oboe-as-cockerel and a bucolic aria with horn obbligato for Simon (the inspiration for the 'Shepherds' Thanksgiving' in Beethoven's 'Pastoral' Symphony), to a chorus hymning the sun. This opens with a sunrise, as overwhelming in its way as the very different sunrise in *The Creation*, and closes, after another lyrical interlude for the solo trio, in a riot of fugal laughter.

In the second part of 'Summer', drought and torpor, marvellously evoked in Lukas's recitative and cavatina, find relief in Hanne's enchanting woodland scene: first in a pictorial recitative, then in a two-section aria, beginning as a languorous duet for soprano and oboe and ending with ecstatic coloratura flourishes. The scene now darkens in a baleful recitative, punctured by distant thunder. Then, with forked lightning on the flute, the thunderstorm erupts. In this, the first great Romantic picture-in-sound of the warring elements, Haydn creates a musical counterpart to the cataclysmic tempests that Turner would paint a quarter of a century and more later. After a fugue on a drooping chromatic subject, the tempest recedes amid distant, desultory lightning flashes. Normal rustic life reasserts itself in the final trio and chorus, opening with Haydn's 'Frenchified trash' (bellowing cattle, croaking frogs, chirping quails, all evoked with charm and humour) and closing with a graceful chorus of villagers that transmutes the storm's ominous tremolandos into drowsy murmurs.

Following the minuet-like introduction to 'Autumn', the trio and chorus in praise of industry is Haydn's supreme triumph over a recalcitrant text: a noble, powerfully organised movement initiated by Simon alone, with delightful woodwind commentaries, and crowned by a choral fugue that climaxes in a stunning harmonic 'purple patch'. The tension relaxes with the rustic love duet, then gradually increases during the hunting scenes, portrayed with detailed relish by Haydn – an enthusiastic hunter himself (on foot rather than horseback) in earlier days. After the bird shoot, opening as a quasi-Handelian bass aria with a burbling bassoon obbligato, and the hare-coursing comes the most spectacular of all hunting choruses, based on traditional hunting calls (courtesy of a quartet of horns) and tracing an audacious tonal journey from D major to E flat. Yet Haydn manages to cap even this sensational movement in the wine harvest, memorably described by the German critic Karl Schumann as 'a feast of Bacchus in the Burgenland, painted by a musical Breughel'. Haydn rejected Swieten's idea of various dance bands playing simultaneously, à la *Don Giovanni*. Instead, an increasingly unruly German dance, complete with pipe, drums, bagpipes and skirling fiddles, spills over into music's first 'drunken fugue' where the singers are so far gone that they can only blurt out fragments of the fugue subject.

In stark contrast to this C major revelry is the depiction of 'thick fogs' that opens 'Winter', a piece of near-impressionistic orchestral tone-painting to set alongside 'Chaos' from *The Creation*. The season's grim aspects are explored further in Hanne's beautiful cavatina, and the tenor aria, with its graphic portrayal of the wanderer's mounting anxiety in the frozen landscape. But, unlike Thomson's doomed traveller (and for that matter the protagonist of Schubert's *Winterreise*), Swieten's wanderer finds refuge in a tavern in which the villagers cheerfully pursue their winter tasks: a cue for a rustic spinning scene (to a text filched from Gottfried August Bürger) that, as Tovey observed, foreshadows Schubert's 'Gretchen am Spinnrade' and, beyond that, the spinning chorus in Wagner's *Der fliegende Holländer*. Next Hanne entertains the company with a quasi-folk tale in which country girl outsmarts a philandering aristocrat, to words taken from a German translation of a romance by Mme Favart. The chorus chips in after each verse, finally erupting in peals of laughter as the girl makes off on the young lord's horse. Though more artful in its structure and orchestral accompaniment (inventively varied from verse to verse), Hanne's song is cut from the same cloth as Papageno's 'Ein Mädchen oder Weibchen'.

There are further Mozartian resonances in the profound closing numbers of 'Winter'. In the valedictory bass solo 'Erblicke hier, betörter Mensch', where the declining year becomes an allegory for old age, Haydn poignantly quotes the slow movement of Mozart's Symphony No. 40. (When Haydn's pupil Sigismund Neukomm expressed his admiration, the composer responded, 'This aria refers to *me*.') At the end of the aria's fast section the music dissolves in insubstantial woodwind chords. 'Nur Tugend bleibt' – 'virtue alone remains' – asserts Simon in his new role of philosopher-moralist, a notion expanded in the final trio and chorus. There are Masonic overtones here, too. Indeed the antiphonal question-and-answer passages for the two choirs, and several melodic phrases, echo the dialogue between Tamino and the Speaker in *Die Zauberflöte*. Swieten proposed that Haydn should end with an eight-part fugue for double chorus. Again the composer ignored the suggestion. Instead he celebrates the certainty of salvation in a magnificently rugged four-part fugue that builds inexorably to a resplendent homophonic climax, replete with proto-Wagnerian brass fanfares, at the vision of 'the holy hill of heavenly bliss'.

Smaller secular vocal works with orchestra

Destatevi, o miei fidi (Hob. XXIVa: 2)
Al tuo arrivo felice (Hob. XXIVa: 3)
Qual dubbio ormai (Hob. XXIVa: 4)
The Storm (Hob. XXIVa: 8)
Invocation of Neptune (Hob. XXIVa: 9)

Haydn composed several congratulatory cantatas for Prince Nicolaus Esterházy, of which only three have survived. Two, *Destatevi* and *Qual dubbio ormai*, were designed for the prince's name-day festivities in 1763 and 1764; *Al tuo arrivo felice*, comprising a recitative and a vaudeville-style chorus, celebrates his return to Eisenstadt in April 1764 from the Frankfurt coronation of Archduke Joseph (the future Emperor Joseph II). The texts, as usual in such works, are toe-curlingly sycophantic. But Haydn's music is full of bold, fiery gestures à la Vivaldi and *opera seria*-style virtuosity for the soloists (soprano in *Qual dubbio ormai*, two sopranos and tenor in *Destatevi*). Highlights include a spectacular soprano and tenor duet and a brief D minor 'storm' aria in *Destatevi*, and an aria in *Qual dubbio ormai* where soprano and solo harpsichord spur each other on to extravagant coloratura flights.

The other two works in this Hoboken grouping date from the London years. Composed to words by Peter Pindar (the pseudonym of John Wolcot) and premiered in February 1792, the so-called 'madrigal' *The Storm*, for chorus and large orchestra, was Haydn's first setting of an English text. Though in 3/4 rather than 4/4 time, its alternation of minor-key tempest and hymn-like major-key calm echoes the even more violent storm chorus 'Svanisce in un momento', from *Il ritorno di Tobia*, better known as the motet *Insanae et vanae curae*. One especially effective dramatic stroke is the 'premature' entry of the choir over the final bars of the orchestral introduction. Robbins Landon has pointed out the kinship between the graceful melody of the 'calm' and several of Haydn's English Psalms.

After the premiere, the *Morning Herald* described *The Storm* as 'a very wonderful composition . . . in which he combined the strongest effects of his art, horror and pity.' It made Haydn's reputation in England as a choral composer, and helped sow the seeds for *The Creation*.

A London curiosity is the fragmentary *Invocation of Neptune*, whose text had formed the preface to a seventeenth-century treatise, *Mare Clausum*, enshrining Britain's rightful sovereignty of the sea. The ode was commissioned in 1794 by Lord Abingdon, and abandoned when the notoriously outspoken earl was arraigned for libel (his unwise target 'those locusts of the law, the Pettifogging Attornies of this country') and sentenced to three months' imprisonment. The crudely tub-thumping verses should make even the most hardened Europhobe blush. But the two completed numbers are in Haydn's ripest style: a noble F major bass aria for Neptune, with rich woodwind writing, and a D major chorus whose verve and contrapuntal power presage the late oratorios and masses.

Operas and dramatic music

In his Autobiographical Sketch of 1776, Haydn proudly nom-
inated his three most recent operas, *Le pescatrici*, *L'infedeltà
delusa* and *L'incontro improvviso*, together with *Il ritorno di Tobia*
and the *Stabat mater*, as 'the works of mine that have received
the most approbation'. A few years later, in 1781, responding
to the success of the *Stabat mater* in Paris, he lamented to
Artaria that his operas were so little known beyond the
Esterházy court: 'If only they [the Parisians] could hear my
Operette *L'isola disabitata* and my most recent opera *La fedeltà
premiata*, for I assure you that such a work has not been heard
in Paris, and perhaps not in Vienna either. It is my misfortune
to live in the country.' Like almost every composer *c.*1780,
Haydn valued his vocal works, particularly his operas, above
his instrumental music; and for nearly two decades from the
opening of the Eszterháza opera house in 1768, his life was
dominated by opera. During these years he not only composed
ten operas, mainly comedies of increasing musical sophistication, plus several *Singspiele* for Prince Nicolaus's marionette
theatre, but was also responsible for engaging and coaching
the singers, adapting other composers' operas for Eszterháza
forces, supervising rehearsals and conducting performances.

By the mid-1780s the balance had shifted. Though *La
fedeltà premiata* and *Orlando paladino*, especially, had some
success beyond Eszterháza, Haydn composed no more operas
for the court after his first full-blown *opera seria*, *Armida*, premiered in 1784. As he increasingly realised, his operas were
too intimately tied to the circumstances and available forces
at Eszterháza to make their full effect in the international
market place. In 1787 he turned down an invitation to perform one of his comic operas in Prague, partly because of
this, partly because he seems to have accepted that, in the
Bohemian capital, of all places, 'scarcely any man could brook
comparison with the great Mozart'.

Whether or not Haydn had really developed an operatic inferiority complex (his remark can also be seen in the light of his exasperation that his younger friend had not found a permanent position), his own stage works soon dropped from view altogether. His London opera of 1791, *L'anima del filosofo*, lay unperformed until 1951. And in the tepid centenary celebrations of 1909, many music-lovers were surprised to learn that Haydn had written any operas at all. There have been fitful professional stagings in Europe and the USA since the late 1950s, and from the early 1990s more or less regular productions at the specialist venues of Eisenstadt and Garsington. Yet while Rupert Christiansen, in the *Faber Pocket Guide to Opera*, exaggerates when he says – perhaps thinking of the 1979 Glyndebourne *La fedeltà premiata* and the 2001 Covent Garden *L'anima del filosofo* – that 'their occasional modern revivals have fallen flat', it is true that none of the operas has established itself in the repertoire. Those who know them do so primarily through the recordings conducted by Antál Dorati (a pioneering 1970s series of eight Eszterháza operas), Nikolaus Harnoncourt (*Orlando paladino* and *Armida*) and Christopher Hogwood (*L'anima del filosofo*).

As Haydn himself may have felt by the late 1780s, in opera, more than anywhere, he has suffered for not being Mozart. In one sense comparisons are unjust, since Mozart's most famous operas, from *Figaro* onwards, postdate Haydn's last comic opera, *Orlando paladino* (1782). Chronologically, a truer yardstick would be other *opera buffa* composers working in the 1760s and 1770s: Gassmann, Anfossi, Cimarosa, Paisiello and Sarti, all of whose works were produced at Eszterháza. Pitted against these, Haydn's operas stand up well. Those who know only the symphonies and quartets of these years may be surprised at his mastery of fluent, shapely Italianate melody, of the kind we habitually dub 'Mozartian'. An inveterate 'developer', he tends to elaborate his material far beyond the capacity of his Italian contemporaries, often with a striking richness of harmony and orchestration. As the American musicologist Mary Hunter has noted, it was Haydn's achievement in these later operas 'to integrate typically sonata elements – long-range tonal tension and resolution, thematic development and return, etc. – into arias', as Mozart was to do even more powerfully in his three Da Ponte operas. Haydn made much of his artistic 'isolation' at Eszterháza. Yet as impresario-adapter he was thoroughly au fait with current operatic trends. This is reflected in the new complexity of the act finales from *La vera costanza* (1778–9) onwards, an increasingly fluid intermingling of comic and serious, high- and low-born characters, and – in the two wholly serious works, *L'isola disabitata* and *Armida* – a concern for dramatic and musical continuity, à la Gluck. But *opera buffa*, in particular, was evolving fast in the early 1780s, with new emphasis on dramatic realism epitomised by the quickfire conversational ensemble. Then, with *Figaro* in 1786, the genre moved on to a different plane altogether: as Julian Rushton put it in *The New Grove Dictionary of Opera*, 'the symbiotic harmony between music and drama is complete'.

Given the superficial similarity of idiom, it is hard for modern listeners to suppress thoughts of *Figaro* or *Così fan tutte* when hearing, say, *L'infedeltà delusa* or *La vera costanza*. Unfair, of course. But the fault is not all Mozart's. Haydn seems to have had little critical sense when setting a text. He certainly never learnt to reject a bad libretto, as Mozart had done with his aborted comedies *L'oca del Cairo* and *Lo sposo deluso* of 1783–4. As we know from his letters during the composition of *Idomeneo* and *Die Entführung*, Mozart, a born theatre animal, chivvied his librettists until he got the text he wanted. Haydn was far more passive, content to use often implausible and flimsily motivated existing librettos, adapted as necessary to Eszterháza resources. As Griesinger remarked, 'Haydn seems to have been predestined to bad texts.' Beyond this, the dominance of aria over ensemble, typical of Italian comic opera before 1780, and Haydn's propensity to symphonic elaboration mean that his comic operas tend to proceed at the stately pace of *opera seria*. This was very much to the taste of Prince Nicolaus, for whom, according to

Haydn, 'nothing could ever be too long'. But this static quality, alongside some creaky dramaturgy, represents the most serious challenge to producers today. Only in the multi-sectioned finales do the characters interact in ensemble, though even here we rarely find the close contrapuntal interplay of Mozart's great opera ensembles and Haydn's own string quartets.

Yet as recordings have revealed, individual numbers, even whole scenes, can be masterly: richly worked (Haydn's leisurely pacing is, of course, less problematic on disc than on stage), sharply characterised, sometimes – as in the ravishing 'dream' trio in the harem opera *L'incontro improvviso* – of a sensuous lyric beauty not readily associated with Haydn. Stock-in-trade comic characters, usually male, are effectively, if not always economically, drawn. Especially vivid are the foppish, preening Perruchetto in *La fedeltà premiata*, and the garrulous Pasquale in *Orlando paladino*. As in Mozart's operas, though, it is the women, often stereotypes in the libretto, who inspire Haydn's most psychologically penetrating music: Sandrina in *L'infedeltà delusa*; the 'sentimental' heroine Rosina in *La vera costanza*; or the shepherdess Celia and the haughty yet vulnerable Amaranta in *La fedeltà premiata*. Most memorable of all is the seductive, vengeful, ultimately tragic sorceress Armida, heroine of Haydn's only *opera seria* for Eszterháza. All the more frustrating, then, that *Armida*'s inert pacing (Handel's *opere serie* positively rattle past by comparison) makes it a headache for any producer. Yet if Haydn's comic operas are unlikely to enter the mainstream, wittily inventive, stylishly sung productions in small-scale venues such as Garsington have shown that they can still give delight to sympathetic audiences in the theatre.

Acide e Galatea

Habsburg celebrations would often include a specially composed *azione teatrale* or *festa teatrale*: a relatively brief opera with a mythological pastoral setting and an obligatory happy ending. Gluck's *Orfeo*, premiered in October 1762, is the most famous example. Never knowingly outshone by the imperial dynasty, Prince Nicolaus Esterházy commissioned his own *festa teatrale* for the wedding festivities of his eldest son Count Anton and Countess Marie Erdödy. The upshot was *Acide e Galatea*, first performed in the new glass-house theatre in the Eisenstadt palace grounds in January 1763.

The libretto, by Metastasio's amanuensis Giovanni Ambroglio Migliavacca, treats the Ovid-inspired story familiar from Handel's *Acis and Galatea*. To the three principal roles of the shepherd Acis, the water nymph Galatea and the cyclops Polyphemus, Migliavacca added two subsidiary parts: Glauce, who deflects Polyphemus's grotesque advances from her friend Galatea; and Tetide, the sea nymph who restores Acis to life in an obligatory *lieto fine*. Around half the music for *Acide* was lost in the Eszterháza fire of 1779. The numbers that survive – Haydn's earliest extant stage music – are an Italianate three-movement overture, like an early Haydn symphony, four extended arias, an accompanied recitative for Acis and a final quartet. We also have three numbers from Haydn's revised version of 1773–4: a tonally wide-ranging accompanied recitative and part of an aria for Galatea, and a coloratura bass aria for Neptune, replacing Tetide as the *deus ex mare*.

If the later pieces are more sophisticated in technique, the 1763 numbers show how well the young Haydn had absorbed the language of *opera seria* as perfected by Jommelli, Galuppi and Hasse. The extravagant virtuosity of Acis's heroic C major aria is a tribute to Haydn's leading tenor, Carl Friberth, while Tetide's aria charmingly sets the voice against a pair of carolling flutes. In Polyphemus's aria, a vigorous Allegro replete with syncopations and self-important horn fanfares, the cyclops's attempts at ardour result merely in hyperactive bluster.

La marchesa nespola

In 1762 or 1763 Haydn wrote nine Italian arias for *La marchesa nespola*, a play with music performed by the theatrical troupe of

Giralomo Bon. Three or four similar works from the early 1760s are lost. As Robbins Landon has pointed out, the nonsense title – 'Marchioness of the Loquat', a fruit only edible after it has started to decay – is typical of Venetian comic dramas. Like *Acide*, *La marchesa* exists only as a fragment, with the spoken dialogue (which would have been in German) and several arias lost. In the Venetian tradition the play mixed serious and *commedia dell'arte* characters, all aptly portrayed by Haydn in the five complete surviving arias.

The *seria* parts are Signora Barbara, who sings a half-dignified, half-agitated aria on the time-honoured metaphor of a boat tossed by the waves; and Leopoldo, whose 'Trema, tiran regnante' is in the same heroic vein as Acis's aria in *Acide*, with huge vocal leaps and flashy coloratura. In contrast, each of the *commedia dell'arte* figures, Columbina, Scanarello and Pantalone, has an aria in perky, short-breathed *buffo* style. Scanarello's is a comic patter song, Columbina's a typical soubrette aria spiced by its wayward phrasing and teasing interjections from flutes and horns.

La canterina

Dated 1766, and probably first performed that July during the name-day celebrations of Count Anton Esterházy, the amusing little *intermezzo in musica*, *La canterina* (The diva) is Haydn's first stage work to survive virtually complete (only a brief section in the Act Two finale is missing). The libretto, taken from an intermezzo in Piccinni's 1760 opera *L'Orgille*, is in the same comic tradition as Pergolesi's *La serva padrona*, with a clever soubrette outwitting a lascivious older man. All the characters are stereotyped *commedia dell'arte* figures: the aspiring diva, Gasparina, manipulative, money-grubbing and anything but innocent; her companion (procuress?) Apollonia, masquerading as her 'mother' – a role originally played in drag, and perhaps sung in falsetto, by tenor Leopold Dichtler; the lecherous singing teacher Don Pelagio, a proto-Don Basilio, in whose studio the women are living rent-free;

and the wealthy merchant's son Don Ettore (another cross-dressing role, sung by Dichtler's wife Barbara), who is finally promised Gasparina's hand.

After Apollonia's self-admiring opening aria at her dressing table, her vanity mocked by mincing staccato figures, Pelagio (sung in 1766 by Carl Friberth) begins the singing lesson with a parody of an *opera seria* aria, complete with obbligato parts for oboes and horns. During the lesson-as-seduction, a genuinely funny scene, the racing, blustering scale figures make clear his intentions, while Gasparina (soprano Anna Maria Weigl) can't even sightread the first phrase of the aria he has written for her. Apollonia chips in with her own advice, to Pelagio's intense irritation. He is even more incensed when he hears Gasparina and Don Ettore planning to cheat him. Pelagio orders the women to leave his house; and the first act ends with a brief, fast-paced quartet of mounting indignation and consternation.

Act Two opens with Don Pelagio ordering the removal men to evict the women, though not for the last time in Haydn's operas, his aria sounds too easy-going for the situation. Gasparina then launches into a C minor aria that mocks the tragic style, and tragic divas, with cors anglais replacing oboes, and the singer protesting with comical vehemence 'più voce non ho' (I've lost my voice). She caps this by fainting. Pelagio is predictably softened, and brings her round with the time-honoured remedy of a bulging purse. At the start of the finale Don Ettore, though under no illusions about Gasparina, trumps this with a gold ring. And in the closing 3/8 Presto, which resembles a typical early Haydn symphony finale, all celebrate the apparently happy outcome, with Pelagio confident that he will not be left out in the cold.

Lo speziale

For the opening of the new Eszterháza opera house in September 1768, Haydn composed the first of his three operas to librettos by the popular Venetian satirist of contemporary mores, Carlo Goldoni (1707–93). Goldoni's *Lo speziale* (The pharmacist), first set to music in the mid-1750s jointly by Domenico Fischietti and Vincenzo Pallavicini, contained seven characters. For practical reasons Haydn, probably with the help of tenor-cum-librettist Carl Friberth (who played the title role, Sempronio), whittled the cast down to just four, omitting two serious parts and an insignificant comic figure. Although only two numbers from Act Three have survived, *Lo speziale* became the first Haydn opera to be revived since the composer's lifetime when the Viennese music critic Robert Hirschfeld created a one-act German version, as *Der Apotheker*, for a Dresden performance in 1895. Further performances conducted by Mahler (Hamburg, 1896) and Weingartner (Vienna, 1899) followed; and Hirschfeld's version remained on the fringes of the repertoire in Germany and Austria for much of the twentieth century. Since the 1980s, performances have usually gone back to Haydn's Italian original, filling out the missing portions with newly composed recitative, as at Eisenstadt in 2001, when *Lo speziale* was given as a double bill with *La canterina*.

In Goldoni's play *Il teatro comico*, one of the characters speaks for the author when he declares: 'Comedy was created to correct vice and ridicule bad customs.' In *Lo speziale* the prime objects of ridicule are the foppish dandy Volpino (another trousers role for Barbara Dichtler) and the pharmacist Sempronio, a pompous bore who spends most of the time with his head in the newspapers parroting tedious facts and fantasising about distant lands. Both characters lust after Sempronio's pretty and knowing ward, Grilletta (soprano Magdalena Spangler). She, though, has other ideas, in the shape of Mengone (Leopold Dichtler), an apprentice in Sempronio's dispensary, whose incompetence with a pestle and mortar is parodied in his opening aria.

The next two numbers likewise trade on broad comic effects. In Sempronio's 'newspaper' aria, extravagant long-held notes and vertiginous leaps send up his fascination with the dimensions of the arena at Verona and the tower at

Cremona. Mengone then sings an aria depicting stomach ache (with a 'cramped' melodic line and stabbing dissonances) and the powers of a good laxative (cue for increasingly rapid runs). Volpino enters with designs on Grilletta, only to be mocked in her lilting aria, where flutes, replacing oboes, give a soft, bright sheen to the texture. His desire turns to anger in a G minor aria that begins in *Sturm und Drang* style but then undercuts Volpino's dignity with short-winded *buffo* patter. The finale is a simple but effective 'chain' ensemble, of the kind first developed by Baldassare Galuppi in his Goldoni settings. The tempo increases from a conspiratorial Andante to an excited Allegro as Sempronio exits, leaving Mengone and Grilletta free to declare their love. When he re-enters unexpectedly and catches them hand in hand, he bullies the music into a new key, and the exchanges become terse and flustered. Finally, a brief, frenzied 6/8 Presto 'freezes' the action.

The arias in Act Two, while effective enough, are less sharply characterised: a siciliano-style song in which Volpino tries to ingratiate himself with Sempronio, en route to winning Grilletta; Sempronio's strutting aria proclaiming that only a stick can bring a girl back to her senses; then, after a quarrel between Mengone and Grilletta, a playful aria in which she pretends to reject him. The finale puts a new slant on convention by introducing *two* fake notaries, aka Mengone and Volpino, each ostensibly writing the contract for Grilletta's marriage to Sempronio while inserting their own names on the contract. After a rondo-like alternation of Adagio (with the *parlando* vocal parts counterpointed by a solo oboe) and Allegro sections, the ruse is discovered; and a Presto coda ends the act in mutual recrimination and general mayhem.

In the sole surviving aria for Act Three, Volpino disguises himself as the Sultan of Turkey's ambassador and offers Sempronio a fabulously rewarded job as the Sultan's pharmacist. The upshot is a nonsense aria in mock-'Turkish' style – in fact, derived from a type of Hungarian popular dance featuring pounding rhythms, pizzicato effects and 'primitive' harmonic progressions. Sempronio, now far more excited by the lure of the Orient than by Grilletta, has agreed with Volpino that she is to marry 'a Turk'. Volpino is convinced of his triumph. But Mengone, also in Turkish disguise, and Grilletta have already outfoxed him. In the finale ensemble the lovers celebrate their victory while Volpino and Sempronio are left to rue their folly.

Le pescatrici

Haydn's next opera, *Le pescatrici* (The fisher-girls), also sets a Goldoni *dramma giocoso*. This time, though, the increased forces at his disposal allowed him a cast of seven, with five comic and two serious characters. The result was Haydn's first full-length opera. Its central theme – that those of blue blood have an innate dignity and nobility of spirit, in contrast to the frivolous, fickle peasantry – made *Le pescatrici* a shrewd choice for the wedding celebrations of Prince Nicolaus's niece, Countess von Lamberg, and Count Pocci on 16 September 1770. Like *Lo speziale*, the opera suffered in the Eszterháza fire of 1779, though here the loss was more serious, amounting to over a third of the music in the first two acts. A viable performing version was created by Robbins Landon for the 1965 Holland and Edinburgh festivals, the first known stagings since the composer's lifetime.

Goldoni sets the action in Taranto, a fishing village in southern Italy. A jolly 'chorus of fishermen' introduces the comic lovers, all sporting typical *buffo* names: Burlotto and Frisellino (sung by tenors Leopold Dichtler and Carl Friberth) are paired with each other's sisters, Nerina and Lesbina (played, doubtless to the court's amusement, by the tenors' wives, Barbara Dichtler and Magdalena Friberth). Burlotto then hymns a fisherman's endurance of the elements in a vast aria that simultaneously showcases Dichtler's coloratura prowess and apes the heroic manner. Frisellino sings an equally extended aria parading the instruments that will feature at his wedding, giving colourful opportunities to the unusually large wind contingent (for 1770) of flute, oboes, bassoon and horns.

Both girls reveal themselves as minxes. Nerina's aria, in typical soubrette style, alternates slow and fast tempos, while Lesbina sings an insinuating minuet song coloured by cors anglais. Haydn's leisurely preamble also includes a fragment of an aria for Eurilda (mezzo-soprano), presumed daughter of the wily old fisherman Mastricco (bass). The action proper, a variation on the Cinderella story, is kick-started by the entry of Prince Lindoro (baritone Christian Specht). After announcing that he is seeking a lost princess brought to the village years ago to escape her father's murderer, he recounts his perilous voyage in a splendid (though incomplete) D minor aria replete with syncopations, frenzied string writing and gigantic vocal leaps. The girls immediately eye their chance, with Lesbina assuming extravagant airs at the close of her fragmentary aria 'Ti miro fisso'. After a gravely beautiful E flat ensemble extolling the delights of a shady grove and cooling breezes (echoes here of 'Virgo virginum praeclara' in the *Stabat mater*), the first act ends with a quartet in which Burlotto and Frisellino mock their girlfriends' pretensions to nobility.

Act Two opens with the fishermen out for revenge. To get his own back on Nerina, and claim the prince's promised reward, Burlotto tells Lindoro that his sister Lesbina is the princess he seeks; Frisellino, in a tripping comic aria, makes the same claim for Nerina. The girls renew their efforts to impress Lindoro with their aristocratic credentials, though Lesbina betrays her true status when her aria switches from over-the-top coloratura to *buffo* patter. In a scene for which no music survives, Eurilda, like a latter-day Perdita in *The Winter's Tale*, is revealed as the lost princess. The finale is again a quartet for the warring lovers, following the Goldoni tradition that first- and second-act finales should only involve comic characters. The girls beg forgiveness and successfully worm their way back into their boyfriends' affections. Or so it seems in the bouncy Presto coda.

For the opening of Act Three the location changes to a temple dedicated to Neptune, duly celebrated in a rousing C major ensemble. Eurilda sings of her love for Lindoro in a Cavatina whose chaste, unadorned lines contrast with the extravagances of the fisher-girls. In a further plot twist, Burlotto and Frisellino now decide to have some fun at the girls' expense. Disguising themselves as 'cavaliers', they succeed with alarming ease in wooing their own girlfriends. Though Goldoni's pairings are unchanged (otherwise the men would have been courting their sisters), the *Così fan tutte* parallels are unmissable. With Burlotto and Frisellino still in disguise, all wish Eurilda and Lindoro a tranquil voyage in an ensemble evocative of murmuring zephyrs – music that foreshadows the chorus 'Placido è il mar', in the same key of E major, in Mozart's *Idomeneo*. When the ruse is revealed, Mastricco engineers an improbably swift reconciliation. The noble couple set sail. And in the finale the lovers and the old fisherman invoke Cupid's blessing on a triple wedding.

If the structure of *Le pescatrici* is typically loose, with minimal interaction between the high- and low-born characters, the surviving music is often delightful, and the orchestration colourful and varied. Further variety comes from the unusual number of ensembles. Apart from the comic finales to Acts One and Two, these are 'choruses' in homophonic style, with the principals probably reinforced by choristers from Eisenstadt, rather than lively action pieces à la Mozart. With its many missing chunks, *Le pescatrici* will always be a problem piece, and has yet to be recorded. Yet the witty 1997 production at Garsington showed that if its occasional longueurs are pruned, it can still make for an entertaining evening in the theatre.

L'infedeltà delusa

L'infedeltà delusa (Deceit outwitted) was premiered on 26 July 1773 to celebrate the name-day of Prince Nicolaus's widowed mother, Princess Maria Anna. On 1 September there was a repeat performance during the ostentatious festivities in honour of Empress Maria Theresa, after a banquet at which three game birds shot by Haydn were presented on the Empress's plate. Maria Theresa, hitherto barely aware of Haydn's music, was delighted at the new work – though it is doubtful whether she ever spoke the much-quoted words, 'If I want to hear a good opera, I go to Eszterháza.' Billed as a *burletta per musica*, *L'infedeltà delusa* lies somewhere between a comic intermezzo and a full-blown *opera buffa*. There are two acts only, relatively few arias and just five characters. Partly because it is easy to stage, *L'infedeltà delusa* has been revived fairly regularly, beginning with productions at the State Opera, Budapest (1959) and the Holland Festival. Its British stage premiere was at St Pancras Town Hall in 1964.

The text was adapted, probably by Carl Friberth (who took the role of Filippo), from a libretto by Maria Theresa's one-time court poet Marco Coltellini. In the Goldonian *buffo* tradition, cunning, greed and paternal bullying are thwarted, and young love duly rewarded. But whereas Goldoni's librettos, like Da Ponte's for Mozart, typically mix comic and serious parts, upper and lower classes – and, as in *Le pescatrici*, ultimately affirm the social *status quo* – *L'infedeltà delusa* deals exclusively with peasants, from Coltellini's native Tuscany. As in *La canterina* and *Lo speziale*, all are stock *commedia dell'arte* figures, though Haydn's music, especially that for Sandrina, injects them with a certain individuality.

Goldoni's comic opera librettos typically begin with an ensemble that sets the scene and gives an inkling of the action to follow. Coltellini does likewise in *L'infedeltà delusa*: a cue, firstly, for an idyllic evocation of Tuscan sunset calm; and then for a frisky 3/8 Allegro where Sandrina (billed as a 'ragazza semplice') enters, alarmed by her father Filippo's plans to marry her off to the rich peasant Nencio – an abnormally wide-ranging part, tailored to the voice of Leopold Dichtler.

When, in a typically expansive aria, Filippo insists that Sandrina marries the man of his choice rather than the peniless Nanni (bass Christian Specht), she erupts in a Presto aria

('Che imbroglio è questo!') in full sonata form, whose nervy, jagged lines and abrupt swerves from major to minor vividly articulate her agitation. Nanni vents his bitterness in a strenuous, driving F minor Allegro di molto, though tension evaporates with the comic 6/8 coda in F major. Enter Nanni's sister Vespina (literally, 'little wasp'). Her feisty ingenuity will drive the whole plot, though her first aria, bemoaning her Nencio's faithlessness, seems demurely jaunty. Brother and sister then proclaim revenge in a marvellous, quicksilver duet (the only duet in the opera) that makes dramatic capital of jumps to keys a third away from the tonic (A major to F major, D major to B flat). Again, there is a dancing 6/8 coda, anticlimactic to modern ears, though doubtless not to Haydn's audience.

Outside Filippo's house Nencio sings a serenade praising the superiority of fresh-faced country girls to their painted urban sisters – exactly the theme of the Autumn love duet in *The Seasons*. The opening, with pizzicato strings imitating a guitar, suggests an ingenuous siciliano. But, quite apart from its exceptionally wide tessitura, the aria far transcends the conventional serenade in its thematic development, its sudden, grating dissonance on 'guai' – 'woe' – and its bittersweet turn from E flat to C flat (another 'third-related' progression) to point the line 'her heart is as false as her face'. This is surely the longest and most sophisticated serenade in all eighteenth-century opera. Not for the only time in Haydn's operas, musical elaboration takes precedence over dramatic momentum.

Overheard by Vespina and Nanni, Nencio tries to win Sandrina's love, first by persuasion, then by force. Vespina springs out of the shadows and slaps Nencio's face, initiating the first-act finale, a brief ensemble of comic indignation.

In Act Two Vespina sets in motion her plan to ensure Sandrina marries Nanni with assorted ridiculous disguises, prompting a whole series of vocal and instrumental effects. First she appears as an infirm old woman, reproaching Nencio for having married and then abandoned her daughter, in a

limping, syncopated aria broken by coughs and splutters –
another piece that seems over-long for its dramatic function.
At this devastating news, Filippo lashes out at Nencio in a
splenetic C major Presto aria with high horns and timpani
(instruments last heard in the scintillating C major overture),
though the beautiful *dolce* 'second subject' at the words 'without love or compassion' goes right against the sense of
Filippo's sarcastic tirade.

Vespina next appears as the German manservant of the
Marquis di Ripafratta, announcing that 'his' master is going to
marry Sandrina and launching into a tipsy bilingual drinking
song. Nencio is predictably incensed. But when the extravagant 'Marquis' appears in person and declares that Sandrina is
to marry his servant, he expresses his *Schadenfreude* at Filippo's
inevitable reaction in a gleeful D major Allegro, with violins
adding their sarcastic laughter. In a perky aria Vespina, as herself, reassures Nanni of her imminent success. Resigned to
marrying Nencio, Sandrina sings of her longing for a simple
life with Nanni in a warmly textured E flat major aria, whose
broad, serene *cantabile* lines suggest a new strength and depth
of character.

The finale opens with Vespina disguised as a notary, like her
near-namesake in *Così fan tutte*, and preparing the fake marriage contract, with Nanni elaborately attired as the Marquis's
manservant. Vespina and Nanni then reveal themselves, provoking laughter from Sandrina, outrage from Nencio and
Filippo, and a sudden surge in tempo. Filippo and Nencio
accept the inevitable, loose ends are tied up, and to horn and
timpani fanfares, all celebrate the double wedding of Sandrina
and Nanni, and that unlikely pairing, Vespina and Nencio.

Philemon und Baucis

After the performance of *L'infedeltà delusa* on 1 September
1773, celebrations continued until dawn with a fancy-dress
ball during which Prince Nicolaus dazzled the Empress and
her retinue with his new Chinese pavilion. The entertainment

was no less lavish the following evening, when the imperial party attended the premiere of Haydn's marionette opera *Philemon und Baucis, oder Jupiters Reise auf die Erde* (Philemon and Baucis, or Jupiter's journey to earth) in what was probably the official opening of the Prince's marionette theatre: a fantastic grotto-like design, with caves on either side of the auditorium decorated with shells, some adorned with frescoes, others with gushing miniature fountains and sparkling plasterwork to reflect the light of the chandeliers. This 'little play with music' was preceded by a short prologue, *Der Götterrath* (The council of the gods), and ended with an allegorical pageant diplomatically glorifying the Hungarian nation and the Habsburg dynasty.

Virtually all the music for the prologue and pageant is lost, probably destroyed in the Eszterháza fire of 1779. Only the prologue's overture (which Haydn appropriated for the first and second movements of Symphony No. 50) and a short orchestral number have survived. With the exception, again, of the overture – an agitated D minor movement with a D major coda – and a single aria, the opera itself also disappeared, resurfacing only in 1950, when the Haydn scholar Jens Peter Larsen came across a manuscript copy in the Paris Conservatoire. In this, the only extant source, the original marionette opera had been adapted for the stage, tricked out with additional music by Haydn (including an aria from *Il mondo della luna*), Carlo d'Ordoñez and Gluck. H. C. Robbins Landon extrapolated a performing version and quickly arranged a recording of *Philemon und Baucis*, Haydn's only indisputably authentic surviving marionette opera. More recently, in 1996 and again in 2003, a touching production by the Little Angel Theatre, using twelve puppets of assorted sizes, charmed audiences in London and at the Eisenstadt Haydn Festival.

The libretto for *Philemon und Baucis* was adapted from a play by Gottlieb Konrad Pfeffel that reworks an episode from Book VIII of Ovid's *Metamorphoses*. After the opening thunderstorm, the slender 'plot' recounts the visit of Jupiter and

Mercury (both speaking roles) to the home of the pious Phrygian villagers, Philemon and Baucis. Their virtue alone has saved the wicked villagers from the gods' wrath. The couple are mourning the deaths of their son, Aret, and his bride-to-be, Narcissa, struck down by a bolt from heaven. Moved by their simple goodness, Jupiter restores Aret and Narcissa to life. The gods reveal themselves, and grant Philemon's wish that their hut should become a temple and that he and Baucis should end their days as priests of Jupiter. At yet another thunderclap, the neighbours rush in and fall to the ground in terror. Jupiter, pointing to Philemon and his family, admonishes the villagers: 'Let this fate be a great lesson to you, for we do not let honesty go unrewarded.' And to a jubilant C major chorus with trumpets and drums, the gods ascend to heaven in a chariot.

Pfeffel's sentimental homily offered Haydn no scope for character interaction or development, and, except in the opening storm, no opportunity for drama. The four arias, two in succession for Philemon (tenor), one for Baucis (soprano), one for Aret (tenor), and the duet for Narcissa (soprano) and Aret are all gentle in tone and tempo. Most striking are Philemon's second aria, 'Ein Tag, der alle Freude bringt', which turns poignantly to the minor as the old man recalls his son's death, and Aret's delicately textured G minor aria, where solo oboe and tenor sing against rustling muted second violins and pizzicato basses – shades here of Orfeo's unearthly arioso 'Che puro ciel' in Gluck's opera.

L'incontro improvviso

Nearly a century after the Turkish siege of Vienna in 1683, the Ottoman Empire was in gentle decline and far from posing a serious military threat to the West. But Europeans remained both fascinated and repelled by the exotic strangeness of Islam, by what they perceived as its mingled sadism, indolence and (strange thought in 2009) unbridled sexual licence. By the 1770s Austria was experiencing a 'Turkish craze', manifested inter alia in the popularity of music imitating janissary bands and operas with oriental settings, above all Gluck's *opéra comique*, *La rencontre imprévue* – a runaway success ever since its 1764 Viennese premiere. Haydn used Carl Friberth's Italian adaptation of its libretto for his own harem opera, *L'incontro improvviso* (The unforeseen encounter). It was premiered at Eszterháza on 29 August 1775, again as part of a lavish series of entertainments, this time in honour of Archduke Ferdinand, Habsburg governor of Milan, and his Italian wife.

L'incontro improvviso shares many ingredients with Mozart's *Entführung*: a heroine (here Persian rather than European) who has been abducted to a seraglio; her noble lover and his comic servant; a failed rescue attempt; death threats; and a last-minute show of clemency by the Sultan. That the setting here is Cairo would barely have registered in 1775. Cairo, Baghdad, Istanbul: steamy oriental locations were all the same to eighteenth-century opera-goers.

After a brief slow introduction, the main part of the overture (Presto) evokes the exotic milieu with flamboyant 'Turkish' music, complete with cymbals and tambourine. In the opening scenes Friberth indulges in some pretty heavy-handed anti-clerical satire through the figure of the Calender, a fake-dervish who sings a pseudo-oriental nonsense chant – echoes here of Volpino's last-act aria in *Lo speziale*. The Indian Prince Ali of Balsóra (Haydn Sikh?), Friberth's own role, and his comic servant Osmin (played by Leopold Dichtler) have arrived penniless in Cairo in search of Ali's beloved Rezia (Magdalena Friberth), who has been abducted by pirates and is living in the harem as the Sultan's favourite.

After Osmin has thrown in his lot with the Calender and his fellow 'whirling-dervishes' – who beg for alms while privately hoarding food and wine – the scene changes to the harem. Rezia learns that Ali has been sighted in Cairo. She sings of her joy in a graceful A major aria, her anticipation suggested by quivering violins, and then joins with her two confidantes, Balkis (Barbara Dichtler) and Dardane (Maria Elizabeth

Prandtner), in the ravishing trio 'Mi sembra un sogno, che diletta', scored with muted strings and cors anglais. Time stands still in the lingering suspensions and languorously protracted cadences of this dream of future bliss. The music's shimmering sensuality looks ahead to *Così fan tutte*, though Mozart would never have allowed the action to stall for as long as Haydn does here.

Ali, alone and forlorn, is introduced in a dignified accompanied recitative, followed by a slow aria full of broken, sighing phrases. Enter Osmin and the Calender, who reveals the rascally secrets of the 'dervish brotherhood' in another pseudo-Turkish nonsense piece. Osmin then tries to recruit an indignant Ali as a mendicant, listing the wonders of the dervishes' table in an aria punctuated by whirling imitations. Rezia glimpses Ali from a window and tests his constancy by sending Balkis to offer him an assignation with an unknown lady. Balkis cajoles him in a flirtatious, soubrette-style aria; and the first act ends with a trio in three sections, with Balkis flattering, Ali protesting his honour and Osmin drunkenly extolling the delights of sausages and cherry brandy, to his master's increasing irritation.

After a short comic number for Ali and Osmin, Dardane in her turn tries to tempt Ali. But he is unmoved, prompting an aria in heroic *opera seria* style in which she praises his fidelity. Rezia herself now appears – cue, one might think, for a rapturous love duet. Instead she sings a chirpy little *canzonetta* recounting her abduction, in the process lampooning the 'villainous sea captain'. Remembering she is a princess, she follows this with a majestic C major coloratura aria, 'Or vicina a te', that became the opera's most popular number in Haydn's lifetime. Ali then launches into another bravura aria, reinforced with warlike trumpets and drums. After a warmly textured *cantabile* aria for Balkis, Osmin describes the planned escape, with softly tiptoeing strings as they creep out of Cairo, rushing scales as they hurry over land, and vigorous rowing movements as they cross the sea. Rezia and Ali's sensuous, long-awaited love duet leads without a break into the finale.

As the lovers prepare for a feast to celebrate their imminent escape, Balkis and Dardane burst in with the news that the Sultan has returned. Ali and Rezia seem paralysed with terror. But Osmin remembers an escape route via a secret staircase. With a change of key and tempo, all repeat at length that they must fly without delay.

As usual with comic operas at this period, the third act is by far the briefest. In hiding, Rezia begs her guiding star to look kindly upon her in a delicately worked Adagio aria with solo oboe, like a slow movement from a contemporary Haydn symphony: again, musical beauty takes precedence over drama. At the news that they have been betrayed by the Calender, Osmin proposes that they should all save their skins by donning disguises. Ali puts on the smock of an eccentric French painter. A painting is conveniently to hand; and as the Sultan's guards enter, Ali talks the company though each detail of the picture, abetted by comic orchestral effects, from drunken fiddlers to exploding bombs. Ali's impersonation fools no one. But as death sentences are being read out, a note from the Sultan arrives pardoning the fugitives but punishing the treacherous Calender. After a Turkish-style march, the Sultan – who, like Mozart's Pasha Selim, turns out to be a model of Enlightenment clemency – appears in person to give his blessing. The Calender's sentence is commuted from death to banishment. And the opera ends with the regulation ensemble of rejoicing, again enlivened by Turkish percussion.

First staged in Britain at the 1966 St Pancras Festival, *L'incontro improvviso* has many incidental pleasures and, in the trio and love duet, two numbers of transcendent beauty. But Friberth was no Da Ponte, and Haydn was not the man to goad him into creating a tighter, more integrated drama. The pacing is slow, even by the standards of Haydn's other comic operas, characterisation is inconsistent, and key dramatic moments go for little. The potentially climactic lovers' reunion in Act Two takes place in dry recitative. Then Rezia sings two arias on the trot, so contrasted in style that they seem to belong to two different characters. The antics of the

Calender and Osmin are virtually superfluous to the plot, while Ali's slapstick painter turn seems arbitrarily dragged in as a vehicle for Friberth's comic talents. Even the lively stagings at Garsington (1994) and Eisenstadt (2000) could not conceal that in *L'incontro improvviso*, more than in any of his other full-length operas, Haydn seems more concerned to showcase his singers than to create compelling, credible characters.

Die Feuersbrunst

After *Philemon und Baucis* Haydn composed three more German operas for the Eszterháza marionette theatre that have been lost: *Hexenschabbas* (Witches' Sabbath, 1773), *Dido* (?1775) and *Die bestrafte Rachbegierde* (Lust for vengeance punished, 1779). In the Catalogue of his Works, however, Haydn listed another lost 'opéra comique' for the marionette theatre, *Vom abgebrannten Haus* (The burned-down house). Robbins Landon maintains that this work is the same as the two-act Singspiel *Die Feuersbrunst* (The conflagration) discovered in an anonymous copy in Paris in 1935. With the missing spoken dialogue reconstructed by his future wife Else Radant, he prepared a performing edition for the modern premiere – given on stage rather than as a marionette opera – at the 1963 Bregenz Festival. Landon has argued plausibly for a dating of 1776–7, the only years in which clarinets (required in two arias) were available at Eszterháza – though assuming the opera is by Haydn, the clarinet parts could have been added later by another hand. Other scholars have doubted the opera's authenticity, especially since it emerged that the overture is identical to three movements of a symphony by Haydn's pupil Ignaz Pleyel.

Authentic Haydn or not, *Die Feuersbrunst* was aptly described by Landon as 'a piece for the coachmen and servant-girls at Eszterháza': a 'low', knockabout comedy centring on the shenanigans of Hanswurst, that archetypal Viennese pantomime figure who would find his most famous incarnation as Mozart's Papageno. Most of the arias are short strophic songs in jauntily demotic style, sometimes crudely comic, with liberal use of Austrian dialect, though one or two numbers cut deeper, including a lyrical E major aria for Columbine and a love duet for Columbine and Hanswurst. Impressive, too, is the C minor 'Fire' chorus as Columbine's house burns down at the end of Act One – the scene that gives the opera its name.

Il mondo della luna

Il mondo della luna (The world of the moon), the last of Haydn's three Goldoni operas, was performed at the wedding celebrations of Count Nicolaus, Prince Nicolaus's second son, on 3 August 1777, though its premiere may have been a few weeks earlier. Goldoni's satire on human gullibility, rooted as ever in the *commedia dell'arte*, had been set by Galuppi in 1750, and subsequently by several other composers. For a setting by Gennaro Astarita (Venice, 1775), Goldoni's two acts were augmented to three, and the finale to Act Two expanded; and it was this version of the libretto that Haydn appropriated for his new *dramma giocoso*. There had been radical changes at Eszterháza in 1776–7. Carl and Magdalena Friberth left for Vienna, Barbara Dichtler dropped dead on stage, baritone Christian Specht took up the viola, and new singers joined the opera troupe, including two established Italian stars: tenor Guglielmo Jermoli and high baritone Benedetto Bianchi. Haydn tailored the opera's two leading male roles, the bogus astronomer Ecclitico and the credulous Buonafede ('good faith'), to their comic talents. The opera's many short, dream-like dance numbers evoking the moon's delights were probably created for the Schmalügger ballet troupe which Prince Nicolaus had engaged for the summer of 1777.

After the surprisingly serious C major overture, later recycled in Symphony No. 63, the first scene is set on Ecclitico's terrace, decked out with an observatory tower and a sizeable telescope. The fake astronomer and four 'students' hymn the moon in a beautiful, shadowy ensemble in E flat, the key associated with the lunar world throughout the opera. Ecclitico has netted a new victim in the person of rich old Buonafede, father of Flaminia and Clarice. In a linked sequence of short arias, recitative and ballet numbers, Buonafede looks through the telescope and likes what he sees: a young girl caressing an old man, a man beating his wife, and a woman betrayed by her lover – 'if only life were like that here,' he sighs. During this sequence the tonality moves up from D major to the 'lunar' key of E flat. Ecclitico now tells the young nobleman Ernesto (played by the newly engaged castrato Pietro Gherardi) and his servant Cecco (Leopold Dichtler) that he has hatched a plan to cheat Buonafede of his two daughters and his maid, Lisetta. Before the day is out he, Ecclitico, will be betrothed to Clarice, Ernesto to Flaminia (the two *seria* roles) and Cecco to Lisetta. Ernesto sings of his love in a suave minuet aria, while Cecco, one of *opera buffa*'s plebeian philosophers, expresses his ironic amusement at the world's hypocrisy.

The scene shifts to Buonafede's house, where the sisters introduce themselves in contrasting arias. Flaminia (Marianna Puttler) sings of the power of love to conquer reason in a noble C major *aria di bravura*, in sonata form with a beautiful contrapuntal 'development' in C minor. The self-willed Clarice (Catarina Poschwa) defies her bullying father in a spirited aria that juxtaposes short-breathed *buffo* phrases with coloratura flourishes. Lisetta (a role written for soprano Maria Jermoli, and later recast for a mezzo) then perkily resists Buonafede's advances. In an accompanied recitative that drifts from a terrestrial C major to a lunar E flat, Buonafede drinks an elixir that, Ecclitico assures him, will spirit him to the moon. His 'flight' is evoked in the gossamer opening of the Act One finale – one of those ambivalent moments, familiar in Mozart's comedies, where absurdity is transmuted into lambent beauty. Clarice and Lisetta fear the old man is dying. But with a change from Adagio to Presto, tears turn to laughter when Ecclitico reads out Buonafede's 'will'.

Awakening in Ecclitico's garden at the start of Act Two, Buonafede imagines he has indeed landed on the moon. Cecco enters dressed as the emperor of the moon, and sings a catalogue-style aria mingling mock-imperious phrases with reams of patter enumerating the world's follies. The arias that follow, and the duet for Buonafede and Lisetta, barely advance the action, though each number is attractive in itself: a severe, quasi-Baroque G minor aria for Ernesto with an assuaging major-key 'second subject' (Haydn would rework this as the Benedictus of the 'Mariazellermesse'); Buonafede's picturesquely scored 'Che mondo amabile', where the old man whistles in imitation of birdsong; and love songs for Flaminia and Clarice. Flaminia's exquisite 'Se la mia stella', with its piquant solos for bassoon and horns, is one of the opera's plums.

The finale is Haydn's most extended to date, moving in a crescendo of comic tension to an effective climax. After the lunar marriage ceremony, Buonafede realises, too late, that he has been duped. The tempo increases to Presto, and in music of real power that swerves between major and minor, the old man fulminates as the others try in vain to placate him.

Typically, the third act is short and all but redundant dramatically. Buonafede forgives everyone, eats humble pie and gives his daughters their ample dowries. Before the vaudeville finale, Clarice and Ecclitico – not, as we might expect, the serious pair of Flaminia and Ernesto – sing the opera's sole love duet. It opens with a nocturnal Largo whose explicit sexual imagery inspired Haydn to perhaps the most sheerly voluptuous music in all his operas.

An Esterházy family friend, Count Carl Zinzendorf, described *Il mondo della luna* in his Diary as 'une farce pour la populace et pour les enfants'. Perhaps he was echoing the prince's views: unusually, the opera was never revived at Eszterháza. While there are longueurs in Act Two, the delight-ful silliness of the plot and the music's spirit and inventiveness have made *Il mondo della luna*, with *L'infedeltà delusa*, the least neglected Haydn opera in modern times. After circulating in a bowdlerised German version made by Mark Lothar in 1932, the opera as Haydn wrote it was first heard in 1959 at the Holland Festival (conducted by Giulini) and at Aix-en-Provence. More recent performances have included Garsington (1991 and 2000) and Eisenstadt (1997), both emphasising knockabout farce, and a harder-edged 2001 Berlin production set in the 1930s, with Ecclitico played as a *Godfather*-style mafioso and pimp.

La vera costanza

Mixing recognisable *buffo* characters with the spirit of the fashionable *comédie larmoyante*, *La vera costanza* (True constancy) was a new departure for Haydn. The most popular opera in this vein was Piccinni's *La buona figliuola*, on a Goldoni libretto derived from the archetypal eighteenth-century 'sentimental' novel, Samuel Richardson's *Pamela, Or Virtue Rewarded*, whose mingled prurience and primness is hard to stomach today. Richardson's improbably long-suffering heroine – satirised by Jane Austen in the figure of Lucy Steele in *Sense and Sensibility* – also left her mark on the disguised gardener-girl of Mozart's *La finta giardiniera*, and on Rosina in *La vera costanza*. But whereas Piccinni's and Mozart's heroines turn out to be aristocrats after all, Rosina remains 'a virtuous fisherwoman', as billed on the title page, thus inviting audiences to reflect on the claims of nobility of birth versus nobility of spirit.

Using a slightly shortened version of a libretto that Francesco Puttini had written for Anfossi in 1776, *La vera costanza* was premiered at Eszterháza on 25 April 1779. (There is no supporting evidence for Dies's claim that it was commissioned by Joseph II for performance in Vienna.) Though the performing parts were destroyed in the fire later that year, Haydn recreated the opera, partly from sketches, for a 1785 revival. Modern performances have included those in Lyons and Katonah, New York (both 1980), Garsington (1992), Eisenstadt (2002) – a wacky modern-dress affair, entertaining to some, muddled to others – and a staging by Bampton Classical Opera using a raunchy English translation (2004).

Five years before the action begins, Rosina (soprano Barbara Ripamonti) was secretly married to Count Errico (tenor Andrea Totti), billed, with some understatement, as 'an eccentric and fickle young man'. He soon abandoned her; she, unbeknown to him, bore their child. After a storm at sea, rather tepidly evoked in the opening ensemble, Rosina and her fisherman brother Masino (Leopold Dichtler) help ashore two aristocrats, Errico's aunt Baroness Irene (Catarina Poschwa) and Marquis Ernesto (tenor Vito Ungricht), plus Irene's maid Lisetta (soprano Anna Zannini) and a Woosterish buffoon, Villotto (Benedetto Bianchi). The Baroness, a preposterous control-freak, has heard rumours of a liaison between Rosina and her nephew. Determined to spike such a socially unthinkable alliance, she orders an immediate marriage between Rosina and the non-aristocratic Villotto. Rosina is dismayed, while Villotto, impervious to Masino's mockery, can hardly believe his luck. The unbalanced Count Errico first threatens Villotto with a pistol, then encourages him in his conquest of Rosina before going out of his mind with jealousy. Rosina tells Lisetta how the Count wooed and betrayed her. Her devotion and suffering, and Errico's instability, are further explored in the long first-act finale, which moves from comic exchanges between Villotto and Masino, through Rosina's vain pleas to the Baroness, to Errico's sudden change of heart. He and Rosina sing a love duet before the Baroness re-enters with a picture of the (aristocratic) girl she has lined up for him. He admires the portrait, Rosina is again plunged into despair, and the act ends in regulation *buffo* chaos.

After another sideshow for Villotto and Masino, Ernesto – a typical ineffectual tenor – tells Rosina that only if she marries Villotto will the Baroness agree to marry him. The Baroness, Errico, Lisetta and Villotto overhear his final words ('You are my only hope'), imagine he is wooing Rosina, and denounce her in a vaudeville-style quintet. Rosina then gives vent to her anguish, while Errico orders the lily-livered Villotto to kill her and Masino. When Lisetta tells him of

Rosina's constancy, Errico becomes delirious, imagining he is Orpheus seeking Euridice. For this *scena* Haydn lifted music from Anfossi's opera, probably at the request of Andrea Totti who had sung in the 1776 premiere.

In extremis, Rosina takes refuge with her infant son in a ruined tower. The finale – another long 'chain' ensemble – begins with more comic byplay for Villotto and Masino. The Baroness appears, with Ernesto in tow, and everyone rushes off to look for Rosina, clearing the stage for the now penitent Errico. When he sees a small boy weeping he is strangely touched; and as Rosina enters, trembling, his aria blossoms into a love duet. In the final mayhem the others express, variously, outrage and bewilderment, while Errico, hardly a paragon of self-control even in his 'reformed' guise, hurls out threats to his adversaries.

Act Three is predictably brief and anticlimactic. Rosina and Errico quickly see through the forged letters sent to them by the Baroness in a last-ditch attempt to separate them, and sing another, superfluous, love duet – though from what we have seen of Errico, their long-term prospects would seem no better than those of the Almavivas in *Figaro*. The Baroness and Ernesto then enter. Rosina kneels and begs her forgiveness (!), the Baroness graciously admits her deception, blesses their union and pledges herself to Ernesto, and all join in a gavotte-like ensemble in praise of constancy.

La vera costanza is Haydn's most sophisticated opera to date, both in its portrayal of Rosina and its 'chain' finales, which in keeping with contemporary trends are far longer than any in his earlier operas. Both finales are constructed around a central tonality (G major in Act One, D major in Act Two), with the main key returning periodically. Puttini's lax libretto militates against the inexorable build of tension we find in the great Mozart–Da Ponte finales. But if successive sections tend to seem like discrete episodes, individual moments can be strikingly effective. In the penultimate section, where the Baroness shows Errico the picture, Rosina's pain is graphically dramatised with a shift from G major to G minor and a soaring phrase that contrasts eloquently with the short-breathed exchanges of the other characters (until this point the melodic line, as so often in comic opera finales, has been carried by the orchestra). *Buffo* frivolity yields to music of acute poignancy; and the G major final section comes as a necessary resolution of the accrued harmonic tension.

The Act One finale confines itself to the key of G and its nearest relations, C and D. That to Act Two moves further afield. After the fast section of the love duet – one of those naggingly memorable Haydn tunes – the rest of the cast voice their consternation, sotto voce, with a plunge from D to B flat: a harmonic coup that perfectly embodies the dramatic situation, all the more potent for the finale's avoidance of flat keys until this point.

The *buffo* figures – Lisetta, Villotto and Masino – are all neatly depicted in arias that tend to be briefer than in Haydn's previous operas. Lisetta's half-coquettish, half-pathetic Act One siciliano, 'Io son, poverina', is a charming piece of characterisation. The ghastly Baroness asserts her social status in the work's sole coloratura aria, while Errico's aria in Act One is one of the most powerful Haydn ever wrote. Its form is dictated entirely by the Count's precarious mental state. Beginning as a swaggering C major *aria di guerra*, with heraldic high horns, as Errico instructs Villotto in the art of amorous conquest, it suddenly breaks off for a rapt Adagio as he becomes transfixed by Rosina's beauty (symbolised by oboe arabesques). Finally he goes right out of his mind in a frantic C minor Allegro, made all the more violent by lashing syncopations and ominous chromaticisms in the bass.

In Puttini's libretto Rosina is merely an Enlightenment plaster saint, whose devotion in the face of ritual humiliation strains credibility. But Haydn's music endows her with a touching emotional truth: in the minor-key outbursts that disrupt her nostalgic evocation of happiness in her opening aria; in her despairing, breathless F minor aria in Act Two, 'freezing' into stark unisons at 'gelar mi sento' as she thinks of her son; or in her scena later in the same act, where accompanied recitatives (usually reserved for high-born characters) frame a valedictory E major aria of moving simplicity and sincerity. Throughout the opera the unaffected candour of Rosina's music, devoid of both *seria* display and *buffo* patter, underlines her nobility of spirit, and sets her apart from the repulsive, ridiculous or raving figures around her.

L'isola disabitata

A curious one-off in this sequence of comic operas is the relatively brief *azione teatrale*, *L'isola disabitata* (The deserted island), on a Metastasio libretto originally set by Giuseppe Bonno in 1754. The premiere was scheduled for Prince Nicolaus's name-day, 6 December 1779; in the event, the opera-house fire of 18 November meant that the performance had to be moved to the marionette theatre. Haydn's choice of an (almost) entirely serious text may have been prompted by the success of Gluck's celebrated *azione teatrale*, *Orfeo ed Euridice*, at Eszterháza in 1776.

Metastasio's elegant but static libretto combines two favourite eighteenth-century themes: a 'rescue' plot, and an idealised desert island setting (think *Robinson Crusoe*) that allows for philosophical reflection on the comparative merits of nature and civilised society. Thirteen years before the opera begins, Gernando (Andrea Totti), his bride Costanza (Barbara Ripamonti) and her infant sister Silvia (Luigia Polzelli) were marooned on an uninhabited island en route for the Indies. While Costanza and Silvia were asleep, pirates abducted Gernando and his companions, leaving Costanza to believe that she was deliberately abandoned.

In the opening scene Costanza, 'curiously dressed in animal skins, leaves and flowers, with part of a worn-out sword in her hand', is engraving her own epitaph. The adolescent Silvia, a child of nature à la Rousseau, is overjoyed at finding her lost fawn, and cannot understand her sister's grief: life for her is one long idyll. Two men land on the island. With Silvia in hiding, they reveal themselves as Gernando and his friend

Enrico (Benedetto Bianchi). Gernando despairs of finding Costanza, but vows to share her grave. Enrico delivers a typical Metastasian homily on the obligations of friend-ship. Silvia, brought up by Costanza to despise the (to her) unknown male sex, is strangely stirred by the sight of Enrico, in a scene that echoes Miranda's first sighting of Ferdinand in *The Tempest*.

At the start of Act Two Gernando sees Costanza's inscrip-tion and fears she is dead. In the opera's turning point, Silvia and Enrico meet. When he tells her he is indeed a man, she is horrified, and tries to escape. But he reassures her, while she tells him that Costanza is still alive. After they separate to search for Costanza and Gernando, Silvia sings of the 'fierce frenzy' welling up in her heart. In the final scene husband and wife are reunited, not without initial confusion and misunder-standing. Silvia at first rejects Enrico's proposal of marriage. But Costanza tells her that Gernando did not desert her, and that men, or at least some of them, can be trusted after all. Silvia falls into Enrico's arms; and in the vaudeville finale, all celebrate their new-found happiness.

Probably influenced by Gluck's *Orfeo*, Haydn links the arias with orchestrally accompanied rather than dry recitative, sometimes delicately expressive (as in the shuddering tremolandos that evoke first Costanza's and then Gernando's state of mind as they read the carved inscription), sometimes too non-committal in effect. To mitigate the long stretches of recitative, Haydn made most of the opera's seven arias relatively brief. Costanza, a latter-day Ariadne, sings two somewhat Gluckian slow arias, dignified rather than, as their texts suggest, tragic in tone. Enrico has a fine, robust number in heroic style, while Silvia's naivety is characterised in the prancing motifs of her recitatives (Haydn nicely brings out the hint of comedy in her encounter with Enrico) and in her two arias, the first coloured by solo flute and bassoon.

Gernando's music, like Costanza's, is slow and soulful, though anguish cuts through his emotional reserve at the centre of his first aria, 'Non turbar'. His second aria, 'Giacché il pietoso amico', directly echoes the aria Costanza has just sung, before breaking off in confused recitative as he turns and sees her – a touching instance of thematic reminiscence. But the most immediately striking numbers are the contrapuntally strenuous G minor overture, interrupted by a minuet-like episode that evokes Silvia's bucolic idyll, and the splendid, if over-expansive, final quartet. The recitative immediately before the finale had already introduced a solo violin, cello and bassoon to symbolise, respectively, Costanza, Gernando and Enrico. Haydn now adds a flute, used earlier to portray Silvia's innocence, and writes an elaborate *sinfonia concertante* for voices and instruments.

For all its refined, sculpted beauty, *L'isola disabitata* is hamstrung by a libretto that was old-fashioned even in 1779. It was evidently not a favourite of Prince Nicolaus, and dropped out of the Eszterháza repertoire following just one repeat performance. After spasmodic airings in Germany during the composer's lifetime, *L'isola disabitata* lay forgotten until 1909, when, as *Die wüste Insel*, it became an improbable choice for the Vienna Hofoper's Haydn centenary tribute. The result was to reinforce the old cliché that Haydn's operas were hopelessly undramatic. More recent productions in Eisenstadt (1998) and by English Pocket Opera in London in 2003 (the professional UK premiere) beguiled the Haydn faithful without suggesting that the opera could ever gain wider currency. That said, *L'isola disabitata* was a surprising success at the Opéra de Rennes in 2006, prompting one enthusiastic reviewer to dub it 'the most original and moving of all Haydn's operas'.

La fedeltà premiata

For the planned opening of the rebuilt Eszterháza opera house in October 1780 it was back to *dramma giocoso*, and another recycled libretto: Giambattista Lorenzi's pastoral comedy *L'infedeltà fedele* (Faithful infidelity), set the previous year by Cimarosa. Reconstruction fell behind schedule, and the premiere was postponed until 25 February 1781. By then the opera had been renamed *La fedeltà premiata* (Fidelity rewarded) to avoid confusion with Cimarosa's opera and Haydn's own *L'infedeltà delusa*. It became an immediate favourite of Prince Nicolaus, doubtless partly because its references to the chase (including a staged hunt) reflected one of his prime passions. For a revival in 1782 Haydn made various cuts and transposed the parts of Celia (from mezzo to soprano) and Perruchetto (from high bass to tenor) to accommodate new singers. *La fedeltà premiata* was also successful beyond the confines of Eszterháza, with acclaimed German-language performances in Vienna in 1784, possibly attended by Mozart. The first modern revival was at the 1970 Holland Festival, in a staging by Jean-Pierre Ponnelle. Subsequent performances have included John Cox's demurely Arcadian play-within-a-play concept at Glyndebourne in 1979, and David Pountney's 1995 Garsington production, which turned the whole thing into a no-holds-barred romp.

While Lorenzi's libretto sends up pastoral convention – in the hunt scene, for instance, it is the animals who do most of the hunting – and several of the characters are pure *buffo* figures, *La fedeltà premiata* contains some of Haydn's most deeply felt operatic music: not only for the two serious, low-born characters, Celia (Maria Jermoli in 1781) and Fileno (played by her husband, tenor Guglielmo Jermoli), but also for the self-seeking, upwardly mobile Amaranta, (soprano Teresa Taveggia). The opera's tangled action, set in ancient Cumae, parodies classical myths of sacrifice and atonement. Each year the priests of Diana, represented by the devious figure of Melibeo (bass Antonio Pesci), must sacrifice two faithful lovers to the sea monster until 'a heroic soul' offers his own life. Only then will the curse be lifted and peace return to the land. After the hunting-style overture, more familiar as the finale of Symphony No. 73, Melibeo assures Amaranta that priests are exempt from the rules and that she may love him with impunity. The nymph Nerina (soprano Costanza Valdestrula) loves Amaranta's brother Lindoro (Leopold

Dichtler), who inconveniently loves the shepherdess Celia. Amaranta, irritated by Nerina, asks Melibeo to engineer a match between Lindoro and Celia. When the ridiculous Count Perrucchetto (the name means 'little wig'; Benedetto Bianchi) stumbles in, apparently pursued by robbers, and starts to woo Amaranta, she checks out his social status and immediately transfers her malleable affections. Melibeo's veiled threats go right over their heads.

The scene changes to 'a garden', where Fileno laments his lost love, first in a cavatina, then in dialogue with Nerina, who tells him her own unhappy tale. In a nearby grove Fillide, searching for Fileno under the assumed name of Celia, reveals how she was abandoned by her despairing lover when she was bitten by a poisonous snake. After falling asleep, she awakens to find Fileno at her side. But joy is quickly tempered when she glimpses Melibeo – as ever, on the lookout for faithful lovers – and Lindoro, senses danger, and denies knowing Fileno. Things are further complicated when Perrucchetto flirts with Nerina, to Amaranta's indignation. Melibeo guesses the truth, and gives Celia/Fillide the choice of marrying Lindoro, thereby enhancing his own chances with Amaranta, or being sacrificed to the monster. The Act One finale – the longest Haydn ever wrote – is a typical chain of misunderstanding, reproach and confusion. It ends with Fileno in fetters and Celia resisting demands that she marry Lindoro before being abducted by peeved satyrs, evidently a constant peril in pastoral Cumae.

At the start of Act Two Nerina has released Fileno, who in turn has rescued Celia, only to lose her again. Melibeo, in the unlikely role of relationship counsellor, advises Nerina how to win Fileno's love; Fileno then woos her to make Celia jealous. During the hunt in honour of Diana, Perrucchetto, Papageno-like, boasts of killing a wild boar, only to recoil in terror as the beast stirs. The scene then shifts to 'a terrifying grotto'. Carving a message in the bark of a tree, Fileno prepares to end his life; when he departs, Celia sees the inscription and bewails his death. Melibeo, seizing the opportunity to fulfil his malign plan, sends Perrucchetto into the cave with Celia and denounces them as the faithful lovers. Amaranta's first reaction is outrage at her thwarted ambition. In the finale Nerina, Amaranta and Lindoro realise the horror of the situation. Amaranta, prompted by self-interest, and Lindoro belatedly resolve to rescue the doomed pair, who are then led forth as sacrificial victims, in music that parodies the Furies in Gluck's *Orfeo*.

Act Three, brief as usual, opens with a duet in which Celia tries in vain to persuade Fileno of her innocence. When all seems lost, Fileno then throws himself forward as the voluntary sacrifice. A spectacular scenic transformation, characteristic of each of Haydn's last three Eszterháza operas, reveals Diana and her court. Appeased by Fileno's heroism, the goddess lifts the curse, strikes down the corrupt Melibeo and unites Fileno and his Fillide, and Amaranta and Perruchetto.

Lorenzi's convoluted plot, mingling Arcadian artifice, parody and amorous intrigue, is hardly a model of deft dramaturgy. Unlike Haydn's audiences, thoroughly au fait with pastoral conventions, we nowadays find cavorting nymphs and shepherds and arbitrarily marauding satyrs less than riveting. Yet Haydn's music, even more than in *La vera costanza*, is consistently engrossing, while until the perfunctory denouement the dramatic pacing is the most fluent in all Haydn's comic operas. The predominantly elegiac music for Celia and Fileno includes Celia's aria in Act One, hauntingly coloured by a muted horn (the voice of her absent lover?), and two magnificent extended scenes in the second act. That for Celia, with its distant timpani rolls – another novel effect – became famous as an independent cantata, 'Ah come il core mi palpita'.

Inverting operatic norms, the priesthood and aristocracy are portrayed as grotesque and/or plain ludicrous. In Melibeo's first aria snarling brass comically depicts the bulls locking horns, while Perrucchetto's arias quickly deflate his would-be dignity with flustered patter. In the libretto the haughty, self-seeking Amaranta is an out-and-out comic figure. But her arias also suggest a surprising vulnerability and tenderness, so that by the time of her Act Two soliloquy she has become almost sympathetic – redeemed, like Mozart's Donna Elvira, through the beauty and sensitivity of her music.

The chain finales continue the trend of Haydn's previous operas, and of late eighteenth-century comic opera generally, towards ever greater length and sophistication. Taking his cue from Cimarosa's setting of the same libretto, Haydn constructs the vast, 822-bar Act One finale in a sequence of descending thirds, with each new event or change of mood marked by a harmonic 'shock'. The key scheme is B flat–G major (beginning as a poignant solo for Celia, her heartbeats suggested by orchestral tremolos)–G minor (as Celia rebuffs Lindoro with a slap on the face)–E flat (enter an outraged Amaranta)–C major (Amaranta drags Celia in)–A flat, where the despairing Fileno appears in fetters. This Adagio forms the finale's reflective centrepiece. Unlike Cimarosa, Haydn then disrupts the pattern of descending thirds with a striking dip to G minor, as Celia rails against her continuing persecution. The last three sections of this splendidly constructed finale oscillate between B flat (as Nerina enters pursued by satyrs) and G minor (the fight between satyrs and shepherds) before the original B flat returns for a climactic ensemble of chaos and confusion. More than in any of Haydn's other ensembles, we have a powerful sense here of the music articulating the action and propelling it forward to the next phase in the drama.

Orlando paladino

Like *La fedeltà premiata*, *Orlando paladino* – dubbed a *dramma eroicomico* – mixes elements of *opera buffa* and *opera seria* within a series of exotic pastoral settings. Haydn composed *Orlando* rapidly during the spring and summer of 1782 for the anticipated visit to Eszterháza of the Russian Grand Duke and future Tsar Pavel Petrovich. In the event the Duke cried off, and the opera was premiered on 6 December 1782 in celebration of Prince Nicolaus's name-day. It quickly came to rival *La fedeltà premiata* as Haydn's most popular stage work, with performances throughout the German-speaking lands. Like his other operas, it then fell into oblivion for nearly two centuries. *Orlando* was revived, with some success, in Vienna during the 1982 Haydn anniversary, and has since been staged in Eisenstadt (1995) and at the Theater an der Wien in Vienna in 2007. By 2008 it had still received only one fully professional British production, at Garsington in 1990.

The text, reworked by the new Eszterháza house poet/adapter Nunziato Porta from Carlo Badini's libretto for Guglielmi's *Le pazzie d'Orlando* (1771), deals with the same episodes in Ariosto's *Orlando furioso* treated by Lully, Vivaldi, Handel et al. Here, though, the dominant tone is one of parody, sometimes veering into farce, as *opera seria*-style hero-ism is repeatedly punctured. Except for the Stygian ferryman Caronte (Charon), who makes a cameo appearance in an aptly sepulchral aria, all the male characters are in varying degrees ridiculous. In essence, *Orlando* is a send-up of eighteenth-century operatic types and conventions.

Angelica, Queen of Cathay – a wholly serious character, originally sung by Porta's wife, Matilde Bologna – is in love with the Saracen warrior Medoro (tenor Prospero Braghetti), whose wimpish dithering makes Mozart's Don Ottavio look like Indiana Jones. The lovers are in flight from the paladin Orlando (tenor Antonio Specioli), who is raging with frus-trated passion for Angelica and prone to bouts of madness. Meanwhile the braying, bicep-flexing Rodomonte, King of Barbary (baritone Domenico Negri), is scouring the land for his mortal enemy Orlando. He announces himself in a bombastic aria, his empty braggadocio immediately suggested by comically spluttering strings.

In a graceful pastoral cavatina, with solo flute adding a silvery gloss to the muted strings, Angelica laments that she is condemned to spend her life in hiding from a madman. Protection arrives courtesy of the sorceress Alcina (mezzo Costanza Valdesturla), here a good(ish) fairy rather than the man-eating siren of Handel's opera. She parades her powers in a C major aria that begins in sweeping *seria* style and ends in *buffo* patter: even the sorceress's dignity is not sacrosanct. Rodomonte then blusters in and encounters Pasquale, Orlando's squire, an upmarket Leporello with a ready line in self-promotion (baritone Vincenzo Moratti). Pasquale wriggles out of a potential duel when the shepherdess Eurilla (Maria Antoni Specioli) brings news that Orlando, a far more prestigious enemy, is looking for Rodomonte. The squire begins his wooing of Eurilla with a quickfire catalogue song recounting his valorous exploits throughout the world. When Medoro announces his desire to leave Angelica for her own safety's sake, she begs him to stay in an increasingly intense two-part aria, 'Non partir, mia bella face', that ends with a formidable display of coloratura: a reminder that, vulnerable as she is, Angelica is also a queen.

Orlando makes his long-delayed entry in an accompanied recitative. The initial impression is of a curiously brooding, bedraggled figure rather than a frenzied tyrant. But he begins to live up to his reputation when he sees Medoro's and Angelica's names carved into a tree, and swears murderous vengeance on his rival in love. In the mayhem of the Act One finale (more loosely structured than the 'chain' finales of *La vera costanza* and *La fedeltà premiata*), Orlando's derangement is graphically conveyed in melodramatic accompanied recitative. Disaster is only averted when Alcina imprisons him in an iron cage; and the finale ends in general bewilderment, with a parodic reference to Metastasio's favourite 'shipwreck' metaphor.

Inexplicably freed from his cage, though not from his derangement, at the opening of Act Two, Orlando is challenged to a duel by the sabre-rattling Rodomonte. But when Eurilla, always in the know, brings news that Angelica has fled with Medoro, Orlando rushes off baying vengeance, leaving Rodomonte to vent his frustration in another mock-heroic aria. Eurilla discovers Medoro, separated from Angelica and certain he will die a cruel death – cue for an eloquent multi-sectioned aria with muted strings. Significantly, Medoro's last words revert to the original forlorn Adagio; yet, as with all his music, the effect is one of pathos rather than absurdity. Pasquale and Eurilla then express their feelings in a charming *buffo* duet ('Quel tuo visetto amabile'), with the squire initially reduced to comically inarticulate sighs. This became the opera's hit number, and was chosen by Haydn for his London benefit concert in May 1795.

After expressing her despair in a magnificent, harmonically rich aria, Angelica is saved from suicide by Alcina, who transports her to Medoro's arms for a love duet. Predictably, Orlando shatters their idyll. As they flee, Alcina conjures a vision of the furies and warns the paladin not to follow the lovers. After Pasquale, dressed in Parisian finery, has boasted to Eurilla of his musical *savoir faire* in another 'catalogue' aria, complete with castrato imitations, Medoro and Angelica take refuge in Alcina's grotto. The Act Two finale begins with Orlando, nervously accompanied by Pasquale, in search of Angelica. When he threatens Alcina, in another disruptive passage of accompanied recitative, she turns him to stone. Pasquale is reduced to a gibbering wreck as he tries to explain what has happened. Despite Pasquale's protests, Alcina restores Orlando to life, and then immediately entombs him in her grotto. The finale ends with rather premature general rejoicing.

After her various ineffectual cures on Orlando, Alcina at last gets it right in the brief third act, courtesy of the ferryman Caronte and the waters of Lethe. The distant Elysian Fields here may be an ironic allusion to Gluck's *Orfeo*. Orlando awakens, healed of his crazed love for Angelica, and finally fights his duel with Rodomonte. Meanwhile the hapless Medoro has been wounded rescuing Angelica from wild animals. Believing her lover dead, and by now half delirious, she longs for peace in death in another moving scena consisting of accompanied recitative and a two-part (Largo–Allegro) aria. Alcina pops up again with the news that Medoro is still alive. As in most comic operas before *Figaro*, the loose threads are hastily tied in dry recitative; and the opera ends with a vaudeville ensemble in which all the principals, including a bemused Orlando and an improbably civilised Rodomonte, celebrate the double wedding of Angelica and Medoro and the *buffo* pairing of Eurilla and Pasquale.

The dramatic pacing of *Orlando* is more meandering than that of *La fedeltà premiata*, not least in the chain finales of the first and second acts, where any tension is dissipated by beautiful but over-long Adagio sections. Elsewhere the dramaturgy can be awkward: the character of Eurilla's father, Licone, for instance, drops out after the opening scene; and throughout there are too many random entrances and exits. Haydn's characterisation of the anti-hero wavers uncomfortably, from his powerful opening accompanied recitative and final 'sleep' aria, to the tritely comic 'Cosa vedo!' in Act Two, where from the music alone it would be impossible to guess that Orlando was being tormented by a vision of the Furies. If Haydn is making fun of Orlando here, the joke misfires.

Yet if the shifts of tone between pathos and parody are not always convincingly managed, *Orlando* contains some of Haydn's finest arias and accompanied recitatives: in the heartfelt numbers for Angelica and Medoro (Haydn almost has you sympathising with the mooning, cowardly Saracen), the poetic scene in Act Three where a dazed Orlando awakes from his magic sleep, and the genuinely funny patter songs for the fast-talking Pasquale, last and most irrepressible of the comic servants that thread through Haydn's operas.

Armida

With *Armida*, premiered on 26 February 1784, Haydn abandoned the comedic, parodic spirit of *dramma giocoso* and *dramma eroicomico* and composed his only full-length *opera seria* for Eszterháza. The stimulus seems to have been the production of Giuseppe Sarti's hugely popular *Giulio Sabino* the previous May. Prince Nicolaus, who had hitherto preferred comedies, suddenly developed a taste for serious opera. Haydn, savouring a new challenge, was quick to respond, beginning work in the summer of 1783; and the upshot was his most successful opera at Eszterháza, with fifty-four performances in five years. Outside Eszterháza, though, it had far fewer performances than *La vera costanza*, *La fedeltà premiata* or *Orlando paladino*. Spasmodic modern revivals have included a Peter Sellars production, set in Vietnam (where else?), at the 1981 Mondanock Festival, New Hampshire, and an abstract staging by Christoph Loy in the uncongenial setting of Salzburg's cavernous Felsenreitschule in 2007.

The story of the Saracen sorceress Armida and the Christian warrior Rinaldo, an archetypal love-versus-duty conundrum derived from Tasso's Crusade epic *Gerusalemme liberata*, probably spawned more operas than any other. In the late seventeenth and eighteenth centuries alone there were over a hundred settings, most famously by Lully, Vivaldi, Handel (*Rinaldo*) and Gluck. For Haydn's opera, magpie librettist Nunziato Porta pilfered various sources, including a text set by Antonio Tozzi in 1775. At the court of King Idreno of Damascus (a high bass role written for Paolo Mandini, brother of Stefano who created the role of Almaviva in Mozart's *Figaro*), his niece Armida (Matilde Bologna) has used her magical arts to ensnare Rinaldo, hero of the Frankish army (tenor Prospero Braghetti). Rinaldo is so besotted he even offers to lead Idreno's army against the Christians. His friend Ubaldo (tenor Antonio Specioli), emblem of simple loyalty, vows to liberate him from Armida's clutches. Another Frankish knight, Clotarco (Leopold Dichtler), is beguiled by the alluring Zelmira (Costanza Valdesturla), daughter of the Sultan of Egypt. In the castle Ubaldo is horrified to find Rinaldo 'basely prating of love', and urges him to take up arms. Rinaldo, as ever, vacillates; and the first act ends with an uneasy love duet for him and Armida.

At the start of Act Two Zelmira, in love with Clotarco, defies Idreno's demand that she lures him and Ubaldo into a fatal ambush. Clotarco entreats Idreno to end the bloodshed, the king simulates friendship, and Ubaldo again tries to win

Rinaldo back to the Christian cause. He, predictably, wavers, then finally departs with Ubaldo, provoking Armida to paroxysms of grief and fury. In the trio that ends the act, a bewildered Rinaldo is taunted by Armida and Ubaldo in turn.

Act Three – here no perfunctory add-on, as it usually is in Haydn's comic operas – is set in Armida's enchanted forest, inviting the kind of spectacular scenic effects deployed in *La fedeltà premiata* and *Orlando paladino*. Determined to cut down the myrtle tree that embodies Armida's power, Rinaldo is instead intoxicated by the forest's sounds and perfumes. Zelmira, disguised as a nymph, tries to lure him back to Armida; when she fails, the sorceress herself first implores him, then unleashes the Furies. Rinaldo prays for courage, braves the Furies and fells the myrtle. The forest vanishes. But Armida is still not finished. Ignoring the dithering Rinaldo's promise to return, she summons her infernal chariot and curses him in a splendidly fiery final sextet that pits the three infidels (Armida, Zelmira and Idreno) against the three tenors.

The static nature of the first two acts, in essence a single situation stretched over nearly two hours, is doubtless the prime reason why *Armida* is so rarely staged. Yet musically it is arguably the richest of all Haydn's operas, as recordings by Dorati (with Jessye Norman as the sorceress) and, especially, Harnoncourt (with Cecilia Bartoli) have confirmed. Even the numbers for Idreno, Clotarco and Ubaldo, virtual ciphers dramatically, rise well above *opera seria* routine, though neither of Idreno's bluff, martial arias suggests the character's underlying treachery. Ubaldo has a fine scena in the first act. Two accompanied recitatives enfold an aria that begins with 'military' dotted rhythms in dreamy slow motion – the bemused soldier has here become a stranger to himself – and continues with sinuous woodwind figures evoking the sorceress's dangerous lure. Zelmira's music is all caressing, cajoling grace, epitomised in her minuet-like opening aria, with its soft bassoon colouring and insinuating dip to the minor key.

Armida's chief glory, though, lies in Haydn's characterisation of the sorceress, by turns passionate, anguished and ferociously vindictive, and in the magnificent scene complexes in Acts Two and Three. Influenced by Gluck's 'reform' operas, Haydn here elides accompanied recitatives and arias to create fluid, continuous dramatic sequences, as Mozart had done three years earlier in *Idomeneo*. That in Act Two begins with a highly charged accompanied recitative for Rinaldo, with rich woodwind scoring (a feature of the whole opera), before moving into a beseeching, then increasingly tortured aria in ever-quickening tempos. As the aria peters out, Armida hurls out a contemptuous 'Barbaro!', sinks into despair and finally erupts in a violent E minor aria. In the middle, and again at the end, disorienting chromaticism and a blurring of the pulse suggest a woman going out of her mind with rage and grief – shades here of Electra's first aria in *Idomeneo*, a work Haydn could not have known in 1783.

The climactic scene in Armida's enchanted forest encompasses no fewer than eight continuous sections, symmetrically framed by accompanied recitatives for Rinaldo in E flat. In the rustling trees, murmuring stream and bird-calls of the opening, Haydn displays his love of tone-painting familiar from *The Creation*; then, as the forest is suffused with seductive scents, the music drifts from E flat, through F minor to a dazzlingly remote A major. After Zelmira's sweet pastoral aria and Armida's final plea – the most piercingly beautiful number in the opera – the Furies are evoked in another graphic piece of descriptive writing. Like Zelmira's aria, their music derives directly from the overture, where, with a nod to Gluck's *Alceste*, Haydn writes a miniature tone-poem encapsulating the essence of the drama.

L'anima del filosofo

Haydn's final opera, the ill-starred *L'anima del filosofo* (The spirit of the philosopher), was a casualty of the absurd rivalry between George III and the Prince of Wales. Commissioned by Sir John Gallini, manager of the newly rebuilt King's Theatre, Haymarket, the opera was due to be premiered in

May 1791. But the King's Theatre, under the patronage of the Prince of Wales, was in direct competition with the Pantheon, supported by King George. The king, predictably, refused to grant Gallini a licence; and at the first rehearsal royal emissaries marched in and terminated proceedings. So with the opera possibly still unfinished – though as Carlo Badini's libretto is lost it is impossible to say what, if anything, is missing – Haydn immediately downed tools.

Eleven numbers were published in 1807, under the opera's alternative title *Orfeo ed Euridice*. But *L'anima del filosofo* had to wait 160 years for its first staging, in Florence on 9 May 1951 as a vehicle for Maria Callas, with Boris Christoff, no less, in the role of Euridice's father Creonte, and Erich Kleiber conducting. A few months earlier a recording had appeared from the Haydn Society. Joan Sutherland and Nicolai Gedda starred in a 1967 staging in Edinburgh, Vienna and New York. Then the opera drifted back into obscurity until the Harnoncourt–Bartoli axis resuscitated it for the 1995 Vienna Festival and later in Zurich, in the pretentious, symbolist Jürgen Flimm production reused for Bartoli's Covent Garden debut in 2001. Like Callas and Sutherland, Bartoli doubled the roles of Euridice and the 'Genio' or Sibyl, positing that the Sibyl is Orpheus's alter ego, or rational, philosophical self.

Haydn informed Prince Anton Esterházy that the opera was to be in five acts and 'entirely different from Gluck'. Indeed, Badini seems to have sedulously avoided comparison with Gluck's masterpiece. His version of the myth, drawing closely on Ovid's *Metamorphoses* and Virgil, begins much earlier, with Euridice fleeing the advances of Prince Arideo, whom Creonte is forcing her to marry against her will. Lost in a dark forest, she is captured by wild shepherds who prepare to sacrifice her to their gods. Orpheus (a role intended for the famous tenor Giacomo Davide) arrives in the nick of time to charm the savages with his lyre – cue for Haydn's only harp solo and an eloquent two-part aria, 'Cara speme'. News of Euridice's rescue reaches Creonte. The lovers return, receive his blessing and sing an extended love duet.

At the start of Act Two Orpheus and Euridice find themselves in 'an idyllic landscape' surrounded by Cupids. Their blithe chorus, reworked from the finale of *Orlando paladino*, dips to the minor key for a chill warning of Orpheus's end. When Orpheus goes off to investigate a disturbance, Arideo and his henchmen rush in to abduct Euridice. In the ensuing commotion she is bitten by a poisonous snake. Orpheus discovers her lifeless body and erupts in an anguished recitative and aria. Creonte then sings a bellicose 'vengeance' aria, reinforced midway through by onstage trumpets.

Act Three opens with a chorus of mourning, continues with another moralising aria for Creonte and then introduces the figure of the Sibyl, who tells Orpheus in a huge C major coloratura aria (which Haydn apparently intended for an unnamed castrato soprano) that 'You will see her again if you can restrain you passion'. In the final act Orpheus and the Sibyl pass the Unhappy Shades and the Furies en route to Pluto, who is duly moved by his pleas. As in all versions of the myth, he cannot refrain from looking at Euridice as he leads her from the underworld, lured here by a direct quotation from 'Che farò' in Gluck's *Orfeo*. He loses her for a second time. In the final scene Badini eschews the *deus-ex-machina*-contrived happy ending of Gluck's opera. Instead he follows classical sources by having Orpheus poisoned by the pleasure-loving Bacchae whose blandishments he has spurned. As the Bacchae set off for 'the island of delight', they are drowned in a storm.

This tragic outcome, almost without parallel in operas of this period, is curiously at odds with the cool, rational tone that permeates the libretto, above all in the moralising of the 'philosophers', Creonte and the Sibyl. Whether or not Badini intended the tragic end to stand, he and Haydn would probably have revised the fourth act, at least, had the project not been aborted. As it is, Orpheus and the Sibyl stroll through Hades with comical ease, overcoming the Furies and Pluto in a few bars of perfunctory dry recitative. And Euridice's second death, again dealt with in bare recitative, is a candidate for the most anticlimactic moment in all opera.

However much he tried to minimise comparisons, Badini's libretto, long on philosophy, woefully short on action, cannot hold a candle to the swift, economical drama Calzabigi created for Gluck. Despite all his operatic experience, Haydn set it uncritically, even in places perversely. Why the placid, decorous minuet in Act Three, when Creonte sings about life not being worth living without love? Or the oddly neutral opening of Orpheus's 'Mi sento languir', after Euridice's second death? And with, say, the entry of the Queen of Night in mind, who can imagine Mozart introducing the Sibyl as casually as Haydn does? Even the apparently flexible mingling of accompanied recitative, chorus and short arias tends to sound stiffly additive rather than cumulative. When the voltage does increase, as in the intrusion of Arideo's henchmen, tension is quickly dissipated. As so often in Haydn's operas, the whole is less than the sum of the parts.

Yet the individual numbers can be glorious. For the first time in an opera he had at his disposal a substantial chorus, representing in turn shepherds, Cupids, mourners, Shades, Furies and Bacchae. Their music ranges from the gentle funeral lament for Euridice, with its mellow clarinet colouring, to the tremendous final storm, ending eerily with a *decrescendo* drumroll and two flutes in their hollow lowest register as the waves engulf the Bacchae. Memorable, too, are the choruses of Unhappy Shades and Furies, the one a contrapuntal F minor movement of sorrowful grace that glides with Schubertian poignancy to the relative major, the other a violent D minor outburst with lashing strings and howling trombones.

Euridice's first aria, 'Filomena abbandonata', and the love duet have a rather formal, chiselled elegance and resort too readily to routine coloratura. Even the Sibyl's C major showstopper is a superior example of typical late eighteenth-century *aria di bravura*. (Compare, say, Flaminia's 'Ragion nell'alma siede' in *Il mondo della luna*.) But Haydn is at his most inspired in Euridice's first death in Act Two, a recitative and cavatina of sublime simplicity and emotional truth, coloured in the closing bars by the plangent sound of cors anglais in their deepest register; in the F minor aria for Orpheus that follows, veering between despair and regretful tenderness (and echoing the main theme of the overture); and in the hero's own death scene, where the poison seeps through his body in a mesmerising harmonic sequence that slips from A major/minor through F minor, D flat major, C sharp minor and D major/minor to F major. Even the tedious Creonte has his moment of glory in his E major Act One aria, whose serene beauty is clouded by a sudden shift to E minor and a plaintive flute solo. As Robbins Landon has noted, this is one of several moments early in the opera (the others are in Orpheus's 'Cara speme', the love duet and the chorus of Cupids) where an ominous darkening of the harmony presages the tragedy to come.

Other vocal music

Arias, scenas, ensembles and incidental music

'Insertion' arias and ensembles
Scena di Berenice, Hob. XXIVa: 10
'Miseri noi, misera patria!', Hob. XXIVa: 7
'Solo e pensoso', Hob. XXIVb: 20
Alfred, König der Angelsachsen, Hob. XXX: 5

As a pragmatic operatic Kapellmeister, Haydn would routinely adapt other composers' works, usually *opere buffe*, to suit
the forces at his disposal. This often meant composing additional or substitute arias tailored to a particular singer. Mozart
did likewise for the Italian opera company in Vienna. Some
twenty of Haydn's 'insertion arias' have survived, all dating
from the years 1777–89. Several, such as the demure 'Chi vive
amante' and the charming Despina-ish 'Son pietosa' (one of
three Haydn contributions to a 1789 pasticcio, *La Circe*), were
fashioned for the modest soubrette talents of Haydn's mistress
Luigia Polzelli. Other arias for soprano are musically and
technically more ambitious, including 'Infelice sventurata',
written for the lovelorn Beatrice in Cimarosa's comedy *I due
supposti conti*, and 'D'una sposa', a coloratura showpiece with
oboe obbligato for the rich and haughty Donna Stella in
Paisiello's *La Frascatana*.

A handful of arias for tenor and bass includes the cynical
'Dice benissimo', complete with cuckold's horns, for the servant Lumaca in Salieri's *La scuola de' gelosi*, and a fine, agitated
recitative and aria (in F minor), 'Ah, tu non senti, amico', for
Orestes in Traetta's *Ifigenia in Tauride*. In lighter mood is
'Levatevi presto', an effervescent trio for two tenors and bass
from *La Circe* with a distinct whiff of Rossini in its comic
repartee and sly woodwind chuckles.

Nothing is known about the origins of the solo cantata 'Miseri noi, misera Patria', a setting from around 1784–5 of an anonymous *opera seria*-style text on the devastation of a city in war. Perhaps, as has often been suggested, Haydn wrote it for Nancy Storace, who sang in the 1784 revival of *Il ritorno di Tobia* and would create the role of Susanna in *Figaro* in 1786. To twenty-first-century ears, Haydn's stately music – a recitative followed by an aria in two sections – seems an oddly equable response to the horrors enumerated in the text.

The highlights of Haydn's gargantuan benefit concert on 4 May 1795 were his new Symphony No. 104 and what the programme billed as a 'New Scene. Madame Banti. Haydn'. Brigida Giorgi Banti, the theatre's principal soprano, was probably the most famous diva of the 1790s. For her Haydn created his most beautiful, harmonically daring operatic scena. The text comes from Metastasio's libretto *Antigone*. Like Ariadne, the heroine, Berenice, has been abandoned by her lover and becomes half crazed with grief. In the opening recitative disorienting shifts of key mirror her tottering reason. The recitative elides into an E major aria of chaste beauty in which Berenice entreats her lover not to cross Lethe without her. After another astonishing 'enharmonic' modulation, she vents her hysterical despair and death-longing in a searing F minor aria, coloured, for the first time in the work, by clarinets.

Haydn composed what Robbins Landon calls his 'rather nostalgic and wistful farewell to the Italian aria', 'Solo e pensoso', in 1798, at the behest of an unknown Russian Grand Duke. Scored for the mellow combination of clarinets, bassoons, horns and strings, this touching setting of Petrarch's sonnet No. 28 ('Alone and pensive I walk the fields with dragging steps') is laid out in the usual two sections: a reflective Adagio that opens with the same gambit as the Agnus Dei of the contemporary *Missa in angustiis*, and a tripping Allegretto whose folk-like charm (rather at odds with the introspective text) is deepened by a typical late-Haydn dip from the home key, B flat, to D flat major.

A curiosity among Haydn's dramatic works is the incidental music for a German translation of Alexander Bicknell's tragedy *The Patriotic King; or Alfred and Elvida*, performed during Princess Marie Hermenegild's name-day celebrations in September 1796. The first of the three numbers is a cheerfully bellicose chorus of Danes, the last a duet for two tenors, with solo violin, that breaks off with spoken text. In between comes a solemn E flat soprano aria for the Guardian Spirit, warmly scored for a sextet of clarinets, bassoons and horns (shades here of the music for the Three Boys that opens the Act Two finale of *Die Zauberflöte*). Uniquely in Haydn's music, the aria uses the technique of melodrama, superimposing Queen Elvida's spoken lines over the instrumental interludes.

Songs, duets and cantatas with keyboard

12 Lieder für das Clavier (Hob. XXVIa: 1–12)
1. 'Das strickende Mädchen'
2. 'Cupido'
3. 'Der erste Kuss'
4. 'Eine sehr gewöhnliche Geschichte'
5. 'Die Verlassene'
6. 'Der Gleichsinn'
7. 'An Iris'
8. 'An Thyrsis'
9. 'Trost unglücklicher Liebe'
10. 'Die Landlust'
11. 'Liebeslied'
12. 'Die zu späte Ankunft der Mutter'

12 Lieder für das Clavier (Hob. XXVIa: 13–24)
13. 'Jeder meint, der Gegenstand'
14. 'Lachet nicht, Mädchen'
15. 'O liebes Mädchen, höre mich'
16. 'Gegenliebe'
17. 'Geistliches Lied'

18. **'Auch die sprödeste der Schönen'**
19. **'O fliess, ja wallend fliess in Zähren'**
20. **'Zufriedenheit'**
21. **'Das Leben ist ein Traum'**
22. **'Lob der Faulheit'**
23. **'Minna'**
24. **'Auf meines Vaters Grab'**

The Lieder Haydn published in 1781 and 1784 rarely feature
in recital programmes today. Yet despite their often coy
or arch texts, the best of them have a grace, wit and depth of
feeling that go beyond mere rococo charm. This was a time
when Joseph II was vigorously promoting German-language
culture at the expense of French and, especially, Italian.
Joseph founded his German National Singspiel in 1778; and
the same year the *Hofklaviermeister* Joseph Anton Steffan published his first collection of 'Lieder für das Clavier', reflecting
the growing popularity of German songs in Viennese salons.
Three years later Haydn followed suit.

He wrote to Artaria in May 1781 that his Lieder, 'through
their variety, naturalness and beautiful and grateful melodies
will perhaps eclipse all my earlier ones' – and, we might add,
those of other composers, especially Leopold Hofmann,
whose Lieder he dubbed 'street songs, without ideas or
expression, much less, melody'. As the possessor of a light,
pleasing tenor well above the average *voix de compositeur*,
Haydn also announced his intention of singing the songs
himself, 'in the best houses. A master must see to his rights by
his presence and by correct performance.' (Griesinger reports
how Haydn late in life criticised composers who had never
learnt how to sing.) Haydn played and sang his Lieder in
salons like those held at the fashionable Mehlgrube home of
Franz Sales von Greiner, who regularly advised him on his
choice of texts.

For the second set, published in 1784, Haydn asked Greiner
for 'three tender new texts, because almost all the others
are merry in spirit; the subject matter should also embrace

sadness, so that there is light and shade, as with the first twelve'. While all twenty-four are in strophic form (i.e., with the same music repeated for each verse), and, with rare exceptions, the keyboard's right hand doubles the voice throughout, these songs are indeed as varied as their essentially domestic medium allows.

The pieces in the first set range from melodious trifles like 'An Iris', the cheery 'Die Landlust' (Joy in the country), and 'Das strickende Mädchen' (where the suitor woos Phyllis in a graceful Adagio, complete with twittering birdsong, while she continues her impassive knitting in a matter-of-fact Allegro), to two beautiful minor-key songs: the miniature operatic scena 'Die Verlassene' (The forsaken girl), and the melancholy 'Trost unglücklicher Liebe' (Consolation of unhappy love), one of three songs written to poems already set 'miserably' (Haydn's verdict) by Hofmann. Haydn here writes a long-spanned melody of Schubertian pathos, expanding its second and third phrases from four to five bars, and colouring the crucial word 'tötet' (kills) with increasing intensity.

In lighter mode are 'Der Gleichsinn' (Indifference), whose contredanse tune is playfully embellished in the little keyboard interludes; the witty 'Cupido', where the voice's innocent melody is gradually drawn into the teasingly ornamental style of the piano introduction; and 'Eine sehr gewöhnliche Geschichte' (An all-too common story) and 'Die zu späte Ankunft der Mutter' (Mother came too late), two droll songs in the mildly risqué Viennese tradition that carried through to Schubert and beyond. Haydn would remember 'Eine sehr gewöhnliche Geschichte', where the piano's repeated notes depict the boy knocking at his sweetheart's door, when he came to write Hanne's sly tale of thwarted seduction in *The Seasons*. Typically deft touches in the jaunty 'Die zu späte Ankunft der Mutter' are the voice's almost casual entry a bar later than expected, with a sense of 'and, incidentally', and the artful sharing of the melodic line between singer and keyboard.

On the whole the twelve songs that appeared in 1784 are indeed more 'merry' than the 1781 set. 'Lachet nicht, Mädchen'

(Do not laugh, girls), with its lopsided three-bar phrases and horn imitations, 'Auch die sprödeste der Schönen' (Even the most aloof beauty), 'Minna' and 'Zufriedenheit' (Contentment) are all in Haydn's insouciant *faux-naïf* vein. The lover's yearning in Bürger's poem 'Gegenliebe' (Mutual love), later set by Beethoven, would seem to suggest a more tender response than Haydn's cheerful, perhaps ironic, setting provides. Its tripping melody turns up in more reflective guise in the Andante of Symphony No. 73 ('La chasse'). Haydn's famed sense of humour is on display in the setting of Gottfried Lessing (a first-rate writer, for once), 'Lob der Faulheit' (In praise of idleness). Here the satirical verses find their perfect musical counterpart in slithering chromaticisms in the piano part – more independent than is usual in these songs – and a yawning, halting vocal line that reluctantly drags itself up step by step before flopping down on 'besingen' (sing). With the right singer this can be one of the funniest songs in the repertoire.

The two finest 1784 songs, though, are serious in tone. 'Das Leben ist ein Traum' (Life is a dream), which like 'Lob der Faulheit' is written on three staves, with a substantially independent piano part, has a distinct aura of *opera seria*: in the broad, stately vocal line, the rhetorical, almost orchestrally conceived climax at 'bis wir nicht mehr an Erde kleben' (until we no longer cling to this earth), and the dramatic pauses near the end, where Haydn reinforces the question 'Was ist's?' with a shift from major to minor. Equally impressive is the richly textured 'Geistliches Lied' (Sacred song), whose lofty pathos prefigures the *Seven Last Words* and some of the late part-songs.

'Beim Schmerz, der dieses Herz durchwühlet',
   Hob. XXVIa: 37
'Der schlaue und dienstfertige Pudel', Hob. XXVIa: 38
'Trachten will ich nicht auf Erden', Hob. XXVIa: 39

'Beim Schmerz, der dieses Herz durchwühlet' (With this sorrow that burrows through my heart), probably from the late 1760s, is Haydn's earliest surviving song, though its scale (a seventy-bar Adagio, with a long keyboard introduction) and style, including flights of coloratura, suggest that it was part of a lost opera. There is a charming story attached to another unsnappily titled song, 'Der schlaue und dienstfertige Pudel'. Around 1780 an officer's daughter from Coburg sent Haydn a ballad poem (running to twenty verses!) about an abnormally clever poodle that helps an army captain win a bet. Enclosing some money, the girl hoped Haydn would set the tale to music. The composer obliged with a song in aptly blithe, folk vein, but returned the money, asking that the girl knit him a pair of garters instead. Which she duly did. 'Trachten will ich nicht auf Erden' (I have no desire for earthly wealth) was probably the last music Haydn composed before setting off for London in December 1790: a touching Adagio that grows to finely calculated climax as the singer proclaims his trust in God. Haydn may have intended the song as a farewell gift, perhaps for Maria Anna von Genzinger.

Six canzonettas (Hob. XXVIa: 25–30)
'The mermaid's song'
'Recollection'
'A pastoral song'
'Despair'
'Pleasing pain'
'Fidelity'

Six canzonettas (Hob. XXVIa: 31–36)
'Sailor's song'
'The wanderer'
'Sympathy'
'She never told her love'
'Piercing eyes'
'Content'

Unlike the German Lieder, the two sets of 'Original Canzonettas' Haydn composed in London in 1794 and 1795 retain a foothold in the recital repertoire, if only as aperitifs to meatier Romantic fare. Again, they were written primarily for the profitable domestic market, far longer established in London than in Vienna. The initial impulse for the canzonettas came from Haydn's friend Anne Hunter, widow of the famous surgeon Sir John Hunter, who was renowned for her polished, if hardly original, verses in the taste of the day: usually sentimental, but also mining a fashionable vein of Gothic gloom (as in 'The wanderer' and 'The spirit's song', one of two English songs published separately). Hunter provided the poems for all the canzonettas in the first set of six, which are dedicated to her.

The English canzonettas, written on three staves throughout, have richer, more independent keyboard parts and range more widely in mood than the German Lieder. Heading each set of six is a tribute to the maritime prowess of Haydn's host nation. In 'The mermaid's song', playful, pearly triplets evoke the mermaid frolicking, while the line 'Come with me, and we will go' is a cue for a charming passage of canonic imitation. Haydn also included two songs in pastoral 6/8 metre in each set. 'Pleasing pain' tellingly varies the simple strophic form: while the first and third verses darken from G major to G minor at the words 'dear anxious days' and 'nor sad regrets', the second verse remains in an unclouded G major as the poet yearns for a return of 'the smiling hours'. In the famous 'Pastoral song' ('My mother bids me bind my hair'), beloved of Jenny Lind and many a Victorian amateur soprano, the keyboard textures have the refinement and transparency of a string quartet.

The textures of two of the most heartfelt songs, 'Recollection' and 'Despair', also suggest strings – in, say, the 'cello' solo at 'Why cannot I the days forget' in 'Recollection' (Hunter may have intended this poem as a memorial to her husband). Though 'Despair' expresses the self-pitying text with a dignified restraint, the temperature does rise at the words 'Despair at length reveals the smart'. In both these songs, the keyboard part could virtually stand alone as an eloquent slow movement.

Similarly, the last song of the set, the impassioned F minor 'Fidelity', could with little alteration be performed as a *Sturm und Drang* keyboard piece. Here Haydn seems less concerned with mirroring the shape of the poem than in using the general sense of the words to create a free sonata-form structure – another testament to the power of the sonata principle in all Haydn's music by the 1790s.

In the second set of canzonettas (1795), only one of the poems, 'The Wanderer', is by Anne Hunter. For the others, Hunter selected a text by Shakespeare, one by Haydn's famous neighbour from the Michaelerhaus, Metastasio ('Sympathy'), and three anonymous poems: 'Sailor's song', 'Piercing eyes' and 'Transport of pleasure'. The canzonettas' dedicatee, Lady Bertie, Countess of Abingdon, apparently found this last song, which reuses music Haydn had composed to German words, 'Der verdienstvolle Sylvius', too erotically explicit; and for a later edition it was fitted with a more decorous (and frankly, pretty dreadful) text, 'Content'.

In the rollicking 'Sailor's song' – once a favourite of Elisabeth Schumann, and long popular as a tenor recital opener – the onomatopoeic accompaniment, depicting bugle calls, cannons, 'rattling ropes' and the like, rumbustiously exploits the sonority and compass of the new Broadwood fortepiano. At the opposite end of the spectrum is 'She never told her love', which sets Viola's words from *Twelfth Night* as a free arioso, full of bold, rhetorical contrasts and unusually elaborate dynamic and expression markings. Two especially inspired touches are the overlapping of the vocal entry with the close of the piano introduction, and the voice's twice-repeated lingering cadence near the close, the first time culminating in a stabbing discord – a perfect musical embodiment of 'Smiling at grief'.

'Piercing eyes' is a bucolic counterpart to 'A pastoral song' and 'Pleasing pain' in the first set, and looks ahead to Simon's shepherd's song in *The Seasons*. Another song in 6/8 time, 'Sympathy', is more reflective in tone, with a dramatic change from major to minor at 'When thou art griev'd'. But the most haunting song in the set, with 'She never told her love', is 'The wanderer', an early example of a topic beloved of the Romantics. As in 'Pleasing pain', Haydn subtly varies the regular strophic structure. Though the voice part is identical in the second verse, the bare two-part keyboard texture is enriched with a new countermelody in the alto (or viola) register – another example of Haydn's 'string' thinking in these songs. In the aching 'Neapolitan' cadence at the end of each verse Haydn may have remembered the close of Pamina's aria in *Die Zauberflöte*, in the same key of G minor.

'The spirit's song', Hob. XXVIa: 41
'O tuneful voice', Hob. XXVIa: 42
'The lady's looking glass', Hob. XXXIc: 17

If Haydn at times seems to be thinking instrumentally in the two sets of canzonettas, the two independently published songs to poems by Anne Hunter, 'O tuneful voice' and, especially, 'The spirit's song', show a true fusion of poetry and music, with the musical form reflecting and enhancing the emotional progression of the verses. Both songs, too, poetically exploit the device of the surprise vocal entry found in 'She never told her love'. The darkly brooding atmosphere of 'The spirit's song' is heightened by ominous pauses and a bleak piano interlude that later accompanies the singer's final 'My spirit wanders free' and then reappears in the coda, deep in the bass against a falling chromatic line. Anne Hunter wrote 'O tuneful voice' as a farewell tribute to the composer before his final departure from England in August 1795. Haydn's setting, possibly composed in Vienna that autumn, combines a fervent *bel canto* line with a wonderful freedom of modulation that, as so often in late Haydn, prefigures Schubert.

In this company, 'The lady's looking glass', probably composed, as Robbins Landon suggests, as a 'hostess gift' (other such *bonnes bouches* may be lost), is absurdly slight: an ingenuous tune, like a folk song, followed, oddly, by a skittish little

keyboard dance. The English musicologist Derek McCulloch
has shown that the tune is not Haydn's at all, but derives from
a 'round' by the Earl of Abingdon. Haydn also paid his friend
the compliment of using his melody in the second of the
'London trios' for flutes and cello.

'Gott erhalte Franz den Kaiser', Hob. XXVIa: 43

Inspired by 'God save our King', the court official Franz
Joseph von Saurau was determined that Austria should have a
comparably stirring patriotic song at a time of national crisis.
He commissioned verses from the poet Lorenz Leopold
Hashka, and then approached Haydn to set them to music.
The upshot was his most famous melody, 'Gott erhalte Franz
den Kaiser' (God preserve Franz the Emperor), written
initially with piano accompaniment and then orchestrated for
its official premiere on the Emperor's twenty-ninth birthday,
12 February 1797. With its sublime Classical simplicity (hard-
won, as sketches reveal), the 'Emperor's Hymn' immediately
became the Austrian national anthem, and was shortly afterwards used by Haydn in his 'Emperor' Quartet, Op. 76 No. 3.
Best known in the English-speaking world as the hymn
'Glorious things of thee are spoken', Haydn's melody became
the German national anthem in 1922, with the words
'Deutschland, Deutschland über alles'. A decade later it was
appropriated by the Nazis. After pressure from the Allied
Commission it was dropped, with few objections, as Austria's
anthem in 1945. Shorn of its chauvinist first verse, it has survived its Nazi associations to remain Germany's national
anthem.

'Als einst mit Weibes Schönheit', Hob. XXVIa: 44
'Ein kleines Haus', Hob. XXVIa: 45
'Antwort auf die Frage eines Mädchens', Hob. XXVIa: 46

Some time between his return to Vienna in 1795 and 1800
Haydn wrote three charming songs to anonymous poems, all

of them through-composed. While the first two – a man's jocular homily to a wife on the need to combine beauty and virtue, and an evocation of snug domestic content – are innocently bucolic, 'Antwort auf die Frage eines Mädchens' (Answer to a girl's question) is an eloquent avowal of everlasting love.

Arianna a Naxos, Hob. XXVIb: 2
'Saper vorrei', Hob. XXVa: 2
'Guarda qui che lo vedrai', Hob. XXVa: 1
'Lines from *The Battle of the Nile*', Hob. XXVIb: 4
'Dr Harington's compliment', Hob. XXVIb: 3

'I am delighted that my favourite *Arianna* is well received at the Schottenhof,' wrote Haydn to Maria Anna von Genzinger on 14 March 1790, 'but I do recommend Fräulein Pepperl to articulate the words clearly, especially the passage "chi tanto amai".' He had probably composed his dramatic cantata the previous year; and though it is unlikely that he intended it primarily for 'Pepperl', Maria Anna's sixteen-year-old daughter, the cantata's limited vocal compass and modest virtuosity suggest that, like Haydn's songs, it was conceived for the cultured amateur rather than the professional. *Arianna* fast became one of his most popular works. Haydn planned to orchestrate the expressive keyboard accompaniment but never got round to it. His pupil Neukomm and, later, others did the job for him.

Following the typical pattern of the eighteenth-century Italian cantata, *Arianna* alternates recitative and aria in four sections. The opening recitative depicts the abandoned Ariadne's voluptuous awakening and her mingled languour and impatience for Theseus's return. In a slow aria, opening with a sensuous phrase that recalls the Countess's 'Dove sono?' from *Figaro*, she begs the gods to bring him back to her. (Haydn was planning to produce *Figaro* at Eszterháza in autumn 1790.) The aria breaks off for the increasingly agitated second recitative, with graphically descriptive keyboard writing. The daughter of Minos momentarily recovers her regal dignity in the F major opening of the second aria. But her anguish and outrage erupt in an F minor Presto, with its yearning repetitions of the key phrase 'Chi tanto amai'– the words Haydn cited in his letter to Frau von Genzinger. The piano's last-second swerve to F major ('normalised' to F minor in several editions) has an air of grim, mocking finality.

The pastoral duets 'Saper vorrei' and 'Guarda qui che lo vedrai' for those ubiquitous Arcadian lovers Tirsi and Nisa (1796), and the recitative and aria 'Lines from *The Battle of the Nile*' (1800) are the most occasional of occasional works. Yet by this time Haydn was incapable of writing dully; and even these trifles are full of shapely, *echt*-Haydn melody and artful touches of chromaticism and counterpoint. The jingoistic text of the Nelson tribute 'Lines from the *Battle of the Nile*' is by Cornelia Knight, a companion of Nelson and the Hamiltons on their visit to Eisenstadt in September 1800. Haydn dedicated this little cantata to Emma Hamilton, who first sang it, to the composer's accompaniment, at a concert in the Esterházy palace in the presence of both her lover and her husband. 'The effect was grand', noted Cornelia Knight in her memoirs, though other reports of Lady Hamilton's singing suggest that she habitually sang out of tune.

Finally in this group, a curio from the composer's second London visit: 'Dr Harington's compliment', for soprano, vocal quartet or chorus and keyboard. The Bath physician and part-time composer Henry Harington had penned a dignified glee in praise of Haydn, 'What art expresses and what science praises, Haydn the theme of both to heaven raises'. Haydn charmingly returned the tribute by presenting the glee both as a solo song and as a part-song, interspersed with keyboard variations, including a surprisingly serious contrapuntal one in the minor.

Part-songs (Mehrstimmige Gesänge)

'Der Augenblick' (Hob. XXVc: 1)
'Die Harmonie in der Ehe' (Hob. XXVc: 2)

'Alles hat seine Zeit' (Hob. XXVc: 3)
'Die Beredsamkeit' (Hob. XXVc: 4)
'Der Greis' (Hob. XXVc: 5)
'An den Vetter' (Hob. XXVb: 1)
'Daphnens einziger Fehler' (Hob. XXVb: 2)
'Die Warnung' (Hob. XXVc: 6)
'Betrachtung des Todes' (Hob. XXVb: 3)
'Wider den Übermut' (Hob. XXVc: 7)
'An die Frauen' (Hob. XXVb: 4)
'Danklied zu Gott' (Hob. XXVc: 8)
'Abendlied zu Gott' (Hob. XXVc: 9)

These thirteen exquisite part-songs for voices and keyboard of 1796–9 are among Haydn's best-kept secrets. Written, as he told Griesinger, 'con amore, in happy hours, not to commission', they seem to have been inspired by the catches and part-songs Haydn had heard in London glee clubs. They were first performed in intimate, informal musical gatherings in Eisenstadt and Vienna; and they consolidated a tradition of convivial Viennese vocal chamber music that would stretch via Schubert to Brahms's *Liebeslieder* waltzes and beyond.

The part-songs range from satirical comedy and drinking songs to religious contemplation. Yet even the lightest pieces are touched by nonchalant mastery. As James Webster put it in *The New Grove Haydn*, 'their fusion of easy intelligibility and wit with the highest art and their ravishing part-writing almost suggest string quartets for voices'.

Haydn set four of the songs as trios: the sportive 'An den Vetter' (To the cousin), with its Don Alfonso-ish cynicism, and 'An die Frauen' (To women); the suavely wistful 'Daphnens einziger Fehler' (Daphne's sole failing – which turns out to be her inability to love); and 'Betrachtung des Todes' (Contemplation of death), one of four religious songs to verses by Haydn's favourite poet, Christian Fürchtegott Gellert. This memento mori unfolds as a desolate A minor siciliano, with chilling pauses and a disorienting deflection from C major to C sharp minor to paint the word 'Irrtum' – error.

The remaining nine songs are quartets. Two of the wittiest are 'Die Warnung' (Warning), with its slithering chromaticisms evoking the lurking scorpions, and the wry 'Die Harmonie in der Ehe' (Marital harmony). Perhaps thinking of his own sour marriage, Haydn each time sets the crucial word 'Harmonie' to a pungent discord. Both 'Alles hat seine Zeit' (Everything has its time) and 'Die Beredsamkeit' (Eloquence) avoid the lederhosen heartiness that was de rigueur in most later drinking songs, Schubert's included. 'Alles hat seine Zeit', to a text translated from the ancient Greek of Athanaeus, is a madrigalesque scherzo, with fragments of melody bandied airily between the four voices. 'Die Beredsamkeit' sets a comic poem by Lessing: water makes us dumb – just look at the fish; but with wine it's quite the opposite. Haydn gleefully depicts the babbling drunkards, and reserves a nice joke for the end, when the singers merely mime the final 'stumm'.

In extreme contrast is the gently solemn 'Der Greis' (The old man), whose halting melodic line touchingly conveys the idea of failing strength. In 1806 Haydn engraved on his visiting card the opening of the soprano part: 'Hin ist alle meine Kraft! Alt und schwach bin ich' (Gone is all my strength. Old and weak am I). In 'Der Augenblick' (The moment), the music has a more serious cast than you would guess from the verses. The sentiments – that 'love' is nothing to do with tenderness, but purely a matter of a chance, off-guard moment – could again have been mouthed by Don Alfonso. But Haydn takes his cue from the opening words, 'Innbrunst' (ardour) and 'Zärtlichkeit' (tenderness), and writes music whose depth of feeling evokes the contemporary late masses. In similar vein are the three religious songs at the end of the collection: 'Wider den Übermut' (Preserve me from arrogance); the majestic, sonorous 'Danklied zu Gott' (Song of thanksgiving to God), which Goethe's musical guru Carl Friedrich Zelter later arranged for full chorus; and, finally, 'Abendlied zu Gott' (Evening hymn to God), which opens as a gentle three-part canon, flowers into joyous melismas at 'Treue' (faith) and ends with soft, diminished harmonies. In its mingled awe, humility and serene confidence, this beautiful song encapsulates the composer's own religious faith.

Folk-song arrangements

Haydn's arrangements of Scottish and Welsh folk songs – nearly four hundred in total – began as an act of charity and ended as one of Arthur Daley's 'nice little earners'. In the 1760s translations of the melancholy, mist-shrouded outpourings of the third-century Gaelic bard Ossian, son of Fingal, helped fuel a European craze for Celtic primitivism – though 'Ossian' and his English translator James Macpherson would later turn out to be one and the same person. When the London publisher William Napier went bankrupt in 1791, Haydn offered to assist him by providing, apparently without payment, accompaniments for piano, violin and (optional) cello to a hundred folk songs, issued as 'A Selection of Original Scots Songs in Three Parts. The Harmony by Haydn'. Not all the tunes were quite as 'original' as the publisher implied. But these 'wild and expressive melodies' (Napier's words), adorned and 'civilised' for the eighteenth-century salon, were such a success that Napier's business was saved, and he was even able to pay Haydn fifty pounds. The publisher immediately requested another fifty arrangements, which he issued during the composer's second London visit in 1795.

All went quiet on the Scottish front until October 1799, when the Edinburgh publisher George Thomson, friend of Robbie Burns and an avid folk-song collector, offered Haydn the tempting rate of two ducats per song for a series of Scottish and Welsh (plus a few Irish) song arrangements. He sent Haydn the tunes, usually without words, in regular batches; and over the next four years the ageing composer obliged with nearly two hundred settings. Thomson was delighted, writing to Anne Hunter in London that 'the Accompaniments which Haydn has composed for the Airs in general are beyond all praise'. The publisher would later do similar mutually profitable business with, inter alia, Beethoven, Hummel and Weber. Between 1802 and 1804 Haydn also provided sixty-five arrangements, all of Scottish songs, for the Edinburgh bookseller and publisher William Whyte, though we now know that as his strength declined he sub-contracted some of the Thomson and Whyte settings to pupils, especially Sigismund Neukomm. The usually appreciative Thomson could occasionally be critical of the settings, one of which, 'O gin my Love', he found 'learned dry & ugly'. Unbeknown to him, this was in fact entirely Neukomm's work.

While they respect the character of the original melodies as far as possible, the folk-song settings for Thomson and Whyte are altogether more elaborate than those for Napier. The trio textures are more inventive (the cello is now indispensable), and at the publishers' request he provided framing instrumental 'symphonies' – i.e. preludes and postludes – often with a strong chromatic flavour. The reflective songs characteristically end with nostalgic diminished harmonies, like so many late-Haydn slow movements. These shavings from the composer's workshop include a delightfully spry 'Auld lang syne' (no hint here of slurred New Year mawkishness), a powerful setting of 'John Anderson, my jo', a handful of spirited duets, and a beautiful arrangement of the Welsh song 'The March of Rhudden', which in mood, key (G minor) and texture recalls 'The Wanderer' from the second set of English canzonettas.

Canons

The vocal canons Haydn wrote in London and Vienna between 1791 and 1799 range from the sacred to the bibulous, though they have none of the scatological bawdiness of the canons Mozart composed for similar domestic gatherings. From his two London visits date *Die heiligen zehn Gebote* (The Ten Commandments, Hob. XXVIIa: 1–10), in three, four and five parts, reusing for the first commandment a 'crab canon' (where the imitating voice sings the tune backwards) Haydn had recently sent to Oxford University. No. 5, 'Thou shalt not kill', has an aptly stern, tortuous subject, with harsh discords on 'töten' (kill); while No. 6, 'Thou shalt not yield thee to lewdness', in a skipping 6/8 metre, takes, not surprisingly given Haydn's track record, an ironically witty view of adultery. There is cynical humour, too, in the stealthy setting of No. 9, 'Thou shalt not go lusting for thy neighbour's wife'. At the furthest extreme is the gravely impressive No. 7, 'Thou shalt not steal', beginning in 'Palestrina style' and developing ever more scrunchy dissonances. Pohl maintained that Haydn jokingly 'stole' No. 7's theme from another composer, though no one has yet discovered the source of the theft.

Griesinger relates how Haydn decorated the 'best room' in his house in Gumpendorf with the manuscripts of many of his secular canons, forty-six in total, including two in English, one in Italian and one in Latin (Hob. XXVIIb: 1–46). When his wife accused him of not leaving enough money behind for a proper burial, he pointed to the canons and assured her that any publisher would be only too glad to fork out the necessary sum. In 1810 the *Allgemeine musikalische Zeitung* praised the canons, mostly in three or four parts, for combining 'an admirable, mathematically refined art with the most beautiful inspiration and naturalness'. Among the most vivid are the comically chattering 'Der Esel und die Dohle' (The ass and the jackdaw), the witty drinking song 'Die Gewissheit' (Certainty), the solemn F minor 'Tod und Schlaf' (Death and sleep), and 'Gott im Herzen, ein gut Weibchen im Arm' (God in your heart, a good little wife in your arms), music of exquisite tenderness that found a more elevated home as the 'Et incarnatus est' of the *Missa Sancti Bernardi von Offida*.

Further reading

'In the history of music no chapter is more important than that filled by the life-work of Joseph Haydn,' declared Donald Tovey at the head of his majestic article on the string quartets in Cobbett's 1929 *Cyclopedic Survey of Chamber Music*. Yet before the Second World War there was barely a volume about Haydn in English worth reading, and certainly none to make you actually want to play or listen to the music. Even after the huge advances in Haydn scholarship and the wide exposure of his works during the last sixty years, the literature, in English, German or French, remains modest. The books listed below, all in English, are ones I have found illuminating in varying degrees. Those with specialist interests who read German may like to refer to the critical commentaries in the ongoing complete edition of Haydn's works (*JHW*), issued (from 1958) by the Joseph Haydn-Institut, Cologne, and published by G. Henle Verlag. Frustratingly, H. C. Robbins Landon's *The Collected Correspondence and London Notebooks of Joseph Haydn* (Thames and Hudson, 1959) has long been out of print, though copies occasionally come up for sale on the internet.

Life and works

Haydn: Two Contemporary Portraits, ed. Vernon Gotwals (revised edition; University of Wisconsin Press, 1968) English translations, with annotations, of the two early biographical sketches of Haydn, by G. A. Griesinger and A. C. Dies, both published in 1810.

Haydn: A Creative Life in Music, Karl Geiringer, in collaboration with Irene Geiringer (University of California Press, 1946; revised edition, 1982)

Drawing on the three-volume biography (1875, 1882, 1927) of Carl Ferdinand Pohl, and carefully updated in the light of modern research, the sections on the life are well worth reading, though Geiringer's discussion of the music can be superficial.

Haydn (Master Musicians), Rosemary Hughes (Dent, 1950; sixth edition, 1989)
A graceful stylist, Hughes covers Haydn's life succinctly and writes more discerningly on the music than Geiringer. She is especially good on the string quartets, though her opera chapter is a rather breathless later addition, and her discussion of the symphonies vitiated by too many slighting comparisons with Mozart.

Haydn: Chronicle and Works, H. C. Robbins Landon, i: *Haydn: The Early Years* 1732–1765 (Thames and Hudson, 1980); ii: *Haydn at Eszterháza* 1766–1790 (1978); iii: *Haydn in England* 1791–1795 (1976); iv: *Haydn: The Years of 'The Creation'* 1796–1800 (1977); v: *Haydn: The Late Years* 1801–1809 (1977)
A monumental achievement: the definitive, if rather chaotically organised, life and works by the doyen of twentieth-century Haydn scholars. The five massive volumes (with cover prices to match) are an indispensable documentary source; and while Landon's analyses of Haydn's music vary in rigour, his mingled erudition and enthusiasm always make for engaging reading.

Haydn: His Life and Music, H. C. Robbins Landon (life), David Wyn Jones (music) (Thames and Hudson, 1988)
A life filleted from Landon's magnum opus (see above), interleaved with excellent chapters on the music, including a perceptive assessment of Haydn's operatic achievement.

The New Grove Haydn, James Webster, with Georg Feder (work list) (Grove/Macmillan, 2002)
A concise distillation of up-to-date Haydn scholarship, with a judicious overview of the music and, not least, a comprehensive and accurate work list.

Guides

The Oxford Composer Companion to Haydn, ed. David Wyn Jones (Oxford University Press, 2002)
A highly readable guide to all things Haydn, using A–Z dictionary format. The 520 pages allow plenty of scope for in-depth treatment of individual topics by some forty authors; and there is barely an aspect of Haydn's music, life, milieu and influence that eludes David Wyn Jones's shrewd editorial eye.

Studies of the music

The Great Haydn Quartets, Hans Keller (Dent, 1986)
Keller's trenchant, gloriously opinionated discussion of the forty-five quartets he deemed 'great' is aimed primarily at string players (Keller's 'insiders'), though there is plenty of illumination (plus occasional exasperation) for the dedicated eavesdropper.

Haydn and the Enlightenment: The Late Symphonies and their Audience, David P. Schroeder (Oxford University Press, 1990)
Schroeder examines the 'Paris' and 'London' symphonies and their impact on audiences in the context of contemporary aesthetic theories, and makes a convincing case for Haydn as a conscious propagator of Enlightenment ideals.

Haydn's 'Farewell' Symphony and the Idea of Classical Style, James Webster (Cambridge University Press, 1991)
Webster proposes, usually convincingly, that many of Haydn's symphonies and quartets are 'through-composed', their four movements interlinked by common motifs and stategies. His argument centres on multifaceted analyses of the 'Farewell' Symphony and its numerical companion, No. 46. He also makes a strong case for Haydn's pre-1770 music, 'down-graded' by Rosen, Keller and others.

Cambridge Music Handbooks (all published by Cambridge University Press)
Haydn: The Creation, Nicholas Temperley (1991)

Haydn: String Quartets, Op. 50, W. Dean Sutcliffe (1992)
Haydn: The 'Paris' Symphonies, Bernard Harrison (1998)
Each of these stimulating handbooks offers background, context and detailed yet not dauntingly technical musical analysis. All three are written with passionate enthusiasm. In the *Creation* volume the section on reception history is especially valuable.

Mozart, Haydn and the Viennese School, 1740–1780, Daniel Heartz (Norton, 1995)
Heartz provides a useful, if sometimes rather dry, survey of most of Haydn's output pre-1780, and is excellent on the mid-century Viennese cultural background.

The Classical Style, Charles Rosen (third edition, Norton/Faber, 2005)
First published in 1971, this is a dazzling study of Haydn (primarily the symphonies, quartets and piano trios from 1780 onwards), Mozart and Beethoven that has rightly become a modern classic. Rosen illuminates Haydn's creative processes with a series of probing, original yet always lucid analyses.

Haydn and his World, ed. Elaine Sisman (Princeton University Press, 1997)
A collection of essays by US scholars examining aspects of Haydn's music within a wider cultural context. Some of the writing is tough going, though James Webster on *The Creation* and Leon Botstein on *The Seasons* are outstanding.

Haydn Studies, ed. W. Dean Sutcliffe (Cambridge University Press, 1998)
Several of the same scholars, including Webster and Botstein, crop up from the Sisman volume (see above). One or two of the essays are post-structural musicology at its most jargon-ridden, though Webster, Botstein and editor Dean Sutcliffe (on the trios) are all compelling, while Robin Holloway's 'Haydn: the Musician's Musician' brilliantly encapsulates the paradoxes and ambiguities of Haydn's art.

The Cambridge Companion to Haydn, ed. Caryl Clark (Cambridge University Press, 2005)
Another multi-contributor volume, with mainly US authors, this includes vigorous chapters on reception history, contemporary aesthetics and Haydn and his fellow composers. The brief sections on individual musical genres are more variable and, again, not free from academic jargon.

Haydn on CD

Listed below is a personal selection of Haydn recordings, though given the notorious volatility of the classical CD catalogue, their ongoing availability cannot be guaranteed. At the time of writing Brilliant Classics are plotting a mammoth 160-CD anniversary set covering around 80 per cent of Haydn's oeuvre, including the complete piano trios and solo piano works, most of the string quartets (though not, apparently, Op. 76!), all the symphonies (in the usually excellent performances by Adám Fischer's Austro-Hungarian Haydn Orchestra), and the first-ever recordings of the complete baryton trios and the complete string trios. The Brilliant Classics Haydn edition is due for release in November 2008.

Symphonies

Symphonies Nos 1–104, Austro-Hungarian Haydn Orchestra/ Adám Fischer, Brilliant Classics 99925 (33 CDs)

Symphonies Nos 6–8, Freiburg Baroque Orchestra, Harmonia Mundi HMC90 1767

'*Sturm und Drang*' *Symphonies: Nos 26, 35, 38, 39, 41–52, 65*, English Concert/Trevor Pinnock, Archiv 463 731-2 (6 CDs)

'*Paris*' *Symphonies, Nos 82–87*, Vienna Concentus Musicus/ Nikolaus Harnoncourt Deutsche Harmonia Mundi 82876 60602-2 (3 CDs)

Symphonies Nos 88–92, *Sinfonia Concertante*, Berlin Philharmonic/Simon Rattle, EMI 394 237-2 (2 CDs)

Symphonies Nos 93, 94, 97, 99–101, Concertgebouw Orchestra/ Colin Davis, Philips 442 614-2 (2 CDs)

Symphonies Nos 95, 96, 98, 102–104, Concertgebouw Orchestra/Colin Davis, Philips 442 611-2 (2 CDs)

Symphonies Nos 99–104, Royal Philharmonic Orchestra/ Thomas Beecham, EMI 585513-2 (2 CDs)

Concertos

Cello Concertos, Sinfonia Concertante, Steven Isserlis, Chamber Orchestra of Europe/Roger Norrington, RCA 09026 68578-2
Cello Concertos, Truls Mørk, Norwegian Chamber Orchestra/Iona Brown, Simax PSC 1078
Keyboard Concertos Hob XVIII: 3, 4, 11, Leif Ove Andsnes, Norwegian Chamber Orchestra, EMI 556960-2
Violin Concertos, Christian Tetzlaff, Northern Sinfonia/Heinrich Schiff, Virgin 759065-2
Trumpet Concerto (with trumpet concertos by Leopold Mozart and Michael Haydn), Crispian Steele-Perkins, King's Consort/Robert King, Hyperion CDA 67266
Concertos for lira organizzata, Vienna Haydn Sinfonietta/Manfred Huss, Koch 313792

String quartets

Complete String Quartets, Angeles Quartet, Philips 464 650-2PX21 (21 CDs)
String Quartets Op. 20, Mosaïques Quartet, Naïve E8802 (2 CDs)
String Quartets Op. 33, Mosaïques Quartet, Naïve E8801 (2 CDs)
String Quartets Op. 50 Nos 1–3, The Lindsays, ASV GLD4007
String Quartets Op. 50 Nos 4–6, The Lindsays, ASV GLD4008
String Quartets Op. 54, The Lindsays, ASV CDDCA582
String Quartets Op. 55, The Lindsays, ASV CDDCA906
String Quartets Op. 64 Nos 1, 3, 6, Mosaïques Quartet, Naïve E8886
String Quartets Op. 64 Nos 2, 4, 5, Mosaïques Quartet, Naïve E8875
String Quartets Op. 71, The Lindsays, ASV GLD4012
String Quartets Op. 74, The Lindsays, ASV GLD4013
String Quartets Op. 76, Mosaïques Quartet, Naïve E8665 (2 CDs)—Quatuor Elysée, ZigZag ZZT030802 (2 CDs)
String Quartets Op. 77 and 103, The Lindsays, ASV GLD4010

Keyboard trios

Complete Keyboard Trios, Beaux Arts Trio, Philips 454 098-2PB9
(9 CDs)
Trios Nos 18, 24, 25, 29, Vienna Piano Trio, Nimbus NI535

Other chamber music

Baryton Trios Nos 71, 96, 113, 126, J. Hsu, D. Miller, F. Arico,
ASV CDGAU109
Baryton Trios Nos 87, 97, 101, 111, J. Hsu, D. Miller, F. Arico,
ASV CDGAU104
Six Duos for Violin and Viola, I. Hajdu, G. Déri, Hungaraton
HCD 31474
Divertimentos for wind and strings, Berlin Haydn Ensemble,
Campion C130069

Keyboard music

Complete Keyboard Sonatas, John McCabe, London 443 785-
2LC (12 CDs)
*Sonatas Nos 20, 32, 34, 37, 40, 42, 48–52; Fantasia in C, Variations
in F minor*, Alfred Brendel, Philips 416 643-2 (4 CDs)
Sonatas Nos 20, 34, 40, 44, 48-52, Fantasia in C, András Schiff,
Teldec 0630-17141-2 (2 CDs)
Sonatas Nos 20, 33–37, 39, 48–52, Andreas Staier, Deutsche
Harmonia Mundi 82876 67376-2 (3 CDs)
Sonatas Nos 23, 24, 32, 37, 40, 41, 43, 46, 50, 52, Marc-André
Hamelin, Hyperion CDA67554 (2 CDs)
Sonatas Nos 26, 32, 36–7, 49, Leif Ove Andsnes, EMI 556756-2
Sonatas Nos 33, 36, 43, 45, 46, Emanuel Ax, Sony SK89363

Sacred music and oratorios

Missa Cellensis (Cäcilienmesse), Missa sunt bonae mixta malis,
Soloists, Collegium Musicum 90/Richard Hickox, Chandos
CHAN0667

Missa in honorem BVM (Grosse Orgelsolomesse); Missa Cellensis (Mariazellermesse), Soloists, Collegium Musicum 90/Richard Hickox, Chandos CHAN0674

Missa Sancti Nicolai; Missa Sancti Bernardi von Offida (Heiligmesse), Soloists, Collegium Musicum 90/Richard Hickox, Chandos CHAN0645

Missa brevis Sancti Johannis de Deo (Kleine Orgelsolmesse); Mass in B flat (Theresienmesse), Soloists, Collegium Musicum 90/Richard Hickox, Chandos CHAN0592

Missa in tempore belli (Paukenmesse); Salve regina in G minor, Soloists, Arnold Schoenberg Choir, Vienna Concentus Musicus/Nikolaus Harnoncourt, Teldec 0630-13146-2

Mass in D minor (Nelsonmesse), Te Deum in C, Hob. XXIIIc: 2, Soloists, English Concert Choir, English Concert/Trevor Pinnock, Archiv 423 097-2

Mass in B flat (Schöpfungsmesse); Mass in B flat (Harmoniemesse), Monteverdi Choir, English Baroque Soloists/John Eliot Gardiner, Philips 470 297-2 (2 CDs)

Stabat mater in G minor, Soloists, English Concert Choir, English Concert/Trevor Pinnock, Archiv 429733-2

Il ritorno di Tobia, Soloists, VokalEnsemble Köln, Capella Augustina/Andreas Spering, Naxos 8.570300-02 (2 CDs)

The Seven Last Words (choral version), Soloists, Arnold Schoenberg Choir, Vienna Concentus Musicus/Nikolaus Harnoncourt, Warner Elatus 2564 60808-2

The Creation (in German), Soloists, Monteverdi Choir, English Baroque Soloists/John Eliot Gardiner, Archiv 449 217-2 (2 CDs)

The Creation (in English) Soloists, Gabrieli Consort and Players/Paul McCreesh, Archiv 477 7361 (2 CDs)

The Seasons, Soloists, RIAS Chamber Choir, Freiburg Baroque Orchestra/René Jacobs, Harmonia Mundi HMC 801829.30 (2 CDs)

Songs, arias and cantatas

Cantatas for the House of Esterházy, Soloists, Vokal Ensemble Köln, Capella Coloniensis/Andreas Spering, Harmonia Mundi HMC 901765

Arias and cantatas (including *Scena di Berenice, Miseri noi, Arianna a Naxos*), Arleen Auger, Handel and Haydn Society/ Christopher Hogwood; Avie AV 2066

English canzonettas, Arianna a Naxos, Lisa Milne, Bernarda Fink, John Mark Ainsley, Roger Vignoles, Hyperion CDA67174

Scottish and Welsh Folksong arrangements, Lorna Anderson, Jamie MacDougall, Haydn Trio, Brilliant Classics 92542 (4 CDs); 93453 (3 CDs)

Operas

The pioneering Dorati series of eight Eszterháza operas, from *L'infedeltà delusa to Armida,* is unavailable at the time of writing, though it is hoped that Philips will reissue these starrily cast recordings for the 2009 Haydn anniversary.

La canterina, Soloists, Palmer Chamber Orchestra/Rudolph Palmer, Newport NPD85595

Lo speziale, Soloists, Neue Deutsche Kammerakademie/ Johannes Goritzki, Berlin Classics 0017 122BC

L'isola disabitata Soloists, Academia Montis Regalis/ Alessandro de Marchi, Opus 111 OP30-319 (2 CDs)

Orlando paladino, Soloists, Vienna Concentus Musicus/ Nikolaus Harnoncourt, Deutsche Harmonia Mundi 82876 73370-2 (2 CDs)

Armida, Soloists, Vienna Concentus Musicus/Nikolaus Harnoncourt, Teldec 8573-811808-2 (2 CDs)

L'anima del filosofo, Soloists, Academy of Ancient Music Choir, Academy of Ancient Music/Christopher Hogwood, L'Oiseau Lyre 452 668-2 (2 CDs)

Acknowledgements

Thanks, firstly, to Harriet Smith, Florence Cooke, Richard Stamp, David Threasher, Robert Avery and Denis McCaldin, all of whom read parts of the manuscript and gave valued feedback. Hugh Macdonald bravely offered to wade through the whole guide – not primarily designed for cover-to-cover reading – and made many stimulating suggestions. My partner Alison Cooke read the initial draft of each section, and saved me from errors of style and repetition. Michael Downes was a keen-eyed copy editor. Thanks, too, to my supportive editors at Faber: Elizabeth Tyerman, and Belinda Matthews, who commissioned the book. Mistakes that remain are, of course, mine alone. If you spot any, I should be delighted to hear about them for future editions.

Translations of letters and documents are my own where I have had access to the German originals, though I have drawn freely, with relatively little emendation, on Vernon Gotwals's translations of the biographical sketches of Griesinger and Dies (Wisconsin University Press, 1968). I am also indebted, as any writer on Haydn must be, to the copious documents reproduced in H. C. Robbins Landon's monumental five-volume *Haydn: Chronicle and Works* (Thames and Hudson), in German and (from Haydn's London years) English. It was Robbins Landon's great book on the symphonies (published by Universal Edition and Rockliff in 1955, and long out of print), together with recordings of the late symphonies by Beecham, Jochum and Hans Rosbaud, that first inspired my teenage passion for Haydn. Three decades later, I visited 'Robbie' and his partner Marie-Noëlle at their château in the Tarn to interview him for a BBC Radio Three series on the post-war Haydn renaissance. It was one of the most inspiring weekends, musically and gastronomically, of my life.

Richard Wigmore
Kingston-upon-Thames
August 2008

Index of Haydn's works

The main entry for each work is in **bold** type

All works are listed under their first letter, even if they begin
with the definite or indefinite article (e.g. under I for *Il
ritorno di Tobia* or under L for *La canterina*)